BESTSELLING BOOK SERIES

London For Dummies®
5th Edition

W9-CEW-634

A Glossary of English Food Terms

When you're in England, you speak English. American English is perfectly fine, of course. Like a major credit card, it's accepted everywhere. But you may come across a few unfamiliar terms, particularly when the subject is food. The following "translations" can help (see the reverse side for general terms):

British English	American English	British English	American English
Afters	Dessert	Jacket potato	Baked potato served with various toppings
Aubergine	Eggplant	Jelly	Jello
Bangers	Sausages	Joint	Meat roasted on the bone
Bap	Soft sandwich bun	Kipper	Smoked fish
Biscuit	Cracker or cookie	Liquor	Green, salty, parsley-based gravy
Black or white	Refers to coffee; white is coffee with cream	Mange tout	Snow peas
Broad bean	Lima bean	Marrow	Squash
Bubble and Squeak	Mashed potatoes mixed with cabbage or meat and then fried	Mash	Mashed potatoes
Chicory	Endive	Mince	Ground meat, usually beef
Chips	French fries	Ploughman's lunch	Pub grub consisting of crusty bread with cheese or pâté
Cornish pasties	Pastry filled with meat, onion, and vegetables	Pudding	Dessert
Cottage pie	Ground meat and mashed potatoes baked in a pie	Rasher	Slice of bacon
Courgettes	Zucchini	Rocket	Arugula
Crisps	Potato chips	Salt beef	Corned beef
Crumpet	Holier version of an "English muffin"	Scotch egg	Hard-boiled egg fried in a jacket of ground sausage and bread crumbs
French beans	Green beans	Shepherd's pie	Baked pie of meat and vegetables covered with gravy and mashed potatoes
Fry-up	Big English breakfast of eggs, sausage/bacon, baked beans, tomatoes, and more	Spotted dick	Sponge cake with fruit and raisins steamed and served with custard sauce
Gateau	Cake	Sticky toffee pudding	Spotted dick (see above) without the fruit and served with warm butterscotch sauce
Haricots vert	Green beans	Steak and kidney pie	Pastry-topped pie of steak, kidneys, and mushrooms in gravy

(continued)

(continued)

British English	American English	British English	American English
Sultana	Raisin	Trifle	Sponge cake soaked in sherry, layered with raspberry preserves, covered with custard sauce, and capped with whipped cream
Sweet	Dessert	Welsh rarebit	Melted cheddar cheese and mustard or Worcestershire sauce served on toast
Treacle	Molasses	Whitebait	Small, whole, deep-fried fish

Minding Your Teas and Queues

British English differs a bit from the English spoken in the New World. You may encounter the following "foreign" words and phrases, which are listed below with their American-English translations (see the reverse side for food terms):

British English	American English	British English	American English
Bonnet	Hood of a car	Mac (mackintosh)	Raincoat
Boot	Trunk of a car	Mate	Male friend
Brilliant	All-purpose, enthusiastic superlative	Nappy	Diaper
Brolly	Umbrella	Peckish	Hungry
Cheers	Goodbye (or said when raising a glass in a toast)	Petrol	Gasoline
Cinema	Movie ("theatre" is only live theater)	Queue	To line up (The Brits are excellent queuers.)
Coach	A long-distance bus	Quid	One pound sterling (£)
Concessions	Special discounts for students, seniors, and the disabled	Return ticket	Round-trip ticket
Cooker	Stove (sometimes called an Aga, a brand name)	Ring	Call on the phone ("Ring me in the morning.")
First floor	Second floor (and so on)	Rubber	Eraser
Flat	Apartment	Serviette	Napkin
Fortnight	Two weeks	Single ticket	One-way ticket
Ground floor	First floor	Subway	Underpass
Jumper	Sweater	Ta	Thanks
Knackered	Tired	Teatime	Period between 3:30 and 6 p.m.
Knickers	Underwear ("Don't get your knickers in a twist.")	Tights	Pantyhose
Lift	Elevator	Torch	Flashlight
Loo	Toilet/restroom ("I need to use the loo.")	Underground/ Tube	Subway
Lorry	Truck		

FOR DUMMIES®

The fun and easy way™ to travel!

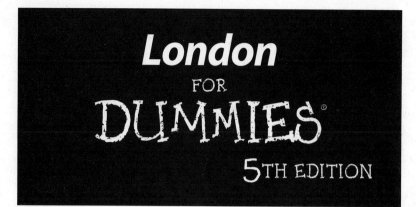

London

FOR

DUMMIES®

5TH EDITION

by Donald Olson

WILEY

Wiley Publishing, Inc.

London For Dummies,® 5th Edition

Published by
Wiley Publishing, Inc.
111 River St.
Hoboken, NJ 07030-5774
www.wiley.com

Copyright © 2008 by Wiley Publishing, Inc., Indianapolis, Indiana

Published simultaneously in Canada

For general information on our other products and services, please contact our Customer Care Department within the U.S. at 800-762-2974, outside the U.S. at 317-572-3993, or fax 317-572-4002.

For technical support, please visit www.wiley.com/techsupport.

Wiley also publishes its books in a variety of electronic formats. Some content that appears in print may not be available in electronic books.

Library of Congress Control Number: 2008920771

ISBN: 978-0-470-16562-1

Manufactured in the United States of America

10 9 8 7 6 5 4 3 2 1

WILEY

About the Author

Donald Olson is a novelist, playwright, and travel writer. His newest novel, *Memoirs Are Made of This,* was published in the U.K. by Hodder-Headline in 2007 under the pen name Swan Adamson. Two earlier Swan Adamson novels, *My Three Husbands* and *Confessions of a Pregnant Princess,* were published in the U.S. and translated into French. Donald Olson's novel, *The Confessions of Aubrey Beardsley,* was published in the United Kingdom by Bantam Press, and his play, *Beardsley,* was produced in London. His travel stories have appeared in the *New York Times, Travel + Leisure, Sunset, National Geographic* books, and many other publications. His additional guidebooks *England For Dummies, Best Day Trips from London, Irreverent London, Germany For Dummies,* and *Frommer's Vancouver & Victoria* are all published by Wiley. London is one of Donald's favorite cities, and England is one of his favorite countries. *England For Dummies* won a 2002 Lowell Thomas Travel Writing Award for best guidebook.

Dedication

This book is dedicated to all those Americans who love London as much as I do. And to my witty and convivial London friends, Stephen Simpson, Didi Morris, David Gwillim, Caroline Montgomery, Antonia Till, and Lady Val.

Author's Acknowledgments

I would like to thank my partner, Gary Larson, for his help and comradeship while I was researching this new edition of *London For Dummies.*

Publisher's Acknowledgments

We're proud of this book; please send us your comments through our Dummies online registration form located at www.dummies.com/register/.

Some of the people who helped bring this book to market include the following:

Acquisitions, Editorial, and Media Development

Editors: Project Editor, Jonathan Scott; Development Editor, Melinda Quintero

Copy Editor: Elizabeth Kuball

Cartographer: Guy Ruggiero

Editorial Manager: Tamara Ahrens

Editorial Assistant: Jennifer Polland

Senior Photo Editor: Richard Fox

Cover Photo: A trio of well-dressed Londoners, © Vassilis Constantineas/IML Image Group/drr.net

Back Photo: Pub exterior, © Steve Vidler/Jupiter Images

Cartoons: Rich Tennant (www.the5thwave.com)

Composition Services

Project Coordinator: Kristie Rees

Layout and Graphics: Claudia Bell, Carl Byers, Ronald Terry, Christine Williams

Proofreaders: Laura Albert, Jessica Kramer, Christine Sabooni

Indexer: Slivoskey Indexing Services

Publishing and Editorial for Consumer Dummies

Diane Graves Steele, Vice President and Publisher, Consumer Dummies

Joyce Pepple, Acquisitions Director, Consumer Dummies

Kristin A. Cocks, Product Development Director, Consumer Dummies

Michael Spring, Vice President and Publisher, Travel

Kelly Regan, Editorial Director, Travel

Publishing for Technology Dummies

Andy Cummings, Vice President and Publisher, Dummies Technology/General User

Composition Services

Gerry Fahey, Vice President of Production Services

Debbie Stailey, Director of Composition Services

Contents at a Glance

Maps at a Glance

Table of Contents

Introduction

● ●

*F*or all its historic panache, time-honored traditions, quaint corners,
and associations with royal pomp and ceremony, London is very
much a modern European city. London is a rich blend of the very old
and the very new, with attractions ranging from the Tower of London,
begun in 1066, to the Tate Modern gallery, which opened in 2000. It's big,
too, both in size and population; more than 9 million people reside in the
1,611-square-kilometer (622-sq.-mile) megalopolis known as Greater
London.

For first-time visitors, London can be a bit of a challenge. But with some
advance planning and useful information under your belt, making the
trip will be easier and even more enjoyable than you thought. London
may be far from where you live, but for many people, a trip to England is
like going home.

About This Book

London For Dummies, 5th Edition, is meant to be used as a reference.
You can start at the first page and read all the way through. If you do,
you'll end up with an unusually complete knowledge of London essentials. On the other hand, you may not need parts of this book because
you've already been to London or know the basics of international
travel. You're after quick, easy-to-find specifics. In that case, you can
easily flip to the part that you need or home in on a specific chapter. The
philosophy behind this book is quite simple: I wanted to create the kind
of guide that I wished I'd had on my first trips to London — informative,
practical, down-to-earth, and fun.

When you travel, unexpected surprises create the most memorable
moments and provide the stories that you take back with you. But the
other side of travel is details and planning. Questions about where to eat
and sleep aren't small issues when you're away from home. They can
make or break a trip — I know that. So what I offer here is based on my
own experience in traveling, living, and working in London.

You should know, however, that travel information is subject to change
at any time — especially prices. Therefore, I suggest that you write or
call ahead for confirmation when making your travel plans.

The authors, editors, and publisher cannot be held responsible for the experiences of readers while traveling. Your safety is important to us, however, so we encourage you to stay alert and be aware of your surroundings. Keep a close eye on cameras, purses, and wallets — all favorite targets of thieves and pickpockets.

Conventions Used in This Book

I recently tried to extract some information from a guidebook and found so many symbols that I needed training in hieroglyphics to interpret them all. I'm happy to report that the user-friendly *London For Dummies, 5th Edition,* travel guide isn't like that. I keep the use of symbols and abbreviations to a minimum. Here are the conventions you need to be aware of while using this book:

- ✔ The credit card abbreviations are AE (American Express), DC (Diners Club), MC (MasterCard), and V (Visa).

- ✔ I include the London postal area (SW7, for example) in all street addresses, in case you want to look up the street in a *London A–Z* or other London street reference map.

- ✔ I give the nearest Tube/Underground (subway) stop for all destinations (for example, Tube: Piccadilly Circus).

- ✔ I list all prices first in British pounds sterling (£), and then in U.S. dollars ($) rounded to the nearest dollar (when prices are under $10, I round them to the nearest nickel). Although the exchange rate fluctuates daily, in this book, I use the rate £1 = $2.

- ✔ The London city code, 020, precedes all London telephone numbers in this book (a different toll-free or charge-for-call code applies in a few cases, which I note). The local London number follows the city code. If you're calling London from outside the United Kingdom, you must dial the U.K. country code (44), followed by 20 and the local number. If you're calling London from elsewhere within the United Kingdom, dial 020 before the number. If you're calling London from within London, just dial the local number.

I also apply a few conventions to the listings of hotels, restaurants, and attractions, as follows:

- ✔ I list the hotels, restaurants, and top attractions in alphabetical order, so you can easily move among the maps and descriptions.

- ✔ For those hotels, restaurants, and attractions that you can find on a map in this book, I include a page reference in the listing information. If a hotel, restaurant, or attraction is outside the city limits or in an out-of-the-way area, it may not be mapped.

- ✔ I give exact prices for every hotel, restaurant, and attraction. Please note, however, that prices are subject to change. Also, an additional 17.5 percent *VAT* (value-added tax) is added to restaurant meals and may be added to hotel bills. (I note in the individual hotel listings if the price does not include VAT.)

✔ I use a system of dollar signs ($) to show a range of costs for hotels or restaurants. The dollar signs for hotels correspond to *rack rates* (nondiscounted standard rates) and reflect a hotel's low to high rates for a double room. For restaurants, the dollar signs denote the *average* cost of dinner for one person, including appetizer, main course, dessert, a nonalcoholic drink, tax, and a tip. Check out the following table to decipher the dollar signs:

Cost	Hotel	Restaurant
$	₤100/$200 or under	₤13/$25 or under
$$	₤101–₤150/$201–$300	₤13–₤25/$26–$50
$$$	₤151–₤200/$301–$400	₤26–₤38/$51–$75
$$$$	₤201–₤250/$401–$500	₤39/$76 and up
$$$$$	₤251/$501 and up	

✔ I divide the hotels into two categories — my personal favorites and those that don't quite make my preferred list but still get my hearty seal of approval. Don't be shy about considering these "runner-up" hotels if you can't get a room at one of my favorites or if your preferences differ from mine — the amenities that the runners-up offer and the services that each provides make all these accommodations good choices to consider as you determine where to rest your head at night.

Foolish Assumptions

As I wrote this book, I made some assumptions about you and what your needs may be as a traveler:

✔ You may be an inexperienced traveler looking for guidance when determining whether to take a trip to London and how to plan for it.

✔ You may be an experienced traveler, but you don't have a lot of time to devote to trip planning, or you don't have a lot of time to spend in London after you get there — you want expert advice on how to maximize your time and enjoy a hassle-free trip.

✔ You may be looking for a carefully selective guidebook, one that focuses only on the places that will give you the best or most unique experiences in London.

If you fit any of these criteria, then *London For Dummies,* 5th Edition, has all the information you're looking for!

How This Book Is Organized

This book has six parts, plus an appendix. You can read all the parts independently — so if you want to zero in on restaurants or hotels, you can turn right to that part. Or you can read the book sequentially to find out all that you need to know about planning and visiting the City by the Thames. The parts include the following:

Part I: Introducing London

This part introduces London and gives you some excellent reasons for going there. I give you a rundown of the best London has to offer, from hotels to historic sights, and then take you deeper into the city's culture, providing information to help you appreciate London's history, architecture, and cuisine. You can use this part to help you decide on the best time of year for your visit, and I recommend some books and movies that may whet your appetite and enhance your enjoyment of London.

Part II: Planning Your Trip to London

This part helps take some of the wrinkles out of trip planning. First, you can get some tips on managing your money and planning a realistic budget. You can also find information on getting to London by air or by crossing over (or under) the English Channel from Europe. Included here are all the options for airlines, tips on how to get the best fare, plus the lowdown on package tours and whether they can really save you money. I provide special tips for families, travelers with disabilities, seniors, and gays and lesbians. This part also covers the details that you need to take care of or consider before your trip begins — from passports to health insurance.

Part III: Settling into London

This part tells you what you need to know after you arrive. A bit of orientation is in order, including detailed information on the ways, means, and costs of getting from the airport into the city. The thumbnail sketches of London neighborhoods can help you decide where you want to stay and what areas you may want to explore. You can find everything that you need to know about getting around town — whether you travel on foot, by public transit, or in a taxi. I explain what kind of accommodations you can expect for your money and describe London's best hotels and B&Bs. After that, I talk about the city's dining scene, provide you with an appetizing survey of London's best restaurants, and provide a list of places for quick, casual meals; down-to-earth fish-and-chips joints; simple or glamorous teas; and picnic possibilities.

Part IV: Exploring London

This part is dedicated to seeing the sights — from the absolute must-sees to lesser-known haunts and fascinating places that are only a quick train or Tube ride away. You can find all kinds of guided tours and shopping coverage that steers you to a whole range of big stores (yes, including Harrods) and small specialty shops. I also provide four sample itineraries that maximize your sightseeing but won't leave you gasping for breath. And if you want to explore beyond London, check out my six great day trips — to Bath, Stonehenge, and more.

Part V: Living It Up after Dark: London Nightlife

This part introduces you to the performing arts, with an emphasis on London's fabulous theater scene, and all manner of after-dark entertainment possibilities. I clue you in to the best sources for finding out what's going on around town and tell you how to get tickets. I also fill you in on some of the city's best pubs, clubs, bars, and discos.

Part VI: The Part of Tens

This part allows me to squeeze in some extra people, places, and things that you may want to know about but that don't really fit in elsewhere in the book. My lists include ten famous London statues, ten special London churches, ten historic pubs, and ten important royals — past and present.

Quick Concierge

This appendix includes an A-to-Z directory of fast facts that you need to know, such as how the telephone system works, what numbers to call in an emergency, and what taxes you must pay. I also provide a list of toll-free telephone numbers and Web sites for airlines and hotel chains serving London, and tell you where to go to find more information on London.

Icons Used in This Book

These six icons appear in the margins throughout this book:

Bargain Alert is my favorite icon — and I suspect it may be yours, too. I'm not cheap, but I love to save money and find out about special deals. Every time I tell you about something that can save you money, I include the Bargain Alert icon.

The Best of the Best icon highlights the best London has to offer in all categories — hotels, restaurants, attractions, shopping, and nightlife.

I'm not an alarmist, so you won't find too many Heads Up icons in this book. If you see one, it means that I want you to be aware of something, such as ticket agencies claiming to sell "reduced-price tickets" or the double-tipping scam that you may encounter in a restaurant. London, you'll be pleased to know, isn't the kind of city that requires too many warning labels.

Traveling with children? Keep your eyes peeled for the Kid Friendly icon. If the icon is in front of a hotel name, the hotel welcomes families with children and may even provide extras for kids. If it's in front of a restaurant name, the kids will enjoy the food or the atmosphere, and the staff will be welcoming to youngsters. And if the icon is in front of an attraction name, kids will (probably) enjoy something about the place.

 When was the last time you read a travel book that filled you in on local gossip, as well as all the mundane facts? For the London Tattler icon (named after the famous London newspaper, *The Tatler,* published from 1709 to 1711), I include only the most newsworthy scandals — I mean stories — to report on. I throw in these tidbits about well-known Londoners and curious bits of London lore just for the fun of it.

 The Tip icon highlights useful bits of information that can save you time or enhance your London experience. A Tip alerts you to something (like a special guided tour or a way to avoid standing in long lines) that you may not otherwise consider or even know about.

Where to Go from Here

To London, of course! This book gives you the tools you need to make the most of your trip, making it a very good place to start your journey. Because the book covers all the basics, it's an excellent guide to help you plan, anticipate, and understand exactly what you want to see and do in London. Whatever your plan, I hope that you think of me as your guide or companion on the journey. I love London. My goal is to help you have a great time while you're there.

Part I
Introducing London

The 5th Wave   By Rich Tennant

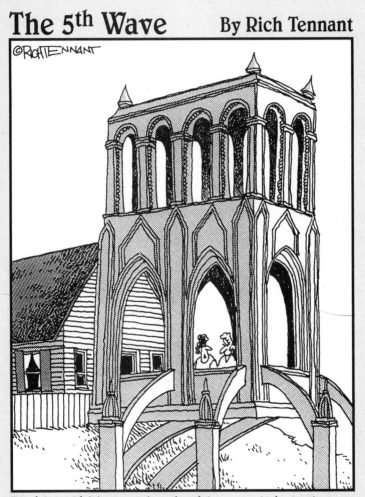

"I think Philip was inspired by our trip last year touring the Great Gothic Decks of London."

In this part . . .

Are you a stranger to London? Well, now's the time to be properly introduced. This part helps you put a face to the place. In Chapter 1, I give a general overview of the best this great city has to offer, sketching in some details so you know what you can find there — including the newest attractions. Chapter 2 helps you understand London from a historical, architectural, and gastronomical perspective and gives you a few suggestions for books and movies that may add to your London knowledge. If you haven't decided when to go, turn to Chapter 3, where I fill you in on what London offers during each season and why you may find some times better than others for a visit.

Chapter 1

Discovering the Best of London

So, you're going to London. Gives you a thrill just thinking about it, right? The capital of the United Kingdom is one of the world's top destinations, visited year-round by millions from all corners of the globe. In fact, international travel surveys consistently rank London as one of the most popular holiday destinations in the world. After you arrive, you'll be making your way through one of the most historic, cultured, and exciting cities on Earth. You have every reason to feel a tingle of anticipation.

This chapter gives you an at-a-glance reference to the absolute best — the best of the best — that London has to offer. In the categories that I outline, you'll find some of the things that make visiting London so much fun and so endlessly fascinating. I discuss each of these places in detail later in this book; you can find them in their indicated chapters, marked with a Best of the Best icon.

The Best Places to Soak Up London's History

The great historic landmarks in London never fail to stir the imagination: They've been witness to so much — from glorious triumphs to bloody tragedies — that it's almost impossible to remain unmoved when visiting them. In Chapter 11, you'll find more details on London's top attractions; here are my picks for the best of the best:

> ✔ An almost perceptible aura of legend pervades the **Tower of London,** which was built over 900 years ago. When visiting the Tower, you tread the ground where the great dramas and terrors of

a turbulent kingdom were played out, where Elizabeth I was held captive while still a princess, and where Sir Thomas More and Anne Boleyn (second wife of Henry VIII and mother of the future Elizabeth I) were beheaded.

✔ No less venerable is **Westminster Abbey,** a magnificent Gothic church that ranks as the most historically significant religious structure in England. Stepping into Westminster Abbey, you enter the place where England's kings and queens have been crowned since William the Conqueror claimed the throne in 1066 and where some of England's greatest figures are buried or memorialized.

✔ Many of London's most historic sites are or were royal domains, and royal watching is a sport almost as popular as horse racing. Okay, so you're probably not going to get invited to the queen's garden party, but you can see where those famous parties take place — and stroll through the royal staterooms — by visiting **Buckingham Palace,** the queen's London residence and a seat of today's royal power and intrigue.

✔ If you missed the Changing of the Guard at Buckingham Palace or want another dose of that royal pomp and pageantry, **Windsor Castle** is less than an hour away. Reputedly the queen's favorite castle, Windsor has a 900-year history that stretches back to the time of William the Conqueror. Many of the rooms that you visit today were remodeled in the time of Queen Victoria.

✔ **Hampton Court Palace** is one of the most magnificent of former royal palaces, and you can easily get there in 30 minutes by train from Central London (or, more romantically, by taking a boat on the Thames). In addition to visiting dozens of staterooms in this 16th-century Tudor palace where Henry VIII once resided, you can enjoy the splendid gardens with their famous maze.

✔ Although you can't see the rooms where the late Princess Diana actually lived, you can get into her former home, **Kensington Palace,** situated at the western side of Kensington Gardens. In addition to the vast, visitable staterooms, this mostly 18th-century palace, where Victoria was born in 1819, houses a remarkable costume exhibit that includes royal raiment through the ages.

✔ Occupying a spot right on the River Thames, the **Houses of Parliament** and their landmark clock tower containing Big Ben have been a familiar sight to Londoners for over 150 years. In the summer, fascinating tours of this seat of power let you see the House of Commons and the House of Lords. Or you can just admire the buildings from the outside and wait for the hourly boom of Big Ben.

✔ **St. Paul's Cathedral,** with its landmark dome, is dear to the hearts of Londoners and is used for events of national significance. A masterpiece by the architect Sir Christopher Wren, the cathedral was built following the Great Fire that swept through London in 1666.

Pomp, ceremony, and scandal: The royals

In London, the royals are spied on the way movie stars are in the United States. The paparazzi furor lessened a bit after Princess Diana's death, but it still exists.

I never gave much thought to royalty, except as a footnote to history, until one day, years ago, when I was passing St. James's Palace and saw Princess Diana and Princess Anne being hustled into a waiting limo. There they were, two princesses, going about the mysterious routines of royalty. I saw them for maybe three seconds and stood there like a slack-jawed yokel as the limo pulled away.

From the queen on down, the monarchy is a huge business (they actually call themselves **"The Firm"**), and you can't avoid it. Buy a London paper any day in London, and you can find some juicy tidbit about Prince Charles, his new wife Camilla Parker-Bowles (the Duchess of Cornwall), Prince William, Prince Andrew, Prince Harry, Princess Anne, or some other member of The Firm. (I provide a few juicy items of my own in this book with my London Tattler asides.)

The Best Museums

If you're a dedicated museum maven, London's selection will keep you going for days, weeks, months, even years. This city is loaded with every conceivable kind of treasure from all over the world. And, amazingly enough, entrance to all the great national museums is free. You can read more about all of London's top museums in Chapter 11; the following are the best of the best:

- ✔ The venerable **British Museum,** with its unparalleled collection of antiquities, comes out on top — the magnificent Parthenon sculptures (formerly called the Elgin Marbles) understandably hold pride of place there, but you'll be amazed by the superlative Egyptian and Roman collections, as well as the ancient treasures found in England.

- ✔ The **National Gallery** houses the nation's greatest collection of British and European paintings from the 13th to the 20th centuries. Here, you find works by Italian masters, such as Leonardo da Vinci and Raphael; canvases by every great French Impressionist; a stunning Rembrandt collection; and paintings by great British artists, such as Turner and Constable.

- ✔ If you tire of the great Western European masterworks hanging in the National Gallery, you can walk next door to see images of pop icons like Elton John and Princess Di in the **National Portrait Gallery.** Here, you'll find a visual who's who of every famous Brit in history, captured in paint, stone, bronze, and photographs.

- ✔ Keen on decorative and applied arts? Then head over to the **Victoria & Albert Museum,** a linchpin in the cluster of great South

Kensington museums. The V&A, as it's called, houses wonderfully decorated period rooms, a comprehensive fashion collection, Italian Renaissance sculpture, and acres more.

✔ The other two outstanding museums in South Kensington are the **Natural History Museum** and the **Science Museum.** Animatronic dinosaurs, including a hungry *T. rex,* are the cold-blooded stars in the Natural History Museum's famed dinosaur exhibit, but while you're there, check out the mind-boggling collection of gems. In the Science Museum, you come face to face with legends from the world of science and technology.

✔ London's South Bank is buzzing with the addition of the stunning **Tate Modern.** Housed in a former power station on the river, the museum exhibits an international roster of contemporary greats.

✔ **Tate Britain** holds the world's greatest collection of British art. Wander through rooms filled with works by William Blake, Turner, Hogarth, Sir Joshua Reynolds, Constable, and all the pre-Raphaelites.

✔ London lovers will love the **Museum of London,** probably the world's most comprehensive city museum, which features an amazing collection of Roman antiquities (the museum incorporates part of a 2,000-year-old Roman wall) and tells the fascinating story of London through the ages.

✔ You can also enjoy masterpieces in museums that were built as private palaces, such as **Spencer House,** former home of Princess Diana's family; **Apsley House,** home of the first Duke of Wellington; and **Hertford House,** home of the Wallace Collection, a national museum.

The Best of British Cuisine

Once upon a time, you could always count on getting lousy meals in London. The nation's dull, insular, uninspired cooking was the joke of Europe. That reputation began to change in the 1980s, with the influx of new cooking trends that favored foods from France and Italy. Since then, London has become a food capital (allegedly with more Michelin-starred restaurants than Paris). For a handy reference guide to English cuisine, see the Cheat Sheet at the front of this book. You can find all of my top London restaurants in Chapter 10; here are my picks for the best the London dining scene has to offer:

✔ London is the best place to find restaurants serving inventive Modern British cuisine. Reserve a table at **Rules, The Ivy, Langan's Bistro, Veronica's, The Oratory,** or **Boxwood Café** — to name just a few — and let your taste buds do the talking.

✔ Traditionalists need not despair: All those wonderful old English faves are still around — eggs, kippers, beans, and fried tomatoes for breakfast; bubble and squeak; roast beef and Yorkshire pudding; meat pies; fish and chips; toad in the hole; cottage pie; sticky toffee pudding; and trifle. You'll find the old English comfort foods at pubs and restaurants such as **The Stockpot, Founders Arms, Simpson's-in-the-Strand, Porter's English Restaurant,** and many others.

✔ Some would say that Indian cooking is the new national cuisine of England. Well, it's certainly one of multiethnic London's faves, and Indian restaurants are often far more affordable than your other options. Like other cuisines, Indian cooking in England has been undergoing many transformations. **Veeraswamy** is the oldest Indian restaurant in London, but the interior is cool and contemporary. You can also find great Indian cooking at **Mela** and **Noor Jahan.**

✔ If French cooking is your idea of heaven, you won't lack for dining options in London. Both traditional and nouvelle French restaurants remain alive and well. You may want to try the classiest of them all, **Aubergine;** other choices include **Oxo Tower Brasserie,** with its stunning river views, **Criterion Bar & Grill,** and **Brasserie St. Quentin.**

✔ And don't forget that London boasts more ethnic restaurants than anywhere else in the United Kingdom, so almost any kind of cuisine can be on the tip of your tongue. For delectable tapas and Spanish/ Moroccan food, go to **Moro.** For slurpy and superlative Japanese noodles, head for **Wagamama.** At **Ken Lo's Memories of China,** you can feast on food inspired by a Chinese master chef. For fresh New Zealand mussels and the most delicious New Zealand dessert, known as Pavlova, **Suze in Mayfair** is your best bet.

The Best Places to Shop in London

It's not just my credit cards talking: I'm here to tell you that London is one of the world's great shopping cities — possibly the greatest. Why? The sheer variety of what's available.

Trend-setting London is to the United Kingdom what New York City is to the United States: the place where it happens first (or ultimately ends up). London is where you can eyeball what's hot, British style. You see the latest hard-core street fashions side by side with the quintessentially traditional.

Not into new? In London, you can hunt for an old engraving, try on a cocktail dress from the '50s, paw through bric-a-brac at an outdoor market stall, or wander through the London silver vaults in your quest for a Georgian soup ladle.

For my complete rundown of London shopping, see Chapter 12; below are some hints on finding London's best stores and shopping districts:

✔ Is **Harrods** the most famous department store in the world? Quite possibly so. See for yourself if it deserves all the hype. And be sure to visit the Food Halls.

✔ **Fortnum & Mason** is the queen's London grocer, and it's probably the only store in the world where you'll see cans of soup displayed on wooden shelves along carpeted aisles. Other departments include china, crystal, leather, antiques, and stationery — plus, you can dine at the store's famous restaurants.

✔ Shopaholics hold **Oxford Street** in very high regard. Lined with major department stores like **Selfridges** and **Marks & Spencer,** and chockablock with dozens upon dozens of moderate to upscale shops, it's a rendezvous point for shoppers of all ages from all over the world. Motto: Big Names, Reasonable Prices.

✔ **Knightsbridge** is a flash-and-cash point of the highest order, home of the aforementioned Harrods, the smaller **Harvey Nichols,** and a lot of luxurious designer boutiques where real and wannabe aristocrats shop for "the season."

✔ Time and money just fly when you visit the super-chic boutiques of **Covent Garden, Bond Street,** and **King's Road** in Chelsea. In these certified shopping zones, you can find everything a true fashionista could ever want.

✔ Hidden away from the hoi polloi, the 200-year-old shops on **Jermyn Street** cater to traditionalists who want the finest goods available. Many of the shops on Jermyn Street have *Royal Warrants* — that is, they're allowed to advertise that they sell to the royal family. Look for custom-made shirts and suits, hand-tooled leather shoes, and fabulous toiletry shops, such as **Floris** and **Taylors of Old Bond Street.**

✔ What reader wouldn't be tempted by the wonderland of bookstores on **Charing Cross Road?** It's a reader's feast and a browser's paradise, with major U.K. independent bookstores like **W & G Foyle,** major U.K. chains like **Waterstone's,** and smaller specialized bookstores like **Murder One** all represented.

The Best of London's Performing Arts

London is a world capital, and that includes being a world capital of the performing arts. When the sun goes down, the curtain comes up. For a description of London's major performing arts venues and companies, see Chapter 15; here are my recommendations for the very best:

✔ For many visitors, going to the **theater** is reason enough to go to London. When actors of the highest caliber are on the boards — as they always are in London — you don't need to think twice about going to the theater; you just go. The London theater scene is phenomenal, and prices are lower than in New York. Take your pick:

long-running international-hit musicals, light comedies, hard-hitting dramas, new works in "fringe" venues, everything from William Shakespeare to Oscar Wilde to Neil LaBute and beyond.

✔ Opera buffs appreciate the fact that London has two major opera companies. International stars appear at the historic **Royal Opera** in Covent Garden, where operas are performed in their original languages. A few blocks away is the **English National Opera,** where every opera is sung in English by mostly British performers and the productions tend to be more adventuresome.

✔ Every night, lovers of classical music have an embarrassment of riches to choose from. London is home to several world-class symphony orchestras. The **London Symphony Orchestra** plays at the Barbican Center, where good seats cost as little as £15 ($30). The **Royal Philharmonic Orchestra** performs at Cadogan Hall and the Royal Albert Hall. The newly refurbished Royal Festival Hall is home to four resident orchestras: the **London Philharmonic,** the **Philharmonia Orchestra,** the **London Sinfonietta,** and the **Orchestra of the Age of Enlightenment.** Other renowned U.K. and European orchestras perform regularly in the city, as do internationally known chamber music ensembles. A summer highlight is the Proms concerts at Royal Albert Hall, featuring an international roster of the best orchestras and soloists in the world.

✔ Dance aficionados can enjoy an evening at the **Royal Ballet** and/or the **English National Ballet,** both of which have regular London seasons. Smaller dance companies, from traditional to cutting edge, are at home in venues throughout the city.

The Best Urban Charms

London is one great city that has actually gotten better over the years. In deference to the millennium year 2000, the city dusted itself off and spruced itself up in ways that have benefited residents and visitors alike. Old museums, such as the Great Court in the British Museum, have been revamped with stunning results, and new museums, such as Tate Modern, have opened (see "The Best Museums," earlier in this chapter). Sleek, new bridges now span the Thames, and riverside areas have seen a flurry of development. Trafalgar Square has been joined to the National Gallery, making pedestrian access a breeze rather than a chore. All in all, London has shaken off its old mantle of hidebound traditionalism, has embraced multiculturalism, and is now high tech and cutting edge.

But the old fabric of London still remains and invites exploration. Despite all the improvements in public transit, London remains a city where walking is a joy that reveals no end of simple urban pleasures; the following are the best among them:

✔ London is blessed with marvelous **parks.** You may have heard of them: **Hyde Park, Kensington Gardens, St. James's Park, Green Park,** and **Regent's Park** (all described in Chapter 11). These carefully groomed havens, where you can stroll beneath stately trees, lounge on the grass, watch ducks in a pond, or admire the color of the springtime daffodils, were former royals-only hunting grounds. Now they're part of every Londoner's life and life's blood, the green lungs of an otherwise congested city.

✔ What could be more fun than just wandering around **London's streets?** Try it. Pick a neighborhood — the City, Soho, Chelsea — then just stroll at will, taking note of the wealth of architectural styles, the curious reminders of days gone by, and the array of local sights, such as the blue, "famous-person-lived-here" plaques on house fronts. On some streets, you can almost hear the horses' hooves clopping on the cobblestones as they did up until about 1915.

✔ The **South Bank** and **Southwark** areas on the "other" side of the river have been opened for pedestrians and show off an ancient area of London that's been completely revitalized. You can enjoy a waterside walk with city views from Westminster Bridge to Tower Bridge.

✔ The variety of **architectural styles** adds to the beauty of the city. Because the Great Fire of 1666 burned down most of medieval London, the building and house styles that you see tend to range from the sober neoclassical of the early 18th century, to the more elegantly light-hearted Regency style of the early 19th century, to the heavier and less graceful Victorian period of the mid- to late 19th century. The human scale of London streets, with their long terraces of attached brick, stone, and stucco homes built around leafy squares, gives the city a charm and character that intrigues and delights the eye. London grew from a series of villages, and you can still find that villagelike character in many London neighborhoods. (For a list of those neighborhoods, see Chapter 8, and for more on London architecture, see Chapter 2.)

Chapter 2

Digging Deeper into London

$\bullet\,\bullet$

In This Chapter

▶ Perusing the main events in London's history
▶ Admiring London's architecture
▶ Discovering English food and beer
▶ Finding books and movies about London

$\bullet\,\bullet$

*T*his chapter helps you find out more about London and deepens your experience of England. I distill the essence of London's complicated and tumultuous past so you can get a clear, quick sense of the major epochs. Then I highlight the main architectural trends, whet your appetite with a primer on English food and drink, and recommend some excellent books and movies about the capital of the United Kingdom.

The Main Events: A Brief History of London

London's history is inextricably intertwined with the larger history of England. Endless tomes have been written on individual monarchs, colorful personalities, architectural styles, and historical epochs in English history. But I'm going to be as brief as a bikini and give you a history that covers only the bare essentials in the following sections.

Prehistory and the arrival of the Romans

Over 2,500 years ago, a Celtic tribe was living beside the River Thames in the region that would later become London.

When the Romans conquered England in A.D. 43, they suppressed or subdued the local Celts. The legendary Queen Boudicca (or Boadicea) was a Celtic warrior queen who fought back the invading Romans. (You can see a statue of her on Westminster Bridge in London.) The Romans brought their building and engineering skills to England and erected a 2.6-square kilometer (1-sq.-mile) fort they called Londinium. This small settlement eventually became the City of London, the earliest area to be developed. In the City, you can still see the remains of Roman walls and a temple where Roman soldiers worshipped a Persian god called Mithras (see Chapter 18).

Northern invaders

With the Roman Empire's breakup in A.D. 410, Jutes, Angles, and Saxons from northern Europe invaded England and formed small kingdoms. For the next 600 years or so, the Anglo-Saxon kingdoms fought off Viking raiders. The capital of England at the time was in Winchester, in the Anglo-Saxon kingdom of Wessex. Because of its strategic position on the Thames, London grew as an important center of trade.

William the Conqueror

The next major transitional period in England — and London — started in 1066, when William of Normandy (1028–1087) fought and killed Harold, the Anglo-Saxon king of England, at the Battle of Hastings. William and his French nobles took over the land, moved their power base to London, and built fortified castles — including Windsor Castle and the Tower of London (both described in Chapter 11) — that still stand today. Every monarch up to the present day claims descent from William the Conqueror and, like him, has been crowned at Westminster Cathedral (see Chapter 11) in London.

Magna Carta

King John, a Plantagenet, signed the Magna Carta in 1215, granting more rights to the nobles. What about the common man and woman? As serfs and vassals in a closed, hierarchical, class-ridden society, their lot wasn't an easy one. Geoffrey Chaucer (1342–1400), who lived and worked in London, was the first writer to give us some recognizable portraits of folks who lived during the medieval period, in *The Canterbury Tales*.

Hundred Years' War

At home and abroad, war and bloodshed tore England apart for more than 300 years. The Hundred Years' War between France and England began in 1337. The War of the Roses, fought between the Houses of York and Lancaster, raged from 1455 to 1487.

Tudor and Elizabethan England

Henry VIII, the Tudor king famous for taking six wives, brought about the next great shift in what had been Catholic England. In 1534, he dissolved all the monasteries and became head of the Church of England. He nabbed Hampton Court Palace (see Chapter 11) from Cardinal Wolsey and made it one of his royal residences. Henry's second wife, Anne Boleyn, was beheaded at the Tower of London in 1536. Henry and Anne Boleyn's daughter, Elizabeth I, ruled during a period of relative peace, power, and prosperity. The Elizabethan period was England's Golden Age, the time when Shakespeare's plays were being performed at the Globe Theatre (see Chapter 15) in London.

Civil War

In 1603, James VI of Scotland became King James I (1566–1625) of England, uniting the crowns of England and Scotland. But conflicts between monarchs and nobles were endless. Charles I (1600–1649), seeking absolute power, dissolved Parliament in 1629. He was beheaded in London after Oliver Cromwell (1599–1658) led a bitter civil war between Royalists and Parliamentarians. Cromwell's armies destroyed churches and Royalist strongholds throughout the country. Cromwell was elevated to Lord Protectorate of the Realm, but by 1660 a new king, Charles II (1630–1685), was on the throne. This time, however, his powers were limited.

Fire, plague, and rebuilding

London, which had been growing steadily, was devastated by two back-to-back catastrophes, the Great Plague of 1665 and the Great Fire of 1666.

Under the brilliant architect Sir Christopher Wren (1632–1723), a new London emerged from the ashes of the Great Fire. Brick and stone replaced timber as the primary building material. Wren's masterpiece, St. Paul's Cathedral (see Chapter 11), was built on the site of the old cathedral, and dozens of Wren churches were erected in the City of London. England's steadily growing naval might was centered at Greenwich (see Chapter 11), where Wren designed the Royal Naval College, today a UNESCO World Heritage Site.

New lines of succession

When James II (1633–1701) tried to reinstate Catholicism in England, he was deposed in 1688 and succeeded by his daughter Mary (1662–1694) and William of Orange (1650–1702), thus ensuring a Protestant line of succession. William and Mary renovated and lived in Kensington Palace (see Chapter 11). The children of Queen Anne (1665–1714), the next monarch, predeceased her, leaving the kingdom without an heir when Anne died. George of Hanover (1660–1727) was chosen to be the next king of England, thus ushering in the reign of the Hanoverians who preceded Victoria.

The Victorian Empire

England reached its zenith of power and prestige during the reign of Victoria (1837–1901), who ruled over an empire so vast that "the sun never set" on it. Victoria was born at Kensington Palace and moved to the grander Buckingham Palace (see Chapter 11) when she was crowned in 1837. Following the death of her husband, Prince Albert of Saxe-Coburg, the queen had the Albert Memorial (see Chapter 11) erected in Kensington Gardens, where it still stands.

The Industrial Revolution spawned major societal changes during this period, moving England away from its agrarian past and into a mechanized future. Charles Dickens (1812–1870) and other social reformers exposed the wretched working and living conditions in Victorian London and throughout England. After a fire, the Houses of Parliament were rebuilt and reopened in 1857. The late Victorian Age was the time of Sherlock Holmes, a fictional London detective created by Sir Arthur Conan Doyle, and Jack the Ripper, a real-life serial killer who terrorized London's East End.

England in the world wars

England suffered terrible losses during World War I (1914–1918) but emerged victorious. During World War II, from the fall of France in 1940 until the United States entered the war in 1941, England stood alone against Hitler. Winston Churchill (1874–1965), the country's prime minister during the war years, frequently held cabinet meetings in a secret warren of underground rooms called the Cabinet War Rooms (see Chapter 11), which are preserved just as they were during his tenure. With strictly rationed food, mandatory blackouts, and terrible bombing raids that destroyed whole sections of London and killed tens of thousands of civilians, life in wartime London had a profound effect on its citizens. Shortages continued for many years afterward.

The welfare state

A major societal shift occurred in 1945 when the Labour Party began to dismantle the empire and introduced the welfare state. Under the National Health System, every citizen in the United Kingdom can receive free healthcare. It wasn't until Margaret Thatcher and the Tory Party came into power during the 1980s that England began privatizing formerly state-run agencies, such as the railroad (with what some say are disastrous results).

Queen Elizabeth II

Queen Elizabeth II ascended the throne in 1952. The fairy-tale wedding of her son Prince Charles to Lady Diana Spencer at St. Paul's Cathedral in 1981 was the last high point for the House of Windsor (which changed its name from the German Saxe-Coburg during World War II). Charles and Diana's subsequent divorce seemed to unleash a floodgate of royal scandals, with the result that the popularity of the British monarchy is at an all-time low. Following her divorce, Diana (1961–1997) lived at Kensington Palace (see Chapter 11), where grieving Londoners left a sea of floral tributes following her death in a car crash.

In 2002, Queen Elizabeth II celebrated her 50th anniversary on the throne.

Recent royal events

In 2005, Prince Charles, the heir to the British throne, finally married his long-time mistress, Camilla Parker-Bowles, in a ceremony that his mother, Queen Elizabeth, did not attend. The wedding was somewhat anticlimactic because Charles had been involved with Camilla throughout his marriage to Princess Diana. On the first anniversary of his marriage to Camilla, Charlie read a poll in the *Times* indicating that 56 percent of Britons did not wish to see his new wife become queen. She will, though, unless the governments of England and 15 Commonwealth nations change the law. In the meantime, the pre-queen is addressed as Her Royal Highness the Duchess of Cornwall.

As the ever-popular Elizabeth enters her twilight years (she turned 81 in 2007), some Britons wonder if the 1,000-year-old British monarchy should end with her — especially with the unpopular Charles next in line for the throne. Just 37 percent of Britons think that Charles should succeed his mother, according to a 2007 poll. In fact, the poll found that 39 percent would prefer that Charles's elder son, Prince William, leapfrog his father for the crown. Poor Charles just can't seem to do anything to win him the respect enjoyed by his mother.

In 2007, Prince Charles was accused by some members of Parliament of overstepping the traditional bounds imposed on the royal family of not interfering in political matters. Soon after, Charles had to read about his second son, Prince Harry, partying with lap dancers as he and his class at Sandhurst military academy finished training. In comparison, Prince William, tall and blond like his late mother, Diana, stays out of trouble and is, by all accounts, quiet and well-mannered. The only semi-bad press William received in 2007 was when he broke off his four-year relationship with Kate Middleton, presumably because her blood wasn't blue enough. Though her parents are self-made millionaires, Kate's mother had once worked as a flight attendant. According to the tabloids, William started to pine for Kate almost as soon as he dumped her, and the two were seen together just two months after their breakup.

William and Harry co-hosted the hugely successful Concert for Diana at Wembley Stadium in London on July 1, 2007 (what would have been Diana's 47th birthday), an event Prince Charles did not attend. The queen, meanwhile, was involved in a PR scuffle when the BBC showed a film clip of her purportedly storming out of a sitting with photographer Annie Leibovitz after Leibovitz asked Her Maj to remove her crown. It turned out that the BBC had manipulated the film footage to suit its story and it was forced to apologize. Soon after, Prince Phillip, the queen's husband, denied reports that he had ever called Diana a "harlot" and a "trollop." Stay tuned. . . .

London at the millennium

In anticipation of the year 2000, London went on an all-out public-relations blitz to show the world that "Rule, Britannia" had become "Cool Britannia." The giant Millennium Dome was a giant fiasco, but the British Airways London Eye (see Chapter 11), an enormous observation wheel, remains one of London's most popular attractions.

Mayor Ken

In 2000, Ken Livingstone, former Labour member of Parliament, was elected to the newly created post of mayor of London (not to be confused with the lord mayor of London, an ancient ceremonial position in the City of London). During his controversial tenure — he was elected for a second term in 2004 — Mayor Ken has instituted major changes in the public transportation system, including the introduction of London's *congestion charge,* a fee that any driver entering Central London during specific hours of the day must pay.

New Labour

In 2001, Tony Blair was elected to a second term as prime minister, and New Labour, with its centrist approach, was firmly in control of the government. But in the 2005 elections, the party lost one-third of its seats as voters expressed their discontent with Blair's continuing support of the U.S.-led war in Iraq. Blair stepped down as prime minister in 2007 and was succeeded by Gordon Brown.

Terrorist bombings

In July 2005, one day after exultant Londoners learned that their city had been chosen to host the 2012 Olympic Games, terrorists detonated bombs in the London Underground and on a double-decker bus, killing 56 people and wounding hundreds more. Londoners stood together and carried on, showing the world that they would not be cowed by acts of violence. A second bombing attempt a week later failed but had tragic consequences when police shot and killed an innocent man suspected of terrorism. In July 2007, police foiled another terrorist plot when they defused bombs in two cars parked in Central London.

Building Blocks: An Overview of English Architecture

The period in which a building was constructed (or reconstructed), is found in its architectural and decorative details. In a country like England, where the age of buildings can span a thousand-year period (a few Anglo-Saxon churches are even older than that), many different styles evolved. The architectural periods are often named for the monarch or royal family reigning at the time. Knowing a few things about the key features of the different styles of London's abundance of historic buildings will add a whole new perspective to your trip. Keep in mind that little remains from before the Great Fire of 1666, which destroyed most of London — Westminster Abbey and the Tower of London are the two most notable exceptions.

The following list gives you a brief primer in English architectural history from Norman to Victorian times:

✔ **Norman (1066–1189):** Round arches, barrel vaults, and highly decorated archways characterize this period's Romanesque style.

✔ **Early English Gothic (1189–1272):** The squat, bulky buildings of the Norman period gave way to the taller, lighter buildings constructed in this style.

✔ **Decorated Gothic (1272–1377):** Buildings in this style have large windows, *tracery* (ornamental work with branching lines), and heavily decorated gables and arches.

✔ **Perpendicular Gothic (1377–1483):** Large *buttresses* (exterior side supports) allowed churches to have larger windows than ever before. Tracery was more elaborate than in previous Gothic buildings, the four-centered arch appeared, and *fan vaulting* (a decorative form of vaulting in which the structural ribs spread upward and outward along the ceiling like the rays of a fan) was perfected.

✔ **Tudor (1485–1553):** During this period, buildings evolved from Gothic to Renaissance styles. Large houses and palaces were built with a new material: brick. England has many half-timbered Tudor and Elizabethan domestic and commercial buildings. This method of construction used brick and plaster between visible wooden timbers.

✔ **Elizabethan (1553–1603):** The Renaissance brought a revival of classical features, such as columns, *cornices* (prominent rooflines with brackets and other details), and *pediments* (decorative triangular features over doorways and windows). The many large houses and palaces of this period were built in an *E* or *H* shape and contained long galleries, grand staircases, and carved chimneys.

✔ **Jacobean (1603–1625):** In England, Inigo Jones used the symmetrical, classically inspired Palladian style that arrived from Italy. Buildings in this style incorporate elements from ancient Greece and Rome.

✔ **Stuart (1625–1688):** Elegant classical features, such as columns, cornices, and pediments, are typical of this period, in which Sir Christopher Wren was the preeminent architect.

✔ **Queen Anne (1689–1714):** Buildings from the English baroque period mix heavy ornamentation with classical simplicity.

✔ **Georgian and Regency (1714–1830):** During these periods, elegant terraced houses were built; many examples survive in Brighton and Bath. Form and proportion were important elements; interior decoration inspired by Chinese motifs became fashionable.

✔ **Victorian (1830–1901):** A whole range of antique styles emerged — everything from Gothic and Greek Revival to pseudo-Egyptian and -Elizabethan. Hundreds of English churches were renovated during the Victorian era.

> ✔ **Modern, postmodern, and contemporary (1946 to present):**
> Massive destruction in World War II bombing raids meant rebuild-
> ing whole sections of London. International modernism, adapted
> from European models, resulted in sleeker and simpler facades.
> The most iconic building from the modernist era is Royal Festival
> Hall, built on the South Bank for the Festival of Britain in 1951.
> Gargantuan and ungainly postmodern office buildings went up in
> the City (London's financial center) in the 1980s, borrowing archi-
> tectural styles and elements from earlier and more gracefully
> coherent epochs. In the past decade, buildings by designer archi-
> tects have popped up on the London skyline, most notably the
> Gherkin, a pickle-shaped City office tower, and the new London City
> Hall, a rounded glass building on the South Bank near Tower
> Bridge, both designed by Lord Norman Foster.

Dining English Style, from Traditional to Modern

London's dining scene can satisfy any taste and budget, and it is the best
place to find restaurants serving inventive modern British and ethnic
cuisines of every sort. In fact, spicy Indian cooking is England's second
"national" cuisine. Scores of Indian and other ethnic restaurants
throughout the city mean there is always something new to try.

But traditionalists in search of all those wonderful old English faves
won't be at a loss. It's true that many Londoners now opt for a latte and
a muffin at Starbucks for their breakfast, but you can still find places
that serve a good greasy fry-up with eggs, kippers, beans, and fried
tomatoes. And old comfort foods like *bubble and squeak* (mashed potatoes mixed with cabbage) and *bangers and mash* (sausages with mashed
potatoes) are still around, too. The great traditional "roasts" are served
at places like Simpson's-in-the-Strand, where a server at your table will
slice your roast beef or roast lamb and dish up your Yorkshire pudding.
When traditional, non-fancy English dishes are done well, they're super-
satisfying and delicious.

Other traditional dishes loved by Londoners include meat and fish pies,
shepherd's pie (ground beef topped with mashed potatoes and baked),
and fish and chips. And for dessert? At restaurants like Porter's English
Restaurant, you can still find *sticky toffee pudding* (sponge cake smoth-
ered in warm butterscotch sauce), *spotted dick* (steamed, raisin-filled
sponge cake covered with custard), and *trifle* (sherry-soaked sponge
cake layered with raspberry preserves, covered with custard sauce,
and topped with whipped cream).

While you're in London, you can also look forward to the world of afternoon tea. Teas can be as simple or as fancy as you want — nothing more
than a cup of tea and a pastry in a patisserie, or an elaborate affair with
scones, clotted or whipped cream, preserves, cakes, and sandwiches.

See Chapter 10 for a list of my recommended London restaurants and spots for tea, and check out the Cheat Sheet at the front of this book for a glossary of English food terms.

Visiting the Local Pub

The pub (short for public house) is an English institution. London is awash with historic pubs where you can sit all evening with a pint of ale, bitter, stout, or cider, and soak up the local color. You can even do a *pub crawl,* walking (upright) from pub to pub and sampling the diverse brews on tap. Although you can get a hard drink at both bars and pubs, when you're in a pub, you're better off confining yourself to beer.

A beer primer: Are you bitter or stout?

Most of the pubs in London and throughout the United Kingdom are tied to a particular brewery and sell only that brewery's beers. (You see the name of the brewery on the sign outside.) Independent pubs can sell more brands than a tied pub. Either way, you still have to choose from what may seem like a bewildering variety. The colorful names of individual brews don't provide much help — you can only wonder what Pigswill, Dogs Bollocks, Hobgoblin, Old Thumper, Pommies Revenge, or Boondoggle taste like. Depending on all sorts of factors — the water, the hops, the fermentation technique, and so on — the brewery crafts the taste of any beer, whether on draught or in a bottle. You can get a few U.S. and international brands, but imports are more expensive than the home-brew.

When ordering beer in a pub, specify the type, the brand, and the amount (pint or half-pint) you want. Asking the bartender to recommend something based on your taste preferences is perfectly okay. Just remember that most English beer is served at room temperature. The following brief descriptions of the most common types of beer will come in handy in a pub:

- ✔ **Bitter** is what most locals drink. It's a clear, yellowish, traditional beer with a strong flavor of hops. *Real ale* is a bitter that's still fermenting ("alive") when it arrives from the brewery; it's pumped and served immediately.

- ✔ **Ale** isn't as strong as bitter and has a slightly sweeter taste. You can order *light* or *pale ale* in a bottle; *export ale* is a stronger variety.

- ✔ **Lager,** when chilled, is probably the closest you can come to an American-style beer. Lager is available in bottles or on draught.

- ✔ **Shandy** is equal parts bitter and lemonade (sometimes limeade or ginger beer); it's for those who like a sweet beverage that's only partially beerlike in taste.

- ✔ **Stout** is a dark, rich, creamy version of ale. Guinness is the most popular brand. A *black and tan* is half lager and half stout.

Parliament has instituted the strict hours that most pubs adhere to: Monday through Saturday from 11 a.m. to 11 p.m. and Sunday from noon to 10:30 p.m. Americans, take note: You *never* tip the bartender in a pub; the best you can do is offer to buy him or her a drink — an acceptable practice in England. Ten minutes before closing, a bell rings, signaling that the time has come to order your last round.

Background Check: Finding London on Page and Screen

Has any country produced as many great and enduring writers as England has? In a brief survey, it's impossible to even scratch the surface. The wonderful thing about London — at least, if you love literature — is that it figures in so many great works. All over the city, you encounter blue plaques on the fronts of buildings identifying what famous person lived there and when. Many of those famous residents were writers. Here are a few of my recommendations:

- ✔ *A History of Britain,* **by Simon Schama:** This highly readable three-volume history of Britain by the noted historian accompanied a program of the same name on the BBC History Channel.

- ✔ *The Cazalet Chronicles,* **by Elizabeth Jane Howard:** The four novels *(The Light Years, Marking Time, Confusion, Casting Off)* in this compulsively readable series chronicle the life of a middle-class family in London and on the south coast of England between the two world wars.

- ✔ *The Diana Chronicles,* **by Tina Brown:** This biography of Diana, Princess of Wales, is highly readable and opinionated — you wouldn't expect less from the former editor of *Tatler, Vanity Fair,* and the *New Yorker.*

- ✔ *The Line of Beauty,* **by Alan Hollinghurst:** A Booker Prize winner, Hollinghurst's brilliantly realized novel sketches a portrait of London during the Thatcher years.

- ✔ *London,* **by Edward Rutherfurd:** London is the main character in this fascinating historical novel that follows the fates of families and fortunes over 2,000 years.

- ✔ *London: A Biography,* **by Peter Ackroyd:** When you get Peter Ackroyd going, you can't shut him up — so it's a good thing he has such fascinating material to so endlessly talk about.

- ✔ *Mrs. Dalloway,* **by Virginia Woolf:** One of Woolf's most accessible and popular books, this novel, written in 1925, takes place during one day in the life of Clarissa Dalloway, an exemplary London hostess, as she prepares for a big party.

- ✔ *Oliver Twist,* **by Charles Dickens:** Dickens set many of his novels in London; one of the most enduring is this story of a boy in Victorian London who survives an almost comically nightmarish world of orphanages and crime.

- ✔ *Saturday,* **by Ian McEwan:** One of McEwan's latest novels, *Saturday* evokes the life of an upper-middle-class family in London today.

- ✔ *Watching the English,* **by Kate Fox:** An entertaining pop-psych book, *Watching the English* deals humorously with the "hidden rules" of English behavior as they relate to class and "Englishness."

- ✔ *White Teeth,* **by Zadie Smith:** This novel is the profoundly hilarious story of two immigrant families in North London.

The Brits are great filmmakers and beat Hollywood cold when it comes to honesty in acting, re-creation of period detail, and human-scale cinematic storytelling. If you've ever watched British television, you know how completely it differs from American TV. The characters actually look like human beings and inhabit recognizable worlds.

Over the past 30 years or so, television imports from the BBC and other U.K. television producers have gained international popularity on *Masterpiece Theatre, Mystery!,* and cable channels, winning legions of fans. Many of these popular series are set in London. They're available on video and DVD:

- ✔ *Absolutely Fabulous:* A hilarious, over-the-top sitcom about two over-the-top women in 1990s London

- ✔ *Cazalet Chronicles:* The fortunes of a middle-class London family between the world wars

- ✔ *The Forsythe Saga:* An Edwardian tale of family intrigue

- ✔ *Upstairs, Downstairs:* Rich London family above, servants below, and stories from both sides at the turn of the 20th century

For a cinematic look at London, you may want to check out the following films:

- ✔ *About a Boy:* You can see a lot of London shots in this well-told story of a narcissistic Londoner (Hugh Grant) who becomes surrogate father to an awkward boy.

- ✔ *Closer:* A chic anomie pervades the lives of four rather unlikable characters whose lives intersect in London today.

- ✔ *Darling:* In this John Schlesinger film from the 1960s, a young Julie Christie stars as a fashionable victim of fashion.

- ✔ *Georgy Girl:* The setting is London in the swingin' '60s, and a young, overweight Lynn Redgrave plays a good-hearted oaf living with a cold-hearted bitch (Charlotte Rampling).

✔ *Love Actually:* Londoners deal with contemporary life and romance in this film starring Hugh Grant, Emma Thompson, Colin Firth, Liam Neeson, Keira Knightley, and others.

✔ *The Madness of King George:* Playwright Alan Bennett wrote the brilliant screenplay for this film about King George III and his bouts with insanity. It features wonderful performances by Nigel Hawthorne, Helen Mirren, and Rupert Everett.

✔ *Midnight Lace:* Doris Day is menaced in London circa 1960 by a mysterious caller; you can see many shots of the city.

✔ *Notes on a Scandal:* Judi Dench is brilliant as an uptight London teacher who falls in with another teacher, the lovely Cate Blanchett, only to discover that her new friend is having an affair with one of her students.

✔ *Notting Hill:* In this romantic comedy, Hugh Grant stars as the owner of a London bookstore and Julia Roberts is an American movie star (quite a stretch).

✔ *The Queen:* Helen Mirren won the Best Actress Oscar in 2007 for her portrayal of Queen Elizabeth II and the crisis following Princess Diana's death in 1997.

✔ *Sunday Bloody Sunday:* In this adult drama from the early '70s, Glenda Jackson and Peter Finch star as Londoners in love with the same guy.

Chapter 3

Deciding When to Go

*L*ondon is one of those cities that's popular year-round. So popular, in fact, that according to VisitBritain (formerly the British Tourist Authority), more than 15 *million* tourists from around the globe visited London in 2005 (the last year for which figures are available).

Arriving in London at any time of year without advance hotel reservations is not a wise idea. If you plan to visit between April and mid-October, making hotel reservations in advance is essential. Although you can find agencies in London that can help you find a hotel or a B&B in peak season (see Chapter 9), you never know quite what you're getting or where it will be, and you will lose some of your precious travel time making arrangements. In Chapter 9, you can find descriptions of my recommended London hotels.

Revealing the Secrets of the Seasons

London weather is what you might call "changeable." Predicting what the weather will be like in any given season is difficult. England is an island, after all, and the seas surrounding it, as well as its northerly location, determine its weather patterns. In general, however, the climate is fairly mild year-round, rarely dipping below freezing or rising above 27°C (80°F), at least for extended periods.

Table 3-1 gives you an idea of London's temperature and rainfall variations. But don't rely on these figures too much: In 2001, London and the rest of England experienced the coldest and wettest winter and spring since written records originated in 1659; and in 2007, London and southern England experienced the warmest spring on record. And every August from 2003 to 2007, the mercury has soared above normal for several days and even reached 32°C (100°F).

Table 3-1	London's Average Temperatures and Rainfall	
Month	*Temp (°C/°F)*	*Rainfall (cm/in.)*
January	4/40	5.3/2.1
February	4/40	4.1/1.6
March	7/44	3.8/1.5
April	9/49	3.8/1.5
May	13/55	4.6/1.8
June	16/61	4.6/1.8
July	18/64	5.6/2.2
August	18/64	5.8/2.3
September	15/59	4.8/1.9
October	11/52	5.6/2.2
November	8/46	6.4/2.5
December	6/42	4.8/1.9

London can be drizzly, muggy, dry and hot, or clammy. It can also be glorious, with clear skies and gentle breezes, or bone-chillingly cold. Some days you get a bit of everything: rain, spots of sun, drizzle, clear skies, and more rain. But whatever the weather, whatever the season, London is well worth seeing. The following sections let you know what's happening in London, season by season, so that you can pick the best time to go for you.

Abloom in the spring

London is at its green, blooming best in April and May. Highlights of the season include the following:

✓ The great London parks and gardens and the surrounding countryside are at their peak of lushness. The Chelsea Flower Show is the quintessential spring event.

✓ Airfares are lower than in summer.

✓ The sky stays light well into the evening.

But keep in mind these springtime pitfalls:

- ✔ During the half-term school holidays in late February and for three weeks around Easter, visitors pour into London. As a result, the major attractions have longer lines (*queues* in Britspeak), and you may have a harder time finding a hotel room.
- ✔ The weather is always unpredictable.
- ✔ Public transportation is reduced during holiday periods.
- ✔ Many museums, stores, and restaurants close on Good Friday, Easter, and Easter Monday (the day after Easter).

Summer fun in the sun

Notoriously chilly London becomes irresistible under the sun. Many tourists flock to London throughout the summer to enjoy the fine weather, but that same weather can turn into rain or a fine, gray drizzle in July and August. The crowds descend in summer for several reasons:

- ✔ Everyone moves outdoors at the slightest hint of good weather, and London buzzes with alfresco theaters, concerts, and festivals (see Chapter 15).
- ✔ The evenings are deliciously long and often cool, even if the day has been hot.
- ✔ The evening stays light until 10 p.m. or even later.

But keep in mind:

- ✔ If you believe the weather statistics, July and August are the months of highest rainfall in London, so skies can stay gray and cloudy.
- ✔ Occasional summer heat waves can drive the mercury toward 30°C, 35°C, and 40°C (the 80s, 90s, and 100s in Fahrenheit), making July and August hot and muggy. Many businesses and budget-class hotels don't have air-conditioning.
- ✔ Aggravated by London's soot, plus gas and diesel fumes, a hot spell can lead to excessive air pollution.
- ✔ Most overseas visitors (30 percent of travelers) converge on the city from July to September. Lines for major attractions can be interminably long.
- ✔ Airfare sales are rare and tickets are the most expensive during the summer peak.
- ✔ Centrally located hotels are more difficult to come by, and their high-season rates apply.
- ✔ Booking your hotel in advance is essential during this time of year (see Chapter 9).

Chock-full of culture in the fall

The golden glow of autumn casts a lovely spell over London. The air is crisp, and the sun gives old stone buildings and church spires a mellow patina. Fall is my favorite time of year to be in London, and I can think of only one disadvantage to counteract the many advantages, which include the following:

- ✔ After mid-September, fewer tourists are around, so the city feels less crowded and you encounter more Londoners than visitors.

- ✔ With the drop in tourism, hotel rates and airfares may go down as well.

- ✔ London's cultural calendar springs to life.

- ✔ Although you may experience rain at this time of year, you're just as likely to encounter what Americans call an "Indian summer," a late stretch of warm weather and clear skies.

One thing to look out for: Like every season in England, autumn can bring rain.

Wonderful in winter

Londoners love to be cozy, and there's no better time for coziness than winter. Although most overseas visitors to London arrive during the warmer months, the number of visitors from *within* the United Kingdom is highest between January and March. What do they know that you should know? Consider the points that make winter wonderful:

- ✔ London in winter is a bargain. London's off-season is November 1 to December 12 and December 25 to March 14. Winter off-season rates for airfares and hotels can sometimes be astonishingly low — airline package deals don't get any cheaper (see Chapter 5). At these times, hotel prices can drop by as much as 20 percent. If you arrive after the Christmas holidays, you can also take advantage of London's famous post-Christmas sales (more on these sales in Chapter 12).

- ✔ Although the winter winds may blow, nothing in London stops — in fact, everything gets busier. The arts — theater, opera, concerts, and gallery shows — are in full swing.

- ✔ London develops a lovely buzz during the Christmas season: The stores are decorated, lights are lit, carols are sung, special holiday pantomimes are performed, and the giant Norwegian spruce goes up in Trafalgar Square.

Naturally, visiting London in the winter has its downside. Consider these points:

  ✔ Although the Yuletide holidays are always jolly, they also add up to another peak tourist season from mid-December to Christmas. You know what that means: bigger crowds and higher prices. The city is virtually shut down on December 25 and 26 and January 1. Stores, museums, and other attractions close, and public transportation is severely curtailed. On December 26 (Boxing Day), you may have problems finding any kind of open restaurant.

  ✔ Wintertime London may be gray and wet for weeks on end; by midwinter, the skies get dark by about 3:30 p.m. The English usually keep their thermostats set quite low, and rather than turn up the heat, they don't their *woollies* (long underwear). You should do the same — or be prepared for a chronic case of goose pimples.

Perusing a Calendar of Events

London hums with festivals and special events of all kinds, some harking back to centuries past. Before you leave for London, write or call **Visit-Britain** (see the Quick Concierge, at the end of this book, for addresses and phone numbers) and request a copy of its monthly *London Planner,* which lists major events, including theater and the performing arts.

January

In January, the **London Parade,** also called the New Year's Day Parade, features marching bands, floats, and the lord mayor of Westminster in a procession from Parliament Square to Berkeley Square. Call ☎ **020/ 8566-8586** for more details. The parade route is mapped out at www. londonparade.co.uk. January 1 from noon to 3 p.m.

February

Late January or early February brings the **Chinese New Year,** marked by colorful street celebrations on and around Gerrard and Lisle streets in Soho's Chinatown. Call ☎ **020/7851-6686** for more information. Date varies.

March

St. Patrick's Day is a big to-do in London, which has the third-largest Irish population, after Dublin and New York. Since 2002, annual parades are held on the weekends around March 17, usually in Trafalgar Square. March 17.

The **King's Road Antiques Fair** draws antiques lovers to Chelsea's Old Town Hall for three days. For more information, visit www.penman-fairs. co.uk. Early March.

April

At the **Oxford and Cambridge Boat Race** between Putney Bridge and Mortlake Bridge, rowing eights from the two famous universities compete for the Beefeater Cup. The Hammersmith Mall makes a good viewing spot. Last Thursday in March or first Saturday in April. (Check the local press for the exact date or go to www.theboatrace.org.)

The **London Marathon,** first held in 1981, has become one of the most popular sporting events in the city. Some 45,000 runners — men and women, champion athletes and first-timers — take part. The 26.2-mile race begins in Greenwich, winds its way past the Tower of London and along the Thames, and finishes in the Mall in front of Buckingham Palace, one of the best viewing spots. For more information, call ☎ 020/ 7902-0199 or check out www.london-marathon.co.uk. Mid-April.

May

The **Football Association FA Cup Final** is held at Wembley Stadium. Remember that *football* in the United Kingdom is what people in the United States call *soccer,* and tickets are difficult to obtain given the sport's popularity. For more information, visit www.thefa.com and www.wembleystadium.com. Mid-May.

One of London's most famous spring events, the **Chelsea Flower Show,** held on the grounds of the Chelsea Royal Hospital, draws tens of thousands of visitors from around the world. You probably want to order tickets at least two months in advance; in the States, you can order them from Keith Prowse at ☎ 800/669-8687 or 212/398-4175 (www.keith prowse.com). For more information, contact the Royal Horticultural Society, Vincent Square, London SW1P 2PE (☎ 020/7834-4333; www.rhs.org.uk). Third week in May.

June

The juried **Royal Academy Summer Exhibition** presents more than 1,000 works of art by living artists from all over the United Kingdom. For more information, call the Royal Academy at ☎ 020/7300-8000 (www.royalacademy.org.uk). Early June through July.

April 21 is Queen Elizabeth's birthday, but her birthday parade, **Trooping the Colour,** takes place in mid-June. The Horse Guards celebrate "Ma'am's" birthday in Whitehall with an equestrian display full of pomp and ceremony. For free tickets (they are scarce, and there's no guarantee you'll get any), send a self-addressed envelope and International Reply Coupon (or U.K. stamps) from January 1 to February 28 to Brigade Major, Headquarters Household Division, Horseguards, Whitehall, London SW1A 5BJ. Mid-June.

The most prestigious horseracing event in England is **Royal Ascot,** held at the Ascot Racecourse (near Windsor in Berkshire, about 30 miles from

London) in the presence of the royal family. For information, call
☎ **01344/876-876** or visit the Web site at www.ascot.co.uk. You
can order tickets online for this event. Mid- to late June.

Kenwood, a lovely estate at the top of Hampstead Heath, is the pastoral
setting for the **Kenwood Lakeside Concerts,** a summer season of
Saturday night, open-air concerts. For more information, call ☎ **020/
8233-7435**. Mid-June to early September.

The world's top tennis players whack their rackets at the **Wimbledon
Lawn Tennis Championships,** held at Wimbledon Stadium. Getting a
ticket to this prestigious event is complicated. From August 1 to
December 31, you can apply to enter the public lottery for next year's
tickets by sending a self-addressed stamped envelope to All England
Lawn Tennis Club, P.O. Box 98, Church Road, Wimbledon, London SW19
5AE; a limited number of tickets is also available on the day of play at
the box office. For more information, call ☎ **020/8944-1066** or 020/
8946-2244 (recorded information), or visit www.wimbledon.com. Late
June to early July.

The **City of London Festival** presents a series of classical concerts,
poetry readings, and theater in historic churches and buildings, including St. Paul's Cathedral and the Tower of London. For more information,
call ☎ **020/7796-4949** or visit www.colf.org. Late June to mid-July.

July
Pride in the Park, the United Kingdom's largest gay and lesbian event,
begins with a march and parade from Hyde Park to Parliament Square,
followed by live music, dancing, and fun. For more information, visit
www.pridelondon.org. Last Saturday in June or first Saturday in July.

The **Henley Royal Regatta,** one of England's premiere sporting and
social events, is a championship rowing event with a long tradition. The
regatta takes place on the Thames just downstream from Henley, an
Oxfordshire town 35 miles west of London. For more information, call
☎ **01491/572-153** or go to www.hrr.co.uk. First week in July.

The **Hampton Court Flower Show,** held on the palace grounds in East
Molesey, Surrey (part of Greater London), shows off one of the loveliest
gardens in England. For more information, call Hampton Court Palace
☎ **0870/7649-1885** or go to www.hrp.org.uk. Second week in July.

In July, you can see the much-loved **BBC Henry Wood Promenade
Concerts.** Known as the Proms, this series of classical and popular concerts is held at the Royal Albert Hall. To book by credit card, call the box
office at ☎ **020/7589-8212** or visit www.royalalberthall.com or www.
bbc.co.uk/proms. Mid-July to mid-September.

August

Buckingham Palace opens to the public August through September. For details and to charge tickets, call ☎ **020/7766-7300.** For more information on visiting the palace, see Chapter 11 or go to www.royal collection.org.uk. August 1 to October 1 (dates vary by a day or two every year).

The **Houses of Parliament** open for guided tours in late summer. You can reserve tickets at the kiosk across from the Houses of Parliament, by phone at ☎ **0870/906-3773** or online at www.firstcalltickets.com. July and August (dates vary by a day or two every year).

During the **Notting Hill Carnival,** steel bands, dancing, and Caribbean fun take over in the streets of Notting Hill (Portobello Road, Ladbroke Grove, and All Saints Road). This enormous street fair is one of Europe's largest. For more information, check magazine listings, call ☎ **020/8964-0544,** or go to www.nottinghillcarnival.org.uk. Last Monday in August.

September

The **Thames Festival** celebrates the mighty river, with giant illuminated floats. For more information, call ☎ **020/7401-2255** or visit www.thames festival.org. Mid-September.

During the **London Open House Weekend,** over 400 buildings usually closed to visitors open their doors for free. For more information, call ☎ **09001/600-061** or visit www.londonopenhouse.org. Third weekend in September.

Since 1950, the Chelsea **Antiques Fair** has drawn lovers of fine antiques to Chelsea Old Town Hall, King's Road, London SW3. For more information visit www.penman-fairs.co.uk. Third week in September.

October

The **Chelsea Crafts Fair** at Somerset House, The Strand, London WC2, is the largest such fair in Europe, with scores of artisans selling handmade crafts of every description. For details, contact the Crafts Council at ☎ **020/7806-2512** or go to www.craftscouncil.org.uk. First week in October.

November

Although based at the National Film Theatre on the South Bank, the **London Film Festival** presents screenings all over town. Call ☎ **020/ 7815-1433** in November for recorded daily updates on what's showing where, or go to www.lff.org.uk. Late October to early November.

On **Guy Fawkes Night,** bonfires and fireworks commemorate Guy Fawkes's failure to blow up King James I and Parliament in 1605. Check the weekly entertainment magazine *Time Out* (www.timeout.com/london) for locations. November 5.

For the **State Opening of Parliament,** the queen in all her finery sets out from Buckingham Palace in her royal coach and heads to Westminster, where she reads out the government's program for the coming year. (This event is televised.) For more information, call ☎ **020/7291-4272** or visit www.parliament.uk. First week in November.

The new lord mayor of London goes on the grand **Lord Mayor's Procession** through the City from Guildhall to the Royal Courts of Justice in his gilded coach; festivities include a carnival in Paternoster Square and fireworks on the Thames. For more information, call ☎ **020/7606-3030** or visit www.lordmayorsshow.org. Early November.

December

Christmas lights go on in Oxford Street, Regent Street, Covent Garden, and Bond Street. Mid-November to early December.

The **lighting ceremony** of the huge Norwegian spruce Christmas tree in Trafalgar Square officially announces the holiday season. First Thursday in December.

Trafalgar Square is the focus of **New Year's Eve** celebrations. December 31.

Part II
Planning Your Trip to London

The 5th Wave   By Rich Tennant

"Welcome to our nonstop flight to London. Will you be sitting among the heather with us, sir, or back in the moors?"

In this part . . .

This part is all about the nitty-gritty of trip planning.
Chapter 4 helps you manage the money side of your
trip — that means planning a workable budget based on real
prices in London and converting your money into English
pounds and pence when you get there; in this chapter, you
can find everything you need to know about using ATMs and
credit cards in London, as well as how to save money by following a few cost-cutting tips. Chapter 5 covers your options
for getting to London by plane, train, or boat, and it gives you
some tips on escorted tours and money-saving package tours.
Chapter 6 is full of special trip-planning advice for London-
bound families, seniors, travelers with disabilities, and gays
and lesbians. Chapter 7 goes through some last-minute details,
such as getting a passport, dealing with travel and medical
insurance, staying healthy while you travel, and more.

Chapter 4

Managing Your Money

• •

In This Chapter

▶ Planning a realistic budget for your trip

▶ Pricing things in London

▶ Uncovering hidden expenses

▶ Using credit cards, traveler's checks, and ATMs

▶ Considering money-saving tips

• •

*O*kay, you want to go to London. You're excited and eager to pack, but can you really afford it? At this point, a financial reality check is in order. London is an expensive city, no two ways about it. But adding everything up, a trip to London can cost about the same as (if not more than) a trip to New York, San Francisco, or Los Angeles.

Planning Your Budget

You can easily budget for your London trip, but holding down costs while you're there may be another matter. (The city's shopping and dining is so enticing — and expensive.) Table 4-1 gives you an idea of some basic costs. The sample hotel rates are undiscounted rack rates, the highest rate you would pay.

Table 4-1	What Things Cost in London
Item	*Cost in U.S. $*
Transportation from Heathrow to Central London by Underground	8
Transportation from Gatwick to Central London by train	30
One-way Underground fare within Central London	8

(continued)

Table 4-1 *(continued)*

Item	Cost in U.S. $
Day Travelcard for unlimited Underground and bus	13
Double room at the Cadogan Hotel	510–710
Double room at Hazlitt's	410–530
Double room with breakfast at St. Margaret's Hotel	190–198
Double room at Luna & Simone Hotel	140–180
Double room at Astons Apartments (self-catering)	198–260
Pub meal for one at The Museum Tavern	15
Lunch for one at Oxo Tower Brasserie, excluding wine	40
Set-price dinner for one at Rules, excluding wine	38
Dinner for one at The Oratory, excluding wine	25
Pizza at Gourmet Pizza Company	14
Afternoon tea for one at the Lanesborough	56
Coffee and cake at Pâtisserie Valerie	12
Pint of beer at a pub	5
Admission to the Tower of London (adult/child)	32/20
Admission to Madame Tussaud's (adult/child)	40/32
Theater ticket	10–100

Note: As a general rule, except for tips in restaurants and for cab drivers (10 percent to 15 percent for both), you don't have to tip excessively in London. But if you stay in an expensive hotel, give the porters who carry your bags £1 ($2) per bag and doormen who hail you cabs £1 ($2) per cab.

Transportation

You may think a trip to London is prohibitively expensive because of the transatlantic flight, but you can often find bargain airfares to this popular spot that are cheaper than what you'd pay when flying to the farthest reaches of your own country. For more specific information on airlines and airfares, see Chapter 5.

I have some other good news that can save you a bundle: You don't need to rent a car in London. (If you want to rent a car to explore the areas surrounding London, see Chapter 14.) The London Underground (called the **Tube**) is fast, convenient, and easy to use. Special reduced-price transportation passes, called London Travelcards, make getting around the city relatively inexpensive; see Chapter 8 for more information.

Lodging

The cost of accommodations takes the biggest bite from your budget. Fortunately, because you have to book your rooms well in advance, you'll know this expense before you leave on vacation.

Chapter 8 gives you an idea of London neighborhoods and their suitability as your home base. Chapter 9 tells you what you can expect for your money, shows you how to get the best rate, and gives you my recommended list of top-notch B&Bs and hotels in all price ranges and locations.

Rates vary considerably according to location and type of hotel or B&B, so I can't really give you a reliable average. For the recommendations in this book, however, the rates are *generally* £100 and under ($200 and under) for an inexpensive property, £101 to £150 ($202–$300) for a moderately priced one, £151 to £200 ($302–$400) for an expensive one, and £201 to £250 ($402–$500) for a very expensive one. After that, you hit the stratosphere of £251-plus ($502-plus) for a luxury B&B or hotel. Keep in mind that many midrange London hotels and all B&Bs include at least a continental breakfast as part of the room rate, so you can save a few pounds there.

The rack rates that I list are not the lowest, special-deal rates that you'll probably be able to find on the hotels' Web sites. You may be surprised at how much you can save off the "official" price of a room.

Britain's version of a sales tax is called the **value-added tax (VAT)**. Brace yourself: The tax amounts to 17.5 percent. The VAT is part of the reason that prices in London are so high (that and the strength of the British pound against the U.S. dollar). The tax is added to the total price of consumer goods (the price on the tag already includes it) and to hotel and restaurant bills. The VAT is not a hidden expense, but not all quoted room rates, especially in the luxury tier, include the tax. Be sure to ask whether your quoted room rate includes the VAT. (In the hotel listings in Chapter 9, I tell you if the rate doesn't include the VAT.)

Dining

In recent years, London has emerged as one of the great food capitals of the world, known for the variety of its restaurants and the overall quality of the cooking. With the current exchange rate, I can't fudge the fact that eating at the top restaurants costs you more than a pretty penny, but countless pubs, local restaurants, cafes, and sandwich shops also exist where you can dine cheaply and well. In addition, many of the best London restaurants offer two- and three-course fixed-price meals that can be real bargains. And if your budget is really tight, you can buy take-out meals at supermarkets for a fraction of what it costs to dine out any-where in London.

If you eat lunch and dinner at the moderately priced restaurants that I recommend in Chapter 10, expect to pay £25 to £50 ($50–$100) per person per day for meals, not including alcoholic drinks (and assuming that breakfast is included in your hotel rate). If you have breakfast at a cafe rather than your hotel and are content with coffee and a roll, expect to pay about £4 to £6 ($8–$12). Depending on the restaurant, an old-fashioned English breakfast with eggs, bacon or sausage, toast, and tea or coffee can run anywhere from £6 to £12 ($12–$24). Likewise, a simple afternoon tea at a cafe sets you back about £5 to £7 ($10–$14), but a lavish high tea at one of the great London hotels will run £25 ($50) or more. For specifics on restaurants, inexpensive cafes and sandwich shops, and places for afternoon tea, see Chapter 10.

On top of the VAT, a few restaurants add a service charge of 12.5 percent to 15 percent to your bill. If they do, the menu and the bill have to state this policy. This charge amounts to mandatory tipping, so if your credit card receipt comes back with a space for you to add a tip, put a line through it.

Sightseeing

Your budget for admission fees depends, of course, on what you want to see. Some of London's top attractions are pricey indeed: an adult ticket to the **Tower of London** costs £16 ($32). But many other outstanding attractions in London — the **British Museum, National Gallery, National Portrait Gallery, Tate Britain,** and **Tate Modern** — are completely free. So are the **Natural History Museum,** the **Science Museum,** and the **Victoria & Albert Museum.** Strolling through London's great parks or viewing **Buckingham Palace** (okay, from the outside) and the **Changing of the Guard** won't cost you a penny. From my suggestions in Chapter 11, you can weed out the must-see sights from the maybes.

Keep in mind that if you're a senior or a student, you can often get a reduced-price admission, and most attractions offer reduced family rates that are good for two adults and two children. Be sure to bring some form of photo identification to prove your senior or student status.

Shopping and nightlife

Shopping and entertainment are the most flexible parts of your budget. You don't have to buy anything at all, and you can hit the sack right after dinner instead of seeing a play or dancing at a club. You know what you want. Flip through the shopping options in Chapter 12 and the entertainment and nightlife venues in Chapters 15 and 16. If anything strikes you as something you can't do without, budget accordingly. (Keep in mind that a pint in a pub sets you back about £2.50/$5, whereas a theater, opera, or concert ticket can cost anywhere from £5/$10 to over £50/$100.)

 If you're not a resident of the European Union, you can get a VAT refund on purchases made in the United Kingdom. (This refund doesn't include hotels, restaurants, or entertainment.) See Chapter 12 for details.

Cutting Costs — But Not the Fun

 Throughout this book, Bargain Alert icons highlight money-saving tips and/or great deals. Check out some additional cost-cutting strategies:

- ✔ **Go in the off-season.** If you can travel at non-peak times (Oct to mid-Dec or Jan to Mar), you'll find hotel prices can be as much as 20 percent less than during peak months.

- ✔ **Travel on off days of the week.** Airfares vary, depending on the day of the week. If you can travel on a Tuesday, Wednesday, or Thursday, you may find cheaper flights to London. See if you can get a cheaper rate by flying on a different day.

- ✔ **Try a package tour.** For popular destinations like London, you can make just one call to a travel agent or packager to book airfare, hotel, ground transportation, and even some sightseeing. You pay much less than if you tried to put the trip together yourself (see Chapter 5).

- ✔ **Reserve a hotel room with a kitchen.** In London, these rooms are called *self-catering units*. With your own kitchen, you can do at least some of your own cooking. You'll save money by not eating in restaurants two or three times a day. Parents traveling with small children may find this strategy particularly useful.

- ✔ **Always ask for discount rates.** Membership in AAA, frequent-flier programs, trade unions, AARP, or other groups may qualify you for discounts on plane tickets, hotel rooms, or even meals.

- ✔ **Always ask if any special room rates are in effect.** Hotels are eager to fill their rooms and now offer many different rates, including "promotional" rates and lower weekend rates. In most cases, you'll find these special rates on the hotel's Web site.

- ✔ **Ask if your kids can stay in your room with you.** A room with two double beds usually doesn't cost any more than one with a queen-size bed. And many hotels won't charge you the additional-person rate if that person is pint-size and related to you. Even if you have to pay a few pounds extra for a rollaway bed, you save hundreds by not taking two rooms.

Ways to save in London and beyond

With a single, one-way fare on the London Underground currently priced at £4 ($8), you'll save lots of money by purchasing a one-day or multi-day Travelcard, good for unlimited travel on the Underground and buses. In the United States and Canada, you can buy a London Travelcard before you leave home by contacting a travel agent; by calling Rail Europe at ☎ 877/272-RAIL in the U.S. or 800/361-7245 in Canada; or by going to www.raileurope.com. Two kinds of cards are available in U.S. dollars: the *All Zone* and the *Central Zone,* which is good for everything in Central London. Both cards are available in one-, three-, or seven-day increments. Prices for the Central Zone card are $15 for adults and $8 for children for one day; $37 for adults and $19 for children for three days; and $52 for adults and $26 for children for seven days. You can also buy various money-saving Travelcards at any London Underground station or ticket machine. These options actually work out to be a bit cheaper. For more information on London Travelcards, see Chapter 8.

If you plan to travel around England by train, consider getting a BritRail pass. These passes offer considerable savings over individual fares, but you must buy them before you arrive (they aren't sold in England). You have many options: a choice of either first or standard class, senior passes for those over 60, travel-time periods from four consecutive days to one month, and Flexipasses allowing you to travel a certain number of days within a set time period. You can also get a London Plus Pass that's great for day trips around London. You can find information on the various rail passes in Chapter 14.

✔ **Use pay phones rather than the phone in your hotel room.** You may find the telephone in your hotel room convenient, but avoid using it if you're on a budget. A local call that costs 40p (80¢) at a phone booth may cost you £1 ($2) or more from your hotel room. If you plan to make a number of calls during your trip, get a phone card (see the details about using phones in the Quick Concierge, at the end of this book) and use pay phones.

✔ **Try expensive restaurants at lunch rather than dinner.** At most top restaurants, prices at lunch are considerably lower than those at dinner, and the menu often includes many of the dinnertime specialties. Also, look for the fixed-price menus.

✔ **Buy takeout meals at supermarkets and sandwich shops.** If you're on a tight budget, skip restaurants and head instead to a nearby supermarket or sandwich shop. Supermarkets in London and throughout England sell sandwiches and all manner of "take-away" meals, so you can create your own picnic.

✔ **Walk a lot.** London is large but completely walkable. A good pair of walking shoes can save you money on taxis and other local transportation. As a bonus, you get to know the city and its inhabitants more intimately, and you can explore at a slower pace.

✔ **Skip the souvenirs.** Your photographs and your memories should be the best mementos of your trip. If you're worried about your budget, do without the T-shirts, key chains, and other trinkets.

Handling Money

Money makes the world go around, but dealing with an unfamiliar currency can make your head spin. In London, you pay for things in pounds and pence, meaning you have to convert your own currency into British pounds sterling. When it comes to carrying money in London, should you bring traveler's checks or use ATMs? What about paying with credit cards? In the following sections, I tell you what you need to know about each option.

Making sense of pounds and pence

Britain's unit of currency is the **pound sterling (£).** Every pound is divided into **100 pence (p).** Coins come in denominations of 1p, 2p, 5p, 10p, 20p, 50p, £1, and £2. Notes are available in £5, £10, £20, and £50 denominations. As with any unfamiliar currency, British pounds and pence take a bit of getting used to. The coins have different sizes, shapes, and weights according to value. Each bank note denomination has its own color and bears a likeness of the queen. All currency is drawn on the Bank of England.

Exchanging your currency

The **exchange rate,** which fluctuates every day, is the rate that you get when you use your own currency to buy pounds sterling (see Table 4-2). In general, $1 = 50p (or £1 = $2). These are *approximate* figures, but they're what I use for all prices in this guide (rounded to the nearest dollar if the amount is over $10, and to the nearest nickel of the amount is under $10). When you're about to leave on your trip, check with your bank or look in the newspaper to find out the current rate.

Table 4-2		Simple Currency Conversions	
U.S. $ to U.K. £		*U.K. £ to U.S. $*	
$1	50p	£1	$2
$5	£2.50	£2	$4
$10	£5	£5	$10
$20	£10	£10	$20
$50	£25	£20	$40
$100	£50	£50	$100

Changing money (either cash or traveler's checks) into a foreign currency makes many people nervous, especially if they're changing money for the first time. You needn't fear. Changing money is a simple operation. Just remember that every time you exchange money, you need to show your passport.

If you want some pounds in hand when you arrive at the airport in London, you can exchange currency before you leave home at many banks and at foreign exchange services at international airports. Otherwise, you can easily change cash or traveler's checks in London by using a currency-exchange service called a *bureau de change*. These services are available at major London airports, any branch of a major bank, all major rail and Underground stations in Central London, post offices, and American Express or Thomas Cook offices. Unless located in a bank or travel agency, most *bureaux de change* are open daily from 8 a.m. to 9 p.m.

Every major bank in Central London has a foreign currency window where you can exchange traveler's checks or cash. Weekday hours for banks are generally 9:30 a.m. to 4:30 p.m., but a few open earlier. Some banks (usually based in busy shopping areas) are open all day Saturday. All banks are closed on public holidays, but many branches have 24-hour banking lobbies with ATMs or ATMs on the street outside. Banks in London and throughout the United Kingdom include **Barclays Bank** (☎ 020/7441-3200; www.barclays.co.uk), **HSBC** (☎ 0845/743-4445; www.hsbc.com), **Midland Bank** (☎ 020/7599-3232; www.midlandnb.com), and **NatWest** (☎ 020/7395-5500; www.natwest.com). These banking companies all have branches throughout the city.

Reputable London banks and *bureaux de change* exchange money at a competitive rate but charge a commission (typically 1 percent to 3 percent of the total transaction) and a small additional fee (usually £3/$6). Some currency-exchange services now guarantee you the same exchange rate when you return pounds for dollars.

All U.K. *bureaux de change* and other money-changing establishments are required to display exchange rates and full details of any fees and rates of commission with clarity and equal prominence. Rates must be displayed at or near the entrance to the premises. Rates fluctuate from place to place, and so do fees, so shopping around sometimes pays.

Steer clear of *bureaux de change* that offer good exchange rates but charge a heavy commission (up to 8 percent). You find them in major tourist sections of London (some are open 24 hours). Some hotels also cash traveler's checks, but their commission is often considerably higher than at a bank or *bureau de change*. Before exchanging your money, always check to see the exchange rate, how much commission you'll have to pay, and whether additional fees apply.

You can avoid paying a second commission fee by using American Express traveler's checks and cashing them at the **American Express** office in London at 6 Haymarket, SW1 (☎ 020/7930-4411; Tube: Piccadilly). Its foreign-exchange bureau is open Monday through Friday from 9 a.m. to 5:30 p.m., Saturday from 9 a.m. to 6 p.m., and Sunday from 10 a.m. to 5 p.m.

Using ATMs and carrying cash

The easiest and best way to get cash away from home is from an ATM. You'll find ATMs, or *cashpoints* as they're sometimes called in England, all over London. The **Cirrus** (☎ 800/424-7787; www.mastercard.com) and **PLUS** (☎ 800/843-7587; www.visa.com) networks span the globe; look on the back of your bank card to see which network you're on, then call or check online for ATM locations in London. Be sure that you know your personal identification number (PIN) before you leave home and find out your daily withdrawal limit before you depart. Some banks will allow you to withdraw cash only from your checking account, not from your savings.

Also keep in mind that many banks impose a fee every time you use your card at a different bank's ATM, and that fee may cost more for international transactions (up to $5 or more) than for domestic ones (where it rarely goes over $1.50). On top of this fee from your bank, the bank from which you withdraw cash may charge its own fee. For international withdrawal fees, ask your bank.

Charging ahead with credit cards

Credit cards are a safe way to carry money. They also provide a convenient record of all your expenses, and they generally offer relatively good exchange rates. You can also withdraw cash advances from your credit cards at banks or ATMs, provided you know your PIN. If you've forgotten yours, or didn't even know you had one, call the number on the back of your credit card and ask the bank to send it to you. It usually takes five to seven business days to arrive by mail, though some banks will provide the number over the phone if you tell them your mother's maiden name or some other personal information.

Keep in mind that when you use your credit card abroad, most banks assess a 2 percent fee above the 1 percent fee that Visa, MasterCard, and American Express charge for currency conversion on credit charges. But credit cards still may be the smart way to go when you factor in things like exorbitant ATM fees and higher traveler's check exchange rates (and service fees).

Some credit card companies recommend that you notify them of any impending trip abroad so that they don't become suspicious when you use the card numerous times in a foreign destination and block your charges. Even if you don't call your credit card company in advance, you can always call the card's toll-free emergency number if a charge is refused — a good reason to carry the phone number with you. But perhaps the most important lesson here is to carry more than one card with you on your trip; a card may not work for any number of reasons, so having a backup is the smart way to go.

Toting traveler's checks

These days, traveler's checks are less necessary because most cities, including London, have 24-hour ATMs that allow you to withdraw cash as needed, with less hassle and with comparable or even cheaper service charges. You can get traveler's checks at almost any bank. **American Express** offers denominations of $20, $50, $100, $500, and (for cardholders only) $1,000. You pay a service charge ranging from 1 percent to 4 percent. You can also get American Express traveler's checks over the phone by calling ☎ **800/221-7282;** Amex gold and platinum cardholders who use this number are exempt from the 1 percent fee.

Visa offers traveler's checks at Citibank locations nationwide, as well as at several other banks. The service charge ranges between 1.5 percent and 2 percent; checks come in denominations of $20, $50, $100, $500, and $1,000. Call ☎ **800/732-1322** or go to www.visa.com for information. AAA members can obtain Visa checks without a fee at most AAA offices, by calling ☎ **866/339-3378. MasterCard** also offers traveler's checks. Call ☎ **800/223-9920** for a location near you.

 If you choose to carry traveler's checks, be sure to keep a record of their serial numbers separate from your checks. If the checks are lost or stolen, you'll get a refund faster if you know the numbers.

 Never pay for hotels, meals, or purchases with traveler's checks denominated in any currency other than British pounds. You get a bad exchange rate if you try to use them as cash.

Dealing with a Lost or Stolen Wallet

Be sure to contact all your credit card companies the minute you discover your wallet has been lost or stolen and file a report with the police. In London, call ☎ **192** for directory assistance, free from public pay phones, to find out the precinct nearest you. Your credit card company or insurer may require a police report number or record of the loss. Most credit card companies have an emergency toll-free number to call if your card is lost or stolen; the company may be able to wire you a cash advance immediately or deliver an emergency credit card in a day or two. Call the following emergency numbers in the United Kingdom:

  ✓ **American Express:** ☎ **01273/696-933**

  ✓ **MasterCard:** ☎ **01702/362-988**

  ✓ **Visa:** ☎ **01604/230-230**

Earning their keep: Royal expenses

Buckingham Palace's accounts revealed that the overall cost to taxpayers of keeping the monarchy rose 4.7 percent in 2006 to £37.4 million ($74.8 million), or about 62p ($1.24) per U.K. resident. Travel expenses accounted for a significant part of the rise. One trip to Egypt, Saudi Arabia, and India by Prince Charles and Camilla, Duchess of Cornwall, cost £304,000 ($608,000). Prince Andrew spent more than £355,000 ($710,000) on a series of visits to destinations including Bermuda, Thailand, and Egypt. He spent £33,405 ($66,810) to charter a plane for two days to travel between Bangkok and the resorts of Hua Hin and Phuket, a two-hour flight with scheduled economy-class seats available for about £80 ($160) round-trip, and he also spent £11,555 ($23,110) to fly from the Isle of Man to St. Andrews for a meeting of the Royal and Ancient Golf Club.

British taxpayers paid £400,000 ($800,000) for wine and spirits for the queen's cellars, while £300,000 ($600,000) was spent on a new kitchen for Windsor Castle. The cost of new security measures at Buckingham Palace came to about £150,000 ($300,000). Utilities for the royal properties totaled £2 million ($4 million), with about £1 million ($2 million) spent on catering and hospitality, including £600,000 ($1,200,000) for garden parties.

Alan Reid, the Keeper of the Privy Purse, was quoted as saying, "Our key aim is not to try and achieve a low-cost monarchy. What we're really after is trying to achieve a high-quality and very efficient monarchy." Buckingham Palace pointed out that the royal family had about 2,700 official engagements across the United Kingdom and overseas in 2006.

If you need emergency cash over the weekend when all banks and American Express offices are closed, you can have money wired to you via **Western Union** (☎ **0800/833-833** in the U.K.; www.westernunion.co.uk).

If you follow four basic rules, you can minimize the risk of a crime happening to you:

✔ Don't keep your wallet in your back pocket or in your backpack, but do keep it out of sight.

✔ Don't leave your purse, briefcase, backpack, or coat unattended in any public place. This isn't only to protect you from thieves. In London, with its stepped-up security, unattended items can be confiscated by the police.

✔ Ladies: Don't hang your purse over the back of your chair in crowded or outdoor cafes or restaurants.

✔ Don't flash your money or credit cards around.

Chapter 5

Getting to London

*N*ow that you've decided to visit London, you'll need to find a way to get there. In this chapter, I discuss your options for direct, non-stop flights and give you some ideas on how you can save money on your flight (and your hotel). I've also got all the information on reaching the United Kingdom via train and ferry, for those travelers who arrive from Europe. What are the pros and cons of taking an escorted tour? You can find answers to your basic travel questions in this chapter.

Flying to London

London's airports are among the busiest in the world, with direct or connecting flights from all over the globe. Finding a flight won't be difficult, but choosing one from the many that are offered may require some research and comparison shopping for the lowest fare.

Finding out which airlines fly to London

Most regularly scheduled international flights from the United States, Canada, Australia, and New Zealand arrive at London's Heathrow and Gatwick airports. Flights from the Continent land at Heathrow, Gatwick, Stansted, or London City. Luton, the smallest of London's five airports, is a destination for charter flights from the Continent.

Here's a brief description of each of the London airports and who flies to them (see the Quick Concierge, at the end of this book, for the contact information of the airlines in this list):

✔ **Heathrow,** the main international airport, is 24km (15 miles) west of Central London. It's served by **Air Canada** (Canadian flights from Calgary, Montreal, Ottawa, St. John's, Toronto, and Vancouver); **Air New Zealand** (Australian flights from Sydney; New Zealand flights from Auckland); **American** (U.S. flights from Boston, Chicago, Los Angeles, Miami, and New York JFK); **British Airways** (U.S. flights from Boston, Chicago, Detroit, Los Angeles, Miami, Newark, New York JFK, Philadelphia, San Francisco, Seattle, and Washington Dulles; Australian flights from Brisbane, Melbourne, Perth, and Sydney; New Zealand flights from Auckland); **Continental** (U.S. flights from Los Angeles, Newark, New York JFK, San Francisco, and Washington Dulles); **Icelandair** (U.S. flights from Baltimore, Boston, Minneapolis/St. Paul, and New York JFK); **Qantas** (Australian flights from Melbourne, Perth, and Sydney; New Zealand flights from Auckland); **United** (U.S. flights from Boston, Chicago, Los Angeles, Newark, New York JFK, San Francisco, and Washington Dulles); and **Virgin Atlantic** (U.S. flights from Chicago, Newark, New York JFK, San Francisco, and Washington Dulles). For information on getting into London from Heathrow, see Chapter 8.

✔ **Gatwick** is a smaller airport about 40km (25 miles) south of London. It's served by **American** (U.S. flights from Boston, Dallas/ Ft. Worth, and Raleigh/Durham); **British Airways** (U.S. flights from Atlanta, Baltimore, Charlotte, Dallas/Ft. Worth, Denver, Houston, Miami, New York JFK, Orlando, Phoenix, and Tampa); **Continental** (U.S. flights from Boston, Cleveland, Houston, Miami, Newark, and Orlando); **Delta** (U.S. flights from Atlanta and Cincinnati); **Northwest** (U.S. flights from Detroit and Minneapolis/St. Paul); **Qantas** (Australian flights from Sydney); and **Virgin Atlantic** (U.S. flights from Boston, Las Vegas, Miami, Newark, Orlando, and San Francisco). For information on getting into London from Gatwick, see Chapter 8.

✔ **Stansted,** 80km (50 miles) northeast of London, handles national and European flights. The Stansted Express train to Liverpool Street Station takes 45 minutes and costs £15.50 ($31).

✔ **London City,** only 10km (6 miles) east of Central London, services European destinations. A new extension of the Docklands Light Railway travels from the airport to Bank Street in Central London, in 22 minutes for £4 ($8); if you're traveling beyond Bank Street by Underground, you'll have to pay an additional fare.

✔ **Luton,** 45km (28 miles) northwest of London, services mostly charter flights. You can travel by free shuttle bus to Luton Airport Parkway station, then take a Capital Connection train to King's Cross Station in central London for £11 ($22); the trip takes 30 to 45 minutes.

Getting the best deal on your airfare

Competition among the major U.S. airlines is unlike that of any other industry. Every airline offers virtually the same product (basically, a coach seat is a coach seat is a . . .), yet prices can vary by hundreds of dollars.

Business travelers who need the flexibility to buy their tickets at the last minute and change their itineraries at a moment's notice — and who want to get home before the weekend — pay the premium rate, known as the *full fare*. But if you can book your ticket far in advance, stay over Saturday night, and travel midweek (Tues, Wed, or Thurs), you can qualify for the least expensive price — usually a fraction of the full fare. The airlines also periodically hold *sales,* in which they lower the prices on their most popular routes. These fares have advance-purchase requirements and date-of-travel restrictions, but you can't beat the prices. As you plan your vacation, keep your eyes open for these sales, which tend to take place in seasons of low travel volume — in England, that's basically October through March. You almost never see a sale around the peak summer vacation months of July and August, or around Thanksgiving or Christmas, when many people fly, regardless of the fare they have to pay.

Consolidators, also known as *bucket shops,* are great sources for international tickets, although they usually can't beat the Internet on fares within North America. Start by looking in Sunday newspaper travel sections; U.S. travelers should focus on the *New York Times, Los Angeles Times,* and *Miami Herald.*

Bucket-shop tickets are usually nonrefundable or rigged with stiff cancellation penalties, often as high as 50 percent to 75 percent of the ticket price, and some put you on charter airlines with questionable safety records.

Several reliable consolidators are worldwide and available online, and most of them offer flights to London. **STA Travel** (☎ 800/781-4040; www.statravel.com), the world's leader in student travel, offers good fares for travelers of all ages. **ELTExpress** (☎ 800/872-8800; www.flights.com) started in Europe and has excellent fares worldwide. Flights.com also has "local" Web sites in 12 countries. **FlyCheap** (☎ 800/FLY-CHEAP; www.1800flycheap.com) is owned by package-holiday megalith MyTravel and has especially good access to fares for international destinations. **Air Tickets Direct** (☎ 800/778-3447; www.airticketsdirect.com) is based in Montreal.

Booking your flight online

The "big three" online travel agencies, **Expedia** (www.expedia.com), **Travelocity** (www.travelocity.com), and **Orbitz** (www.orbitz.com), sell most of the air tickets bought on the Internet. (Canadian travelers should try www.expedia.ca and www.travelocity.ca; U.K. residents can visit www.expedia.co.uk and www.opodo.co.uk; Australians and New Zealanders should try www.expedia.com.au.) Each agency has different business deals with the airlines and may offer different fares on the same flights, so shopping around is wise. Expedia and Travelocity will also send you an **e-mail notification** when a cheap fare becomes available to your favorite destination. Of the smaller travel-agency Web sites, **SideStep** (www.sidestep.com) receives good reviews from users. It's a browser add-on that purports to search over 100 sites at once.

 Great **last-minute deals** are available through free weekly e-mail services provided directly by the airlines. Most of these deals are announced on Tuesday or Wednesday and must be purchased online. Most are only valid for travel that weekend, but some can be booked weeks or months in advance. Sign up for weekly e-mail alerts at airline Web sites or check mega-sites that compile comprehensive lists of last-minute specials, such as **Smarter Travel** (www.smartertravel.com). For last-minute trips, www.lastminute.com often has better deals than the major-label sites.

If you're willing to give up some control over your flight details, use an opaque fare service like **Priceline** (www.priceline.com) or **Hotwire** (www.hotwire.com). Both services offer rock-bottom prices in exchange for travel on a "mystery airline" at a mysterious time of day, often with a mysterious change of planes en route. The mystery airlines are all major, well-known carriers — and the possibility of being sent from Philadelphia to Chicago via Salt Lake City is remote. But your chances of getting a 6 a.m. or 11 p.m. flight are pretty high. Hotwire tells you flight prices before you buy; Priceline usually has better deals than Hotwire, but you have to play their "name our price" game. *Note:* Priceline does have a non-opaque service in its roster. You have the option to pick exact flights, times, and airlines from a list of offers — or opt to bid on opaque fares.

Arriving by Other Means

If you're traveling to London from another destination in Europe, you don't have to fly to get there. Train and car ferries and high-speed hovercrafts cross the English Channel throughout the year from ports in France, Holland, and Belgium. And the Eurostar high-speed train zips beneath the channel through the **Chunnel,** a tunnel beneath the English Channel.

Taking the train

London has several train stations, and the one you arrive at depends on your point of departure from the Continent. The three-hour **Eurostar** service connecting Paris and Brussels to London via the Chunnel arrives at King's Cross/St. Pancras Station. Trains from Amsterdam arrive at Liverpool Street Station. Other London train stations include Euston, Waterloo, Paddington, and Victoria stations.

Several types of Eurostar fares are available. Senior fares for those over 60 and youth fares for those under 26 can cut the price of a first-class fare by 20 percent or more. The same reductions apply for passengers traveling with validated Eurail and BritRail passes. To check out current and special promotional fares for Eurostar, visit RailEurope's Web site at www.raileurope.com.

The trains in England and the rest of the United Kingdom are separate from those in continental Europe, so a Eurail pass isn't valid in the U.K. If you're going to travel within England or the rest of the United Kingdom, check out the various BritRail passes available (see Chapter 14 for more information).

For more information on train schedules, routes, and fares throughout England, go to www.nationalrail.co.uk or call ☎ **0845/484-950.**

Riding a ferry or hovercraft

Crossing times for the car, train, and passenger ferries that regularly crisscross the English Channel can be anywhere from 90 minutes to 5 hours, depending on the point of departure. Various *hovercrafts* (high-speed ferries with propellers that lift them off the surface of the water) skim over the water in as little as half an hour. Frequent train service to London is available from all the channel ports. The following is a list of the major ferry and hovercraft companies:

- ✔ **Norfolk Line** (☎ **0870/870-1020** in the U.K.; www.norfolkline-ferries.com) accepts motorists only — no foot passengers — on its ferries between Dover, England, and Dunkerque, France (crossing time in 1¾ hours).

- ✔ **P&O Ferries** (☎ **0870/598-0333** in the U.K.; www.poferries.com) offers daily ferry/car crossings between Cherbourg and Portsmouth (crossing time is 5 hours) and Le Havre and Portsmouth (5½ hours) and between Calais and Dover (1¼ hours).

- ✔ **Sea France Limited** (☎ **0871/663-2546** in the U.K.; www.seafrance.co.uk) runs ferries between Dover and Calais (crossing time is 1½ hours).

Joining an Escorted Tour

Some people love escorted tours. The tour company takes care of all the details and tells you what to expect at each leg of your journey. You know your costs upfront and don't get many surprises. Escorted tours can take you to the maximum number of sights in the minimum amount of time with the least amount of hassle.

TIP

If you decide to go with an escorted tour, I strongly recommend purchasing travel insurance, especially if the tour operator asks you to pay upfront. But don't buy insurance from the tour operator! If the tour operator doesn't fulfill its obligation to provide you with the vacation you paid for, there's no reason to think that it'll fulfill its insurance obligations either. Get travel insurance through an independent agency. (You can find out more about the ins and outs of travel insurance in Chapter 7.)

When choosing an escorted tour, along with finding out whether you have to put down a deposit and when final payment is due, ask a few simple questions before you buy:

✔ **What is the cancellation policy?** Can the tour operator cancel the trip if they don't get enough people? How late can you cancel if you're unable to go? Do you get a refund if you cancel? If the tour operator cancels?

✔ **How jam-packed is the schedule?** Does the tour schedule try to fit 25 hours into a 24-hour day, or does it give you ample time to relax or shop? If getting up at 7 a.m. every day and not returning to your hotel until 7 or 8 p.m. sounds like a grind, certain escorted tours may not be for you.

✔ **How large is the group?** The smaller the group, the less time you spend waiting for people to get on and off the bus. Tour operators may be evasive about this, because they may not know the exact size of the group until everybody has made reservations, but they should be able to give you a rough estimate.

✔ **Is there a minimum group size?** Some tours have a minimum group size, and the tour operator may cancel the tour if it doesn't book enough people. If a quota exists, find out what it is and how close the operator is to reaching it. Again, tour operators may be evasive in their answers, but the information may help you select a tour that's sure to happen.

✔ **What exactly is included?** Don't assume anything. You may have to pay to get yourself to and from the airport. A box lunch may be included in an excursion, but drinks may be extra. Beer may be included, but not wine. How much flexibility do you have? Can you opt out of certain activities, or does the bus leave once a day, with no exceptions? Are all your meals planned in advance? Can you choose your entree at dinner, or does everybody get the same chicken cutlet?

Here are two companies that offer escorted tours to London and the rest of England (with prices per person, based on double occupancy):

✔ **Globus and Cosmos** (www.globusandcosmos.com) are well-known budget tour companies working in partnership. Current offerings include a four-day/three-night tour of London starting at $499 and an eight-day/seven-night tour starting at $799, airfare not included.

✔ **Trafalgar Tours** (www.trafalgartours.com) provides tours to London and the rest of the United Kingdom. Prices for the Week in London tour start at $1,055, airfare not included. The company also offers an eight-day London, Stratford & Bath tour starting at $1,060, airfare not included.

Choosing a package tour

For a lot of destinations, including London, package tours can be a smart way to go. In many cases, a package tour that includes airfare, hotel, and transportation to and from the airport costs less than the hotel alone on a tour that you book yourself. That's because packages are sold in bulk to tour operators, who resell them to the public.

Package tours vary greatly in what they provide. Some offer a better class of hotels than others; others provide the same hotels for lower prices. Some book flights on scheduled airlines; others sell charters. In some packages, your choice of accommodations and travel days may be limited. Some let you choose between escorted vacations and independent vacations; others allow you to add on a few excursions or escorted day trips (also at discounted prices).

To find package tours, check out the travel section of your local Sunday newspaper or the ads in the back of national travel magazines, such as *Travel + Leisure, National Geographic Traveler,* and *Condé Nast Traveler.* **Liberty Travel** (☎ 888/271-1584; www.libertytravel.com) is one of the biggest packagers in the northeastern United States and usually boasts a full-page ad in Sunday papers.

Another good source of package deals is the airlines themselves. Most major airlines offer air/land packages. Several big **online travel agencies** — Expedia, Travelocity, Orbitz, and Lastminute.com — also do a brisk business in packages.

Locating package tours

Information about package tours is available from a variety of sources. Here are a few companies that offer packages to England:

✔ **British Travel International** (☎ 727/653-5710; www.british travel.com) is a good source for discount packages.

✔ **Liberty Travel** (☎ 888/271-1584; www.libertytravel.com), one of the biggest packagers in the northeastern United States, offers reasonably priced packages.

✔ **Trailfinders** (www.trailfinders.com), another good source for discount packages, has several offices in Australia: Brisbane (☎ 07/3229-0887), Cairns (☎ 07/4041-1199), Melbourne (☎ 03/9600-3022), Perth (☎ 08/9226-1222), and Sydney (☎ 02/9247-7666).

Checking out airline and hotel packages

Airlines are good sources for package tours because they package their flights together with accommodations. The following airlines offer packages to London:

- ✔ **American Airlines Vacations** (☎ 800/321-2121; www.aa vacations.com)

- ✔ **British Airways Holidays** (☎ 800/247-9297; www.baholidays. com)

- ✔ **Continental Airlines Vacations** (☎ 800/525-0280; www. continental.com)

- ✔ **Northwest Airlines World Vacations** (☎ 800/800-1504; www.nwa worldvacations.com)

- ✔ **United Airlines Vacations** (☎ 800/328-6877; www.united vacations.com)

- ✔ **Virgin Atlantic Vacations** (☎ 888/937-8474; www.virgin.com/ vacations)

Chapter 6

Catering to Special Needs or Interests

. . . .

In This Chapter

▶ Visiting London with children
▶ Getting discounts and special tours for seniors
▶ Locating wheelchair-accessible attractions
▶ Finding lesbian- and gay-friendly communities and special events

. . . .

*M*any of today's travelers have special needs or interests. Parents may want to take their children along on trips. Seniors may be looking for special discounts or tours designed especially for them. People with disabilities want to ensure that sites on their itineraries offer wheelchair access. And gays and lesbians may want to know about welcoming places and events. In response to these needs, this chapter offers advice and resources.

Traveling with the Brood: Advice for Families

Traveling with children, from toddlers to teens, is a challenge — no doubt about it. Bringing the brood can put a strain on the budget and influence your choices of activities and hotels. But in the end, isn't sharing your experiences as a family great?

Look for the Kid Friendly icon as you flip through this book. I use it to highlight hotels, restaurants, and attractions that are particularly family friendly. Zeroing in on these places can help you plan your trip more quickly and easily.

In addition, the following resources can help you plan your trip:

> ✔ **About Family Travel** (3555 S. Pacific Hwy., Medford, OR 97501; ☎ 541/778-2022; www.about-family-travel.com) can tailor a tour specifically for families traveling to London. Its services include arranging airfares, hotel rooms, transportation, and theater tickets, as well as providing tips on sights and destinations. Don't

rely on its free online London information, however, because it hasn't been updated in years.

✔ **Family Travel Forum** (www.familytravelforum.com) is a comprehensive site that offers customized trip planning.

✔ **Kids Love London** (http://kids.visitlondon.com), by the London Tourist Board, is a site created to give kids the lowdown on kid-friendly attractions, events, restaurants, and more.

✔ **TravelWithYourKids.com** (www.travelwithyourkids.com) is another comprehensive site full of sound advice for long-distance and international travel with children.

 Admission prices for most London attractions are generally reduced for children 5 to 16 years old. Children under 5 almost always get in for free. If you're traveling with one or two children, always check to see whether the attraction offers a money-saving family ticket, which considerably reduces the admission price for a group of two adults and two children.

Locating family-friendly accommodations and restaurants

Most hotels will happily accommodate your family if you reserve your rooms in advance and make the staff aware that you're traveling with kids. The establishment may bring in an extra cot or let you share a larger room; these types of arrangements are common. Smaller bed-and-breakfasts (B&Bs) may present problems, such as cramped rooms and shared toilet facilities, and some places don't accept children at all. Ask questions before you reserve.

 To keep costs down, you can rent a hotel room with a kitchen (in England these rooms are called *self-catering units*) and prepare your own meals. Another option, when the weather cooperates, is to take the family on a picnic. **Kensington Gardens** or **Hyde Park** may be just the ticket for an enjoyable afternoon (see Chapter 10 for more suggestions). You can also take advantage of pre-theater, fixed-price menus (usually 5:30–7 p.m.), which usually give you a good deal.

London has plenty of American-style fast food places, including **Burger King, KFC, McDonald's,** and **Pizza Hut.** Teens may want to check out the **Hard Rock Cafe** in Mayfair or the scene at the **Pepsi Trocadero** in **Piccadilly Circus,** which offers theme restaurants such as **Planet Hollywood** and the **Rainforest Café** (see Chapter 10). London is also a good place to introduce more adventurous kids to Chinese or Indian cuisine, or to the communal dining experience offered by **Wagamama** Japanese noodle restaurants.

 Expensive restaurants are sometimes less welcoming toward young children. The menus aren't geared to the tastes of youngsters, the prices can be high, and the staff may be less than accommodating.

Planning your trip together

Letting your younger children read *Peter Pan* or *Peter Pan in Kensington Gardens,* and telling them about his statue there, can generate excitement about the trip. Slightly older children may want to read the *Harry Potter* series, which takes place in real and fictional settings in London and around the country. (If your kids have already read the *Harry Potter* series, they know that Harry lives just south of London — in fact, he leaves from King's Cross Station to go off to sorcerer's school.) With the information in this book and some online investigating, you can also incite your kids' curiosity about historic sites such as the **Tower of London** and the **Prime Meridian line** at Greenwich. And most young people enjoy the prospect of a meal at the **Hard Rock Cafe** or a trip to **Madame Tussaud's** wax museum.

Some kid and adult activities can easily overlap. You may want to spend one afternoon in **Kensington Gardens.** After the entire family visits Kensington Palace, the kids can blow off steam in the new **Princess Diana Memorial Playground.** Many kid-oriented activities in London are just as interesting for parents. From the fantastic dinosaur exhibit in the **Natural History Museum** to the animatronic robots re-creating historic scenes at Madame Tussaud's, you *and* your kids have plenty to experience and enjoy together.

Preparing for a long trip

The shortest trip from the United States to London (from New York) is about 6 hours; airtime from Australia may be 25 hours, which is a lot of time for kids to sit still and be quiet. Although children can spend some of the journey time watching a movie (or two) on the plane, come prepared with extra diversions: games, puzzles, books — whatever you know will keep your kids entertained. If your child needs baby food, bring your own and ask a flight attendant to warm it. Dealing with jet lag can be hard on adults but even harder on small children. Don't schedule too much for your first day in London. Get everyone comfortably settled and then take it from there.

Hiring a baby sitter while on your trip

What you really need is a relaxing evening at the opera and a romantic late dinner. But you can't take Junior along. What are your options? Ask your hotel staff if they can recommend a local babysitting service. Most of the hotels marked with a Kid Friendly icon in Chapter 9 can arrange for babysitting. London also has several respected and trustworthy babysitting agencies that provide registered nurses and carefully screened mothers, as well as trained nannies, to watch children. One old and trustworthy babysitting service is **Universal Aunts** (☎ 020/ **7386-8937;** www.universalaunts.co.uk), which charges £11 ($22) per daytime hour, £9 ($18) from 6 p.m. to midnight (three-hour minimum), plus a £19 ($38) agency fee.

A fully licensed 24-hour childcare facility, **Pippa Pop-ins** (430 Fulham Rd., SW6 1DU; ☎ 020/7731-1445; www.pippapopins.com), in Chelsea, provides a lovely toy-filled nursery staffed by experienced caregivers where you can safely park the little ones. Call for rates. Another branch is located in Fulham at 165 New Kings Rd., SW6 (same phone number).

Making Age Work for You: Tips for Seniors

London won't present any problems for you if you're a senior who gets around easily. If you do have mobility issues, be aware when you plan your trip that not all hotels — particularly less expensive B&Bs — have elevators. The steep staircases in some places are a test for *anyone* with luggage. When you reserve a hotel, ask whether you'll have access to a *lift* (an elevator in Britspeak).

In most cities, including London, being a senior often entitles you to some terrific travel bargains, such as reduced admissions at theaters, museums, and other attractions. Carrying ID with proof of age can pay off in all these situations. *Note:* In London and throughout the United Kingdom, you may find that some senior discounts are available only to U.K. residents. But always ask, even if the reduction isn't posted.

The following sources can provide information on discounts and other benefits for seniors:

✔ **AARP** (formerly the American Association of Retired Persons; 601 E St. NW, Washington, DC 20049; ☎ 800/424-3410; www.aarp.org) offers member discounts on car rentals and hotels. AARP offers $13 yearly memberships that include discounts on flights to London when booked through the AARP Web site.

✔ **Elderhostel** (11 Ave. de Lafayette, Boston, MA 02110-1746; ☎ 877/426-8056; www.elderhostel.org) offers people 55 and older a variety of university-based educational programs in London and throughout England. These courses are value-packed, hassle-free ways to learn while traveling. The price includes airfare, accommodations, meals, tuition, tips, and insurance. And you'll be glad to know that you don't receive any grades. Popular London offerings have included "Inside the Parliament," "Legal London," "Classical Music and Opera in London," and "Treasures of London Galleries."

✔ **Grand Circle/Overseas Adventure Travel** (347 Congress St., Boston, MA 02210; ☎ 800/959-0405; www.gct.com) is another agency that offers mature travelers tours to England.

Accessing London: Advice for Travelers with Disabilities

More options and resources are available for disabled travelers than ever before. In London, most hotels and restaurants happily accommodate people with disabilities. London's top sights are wheelchair accessible. Theaters and performing arts venues are usually wheelchair accessible as well (always call first to make arrangements and get directions to special entrances and elevators).

Persons with disabilities are often entitled to special discounts at sightseeing and entertainment venues in Britain. These discounts are called *concessions* (often shortened to *concs*).

Before departing on your trip, contact VisitBritain (see the Quick Concierge, at the end of this book, for addresses and phone numbers) to request a copy of its "Disabled Traveler Fact Sheet," which contains some helpful general information. *Access in London* is the best and most comprehensive London guide for people with disabilities and anyone with a mobility problem. The book provides full access information for all the major sites, hotels, and modes of transportation. You can order it at www.accessinlondon.org or from major online booksellers.

The United Kingdom has several information resources for disabled travelers. The best of these resources include the following:

- ✔ **Artsline** (☎ 020/7388-2227; www.artsline.org.uk) provides advice on the accessibility of London arts and entertainment events.

- ✔ **The Society of London Theatres** (32 Rose St., London WC2E 9ET; www.officiallondontheatre.co.uk) offers a free guide called *Access Guide to London's West End Theatres.*

- ✔ **Holiday Care/Tourism for All Holidays Ltd.** (7th Floor, Sunley House, 4 Bedford Park, Croyden, Surrey CR0 2AP; ☎ 0845/124-9971 in the U.K. or 020/8760-0072 outside the U.K.; www.holiday care.org.uk) offers information and advice on suitable accommodations, transportation, and other facilities in England.

- ✔ **The National Trust** (☎ 020/7447-6742; www.nationaltrust.org.uk) is a British organization that owns and operates hundreds of historic properties (castles, gardens, and more) throughout England. For details on accessibility at each site, download the "National Trust Access Guide" from its Web site. Although not all National Trust sites are accessible, the organization provides powered four-wheeled vehicles free of charge at more than 50 properties; you can drive yourself or have a companion or volunteer drive for you.

✔ **Royal Association for Disability and Rehabilitation** (RADAR; 12 City Forum, 250 City Rd., London EC14 8AF; ☎ **020/7250-3222**; www.radar.org.uk) publishes information for disabled travelers in Britain.

Some other helpful resources in the United States include the following:

✔ **American Foundation for the Blind** (11 Penn Plaza, Suite 300, New York, NY 10001; ☎ **800/232-5463**; www.afb.org) offers information on traveling with Seeing Eye dogs; the foundation also issues ID cards to the legally blind.

✔ **The Society for Accessible Travel & Hospitality** (347 Fifth Ave., Suite 610, New York, NY 10016; ☎ **212/447-7284**; www.sath.org) is a membership organization with names and addresses of tour operators specializing in travel for the disabled. You can call to subscribe to its magazine, *Open World.*

✔ **Travel Information Service** (www.mossresourcenet.org) provides general information and resources for the disabled traveler.

Joining escorted tours

You can find tours designed to meet the needs of travelers with disabilities. One of the best operators is **Flying Wheels Travel** (143 West Bridge, P.O. Box 382, Owatonna, MN 55060; ☎ **507/451-5005**; www.flyingwheelstravel.com), which offers various escorted tours and cruises, as well as private tours in minivans with lifts.

Here are some other tour operators for London-bound travelers with disabilities:

✔ **Accessible Journeys** (☎ **800/846-4537**; www.disabilitytravel.com) offers tours of Britain and London in minibuses or motor coaches.

✔ **The Guided Tour** (☎ **800/783-5841**; e-mail: gtour400@aol.com) has one- and two-week guided tours for individuals, with one staff member for every three travelers.

✔ **Undiscovered Britain** (11978 Audubon Place, Philadelphia, PA 19116; ☎ **215/969-0542**; www.undiscoveredbritain.com) provides specialty travel and tours for individuals, small groups, or families traveling with a wheelchair user.

Dealing with access issues

In October 2004, Part III of the Disability Discrimination Act — which requires anyone offering a service to remove physical barriers that prevent disabled people from accessing it — went into effect throughout the U.K. What this means is that more and more businesses have become accessible, and access in general is easier than ever before. Don't assume, however, that all hotels and restaurants in London provide wheelchair ramps. Most of the less expensive B&Bs and older hotels don't have elevators, or the elevators are too small for a wheelchair. Ask about this when you reserve your room or table.

All the top sights and many of the attractions in Chapter 11 are wheelchair accessible, but in some cases you must use a different entrance. Call the attraction to find out about special entrances, ramps, elevator locations, and general directions. Theaters and performing arts venues are often wheelchair accessible, as well (again, call first).

Trains throughout the United Kingdom now have wide doors, grab rails, and provisions for wheelchairs. The **National Rail** Web site (www.nationalrail.co.uk) has a section on disabled travel and contact information for the various train operating companies.

Disabled travelers will want to keep the following in mind when traveling around London:

- ✔ Although London's streets and sidewalks are generally kept in good repair, the city is old and not all streets have modern curb cuts.

- ✔ Not all the city's Underground (subway) stations have elevators and ramps.

- ✔ Low-floor wheelchair-accessible buses serve most stations in London.

- ✔ The city's black cabs are roomy enough for wheelchairs.

- ✔ Victoria Coach Station in Central London has Braille maps.

The following organizations provide access information and services for disabled travelers in London:

- ✔ **Transport for London** (☎ 020/7222-1234; www.tfl.gov.uk) publishes a free brochure called "Tube Access," which helps travelers with disabilities plan a Tube journey, avoiding stairs and escalators. You can obtain this brochure at Underground stations in London.

- ✔ **Wheelchair Travel** (1 Johnston Green, Guildford, Surrey GU2 6XS; ☎ 1483/233-640 within the U.K. or 1483/237-668 from outside the U.K.; www.wheelchair-travel.co.uk) is an independent transport service for the disabled traveler arriving in London. The organization offers self-drive cars and minibuses (although I strongly discourage anyone, disabled or not, from driving in London) and can provide wheelchairs. Drivers who also act as guides are also available on request. Bring your own disabled stickers and permits from home if you're going to rent a self-drive vehicle.

Taking health precautions

Before you leave on your trip, talk to your physician about your general physical condition and your prescriptions for the time you're traveling, the medical equipment that you need to take, and how to get medical assistance when you're away. Carry all prescription medicines in their original bottles with the contents clearly marked, along with a letter from your doctor.

 Make a list of the generic names of your prescription drugs, in case you need to replace or refill them during your visit. Pack medications in your hand luggage. If you use a wheelchair, have a maintenance check before your trip.

Following the Rainbow: Gay and Lesbian Travelers

London has always been a popular destination for gays and lesbians, even in the days (prior to 1967) when homosexuality was a criminal offense in Britain. Today, with a more tolerant government at the helm and civil partnerships offering same-sex couples the same rights as heterosexual couples, gay pride is prominent. The city government actually spends money to promote gay tourism. You can find gay theaters, gay shops, more than 100 gay pubs, famous gay discos, and gay community groups of all sorts. The official Visit London Web site (www.visit london.com) has information on gay venues and events in London.

Old Compton Street in Soho is the heart of London's Gay Village, filled with dozens of gay pubs, restaurants, and upscale bars/cafes. The **Earl's Court** area, long a gay bastion, is home to many gay pubs and restaurants.

Lesbigay events in London include the **London Lesbian and Gay Film Festival** in March, the **Pride Parade** and celebrations in June, and the big outdoor bash known as **Summer Rites** in August. You can obtain information and exact dates from the **London Lesbian and Gay Switchboard** at ☎ 020/7837-7324 or online at www.llgs.org.uk.

 Brighton (which I describe in Chapter 14) is one of the gayest seaside resort towns in Europe. From London, you can get to Brighton on the train in under an hour.

You may want to check out the following Web sites as you plan your trip. All are specifically geared to gay and lesbian travelers to London and the United Kingdom:

✓ **Gay Britain Network:** www.gaybritain.co.uk

✓ **Gay London:** www.gaylondon.co.uk

✔ **Pink Passport:** www.pinkpassport.co.uk

✔ **UK Gay Guide:** www.gayguide.co.uk

In addition, several gay magazines, useful for their listings and news coverage, are available in gay pubs, clubs, bars, and cafes. The most popular are *Pink Paper* (www.pinkpaper.com), *Boyz* (www.boyz.co.uk), and *QX* (*Queer Xtra;* www.qxmagazine.com). *Gay Times* (www.gaytimes.co.uk), a high-quality, monthly, news-oriented mag, is available at most news agents. Indispensable for its citywide listings (including gay listings), *Time Out* (www.timeout.com), with gay and lesbian listings, appears at newsstands on Wednesdays.

Gay's the Word (66 Marchmont St., WC1; ☎ **020/7278-7654;** www.gaystheword.co.uk; Tube: Russell Square), the city's only all-around gay and lesbian bookstore, was still open as of press time — but it was "under threat" and in danger of closing. The store stocks a fine selection of new and used books and current periodicals.

Chapter 7

Taking Care of the Remaining Details

. . . .

In This Chapter

▶ Crossing borders: Passports
▶ Insuring yourself and your trip
▶ Taking care of your health: Medications and emergencies
▶ Using cellphones and e-mail in London
▶ Getting through airport security

. . . .

*B*efore you depart for London to take that boat ride on the River Thames or visit the Tower of London, you need to take care of some final details. Do you have an up-to-date passport? Have you taken steps to meet your health needs while you're on your trip? Are you wondering how to use a cellphone or access e-mail while in London? Do you think you need to rent a car? This chapter gives you the information you need to answer those lingering questions.

Getting a Passport

A valid passport is the only legal form of identification accepted around the world. You can't cross an international border without one. Getting a passport is easy, but the process takes some time.

The U.S. Department of State's Bureau of Consular Affairs maintains http://travel.state.gov, a Web site that provides everything you ever wanted to know about passports (including a downloadable application), Customs, and other government-regulated aspects of travel.

Applying for a U.S. passport

If you're applying for a first-time passport, follow these steps:

1. Complete a **passport application** in person at a U.S. passport office; a federal, state, or probate court; or a major post office. To find your regional passport office, either check the **U.S. State Department** Web site (http://travel.state.gov) or call the

National Passport Information Center (☎ 877/487-2778) for automated information.

2. Present a **certified birth certificate** as proof of citizenship. (Bringing along your driver's license, state or military ID, or Social Security card is also a good idea.) If you're a naturalized citizen of the United States, you'll have to provide your Naturalization Certificate or Certificate of Citizenship as proof.

3. Submit **two identical passport-size photos,** measuring 2 x 2 inches in size. You often find businesses that take these photos near a passport office. *Note:* You can't use a strip from a photo vending machine because the pictures aren't identical.

4. Pay a **fee.** For people 16 and over, a passport is valid for ten years and costs $97. For children 15 and under, a passport is valid for five years and costs $82.

Allow plenty of time before your trip to apply for a passport; standard processing in 2007 took 10 to 12 weeks. Expedited service, which requires an additional fee, takes 2 to 3 weeks. If you use the expedited service, it's also a good idea to arrange overnight delivery (for an extra charge) to send your passport application and receive your passport.

If you have a passport in your current name that was issued within the past 15 years (and you were over age 15 when it was issued), you can renew the passport by mail for $67. Whether you're applying in person or by mail, you can download passport applications from the U.S. State Department Web site at http://travel.state.gov. For general information, call the **National Passport Agency** (☎ 202/647-0518). To find your regional passport office, either check the U.S. State Department Web site or call the **National Passport Information Center** (☎ 877/487-2778) for automated information.

Applying for other passports

The following list offers information for citizens of Australia, Canada, and New Zealand:

- ✔ **Australians** can visit a local post office or passport office, call the **Australia Passport Information Service** (☎ 131-232 toll-free from Australia), or log on to www.passports.gov.au for details on how and where to apply.

- ✔ **Canadians** can pick up applications at passport offices throughout Canada; at post offices; or from the central **Passport Office** (Department of Foreign Affairs and International Trade, Ottawa, ON K1A 0G3; ☎ 800/567-6868; www.ppt.gc.ca). Applications must be accompanied by two identical passport-size photographs and proof of Canadian citizenship. Processing takes five to ten days if you apply in person or about three weeks if you apply by mail.

✔ **New Zealanders** can pick up a passport application at any New Zealand Passports Office or download it from the office's Web site. Contact the **Passports Office** at ☎ **0800/225-050** in New Zealand or 04/474-8100, or log on to www.passports.govt.nz.

Entering England with your passport

If you're a citizen of the United States, Canada, Australia, or New Zealand, you must have a passport with at least six months remaining until its expiration to enter the United Kingdom. You need to show your passport at the Customs and immigration area when you arrive at a U.K. airport. After your passport is stamped, you can remain in the United Kingdom as a tourist for up to three months. No visa is required if you're going to stay in England or the rest of the United Kingdom for less than three months.

Keep your passport with you at all times. You need to show it only when you're converting traveler's checks or foreign currency at a bank or currency exchange. However, you may be asked to present your passport to the hotel clerk when you check in; after examining it, the clerk will return the passport to you. If you're not going to need your passport for currency exchanges, ask whether the hotel has a safe where you can keep it locked up; there may be a safe in your room.

Dealing with a (gulp!) lost passport

Don't worry; if you lose your passport in England, you won't be sent to the Tower of London, but you need to take steps to replace it *immediately*. First, notify the police. Then go to your consulate or high commission office (they're all located in London — you'll find addresses and phone numbers in the Quick Concierge, at the end of this book). Bring all available forms of identification, and the staff can get started on generating your new passport. Always call first to verify the hours.

Before leaving on your trip, make a few photocopies of your passport photo page. Leave one copy with someone staying at home, and keep another copy with you on your trip, separate from your actual passport. If you do lose your passport, bring the copy to your consulate. It may help speed up the process of getting a new passport.

Renting a Car in London — Not!

Having a car in London is more trouble than it's worth for the following reasons:

✔ Maneuvering through London's congested and complicated maze of streets can be an endurance test even for Londoners.

✔ Finding your way through the city in heavy traffic while driving on the *left-hand* side of the road when you're used to driving on the

right-hand side can turn even the best driver into a gibbering nut
case.

✔ Parking is difficult to find and expensive (street meters cost £1/$2
for 20 minutes).

✔ Congestion pricing (road tolls) makes driving in and out of Central
London pricey.

✔ Gas (*petrol* in Britspeak) costs about £1 per liter (or approximately
$8 a gallon).

✔ Public transportation — especially the Tube — will get you everywhere you want to go at a fraction of the cost.

Do yourself a favor: Forget about renting a car. If you want to be with
Londoners on their own turf (or in their own tunnels), the Tube (Underground) is a great way to do it. Even if you're planning excursions outside London, the trains are a better option. (However, see Chapter 14 for
details on renting a car for day-tripping.)

Playing It Safe with Travel and Medical Insurance

Three kinds of travel insurance are available: trip-cancellation insurance,
medical insurance, and lost-luggage insurance. The cost of travel insurance varies widely, depending on the cost and length of your trip, your
age and health, and the type of trip that you're taking, but expect to pay
between 5 percent and 8 percent of the vacation itself. Here's my advice
on all three:

✔ **Trip-cancellation insurance** helps you get your money back if you
have to back out of a trip, if you have to go home early, or if your
travel supplier goes bankrupt. Allowed reasons for cancellation can
range from sickness to natural disasters to the State Department
declaring your destination unsafe for travel.

✔ For travel overseas, most health plans (including Medicare and
Medicaid) do not provide coverage. Even if your plan does cover
overseas treatment, most out-of-country hospitals, including those
in England, make you pay your bills upfront and send you a refund
only after you've returned home and filed the necessary paperwork
with your insurance company. As a safety net, you may want to
buy **travel medical insurance.** If you require additional medical
insurance, try **MEDEX Assistance** (☎ 410/453-6300; www.medex
assist.com) or **Travel Assistance International** (☎ 800/821-
2828; www.travelassistance.com).

Coping with jet lag

Jet lag is a pitfall of traveling across time zones. If you're flying north–south and you feel sluggish when you touch down, your symptoms will be the result of dehydration and the general stress of air travel. When you travel east–west or vice versa, however, your body becomes thoroughly confused about what time it is, and everything from your digestive system to your brain is knocked for a loop. Traveling east — say, from Chicago to London — is more difficult on your internal clock than traveling west — say, from London to Atlanta — because your body is likely more inclined to stay up late than fall asleep early.

Here are some tips for combating jet lag:

✔ Reset your watch to your destination time before you board the plane.

✔ Drink lots of water before, during, and after your flight, and avoid alcohol on the plane.

✔ Exercise and sleep well for a few days before your trip.

✔ If you have trouble sleeping on planes, fly eastward on morning flights.

Daylight is the key to resetting your body clock. At the Web site for **Outside In** (www. bodyclock.com), you can get a customized plan of when to seek and avoid light.

✔ **Lost-luggage insurance** is not necessary for most travelers. On international flights (including U.S. portions of international trips), baggage coverage is limited to approximately $9.07 per pound, up to approximately $635 per checked bag. If you plan to check items more valuable than the standard liability, see if your valuables are covered by your homeowner's policy, get baggage insurance as part of your comprehensive travel insurance package, or buy Travel Guard's BagTrak product. Don't buy insurance at the airport — it's usually overpriced. Be sure to take any valuables or irreplaceable items with you in your carry-on luggage, because many valuables (including books, money, and electronics) aren't covered by airline policies.

If your luggage is lost, immediately file a lost-luggage claim at the airport, detailing the luggage contents. For most airlines, you must report delayed, damaged, or lost baggage within four hours of arrival. The airlines are required to deliver luggage, once found, directly to your house or destination free of charge.

For more information, contact one of the following recommended insurers: **Access America** (☎ **866/807-3982;** www.accessamerica. com); **Travel Guard International** (☎ **800/826-4919;** www.travel guard.com); **Travel Insured International** (☎ **800/243-3174;** www. travelinsured.com); or **Travelex Insurance Services** (☎ **888/ 457-4602;** www.travelex-insurance.com).

Staying Healthy When You Travel

Getting sick will ruin your vacation, so I *strongly* advise against it. (Of course, last time I checked, the bugs weren't listening to me any more than they probably listen to you.)

 For travel abroad, you may have to pay all medical costs upfront and be reimbursed later. For information on purchasing additional medical insurance for your trip, see the preceding section.

Talk to your doctor before leaving on a trip if you have a serious and/or chronic illness. For conditions such as epilepsy, diabetes, or heart problems, wear a **MedicAlert identification tag** (☎ **888/633-4298;** www.medicalert.org), which immediately alerts doctors to your condition and gives them access to your records through MedicAlert's 24-hour hotline. Contact the **International Association for Medical Assistance to Travelers** (IAMAT; ☎ **716/754-4883** in the U.S. or 416/652-0137 in Canada; www.iamat.org) for tips on travel and health concerns in the countries that you're visiting.

Staying Connected by Cellphone or E-Mail

The three letters that define much of the world's **wireless capabilities** are GSM (Global System for Mobiles), a big, seamless network that makes for easy cross-border cellphone use throughout Europe and dozens of other countries worldwide. In the United States, T-Mobile and AT&T Wireless use this quasi-universal system; in Canada, Microcell and some Rogers customers are GSM; and all Europeans and most Australians use GSM.

Avoiding "economy-class syndrome"

Deep vein thrombosis, or as it's known in the world of flying, "economy-class syndrome," is a blood clot that develops in a deep vein. It's a potentially deadly condition that can be caused by sitting in cramped conditions — such as an airplane cabin — for too long. Symptoms of deep vein thrombosis include leg pain or swelling, or even shortness of breath.

During a flight (especially a long-haul flight), get up, walk around, and stretch your legs every 60 to 90 minutes to keep your blood flowing. Other preventive measures include frequent flexing of the legs while sitting, drinking lots of water, and avoiding alcohol and sleeping pills.

If you have a history of deep vein thrombosis, heart disease, or another condition that puts you at high risk, some experts recommend wearing compression stockings or taking anticoagulants when you fly; always ask your physician about the best course for you.

Healthy travels to you

The following government Web sites offer up-to-date health-related travel advice:

✔ **Australia:** www.dfat.gov.au/travel/

✔ **Canada:** www.hc-sc.gc.ca/index_e.html

✔ **United Kingdom:** www.dh.gov.uk/en/Policyandguidance/Health advicefortravellers

✔ **United States:** www.cdc.gov/travel/

If your cellphone is on a GSM system, and you have a world-capable multiband phone such as many Sony Ericsson, Motorola, or Samsung models, you can make and receive calls across developed areas throughout much of the world, from Andorra to Uganda. Just call your wireless operator and ask for international roaming to be activated on your account. Unfortunately, per-minute charges can be high — usually $1 to $1.50 in England and Western Europe.

That's why it's important to buy an unlocked world phone from the get-go. Many cellphone operators sell locked phones that restrict you from using any removable computer memory phone chip (called a **SIM card**) other than the ones they supply. Having an unlocked phone allows you to install a cheap, prepaid SIM card (found at a local retailer) in England. (Show your phone to the salesperson; not all phones work on all networks.) You'll get a local phone number — and much, much lower calling rates. If you're staying in England for an extended period of time, buying a prepaid British SIM card may be your best bet. Getting an already locked phone unlocked can be a complicated process, but it can be done; just call your cellular operator and say you'll be going abroad for several months and want to use the phone with a local provider.

For many people, **renting** a phone is a good idea. Although you can rent a phone from any number of overseas sites, including kiosks at airports and at car rental agencies, I suggest renting the phone before you leave home. That way, you can give loved ones and business associates your new number, make sure the phone works, and take the phone wherever you go — especially helpful for overseas trips through several countries, where local phone rental agencies often bill in local currency and may not let you take the phone to another country.

However, phone rental isn't cheap. You'll usually pay $40 to $50 per week, plus airtime fees of at least $1 a minute. If you're traveling to England, though, local rental companies often offer free incoming calls within their home country, which can save you big bucks. The bottom line: Shop around.

Surfing at Internet cafes in London

The **easyInternetCafe** chain has several giant Internet cafes in London — but *cafe* is really a misnomer, because the hundreds of screens in the largest locations make them look like telemarketing sweatshops, and you don't hear any conversation, just the clicking of keyboards.

The charging system is radical because surfers buy credit, not minutes. The minimum you'll spend is £2 ($4), and the amount of time you get for that is in inverse proportion to how busy the branch is. The rate is adjusted every five minutes and posted on video screens, a bit like a stock exchange. Your ticket has a user ID, which notes the current rate when you first log on. That becomes your rate. You'll never pay more, but if things quiet down, your credit will buy more time — a pound could be worth up to six hours, or so they claim. easyInternet never closes, so avoid afternoons and early evenings, and surf with the creatures of the night and early morning.

Turn to the appendix for a list of convenient branches. Otherwise, check www.easy everything.com for a complete list. As befitting a large chain, the telephone number for all locations is ☎ 020/7241-9000.

Rent-a-phone (☎ 800/400-7221 in the U.S. or 0800/317-540 in the U.K.) is an international cellphone rental company with offices in the United States and United Kingdom; per-minute charges from England are generally about $1.99 per minute to the United States and Europe, and the phones can be delivered to your door in the U.S. before you leave.

In Terminal 1 and Terminal 2 at Heathrow Airport, you can buy a range of mobile phones and services, including SIM cards, at **Primus** (☎ 020/8607-5960).

Two good wireless rental companies are **InTouch USA** (☎ 800/872-7626; www.intouchglobal.com) and **RoadPost** (☎ 888/290-1606 or 905/272-5665; www.roadpost.com). Give them your itinerary, and they'll tell you what wireless products you need. InTouch will also, for free, advise you on whether your existing phone will work overseas; simply call ☎ 703/222-7161 between 9 a.m. and 4 p.m. eastern standard time or go to www.intouchglobal.com/travel.htm.

You have any number of ways to check your e-mail and access the Internet on the road. Of course, using your own laptop — or even a personal digital assistant (PDA) or electronic organizer with a modem — gives you the most flexibility. But even if you don't have a computer, you can still access your e-mail and even your office computer from cybercafes.

It's hard nowadays to find a city in England that *doesn't* have a few cybercafes, though you won't find any in smaller towns and villages. No definitive directory of cybercafes exists — these are independent businesses, after all — but two places to start looking are at www.cyber captive.com and www.cybercafe.com.

Aside from formal cybercafes, most **youth hostels** nowadays have at least one computer on which you can access the Internet. And most **public libraries** offer Internet access free or for a small charge. If you want to save money, avoid **hotel business centers** unless you can use the service for free. Most major airports now have **Internet kiosks** scattered throughout their gates. These kiosks, which you also see in shopping malls, hotel lobbies, and tourist information offices around the world, give you basic Web access for a per-minute fee that's usually higher than cybercafe prices. The kiosks' clunkiness and high prices mean that you probably want to avoid them whenever possible.

To retrieve your e-mail, ask your **Internet service provider (ISP)** if it has a Web-based interface tied to your existing e-mail account. If your ISP doesn't have such an interface, you can use the free **mail2web** service (www.mail2web.com) to view and reply to your home e-mail. For more flexibility, you may want to open a free, Web-based e-mail account with **Yahoo! Mail** (http://mail.yahoo.com) or **Google** (www.gmail.com). If you have **AOL,** you can access your e-mail online at www.aol.com. (Microsoft's Hotmail is another popular option, but Hotmail has severe spam problems.) You may be able to get your home ISP to forward your e-mail to the Web-based account automatically.

If you need to access files on your office computer, look into a service called **GoToMyPC** (www.gotomypc.com). The service provides a Web-based interface for you to access and manipulate a distant PC from anywhere — even a cybercafe — provided that your "target" PC is on and has an always-on connection to the Internet (such as with Road Runner cable). The service offers top-quality security, but if you're worried about hackers, use your own laptop rather than a cybercafe computer to access the GoToMyPC system.

If you're bringing your own computer with **Wi-Fi** (wireless fidelity), you'll be happy to know that more and more hotels, cafes, and retailers are signing on as wireless Internet hotspots. You can get a Wi-Fi connection one of several ways. Many laptops sold in the last year have built-in Wi-Fi capability. Mac owners have their own networking technology, Apple AirPort. If you have an older computer, you can plug a **Wi-Fi card** (around $50) into your laptop.

You sign up for wireless access service much as you do cellphone service, through a plan offered by one of several commercial companies that have made wireless service available in airports, hotel lobbies, and coffee shops, primarily in the United States (followed by the U.K. and Japan). **T-Mobile Hotspot** (www.t-mobile.com/hotspot) serves up wireless connections at Starbucks coffee shops throughout England. **Boingo** (www.boingo.com) and **Wayport** (www.wayport.com) have set up networks in airports and high-class hotel lobbies. iPass providers also give you access to a few hundred wireless hotel-lobby setups. Best of all, you don't need to be staying at the Four Seasons to use the hotel's network; just set yourself up on a nice couch in the lobby. The companies' pricing policies can be byzantine, with a variety of monthly, per-connection, and per-minute plans, but in general, you pay around $30 a month for limited access — and as more and more companies jump on the wireless bandwagon, prices are likely to get even more competitive.

Some places in cities around the world also provide **free wireless networks.** To locate these free hotspots, go to www.personaltelco.net/index.cgi/WirelessCommunities.

If Wi-Fi is not available at your destination, most business-class hotels throughout England and the rest of the United Kingdom offer dataports for laptop modems, and many offer free high-speed Internet access using an Ethernet network cable. You can bring your own cables, but most hotels rent them for around $10. **Call your hotel in advance** to see what your options are.

In addition, major ISPs have **local access numbers** around the world, allowing you to go online by simply placing a local call. Check your ISP's Web site or call its toll-free number and ask how you can use your current account away from home, and how much it will cost. If you're traveling outside the reach of your ISP, the **iPass** network has dial-up numbers in most of the world's countries. You'll have to sign up with an iPass provider, who will then tell you how to set up your computer for your destination. For a list of iPass providers, go to www.ipass.com and click "Individuals Buy Now." One solid provider is **i2roam** (☎ **866/811-6209** or 920/235-0475; www.i2roam.com).

Wherever you go, bring a **connection kit** of the right power and phone adapters, a spare phone cord, and a spare Ethernet network cable — or find out whether your hotel supplies them to guests.

North American current runs 110V, 60 cycles; the standard voltage throughout Britain is 240V AC, 50 cycles. You need a current converter or transformer to bring the voltage down and the cycles up. Two-pronged North American plugs won't fit into the three-pronged square British wall sockets, so you also need a three-pronged square adapter and converter if you use North American laptops or appliances while in England. Australian and New Zealand plugs won't fit, although the electrical current is the same as England. Plug adapters and converters are available at most travel, luggage, electronics, and hardware stores. Some plug adapters are also current converters. Most contemporary laptop computers automatically sense the current and adapt accordingly.

Keeping Up with Airline Security Measures

With the federalization of airport security, security procedures at U.S. airports are more stable and consistent than ever. Generally, you'll be fine if you arrive at the airport **one hour** before a domestic flight and **two hours** before an international flight; if you show up late, tell an airline employee and she can probably whisk you to the front of the line.

Bring a **current, government-issued photo ID** such as a driver's license or passport. Keep your ID at the ready to show at check-in, the security checkpoint, and sometimes even the gate. (Children under 18 do not need government-issued photo IDs for domestic flights, but they do for international flights to most countries.)

In 2003, the Transportation Security Administration (TSA) phased out **gate check-in** at all U.S. airports. And **E-tickets** have made paper tickets nearly obsolete. If you have an E-ticket, you can beat the ticket counter lines by using airport **electronic kiosks** or even **online check-in** from your home computer (electronic check-in is not available for most international flights, however). Online check-in involves logging on to your airline's Web site, accessing your reservation, and printing out your boarding pass — and the airline may even offer you bonus miles to do so! If you're using a kiosk at the airport, bring the credit card that you used to book the ticket or your frequent-flier card. Print out your boarding pass from the kiosk and simply proceed to the security checkpoint with your pass and a photo ID. If you're checking bags or looking to snag an exit-row seat for the domestic portion of your flight to London, you'll be able to do so using most airline kiosks. Even the smaller airlines are employing the kiosk system, but always call your airline to make sure these alternatives are available. **Curbside check-in** is also a good way to avoid lines, although a few airlines still ban curbside check-in; call before you go. If your trip requires you to fly to another U.S. airport to get your flight to London, chances are that you must check in at the airline counter, showing your passport, for your international flight.

Security checkpoint lines in U.S. airports are generally shorter and faster than they were immediately after September 11, 2001, but when you're returning from London via Heathrow or Gatwick airports, be prepared for long lines and multiple security checks. If you have trouble standing for long periods of time, tell an airline employee; the airline will provide a wheelchair. Speed up security by **not wearing metal objects** such as big belt buckles. If you've got metallic body parts, a note from your doctor can prevent a long chat with the security screeners. Keep in mind that only **ticketed passengers** are allowed past security, except for folks escorting disabled passengers or children.

Federalization has stabilized **what you can carry on** and **what you can't.** The general rule is that sharp things are out, nail clippers are okay. Any liquids or gels must be in 3-ounce or smaller containers and placed in a see-through 1-quart plastic bag, which is put separately through the scanner. (After you've passed through security, you can buy bottled water and bring it on the plane.) Bring food in your carryon rather than checking it, because explosive-detection machines used on checked luggage have been known to mistake food (especially chocolate, for some reason) for bombs. Travelers in the United States are allowed one carry-on bag, plus a personal item (such as a purse, brief-case, or laptop bag). Carry-on hoarders can stuff all sorts of things into a laptop bag; as long as it has a laptop in it, it's still considered a personal item. The Transportation Security Administration (TSA) has issued a list of restricted items; you can find the list at www.tsa.gov (click "For Travelers" and then "Air Travel").

Airport screeners may decide that your checked luggage needs to be searched by hand. You can now purchase luggage locks that allow screeners to open and relock a checked bag if hand-searching is neces-sary. Look for Travel Sentry–certified locks at luggage or travel shops and Brookstone stores (you can buy them online at www.brookstone.com). These locks, approved by the TSA, can be opened by luggage inspectors with a special code or key. For more information on the locks, visit www.travelsentry.org. If you use something other than TSA-approved locks, your lock will be cut off your suitcase if a TSA agent needs to hand-search your luggage.

Part III
Settling into London

The 5th Wave   By Rich Tennant

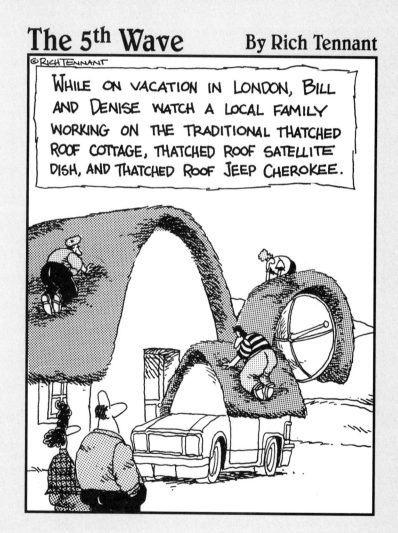

WHILE ON VACATION IN LONDON, BILL AND DENISE WATCH A LOCAL FAMILY WORKING ON THE TRADITIONAL THATCHED ROOF COTTAGE, THATCHED ROOF SATELLITE DISH, AND THATCHED ROOF JEEP CHEROKEE.

In this part . . .

In this part, I help you settle into London. In Chapter 8, I tell you how to get from the airport into the city and introduce you to London's neighborhoods; I also tell you everything you need to know about using public transportation, including ways to save a bundle on bus and Tube tickets. Chapter 9 tells you what you can expect in terms of accommodations and their price ranges, focuses on finding a good hotel for the best possible rate, and gives you my list of London's best hotels, all indexed by location and price. In Chapter 10, I introduce you to London's dining scene, telling you about the variety of cuisines you'll discover and recommending dozens of my favorite London restaurants, from pubs and fish-and-chips joints to the hottest of haute hangouts, all indexed by neighborhood, cuisine, and price so you can easily find what you're looking for. I also give you a list of places for a quick snack or a formal high tea.

Chapter 8

Arriving and Getting Oriented

- -

In This Chapter

▶ Making it through Customs
▶ Traveling from the airport (or train station) to your hotel
▶ Getting familiar with the London neighborhoods
▶ Finding help and information after you arrive
▶ Traveling around the city

- -

*A*lthough London is among the world's largest cities, both in size and population, its neighborhoods were once small, separate villages. With urban roots (and routes) that hark back to Roman times, London isn't always the easiest city to navigate. Streets aren't organized in a grid, and although most have been paved and modernized, a few old lanes here and there still have cobblestones. This quaint, villagelike quality is one reason for London's enduring charm, but charm is little comfort when you're trying to find your way around in a strange city. This chapter helps you get your bearings. Neighborhood boundaries come later in this chapter, too. First, you need to get from the airport or train station into Central London.

Getting through Passport Control and Customs

Have your passport ready because your first stop after deplaning is passport control (for details on getting a passport, see Chapter 7). The procedure is fairly routine. On the plane you fill out a *landing card* that asks for your name, home address, passport number, and the address where you'll be staying in London. Present the completed card with your passport to the official at Passport Control. The official may ask for the following information:

✔ How long you'll be staying (you can only stay up to three months if you don't have a visa)

✔ Where you plan to stay

- Whether the trip is for business or pleasure
- What your next destination will be
- How much money you have with you

Although you may think that the question about your finances is snoopy impertinence, officials have good reason to ask. They want to verify that people entering England won't apply for some kind of welfare or national health-insurance benefits and become a burden on the country.

Officials may stamp your passport without asking a thing. After your passport is stamped, proceed to pick up your luggage. From there, you wind your way out through the Customs Hall.

At the Customs area, you get two choices: "Nothing to Declare" and "Goods to Declare." Chances are you won't be declaring anything, in which case you'll walk right through. Limits on imports for visitors age 17 and older entering England include the following:

- 200 cigarettes, 50 cigars, or 250 grams (8.8 oz.) of loose tobacco
- 2 liters (2.1 qt.) of still table wine
- 1 liter (1 qt.) of liquor over 22 percent alcohol content or 2 liters (2.1 qt.) of liquor under 22 percent
- 2 fluid ounces of perfume

If you fall within these limits, go through the "Nothing to Declare" area at Customs. You may, however, be stopped for a random luggage search. Don't take it personally if this happens. Unless you're smuggling in contraband, you have nothing to worry about.

For details on duty-free shopping and limits on what you can bring back home, see Chapter 12.

Making Your Way to Your Hotel

You're in London! Well, almost. First, you have to get from the airport or train station to your hotel. I fill you in on all your options from each airport in the following sections.

Arriving at Heathrow

About 24km (15 miles) west of Central London, Heathrow (☎ **0870/000-0123;** www.baa.co.uk) is the largest of London's airports, as well as one of the world's busiest, with four passenger terminals (and an additional fifth under construction) serving flights from around the globe. Signposts mark just about everything and moving walkways make the trek through the long corridors easy. You'll probably arrive at Terminal 3 or Terminal 4:

✔ Terminal 3 is for non-British, long-haul flights.

✔ Terminal 4 is for British Airways intercontinental flights.

After clearing Customs (see the section "Getting through Passport Control and Customs," earlier in this chapter), you enter the main concourse of your terminal. You can pick up a free map and general info from the **Tourist Information Centre** in the Underground concourse of Terminals 1, 2, and 3 (open Oct–May daily 8 a.m.–6 p.m. and June–Sept Mon–Sat 8 a.m.–7 p.m.). You can also find ATMs, hotel booking agencies (see Chapter 9), theater booking services, and several banks and *bureaux de change* where you can swap your dollars or traveler's checks for pounds and pence (see Chapter 4 for details on changing money).

You have several options for getting into the city. The **London Underground** (☎ **020/7222-1234;** www.tfl.gov.uk/tube), called the *Underground* or the *Tube,* is the London subway system and the cheapest mode of public transportation for most Central London destinations (see the inside back cover of this book for a map of the Underground system). All terminals at Heathrow link up with the Tube system. Follow the Underground signs to the ticket booth. The Piccadilly Line gets you into Central London in about 45 minutes for a fare of £4 ($8). Underground trains run from all four Heathrow terminals every five to nine minutes Monday through Saturday 5:30 a.m. to 11:30 p.m. and Sunday 6 a.m. to 11 p.m.

The one potential hassle with the Underground is that the Tube trains don't have luggage racks. Stash your bags as best you can — behind your legs, on your lap, or near the center doors where there's more space. Keep in mind that, during rush hour, the trains become increasingly packed as you get closer to London. To reach your hotel on the Underground, you may have to change trains or take a cab from the Underground station closest to your destination.

If the Underground is closed, you can ride the **N97 night bus** from Heathrow to Central London. Buses (located in front of the terminals) run every 30 minutes Monday through Saturday midnight to 5 a.m. and Sunday 11 p.m. to 5:30 a.m. The trip takes about an hour; a one-way fare costs £2 ($4).

The buses operated by **National Express** (☎ **08705/808-080;** www.nationalexpress.com) may be a better alternative to the Underground if you have lots of heavy luggage. The trip from the airport to Victoria Coach Station takes about 75 minutes, and costs £4 ($8; payable on the bus). Up to three buses per hour depart daily from 4 a.m. to 11:23 p.m. from the coach station in front of Heathrow's Terminals 3 and 4.

It's about time! Heathrow's new Terminal 5

Heathrow Airport was initially built to serve about 45 million passengers a year, but for a decade now its four terminals have been processing upwards of 70 million. The overcrowding was so bad that passengers voted Heathrow their least favorite airport worldwide in a 2006 poll by TripAdvisor. Some of that passenger crush should be alleviated in March 2008, when Heathrow opens its new Terminal 5.

The new terminal, which serves British Airways, is a radical departure from the other four. Designed by architect Richard Rodgers, it features light stone floors (instead of much-tramped carpeting) and glass facades (instead of windowless corridors) that provide views of Windsor Castle and Wembley Stadium. With some 112 retail outlets, including upscale stores like Prada and Harrods, shopping is a major component of the new terminal, as are eating and drinking — the terminal is set to include bars, cafes, and a restaurant from celebrity chef Gordon Ramsay featuring a one-hour menu.

When Terminal 5 is up and running, Terminal 2 will be demolished and a new Heathrow East Terminal will be built on its site. When the East Terminal is open, Terminal 1 will be closed and Terminal 3 will be expanded. By that time — a decade or more away — Heathrow will be back to its original four terminals. But what's really needed, say many, is another runway.

The **Heathrow Express** (☎ 0845/600-1515; www.heathrowexpress. co.uk) is a dedicated train line running from all four Heathrow terminals to London's Paddington Station in only 15 minutes. The trains have air-conditioning, ergonomically designed seating, and plenty of luggage space. The Express (standard) class fare costs £16 ($32). You can buy tickets at the airport or onboard the train (for an additional £2/$4 charge). Service runs daily every 15 minutes from 5 a.m. to 11:48 p.m.

If you're travel-weary, you may want the luxury of taking a **taxi** directly to your hotel. Taxis are especially cost effective if four or five people are traveling together. You can order one at the Taxi Information booths in Terminal 3 (☎ 020/8745-4655) or Terminal 4 (☎ 020/8745-7302). Expect to pay about £45 to £50 ($90 to $100), plus tip (15 percent of the total fare), for a trip of about 45 minutes. Cabs are available 24 hours a day. Wheelchair facilities are available at all times for the disabled.

Arriving at calmer Gatwick

Gatwick (☎ 0870/000-2468; www.baa.co.uk) is considerably smaller than Heathrow but basically provides the same services, except that there's no tourist information office here. Gatwick is about 45km (28 miles) south of Central London and handles national and international flights from some U.S. airlines; international flights come in at the South Terminal. Gatwick also has a North Terminal.

If you land at Gatwick rather than Heathrow, you have fewer transportation options into Central London. The highway system from Gatwick into London is far less efficient than from Heathrow, so buses, minivans, or cabs can end up taking two or three hours in heavy traffic.

Your quickest way of getting into Central London from Gatwick is the convenient **Gatwick Express train** (☎ 0845/850-1530; www.gatwick express.co.uk). You can board the train right in the South Terminal, and in about 30 minutes, you'll be at Victoria Station. The trip costs £16 ($32) for Express class; First class, which has reclining chairs and refreshment service, costs £24 ($48). Trains run daily every 15 minutes from 5:50 a.m. to 1:35 a.m.

Southern Train (☎ 08451/272-920; www.southernrailway.com), a local passenger train, runs to Victoria Station in 30 minutes and costs £8.90 ($18). Four trains an hour run during the day; they run hourly from midnight to 5 a.m.

National Express buses (☎ 08705/808-080; www.nationalexpress. com) provide service from the airport to Victoria Coach Station in Central London, departing from both the North and South Terminal. The fare is £6.60 ($13), payable on the bus.

Hotelink (☎ 01293/552-251; www.hotelink.co.uk) runs a minibus service from Gatwick directly to your hotel for £20 ($40).

For 24-hour taxi service between Gatwick and Central London, call

   ✔ Gatwick Airport Cars (☎ 01293/562-291)

   ✔ Gatwick Goldlines Cars (☎ 01293/568-368)

You can order a taxi at the Taxi Information booth when you arrive at Gatwick Airport. Fares for both companies are the same: £65 ($130), plus tip, for the journey that takes about 90 minutes.

Touching down at another airport

If you fly into London from elsewhere in Europe, you may arrive at an airport other than Heathrow or Gatwick. The following sections help you navigate from these less-used facilities.

Stansted: For national and European flights

Stansted (☎ 0870/000-0303; www.stanstedairport.com) is a single-terminal airport used for national and European flights. The airport is about 80km (50 miles) northeast of Central London. The **Stansted Express train** (☎ 0845/600-7245) to Liverpool Street Station takes 45 minutes and costs £16 ($32). Trains run every 15 minutes daily 5:30 a.m. to 11:59 p.m. Taxi fare into the city averages about £60 ($120), plus tip.

London City Airport: European destinations only

London City Airport (☎ 020/7646-000; www.londoncityairport.com) is a mere 10km (6 miles) east of the city center, and it services only European destinations. A new extension of the **Docklands Light Railway** (DLR) travels from the airport to Bank Street, in Central London, in 22 minutes for £4 ($8); the Underground requires an additional fare if you're traveling beyond Bank Street. A taxi to the vicinity of Marble Arch costs about £25 ($50), plus tip.

Luton: Serving European charters

Luton (☎ 01582/405-100; www.london-luton.co.uk) services European charter flights. This small, independent airport is about 45km (28 miles) northwest of the city. Travel by free shuttle bus to Luton Airport Parkway station, then take a **Capital Connection train** to King's Cross Station in central London for £11 ($22); the trip takes 30 to 45 minutes. Taxis into the city cost about £50 ($100), plus tip.

Arriving by train

If you're coming from the Continent, you cross the English Channel and disembark at one of the United Kingdom's Channel ports. The ports closest to London are Dover, Folkestone, and Ramsgate to the east and Newhaven, Portsmouth, and Southampton to the south. The *QE II* cruise ship also docks at Southampton.

Trains connecting with ferries on the U.K. side of the Channel generally go to Liverpool Street Station, Victoria Station, or Waterloo International. Train passage to London is included in the ferry fee. The newly reopened (in 2007) King's Cross/St. Pancras Station is where the Eurostar Chunnel trains arrive from Paris and Brussels. On the Eurostar, you don't have to make any train-to-boat-to-train transfers along the way. (For more on the Eurostar, see Chapter 5.)

All London stations link to the Underground system. Just look for the Underground symbol (a circle with a line through it). The stations connect to the Underground as follows:

- ✔ **Liverpool Street** is on the Circle, East London, Metropolitan, and Central Lines.
- ✔ **Victoria** is on the District, Circle, and Victoria lines.
- ✔ **Waterloo** is linked to the Northern and Bakerloo lines.
- ✔ **King's Cross/St. Pancras** is on the Piccadilly and Northern lines.

Taxis wait outside all train stations. See the "Getting Around London" section, later in this chapter, for more information on the London Underground and taxis.

London's train stations are swarming with activity. You find bookstores, *bureaux de change,* restaurants, newsstands, hotel reservation agencies, and many of the services that airports traditionally offer.

Keep in mind that the United Kingdom, like the rest of Europe, uses the 24-hour clock for rail and other timetables, which means that 0530 is 5:30 a.m., 1200 is noon, and 1830 is 6:30 p.m. Just continue counting up from noon: 1300 = 1 p.m., 1400 = 2 p.m., 1500 = 3 p.m., and so on up to 2400 (midnight). In this book, I stick to the American a.m. and p.m. system. Like most of the rest of the world, London goes on daylight saving time from April through October.

Figuring Out the Neighborhoods

Londoners orient themselves by neighborhood (see the "London's Neighborhoods" map on p. 90). Sounds simple enough, but with London's confusing and sometimes oddly named streets and its seemingly endless plethora of neighborhoods, you may have a hard time telling where one neighborhood begins and another leaves off. For orientation purposes, I give you major streets as boundary markers. But be aware that the neighborhoods frequently bleed beyond these principal arteries.

To help you find your way around, I strongly suggest that you buy a copy of *London A–Z.* (Americans take note: ask for *London A–Zed,* because *z* is pronounced *zed* in the U.K.) You can pick up this indexed London street map at just about any bookstore or newsstand (you may want to get it while you're at the airport).

Although **Greater London** encompasses a whopping 1,610 sq. km (622 sq. miles), the main tourist portion covers only a fraction (65 sq. km/ 25 sq. miles, at the most) of that distance. Most sites within this 65km (25-mile) range are convenient to the Underground system (the Tube). You may have a short (ten-minute or less) walk from the Tube stop to your destination, but London is flat, and for walkers it's a dream.

London is divided into **postal districts.** All London street addresses include a designation such as SW1 or EC3. (In London, the postal districts are related to where they lie geographically from the original post office, which was at St. Martin-le-Grand in the City.) Addresses in the City of London, the easternmost portion of Central London, have designations such as EC2, EC3, or EC4. As you move west, the codes change accordingly to W, WC, SW, NW, and so on.

You don't need to bother yourself with postal districts except when you're mailing something to London or looking up streets in *London A–Z* (many streets in different parts of London have the same name). When you actually hit the streets, the postal district designations aren't as important as the nearest Tube stop.

London's Neighborhoods

London grew up along the north and south banks of the **Thames River,** which snakes through the city in a long, loose *S*-curve. This great tidal river played a fundamental role in London's growth, development, and prosperity. London's major tourist sights, hotels, and restaurants are on the river's north bank, and many of the city's famous performing arts venues are along the south bank.

Central London, on the north bank of the Thames, is considered the city center — the area covered by the Circle Line Underground route. Paddington Station anchors the northwestern corner, Earl's Court marks the southwestern corner, Tower Hill sits at the southeast corner, and Liverpool Street Station anchors the northeastern corner. Central London is divided into three areas: the **City,** the **West End,** and **West London.** In the descriptions that follow, I start at the City and move west from there.

The City of London: The heart of it all

A self-governing entity that extends south from Chiswell Street to the River Thames, the City of London is bounded on the west by Chancery Lane and to the east by the **Tower of London,** the City's most important historic monument.

Fleet Street, associated with printing and publishing since the 1500s but now a little forlorn since the departure of most of its newspaper offices, cuts through the center of the district to Ludgate Circus, where it becomes Ludgate. Follow that road and you get to **St. Paul's Cathedral,** its massive dome beautifully illuminated at night. St. Paul's is just one of the buildings built atop the ancient area known as the City.

Covering the original 2.6 sq. km (1 sq. mile) that the Romans called *Londinium,* the City encompasses the territory between Moorfields to the north and the Thames to the south and from Aldgate to the east and Temple Bar to the west. Today, this area is the Wall Street of England, home to the **Bank of England,** the **Royal Exchange,** and the **Stock Exchange,** as well as the new **Lloyds of London** building and the **NatWest Tower,** London's second tallest building. You also find the **Museum of London,** the remains of the **Roman Temple of Mithras,** the church of **St. Stephen Walbrook** (designed by Sir Christopher Wren), the Wren-designed **Monument** that commemorates the Great Fire of London in 1666, and the **Barbican Centre,** a mega-arts complex of theaters and concert halls.

Liverpool Street Station is the main rail terminus in this area. The major Tube stops are Bank, Barbican, Blackfriars, Liverpool Street Station, Moorgate, St. Paul's, and Tower Hill.

The West End: Downtown London

The West End (that is, west of the City) is "downtown" London. The West End is known for the theater, entertainment, and shopping areas around Piccadilly Circus and Leicester Square. But a host of neighborhoods make up the West End. I describe them briefly in the sections that follow.

Holborn

Abutting the City of London to the west is the old borough of Holborn, the legal heart of London and home to the **Inns of Court, Lincoln's Inn Fields, Old Bailey,** and **Royal Courts of Justice.**

This "in-between" district is bounded roughly by Theobald's Road to the north, Farringdon Road to the east, the Thames to the south, and Kingsway, Aldwych, and Lancaster Place to the west. The major Tube stops are Aldwych, Blackfriars, Holborn, and Temple.

The Strand and Covent Garden

The northern section of the Strand, the area west of Holborn, is Covent Garden, with Shaftesbury Avenue as its northern boundary. Covent Garden has many theaters, eateries, and shops and is home to the **Royal Opera House** and **Covent Garden Market,** one of the busiest shopping areas in London. Covent Garden is an area for strolling, shopping, and stopping for tea or a meal.

Formerly one of the premier streets in England, the Strand (the same name as the neighborhood) runs from Trafalgar Square to Fleet Street; the Strand is the principal thoroughfare along the southern edge, with Charing Cross Road to the west and Kingsway, Aldwych, and Lancaster Place to the east. **Cleopatra's Needle,** an Egyptian obelisk dating from about 1475 B.C. and moved to England in 1878, is located in the Victoria Embankment on the north side of the Hungerford Bridge. The major Tube stops are Charing Cross, Covent Garden, and Leicester Square.

Bloomsbury

Just north of Covent Garden, New Oxford Street and Bloomsbury Way mark the beginnings of the Bloomsbury district, home of the **British Museum** and several colleges and universities, as well as the only surviving London home of novelist Charles Dickens.

This intellectual pocket of Central London was home to the famed Bloomsbury Group, whose members included novelist Virginia Woolf and historian Lytton Strachey. Bloomsbury is bounded to the east by Woburn Place and Southampton Row, to the north by Euston Road, and to the west by Tottenham Court Road. The major Tube stops are Euston Square, Goodge Street, Russell Square, and Tottenham Court Road.

Soho

This lively area is full of restaurants, cafes, bars, pubs, and nightclubs and is popular with the gay community. London's **Gay Village** centers around Old Compton Street. Gerrard Street is one of the main streets of

Chinatown. Much of Soho used to be a down-to-earth Italian neighborhood, but the area later became known for its strip joints and porn palaces. You still see remnants of the sex 'n' sleaze era, but most of it is now gone, and things are going upscale.

The Soho neighborhood occupies the maze of densely packed streets north of Shaftesbury Avenue, west of Charing Cross Road, east of Regent Street, and south of Oxford Street. The major Tube stops are Covent Garden, Leicester Square, and Tottenham Court Road.

Piccadilly Circus, Leicester Square, and Charing Cross

This area, just west of the Strand, is "downtown" London or Theatreland. Piccadilly Circus, with its landmark statue of Eros, is the area's major traffic hub and best-known tourist destination, feeding into Regent Street and Piccadilly. The **Royal Academy of Arts** is just west of Piccadilly Circus. A few minutes' walk to the east puts you at Leicester Square and Shaftesbury Avenue, where you find most of the West End theaters. From Leicester Square, Charing Cross Road runs south to **Trafalgar Square,** with its delightful fountains and four immense bronze lions guarding its corners. Around the square, you see the **National Gallery** and the **National Portrait Gallery. Charing Cross Road** is well known for its bookshops. The Tube stops are Charing Cross, Leicester Square, and Piccadilly Circus.

Mayfair

Elegant and exclusive, Mayfair is luxury-hotel and luxury-shopping land. The area is nestled among Regent Street on the east, Oxford Street on the north, Piccadilly on the south, and Hyde Park on the west. The major Tube stops are Bond Street, Hyde Park Corner, Marble Arch, and Piccadilly Circus.

Marylebone

In a sense, Marylebone (pronounced *mar*-lee-bone) is "Medical London" because the area has several hospitals and the famous **Harley Street Clinic.** But perhaps the most famous street is Baker Street, home of the fictional Sherlock Holmes. **Madame Tussaud's** wax museum is on Marylebone Road.

Marylebone is the neighborhood north of Mayfair and Bloomsbury and is capped to the north by giant **Regent's Park** (Marylebone Road runs south of the park). Great Portland Street is the area's eastern boundary and Edgware Road the western. The major Tube stops are Baker Street, Marylebone, and Regent's Park.

St. James's

St. James's is "royal London," a posh green haven beginning at Piccadilly and moving southwest to include **Green Park** and **St. James's Park,** with **Buckingham Palace** between them and **St. James's Palace** across from St. James's Park.

Pall Mall (pronounced *pell mell*), lined with exclusive "gentlemen's clubs," runs roughly east–west into the area and meets the north–south St. James's Street. Regent Street is the eastern boundary. The Tube stops are Green Park and St. James's Park.

Westminster

East and south of St. James's, Westminster draws visitors to **Westminster Abbey** and the **Houses of Parliament,** the seat of British government.

Westminster extends from Northumberland Avenue just south of Charing Cross to Vauxhall Bridge Road, with the Thames to the east and **St. James's Park** to the west. Victoria Station, on the northwestern perimeter, is a kind of axis for Belgravia, Pimlico, and Westminster. The Tube stops are St. James's Park, Victoria, and Westminster.

Pimlico

The pie-shaped wedge extending west from Vauxhall Bridge Road to Buckingham Palace Road is Pimlico. Crowning the area to the north is Victoria Station. Near the Vauxhall Bridge is the **Tate Britain** gallery. The Tube stops are Pimlico and Victoria.

Belgravia

A posh quarter long favored by aristocrats, Belgravia is where many foreign embassies are located. Beginning west of Victoria Station and Green Park, Belgravia extends south to the river and west to Sloane Street; **Hyde Park** is its northern boundary. The Tube stops are Hyde Park, Sloane Square, and Victoria.

Central London: Parks, museums, and more

West of the West End, you find Central London's residential, cultural, and shopping attractions, including beautiful gardens and popular museums.

Knightsbridge

West of Belgravia is the fashionable residential and shopping district of Knightsbridge, bounded to the north by **Hyde Park** and to the west by Brompton Road. Here you find **Harrods,** the famed department store that has been a London shopping staple for a century and a half. Running through the neighborhood is pretty Beauchamp (pronounced *beech*-um) Place with its expensive boutiques. The Tube stops are Knightsbridge and Sloane Square.

Chelsea

South of Knightsbridge and west of Belgravia, artsy, trendy Chelsea begins at Sloane Square and runs south to Cheyne Walk and Chelsea Embankment along the Thames. The famous King's Road acts as its northern boundary and Chelsea Bridge Road its eastern border. To the west, the area extends as far as Earl's Court Road, Redcliffe Gardens, and Edith Grove. In Chelsea, you find **Carlyle's House** and the lovely and historic **Chelsea Physic Garden.** The annual Chelsea Flower Show is held on the grounds of Chelsea Royal Hospital. The Tube stop is Sloane Square.

South Kensington

Forming the green northern boundary of South Kensington are **Kensington Gardens** and **Hyde Park.** South Ken is London's museum capital, including the **Natural History Museum, Science Museum,** and **Victoria & Albert Museum,** and is packed with hotels and restaurants.

South Kensington is bounded to the south by Brompton Road, to the west by Gloucester (pronounced *gloss*-ter) Road, and to the east by Fulham Road. The Tube stops are Gloucester Road and South Kensington.

Kensington

The residential neighborhood of Kensington fills in the gap between **Kensington Gardens** and **Holland Park,** with Notting Hill Gate and Bayswater Road marking the northern boundary. Kensington Church Street runs north–south between Notting Hill Gate and Kensington High Street. The Tube stop is High Street Kensington.

Earl's Court

This down-to-earth neighborhood has long been a haven for budget travelers (particularly Australians — hence its nickname, Kangaroo Court) and for gays and lesbians. Earl's Court is gradually being renovated, but some streets still look a bit down at the heels. This area offers no major tourist attractions, but it does have some good hotels and B&Bs.

The area begins south of West Cromwell Road and extends south to Lillie Road and Brompton Road. Its western boundary is North End Road, and its eastern boundary is Earl's Court Road. The Tube stop is Earl's Court.

Notting Hill

Beginning north of Holland Park, Kensington Gardens, and Hyde Park (Holland Park Avenue and Bayswater Road run along the northern perimeter of the parks), you find the antiques shops of Notting Hill and the rising sub-neighborhood of Notting Hill Gate.

The area is bounded by Clarendon Road to the west, Queensway to the east, and Wesbourne Grove to the north. The most famous street, Portobello Road, runs north–south through the center. The neighborhood served as a backdrop for the 1999 movie *Notting Hill,* starring Julia Roberts and Hugh Grant. The Tube stops are Bayswater, Notting Hill Gate, and Queensway.

Bayswater and Paddington

Picking up where Notting Hill ends, Bayswater runs east to meet
Marylebone at Edgware Road. The roaring A40 (Westway) highway acts
as its northern boundary. Paddington Station is in the northwestern
corner of Bayswater.

This commercial area isn't much to look at. The neighborhood offers no
major tourist attractions, but it does have many budget B&Bs. The Tube
stops are Edgware Road, Lancaster Gate, Marble Arch, and Paddington.

Shoreditch

London's East End has no exact boundaries but basically extends east of
the City to Canary Wharf. Historically, this part of London has always
been home to working-class and immigrant communities. Today, the
area known as Shoreditch is one of London's hot new trend zones, especially the area around Hoxton Square. The primary tourist attraction in
Shoreditch is the **Geffrye Museum.**

The South Bank

You most likely won't be staying on the South Bank, but you may go
there for a play, an exhibition, or a concert at one of its internationally
known arts and performance venues or museums. The Tube stops are
London Bridge, Southwark, and Waterloo.

The **Hayward Gallery,** the **National Film Theatre,** the **Royal National
Theatre,** and the **South Bank Centre** (which contains **Royal Festival
Hall** and two smaller concert halls) are all clustered beside the river
within easy walking distance of Waterloo Station. Closer to Westminster
Bridge is the city's newest high-rise attraction: the **British Airways
London Eye** observation wheel.

For a scenic route to the South Bank, take the Tube to Embankment, on
the north bank, and walk across the Thames on the new Hungerford
pedestrian bridge. The **Jubilee Walkway,** a breezy riverside path,
extends south from the arts complexes to the **London Aquarium** and
north to the new **Tate Modern,** the **Globe Theatre** (a re-creation of the
Elizabethan outdoor theater used by William Shakespeare), **Southwark
Cathedral,** and **Tower Bridge.** The new pedestrian-only **Millennium
Bridge** spans the Thames from the **Tate Modern** to **St. Paul's.**

Finding Information after You Arrive

You can find hotel and theater booking agencies, a currency exchange,
and numerous free brochures on river trips, walking tours, and day trips
from London at the **Britain & London Visitor Centre,** 1 Lower Regent
St., Piccadilly Circus, SW1 (☎ **08701/566-366;** Tube: Piccadilly Circus),
which provides tourist information to walk-in visitors Monday 9:30 a.m.

to 6:30 p.m., Tuesday through Friday 9 a.m. to 6:30 p.m., and Saturday and Sunday 10 a.m. to 4 p.m. (9 a.m.–5 p.m. June–Sept).

Tourist Information Centres are found in the following locations:

- ✔ **City of London,** St. Paul's Churchyard (☎ **020/7332-1456;** Tube: St. Paul's Cathedral): Open Monday through Saturday 9 a.m. to 5 p.m., Sunday 10 a.m. to 4:30 p.m.

- ✔ **Waterloo International Terminal Arrivals Hall** (☎ **020/7620-1550;** Tube: Waterloo): Open daily 8:30 a.m. to 10:30 p.m.

- ✔ **Leicester Square** (no phone; Tube: Leicester Square): Located at the half-price ticket kiosk, the **London Information Centre** (run by LondonTown.com, an online marketing group) distributes free bus and Underground maps and can help with basic directions or questions; it's open Monday through Friday 8 a.m. to 11 p.m., Saturday and Sunday 8 a.m. to 6 p.m.

Getting Around London

You can choose many ways to get around London. If you travel for any distance, the fastest mode of transportation in this enormous city is the Tube (the subway system). Many of the slower but more scenic buses are double-deckers but you'll also see new, energy-efficient buses. Most convenient (unless you're stuck in a traffic jam) is to go by taxi. But walking is the most fun of all. When you're on foot, you see more and can explore some of the leafy squares and cobbled lanes that contribute to London's enduring charm.

For general London travel information, call **Transport for London** at ☎ **020/7222-1234** or visit its Web site (www.tfl.gov.uk). You can get free bus and Underground maps and buy Travelcards and bus passes at any major Underground station (at the windows or from the machines) or at the London Travel Information Centres in the stations at King's Cross; Liverpool Street; Oxford Circus; Piccadilly Circus; St. James's Park; Victoria; and Heathrow Terminals 1, 2, and 3.

Taking the Underground (subway)

London has the oldest and most comprehensive subway system in the world. The Tube is fast and convenient, and just about everyone but the royals uses it. Everywhere you'll want to go is near a Tube stop, each of which is clearly marked by a red circle with a horizontal line through it. For an Underground map, see the inside back cover of this book.

Using the Underground

Thirteen Underground lines crisscross the city and intersect at various stations where you can change from one train to another. On Underground maps, every line is color-coded (Bakerloo is brown, Piccadilly is dark blue, and so on), which makes planning your route easy. All you need to know is the name of your stop and the direction you're heading. After you figure out which line you need to take, look on the map for the name of the last stop in the direction you need to go. The name of the last stop on the line appears on the front of the train and also on electronic signboards that display the name of the arriving train. (The one exception to this rule is the Circle Line, which runs in a loop around Central London.) Inside the trains, electronic signs, recorded voices, or both, announce the name of each approaching stop.

Traveling to your destination by Underground may require transferring from one Underground line to another. All Underground maps clearly show where various lines converge. Signs in the stations direct you from one line to another. To get from one line to another, you go through tunnels (which the Brits call *subways*), and you may have to go up or down a level or two.

Most of the Underground system operates with automated entry and exit gates. If you have a regular paper ticket or Travelcard, you feed it into the slot; the ticket disappears and pops up again, the gate bangs open; you remove your ticket and pass through. Be sure to keep your ticket during your ride because you'll need it to get out. At the other end, you put your ticket through as you did upon entry, but this time the machine keeps the ticket (unless you have a multiuse Travelcard ticket, which the machine returns to you). A new kind of electronic Tube ticket called the **Oyster** recently went into effect. The Oyster is like a debit card, and a breeze to use: You simply touch the card to the electronic keypad on the turnstile and the gate opens. You won't need an Oyster card unless you're planning to be in London for several days. For stays of one to three days, you'll save considerably by purchasing a Travelcard (see the following section).

 Underground service stops around midnight (a little earlier on less-used lines). Keep this in mind when you're out painting the town red. If you miss the last train, you must take a taxi or one of the night buses.

Buying tickets

You can purchase Underground tickets at the ticket window or from one of the automated machines that you can find in most stations. Machines can change £5, £10, and £20 notes. Tickets are valid for use on the day of issue only.

For fare purposes, the city is divided into zones. **Zone 1** covers all Central London. **Zone 6** extends as far as Heathrow to the west and Upminster to the east. Make sure that your ticket covers all the zones that you're traveling through (no problem if you're staying in Central London), or you may have to pay a £10 ($20) penalty fare.

New pricing guidelines have raised the price of a **one-way single cash fare** within Zone 1 to a whopping £4 ($8) for adults and £2 ($4) for children 5 to 15. If you're making more than one trip by Underground, you can save lots of money by purchasing a **Travelcard** or an **Oyster** card.

Saving with Travelcards

To make the most of London's public transportation system, consider buying a **Travelcard,** which allows unlimited travel by Underground *and* bus. You can purchase these cards at any Tube station window or machine in the following increments:

✔ A **Day Travelcard,** good for one day in zones 1 and 2 (everything in Central London), costs £6.60 ($13) for an adult and £3.30 ($6.60) for children 5 to 15. If you travel off-peak (after 9:30 a.m.), the price of an adult Day Travelcard drops to £5.10 ($10).

✔ The **3-Day Travelcard** for zones 1 and 2 and valid at peak travel times (before 9:30 a.m.) costs £16 ($32) for an adult and £8.20 ($16) for a child.

✔ A **7-Day Travelcard,** valid at peak travel times (before 9:30 a.m.) for zones 1 and 2 (all of Central London) costs £23 ($46) for an adult and £12 ($24) for a child.

Another great way to save money on London transportation is the **London Travelcard,** which you can buy in the United States and Canada before leaving home. Keep in mind, though, that it's actually a bit cheaper to buy Travelcards (including the London Travelcard) when you're in London. (For details, see Chapter 4.)

Riding a bus

Distinctive red double-decker buses are very much a part of London's snarled traffic scene, but not all London buses are double-deckers, and some aren't red. The one drawback to bus travel, especially for first-timers, is that you need to know the streets of London so you can get off at the correct stop. Get a free bus map at one of the Travel Information Centres (see "Finding Information after You Arrive," earlier in this chapter), or you may overshoot your destination. On the plus side, riding the bus is cheaper than taking the Tube; you don't have to contend with escalators, elevators, or tunnels; and you get to see the sights as you travel.

A concrete post with a red or white sign on top reading LONDON TRANSPORT BUS SERVICE clearly marks each bus stop. Another sign shows the routes of the buses that stop there. If the sign on top is red, the stop is a request stop, meaning you must hail the approaching bus as you would a taxi (don't whistle — just put up your hand). If the sign is white, the bus stops automatically. Be sure to check the destination sign on the front of the bus to make certain that the bus travels the entire route. Have some coins with you, because the driver won't change banknotes.

The bus network is divided into two fare zones to simplify cash transactions. **Zone 1** covers all Central London, including all the main tourist sites. The bus fare for adults is £2 ($4). Children 16 and under ride free if traveling with an adult with a valid ticket.

Bus passes, available at most Underground stations, selected news agents, and the Travel Information Centres, can be used all day but aren't valid on *N*-prefixed night buses (see the next paragraph). For adults, a **1-day bus pass** for all Central London costs £3.50 ($7); a **7-day bus pass** for Central London costs £14 ($28). *Note:* Children under 16 travel free with an adult after 9:30 a.m.

At the witching hour of midnight, buses become **night buses** (N), and their routes change. Nearly all night buses pass through Trafalgar Square, Central London's late-night magnet for insomniacs.

Hailing a taxi

Taking a taxi is a safe and comfortable way to get around the city. Riding in the old-fashioned, roomy black taxis is a pleasure. Today, many smaller and newer-model taxis also run. London cabs of any size or color aren't cheap, however. Fares change depending on the time of day, speed, and distance traveled. Fares and any extra charges are also displayed on the meter next to the driver. The basic fare begins at £2.20 ($4.40) and rises in increments of 20p (40¢) every 160 meters or 34.5 seconds. Tip your cabbie 10 percent to 15 percent of the total fare.

You can hail a cab on the street. If a cab is available, the yellow or white FOR HIRE sign on the roof is lit. You can order a **radio cab** by calling ☎ **020/7272-0272** or 020/7253-5000. Be aware that if you call for a cab, you have to pay an additional £2 ($4) service charge.

London is one city where you don't have to worry about whether the cab driver knows where he's going. When it comes to finding a street address, London cabbies are among the most knowledgeable in the world. Their rigorous training, which includes an exhaustive street test called "The Knowledge," gives them an encyclopedic grasp of the terrain.

Walking on your own two feet

If you really want to get acquainted with the charming hodgepodge and monumental grandeur of London, bring along a good pair of walking shoes and explore on foot. Everywhere you turn, you see enticing side streets, countrylike lanes, little *mews houses* (former stables converted into homes), and picturesque garden squares. London's great parks are as safe to walk in as its streets. (In fact, crime is less prevalent in London than in many other major cities, and all the neighborhoods included in this book are safe.)

If you want to follow a detailed stroll or two around the city, perhaps of Dickens's London or of Westminster and Whitehall, check out the 11 tours in *Frommer's Memorable Walks in London* (Wiley Publishing, Inc.).

A 11.25km (7-mile) walk commemorating the life of Princess Diana passes through four of London's royal parks — St. James's Park, Green Park, Hyde Park, and Kensington Gardens. Along the way are 90 plaques that point out sites associated with Diana, including Kensington Palace (her home for 15 years), Buckingham Palace, St. James's Palace (where she shared an office with Prince Charles), and Spencer House (her family's mansion, now a museum). A good place to start is at Kensington Palace, Hyde Park Gate, or Horse Guards Parade (for the Green Park/St. James's section).

When you walk in London (or anywhere in England), remember:

✔ **For North Americans, traffic moves on the opposite side of the street from what you're accustomed to.** This sounds simple enough on paper, but in practice, you need to keep reminding yourself to look in the "wrong" direction when crossing a street. Throughout London, you see Look Right or Look Left painted on street crossings.

✔ **Pedestrian crossings are marked by striped lines (called *zebra crossings*) on the road.** Flashing lights near the curb indicate that drivers must stop and yield the right of way when a pedestrian steps out into the zebra to cross the street.

Chapter 9

Checking In at London's Best Hotels and B&Bs

In This Chapter

▶ Getting the lowdown on London's accommodations types

▶ Knowing what to expect from a hotel in your price range

▶ Finding the best room for the best rate

▶ Reviewing a list of London favorites

*L*ondon hotel rooms run the gamut from a basic tiny bedroom with a shared bathroom down the hall to elegant, sumptuous suites. Many travelers don't care where they stay, as long as they can stay there cheaply. The reasoning is, "I'm only going to be in a hotel room to sleep." That assumption may be true, but I also know that a cheap-at-all-costs hotel room can color your mood and potentially turn a memorable vacation into something unnecessarily dreary.

This chapter is devoted to London hotels and B&Bs. You can find details about what to expect for your money, get the lowdown on how to get the best rooms at the best rates, and check out a list of specific hotels and B&Bs that I heartily recommend.

Getting to Know Your Options

Accommodations in London are available in varying price ranges and degrees of luxury. Places to stay generally fit into one of two categories: hotels and bed-and-breakfast inns (B&Bs). The following sections provide a rundown on the quirks and perks of each.

Understanding the pros and cons of B&Bs

B&Bs are small, family-run hotels with differing degrees of comfort and service. Because B&Bs are often private homes (or what were once private homes), amenities vary widely, especially in the bathroom facilities. Nearly all B&B rooms contain wash basins, but you may have to share a bathroom down the hall. The facilities are usually kept scrupulously clean. Keep in mind that *en-suite* (in the room) baths are generally so small that you feel as if you haven't left the airplane, and the super-small showers can be a trial. In terms of décor, B&Bs tend to be fairly basic — everything you need but without a lot of fuss or froufrou.

Licensed B&Bs, like hotels, are inspected regularly, and the quality of London B&Bs has improved tremendously over the years. I recommend them for people who don't require many extras, although the most successful B&Bs continually upgrade their services or offer some enticing amenities. For example, many B&Bs now provide cable TVs and direct-dial phones in the rooms. Many travelers prefer B&Bs over large hotels because they want friendly service and a personal touch. It's easier to meet people in a small B&B than in a large hotel.

What about the breakfast part of the B&B? Well, gone are the days when the staff of every B&B cooked you up a *full English breakfast* of eggs, sausages, bacon, fried tomatoes, and beans. Some B&Bs still do serve an English breakfast, but others put out a *continental buffet,* which is a breakfast of cereals, fruits, and breads. The B&B descriptions in this book say either "English breakfast included" or "continental breakfast included," so you know what to expect.

If you want to do some additional B&B research, the following three agencies have useful Web sites:

- ✔ **London Bed and Breakfast:** www.londonbandb.com (☎ **800/872-2632** in the U.S. or 020/7351-3445 in London)

- ✔ **London Bed and Breakfast Agency Ltd.:** www.londonbb.com (☎ **020/7586-2768** in London)

- ✔ **Uptown Reservations:** www.uptownres.co.uk (☎ **020/7937-2001** in London)

If you're physically disabled in any way, B&Bs may not be the choice for you. B&Bs usually don't have elevators, so you may have to carry your luggage up steep, narrow stairs. Be sure to check how accessible the B&B is before you make your reservations.

Exploring hotel choices

You find a wide choice of hotels in London. Most of the moderately priced hotels provide breakfast with a room rental. At a 4- or 5-star hotel, you pay a hefty price to eat breakfast on the premises. The rooms in a self-catering hotel are equipped with small kitchens, so you can make your own meals in your room, if you prefer.

Boutique and deluxe hotels

London offers a few *boutique hotels.* These hotels are midrange in size but not price; sumptuously furnished, they offer state-of-the-art amenities and full service. I've included a few in my reviews later in this chapter. The **Montague** in Bloomsbury and **41** in Victoria/Westminster are two of the best.

A more traditional choice is one of London's older deluxe hotels. The **Cadogan Hotel** in Chelsea, **The Gore** in South Kensington, and **Hazlitt's** in Soho have all been around for a century or more. These hotels offer a distinctly English kind of style, full of charm and character.

The older deluxe hotels are offset by the hippest-of-the-hip: the **St. Martin's Lane,** an Ian Schrager concoction in a converted office block.

Chain properties

But maybe you *always* stay at one of the chain hotels — a **Crowne Plaza,** a **Hyatt,** a **Radisson,** or a **Marriott** — places that are basically the same no matter where they are. Chains rely on their brand name and a no-surprise approach to win customers. London is chock-full of chain hotels, if that's what you fancy. Most of them cater to large groups, and you may feel rather anonymous in them. On the other hand, these hotels are usually well equipped for people with disabilities and families with children.

Landmark hotels

At the top of the hotel spectrum, in both price and prestige, are the landmark hotels: **Claridge's,** the **Dorchester,** the **Park Lane Sheraton,** and **The Savoy** (although The Savoy is currently closed for remodeling, so it's not included in this edition). The **Langham Hotel** on Regent Street is London's newest landmark hotel. These famous hotels are among the best in the world. In each of them, you can expect glamorous public salons, a generously proportioned and well-decorated room with a large private bath, an on-site health club or access to one nearby, and top-of-the-line service. I've reviewed all the preceding hotels later in this chapter.

Self-catering options

You can also consider staying at a *self-catering hotel,* where *you* do the cooking in the kitchen in your own hotel room. For short stays and for one or two people, self-catering hotels don't always beat the competition's price. But for families and travelers who can't afford or don't want to eat every meal out, self-catering hotels can be a budget-saver. For comfort and convenience, **Astons Apartments** in South Kensington is among the best, and it's the only self-catering hotel I include. If you're interested in finding other self-catering options in London, visit the Web site www.refresh accommodation.com.

One of the most economical ways to stay in London is to rent a self-catering flat. The owners register their flats with rental agencies; minimum rental time is usually one week. You can find a small studio flat in Central London that sleeps two and is fully equipped for under £500 ($1,000) per week. One of the best agencies to help you find a flat is the **Independent Traveller** (☎ **01392/860-807;** www.gowithit.co.uk).

Finding the Best Room at the Best Rate

The maximum rate that a hotel charges for a type of room is the *rack rate*. If you walk in off the street and ask for a room for the night, the hotel may charge you this top rate. Hotel rates, like airline fares, change all the time, and it's impossible to list the most current "specials" a hotel is offering on its Web site. So the rack rate is what I use as a hotel price guide in this book.

Be aware that you don't have to pay the rack rate — hardly anybody does.Just ask for a cheaper or discounted rate. The result is often favorable when savvy travelers make this request. Hotels in London are eager to fill their beds, and most of them are willing to negotiate a room rate. Read on for more strategies on getting a good rate.

Finding the best rate

The rate you pay for a room depends on many factors, and the way you make your reservation is the most important. The following strategies can help you get the best rate available:

- ✔ **Call around.** If the hotel you're interested in has a toll-free number, call that, but also call the hotel's local London number. The quoted rates can vary so widely that you may save a bundle.

- ✔ **Ask about discounts.** If you make your reservation with a large chain hotel, be sure to mention membership in AARP, frequent-flier programs, and any other corporate rewards program. Budget hotels and small B&Bs rarely offer these organization discounts, but with larger hotels, you never know when the mention may be worth a few pounds off your room rate.

- ✔ **Travel off-season and on weekends.** Room rates change with the season and as occupancy rates rise and fall. You're less likely to receive discount rates if a hotel is close to full, but if it's nearly empty, you may be able to negotiate a significant discount. Expensive hotels catering to business travelers are most crowded on weekdays and usually offer big discounts for weekend stays.

  You may be able to save 20 percent or more by traveling off-season, which is mid-October to mid-December and January to March.

- ✔ **Choose a package tour.** The best rates of all will probably be with an air/hotel package (see Chapter 5). With these packages, which are sometimes astonishingly cheap, you have to choose a hotel that's part of the package. Airline package hotels tend to be larger chains. So what? The money you save may amount to hundreds of dollars over what you'd pay by booking the hotel and flight separately.

- ✔ **Use a travel agent.** A travel agent may be able to negotiate a better room rate than you could get by yourself. The hotel gives the agent a discount in exchange for steering his business toward that hotel.

Surfing the Web for hotel deals

Another great source for finding hotel deals is the Internet. Nowadays, almost all hotels, even those in the budget range, have Web sites. (I list each hotel's Web site with the other hotel information.) Special promotional offers are often available only on the hotel's Web site, so it pays to do some checking.

You can also use search engines to help you locate a London hotel. Although the major travel-booking Web sites (Travelocity, Expedia, Yahoo!, and Smarter Living) offer hotel booking, you may be better off using a Web site devoted to lodging because more-general sites don't list all types of properties. Some lodging sites specialize in a particular type of accommodations, such as bed-and-breakfast inns, which aren't on the more mainstream booking services. Other services, such as TravelWeb (see the following list), offer weekend deals on major chain properties that cater to business travelers and have more empty rooms on the weekends.

Some good all-purpose Web sites that you can use to track down and make online reservations at hotels in London include the following:

✔ **All Hotels on the Web** (www.all-hotels.com) doesn't actually include *all* the hotels on the Web, but it does have tens of thousands of listings throughout the world, including London. Bear in mind that each hotel in the list has paid a fee ($25 and up) for placement, so the list is not objective, but more like online brochures.

✔ **British Hotel Reservation Centre** (www.bhrc.co.uk) lists current and seasonal specials at selected London hotels.

✔ **HotelDiscount.com** (www.hoteldiscount.com) lists bargain rates at hotels in U.S. and international cities, including London. If you click "London" and input your travel dates, the site provides a list of the best prices for a selection of hotels in various neighborhoods.

✔ **Independent Traveller** (www.gowithit.co.uk) lists hundreds of self-catering accommodations in London. These are private flats, not hotels, and are available for a one-week minimum period; they can be a fantastic bargain.

✔ **London Bed & Breakfast** (www.londonbandb.com) can provide inexpensive accommodations in select private homes.

✔ **London Bed and Breakfast Agency Ltd.** (www.londonbb.com) is another reliable B&B-finder in London.

✔ **Londontown** (www.londontown.com) has a long list of hotels to choose from, including some with special offers.

✔ **Refresh Accommodation** (www.refreshaccommodation.com) acts as the booking agent for self-catering flats and hotel rooms throughout London and offers all-inclusive (tax included) prices.

✔ **Seniors Travel Guide** (http://seniorstravelguide.com) is a site for seniors looking for special hotels and other forms of accommodations, including home and apartment exchanges.

✔ **TravelWeb** (www.travelweb.com) lists more than 16,000 hotels worldwide, focusing on chains, such as Hyatt and Hilton. You can book almost 90 percent of the properties online. Its Click-It Weekends, updated each Monday, offers weekend deals at many leading chains.

✔ **Uptown Reservations** (www.uptownres.co.uk) provides listings for dozens of B&Bs in private homes in London.

Reserving the best room

After you know where you're staying, asking a few more questions can help you land the best possible room. For example:

✔ **Ask about staying in a corner room.** They're usually larger, quieter, and brighter, but they may cost a bit more.

✔ **Ask about staying in a room in the back of the building.** In London, traffic noise can be loud and annoying. In the back, you may get a room that overlooks a quiet garden.

✔ **If your London hotel is a high-rise, request a room on a high floor.** Being farther away from the street means your room may be quieter. Plus, a higher room may give you the added bonus of a better view.

✔ **Ask whether the hotel is renovating.** If the answer is yes, request a room away from the renovation work, and make sure you ask again when you check in.

✔ **If you have any physical impairments, be sure to ask whether the hotel has a *lift* (elevator).** Many small and older hotels in London do not have elevators. If the hotel lacks a lift, ask whether a ground-floor (first floor) room is available.

✔ **Inquire about the location of restaurants, bars, and meeting facilities, which can be noisy.**

✔ **If you aren't happy with your room when you arrive, return to the front desk right away.** If another room is available, the staff should be able to accommodate you, within reason.

Arriving without a Reservation

Whatever your hotel choice in London, I want to remind you again: *Booking ahead is a good idea.* Why waste precious vacation time searching for a hotel? If you do arrive without a reservation, your first option is to start calling the hotels directly. Keep in mind that smaller B&Bs may not accept reservations late in the evening. You can also book rooms through the trustworthy agencies in the following list, but the first one doesn't have phone service so you must show up in person.

- ✔ **The Britain & London Visitor Centre** (1 Lower Regent St.; Tube: Piccadilly Circus) is open weekdays 9 a.m. to 6:30 p.m. (from 9:30 a.m. on Mon) and on Saturday and Sunday 10 a.m. to 4 p.m. (Sat June–Sept 9 a.m.–5 p.m.). You have to show up in person to get help reserving a room.

- ✔ **British Hotel Reservation Centre** (☎ 020/7340-1616; www.bhrc. co.uk) offers a 24-hour phone line. The center provides free reservations and discounted rates at all the leading hotel groups and the major independents. This agency operates a reservations desk (open daily 6 a.m. to midnight) at the Underground station of Heathrow Airport.

- ✔ **First Option Hotel Reservations** (☎ 020/7808-3861) is another hotel booking service. This hotel booking agency operates kiosks at the following Central London rail stations: Charing Cross (☎ 020/7976-1171); Euston (☎ 020/7388-7435); Kings Cross, by Platform 8 (☎ 020/7837-5681); Paddington (☎ 020/7723-0184); and Victoria, by Platform 9 (☎ 020/7828-4646).

London's Top Hotels

Every recommended hotel in this chapter has a $ symbol to help you home in on your price limit. These symbols reflect a hotel's high- and low-end rack rates for a double room. Table 9-1 shows what you can expect in terms of accommodations type, room size, and standard amenities in the five price categories.

Table 9-1	**Key to Hotel Dollar Signs**	
Dollar Sign(s)	*Price Range*	*What to Expect*
$	Less than £100/$200	These accommodations are relatively simple and more likely to be found in B&Bs than hotels. Rooms will likely be small, and in-room amenities such as a telephone and televisions are not necessarily provided. You may have to share a bathroom. In a B&B, you will get breakfast.
$$	£101–£150/$202–$300	A bit classier, these midrange accommodations offer more room, more extras (such as irons, hair dryers, or a microwave), and a more convenient location than the preceding category. You probably get breakfast.

(continued)

Table 9-1 *(continued)*

Dollar Sign(s)	Price Range	What to Expect
$$$	£151–£200/$302–$400	Higher-class still, these accommodations begin to look more upscale and service begins to factor in. Many chain hotels are in this category. You'll have a roomier private bathroom, cable TV, and other in-room amenities, and there will probably be a cafe or restaurant on the premises. You may or may not get breakfast.
$$$$	£201–£250/$402–$500	Hotels in this category will generally meet high international standards and be found in upscale neighborhoods. Porter and room service will be available. Think fine furnishings, larger bathrooms with designer toiletries, high-quality bedding, chocolates on your pillow, a classy restaurant, and a knowledgeable concierge. There will be a fine breakfast available, but you'll probably have to pay for it.
$$$$$	£251/$502 and up	These top-rated accommodations generally come with luxury amenities, such as valet parking, 24-hour room service, a gourmet restaurant, on-site spa and health club, large bathrooms, high-end furnishings and high-quality sheets, DVD/CD players, turn-down service — it's all great, and you pay through the nose for it. Breakfast will be available but not included in the price. The great London "name" hotels fall into this category.

Sorry, you can't escape that annoying **17.5 percent value-added tax (VAT).** In general, the quoted room rate includes the VAT (except for rooms at the upper end of the price scale). Be sure to ask, though, so you won't get an unpleasant surprise when you're checking out. Unless I note otherwise, the VAT is included in the rates for my recommended hotels.

The Abbey Court
$$–$$$$ Notting Hill

This small, graceful hotel, with a flower-filled front patio and a rear conservatory where breakfast is served, is located in a renovated mid-Victorian townhouse near Kensington Gardens. The 22 charming guest rooms feature 18th- and 19th-century country antiques and marble bathrooms equipped with Jacuzzi tubs, showers, and heated towel racks. You can enjoy 24-hour room service and take advantage of the services of the concierge, who can help arrange for babysitting.

See map p. 120. 20 Pembridge Gardens, W2 4DU. ☎ *020/7221-7518. Fax: 020/7792-0858.* www.abbeycourthotel.co.uk. *Tube: Notting Hill Gate (then a 5-minute walk north on Pembridge Gardens Road). Rack rates: £110–£170 ($220–$340) double. AE, MC, V.*

Aster House
$$$–$$$$ South Kensington

Found at the end of an early Victorian terrace, this beautifully renovated charmer is a former two-time winner of the London Tourism Bed and Breakfast of the Year Award. Each of the 12 guest rooms is individually decorated in English country-house style, some with four-poster, half-canopied beds and silk wallpaper. The new bathrooms come with power showers. The breakfasts, served in the glassed-in garden conservatory, are more health-conscious than those served in most English B&Bs.

See map p. 118. 3 Sumner Place (near Onslow Square), SW7 3EE. ☎ *020/7581-5888. Fax: 020/7584-4925.* www.asterhouse.com. *Tube: South Kensington (then a 5-minute walk west on Old Brompton Road and south on Sumner Place). Rack rates: £165–£220 ($330–$440) double. Continental breakfast included. MC, V.*

Astons Apartments
$–$$ South Kensington

In three carefully restored Victorian redbrick town houses, Astons offers value-packed self-catering accommodations, some ideal for families. Each studio has a compact kitchenette; a small bathroom; and bright, functional furnishings. The more expensive executive studios feature larger bathrooms, more living space, and extra pizzazz in the décor. If you like the idea of having your own cozy London apartment (with daily maid service), you can't do better. Cots and cribs are available for kids.

See map p. 118. 31 Rosary Gardens (off Hereford Square), SW7 4NQ. ☎ *800/525-2810 in the U.S. or 020/7590-6000. Fax: 020/7590-6060.* www.astons-apartments.com. *Tube: Gloucester Road (then a 5-minute walk south on Gloucester Road and west on Hereford Square; Rosary Gardens is 1 block farther west). Rack rates: £99–£130 ($198–$260) double. Rates don't include 17.5 percent VAT. AE, MC, V.*

London Accommodations Overview

0   1 Mi

0   1 Km

✝ Church

ⓘ Information

⊖ Tube stop

Note: not all Tube stations are featured on this map

ISLINGTON

SHOREDITCH

King's Cross Station

KING'S CROSS ST. PANCRAS

Pentonville Rd.

York Way

Caledonian Rd.

King's Cross Rd.

Gray's Inn Rd.

Euston Rd.

Judd St.

City Rd.

Shepherdess Walk

Goswell Rd.

Lever St.

OLD ST.

Old St.

Gt. Eastern St.

East Rd.

Bethnal Green

Commercial St.

Brick Ln.

See "Hotels in the West End" Map

FINSBURY

ST. PANCRAS

Coram's Fields

Farringdon Rd.

CLERKENWELL

Clerkenwell Rd.

Bath St.

Bunhill Row

Woburn Pl.

Bernard St.

Russell Sq.

Guilford St.

Montague Pl.

Southampton

Theobalds Rd.

RUSSELL SQUARE

Catthorpe St.

Rosebery Ave.

FARRINGDON

Beech St.

Aldersgate St.

CHANCERY LANE

Hatton Gdn.

BARBICAN

The Barbican Centre

Moorgate

LIVERPOOL ST. STATION

Liverpool St. Station

THE EAST END

Mansell St.

Leman St.

Dock St.

British Museum

Bloomsbury

High Holborn

Kingsway

Holborn

HOLBORN

Holborn

Fetter Ln.

Farringdon St.

Via

ST. PAUL'S

MOORGATE

London Wall

ⓘ

Bishopsgate

Houndsditch

ALDGATE

HOLBORN

COVENT GARDEN

Law Courts

St. Paul's ✝ Cathedral

Bank of England

Cheapside

Cornhill

Stock Exchange

Leadenhall St.

Gracechurch St.

TOWER HILL

Leicester Square

ⓘ

COVENT GARDEN

Aldwych

Strand

TEMPLE

BLACKFRIARS STATION

THE CITY

Cannon St.

MONUMENT

Byward St.

Tower Hill East

THE STRAND

National Gallery

Charing Cross Station

LEICESTER SQUARE

Victoria Embankment

Upper Thames St.

CANNON ST. STATION

Lower Thames St.

ⓘ

Tower of London

WAPPING

Trafalgar Square

EMBANKMENT

Hungerford Bridge

Blackfriars Bridge

River Thames

Waterloo Bridge

Millennium Bridge

Globe Theatre ■

Southwark Bridge

London Bridge

LONDON BRIDGE

London Bridge Station

Tower Bridge

London City Hall

DOCKLANDS

Whitehall

Stamford St.

■ Tate Modern

BANKSIDE

Southwark St.

Tooley St.

Bermondsey St.

10 Downing Street

WESTMINSTER

ⓘ

SOUTH BANK

Union St.

SOUTHWARK

THE BOROUGH

St. Thomas St.

Jamaica Rd.

Druid St.

County Hall

WATERLOO STATION

The Cut

BOROUGH

Borough High St.

Long Ln.

Abbey St.

Houses of ✝ Parliament

Westminster Bridge

LAMBETH NORTH

Westminster Bridge Rd.

Borough Rd.

Southwark Bridge Rd.

Kennington Causeway

Harper Rd.

Great Dover St.

Grange Rd.

Westminster Abbey

York Rd.

Waterloo Rd.

Lambeth Bridge

Lambeth Palace Rd.

Blackfriars Rd.

London Rd.

St. George's Rd.

NEWINGTON

New Kent Rd.

Tower Bridge Rd.

WEST-MINSTER

Lambeth Rd.

Kennington Rd.

ELEPHANT & CASTLE (BAKERLOO)

ELEPHANT & CASTLE

Millbank

Tate Britain

Albert Embankment

WALWORTH

Walworth Rd.

Kennington Park Rd.

SCOTLAND

0   100 mi

0   100 km

North Sea

Vauxhall Bridge

VAUXHALL

Harleyford Rd.

KENNINGTON

Kennington Ln.

KENNINGTON

Albany Rd.

Irish Sea

ENGLAND

WALES   London

VAUXHALL

OVAL

English Channel

Avonmore Hotel
$ Kensington

This small hotel is in a quiet neighborhood easily accessible to West End theaters and shops. You'd be hard-pressed to find more for your money: Each of the nine guest rooms offers a tasteful décor and an array of amenities not usually found in this price range. A few years ago, this establishment was voted London's best private hotel by the Automobile Association (AA), and the high standards that earned that honor are still maintained. An English breakfast is served in a cheerful breakfast room; a bar and limited room service are also available, and the hotel can arrange for babysitting.

See map p. 118. 66 Avonmore Rd. (northwest of Earl's Court), W14 8RS. ☎ *020/7603-4296. Fax: 020/7603-4035.* www.avonmorehotel.co.uk. *Tube: West Kensington (then a 5-minute walk north on North End Road and Mattheson Road to Avonmore Road). Rack rates: £60–£90 ($111–$167) double without bathroom, £80–£100 ($160–$200) double with bathroom. English breakfast included. AE, MC, V.*

B+B Belgravia
$$ Belgravia

Close to Victoria Station, this small, comfortable, contemporary B&B favors simple, modern design over the old-fashioned chintzes and furniture of so many London B&Bs. Rooms have a spare, cool look and come with a bath or shower. The lobby is a nice little gathering spot where you can relax and get fresh tea and coffee 24/7. Breakfast is either continental or English, cooked up right in front of your eyes in the open kitchen. Free Wi-Fi and Internet access are among the amenities.

See map p. 115. 64–66 Ebury St., SW1W 9QD. ☎ *020/7259-8570. Fax: 020/7259-8591.* www.bb-belgravia.com. *Tube: Victoria (then a 10-minute walk south on Buckingham Palace Road, west on Eccleston Street, and south on Ebury Street). Rack rates: £107–£117 ($214–$234). English breakfast included. MC, V.*

Bryanston Court Hotel
$$ Marylebone

Located in a neighborhood with many attractive squares, this 200-year-old hotel is one of Central London's finest in the moderate price range. The refurbished hotel has 54 small guest rooms (with equally small bathrooms) that are comfortably furnished and well maintained. You find a welcoming bar with a fireplace in the back of the lounge.

See map p. 120. 56–60 Great Cumberland Place (near Marble Arch), W1H 7FD. ☎ *020/7262-3141. Fax: 020/7262-7248.* www.bryanstonhotel.com. *Tube: Marble Arch (then a 5-minute walk north on Great Cumberland Place to Bryanston Place). Rack rates: £120 ($240) double. Continental breakfast included. AE, DC, MC, V.*

Hotels in Westminster and Victoria

⊖ Tube Stop

Thames

Lambeth Bridge

River

WESTMINSTER ⊖

Millbank

Millbank

Horse Guards Road

King Charles St.

Westminster Abbey

Smith Square

John Islip St.

Marsham St.

WESTMINSTER

Marsham St.

Marsham St.

Old Queen Street

Victoria St.

Tothill St.

Horseferry Rd.

Page St.

Vincent St.

Monck St.

ST. JAMES'S PARK

France

Caxton St.

Street

Regency St.

Douglas St.

ST. JAMES'S PARK

Birdcage Walk

Petty

Victoria

Howick Pl.

Greencoat Pl.

Francis

Willow Pl.

Ambrosden Ave.

VINCENT SQUARE

Vauxhall Bridge Rd.

PIMLICO ⊖

Charlwood Street

Tachbrook St.

Gloucester St.

Belgrave Rd.

Queen Victoria Memorial

The Mall

The Spur

Buckingham Gate

Wilfred St.

Castle Ln.

Palace St.

Stag Pl.

Carlisle Pl.

Wilton Rd.

Warwick Square

St. George

GREEN PARK

Constitution Hill

Buckingham Palace

Bressenden Pl.

Vauxhall Bridge Rd.

Wilton Rd.

Gillingham

8

Warwick Way

St. George St.

2

Grosvenor Gardens

Eccleston Bridge

7

Hugh St.

Alderney St.

BUCKINGHAM PALACE GARDENS

Beeston Pl.

1

Buckingham Palace Rd.

VICTORIA STATION

Victoria Station ⊖

Eccleston Bridge

HYDE PARK CORNER ⊖

Grosvenor Pl.

Hobart Pl.

Lower Belgrave St.

Victoria Coach Station

Semley Pl.

Piccadilly

Chester St.

Wilton St.

Eccleston St.

Ebury St.

4

5

6

Pimlico Rd.

Halkin St.

Chapel St.

3

Eaton Sq.

Chester Sq.

Elizabeth St.

South Eaton Pl.

Eaton Terrace

Chester Row

Chester Terrace

Ebury St.

Graham

HYDE PARK

BELGRAVE SQUARE

BELGRAVIA

Motcomb Street

Chesham Pl.

Lyall St.

Chesham St.

Cadogan Ln.

King's Rd.

Bourne St.

Eaton Terrace

SLOANE SQUARE ⊖

Holbein Pl.

Sloane Square

Place

Lower Sloane St.

Sloane St.

1/4 mi

1/4 km

B+B Belgravia **3**
Cartref House **5**
Ebury House **4**
41 **2**
Goring Hotel **1**
Lime Tree Hotel **6**
Luna & Simone Hotel **8**
Winchester Hotel **7**

Hotels in the West End

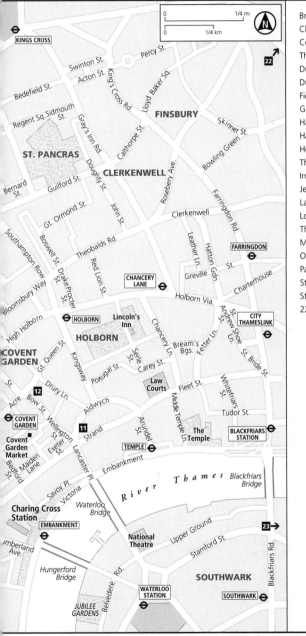

Brown's Hotel **8**
Claridge's **4**
Covent Garden Hotel **13**
The Dorchester **5**
Dukes Hotel **7**
Durrants Hotel **2**
Fielding Hotel **12**
Grange Blooms Hotel **16**
Harlingford Hotel **21**
Hazlitt's **14**
Hotel La Place **1**
The Hoxton **22**
Imperial Hotel **19**
Jenkins Hotel **20**
Langham Hotel **3**
London Bridge Hotel **23**
The Montague **18**
Morgan Hotel **17**
One Aldwych **11**
Park Lane Sheraton Hotel **6**
St. Margaret's Hotel **15**
St. Martin's Lane **10**
22 Jermyn Street **9**

Hotels from Knightsbridge to Earl's Court

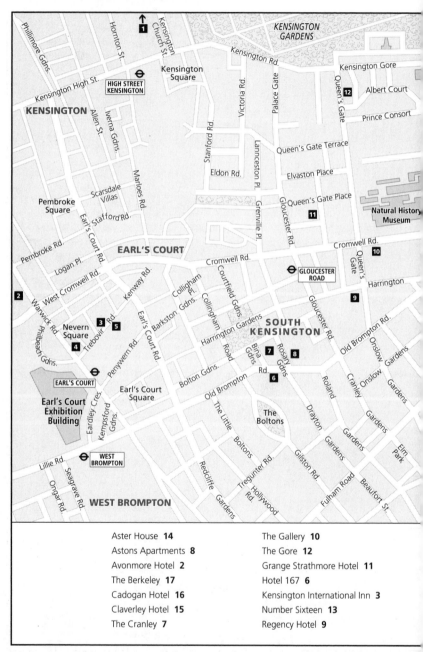

Aster House **14**	The Gallery **10**
Astons Apartments **8**	The Gore **12**
Avonmore Hotel **2**	Grange Strathmore Hotel **11**
The Berkeley **17**	Hotel 167 **6**
Cadogan Hotel **16**	Kensington International Inn **3**
Claverley Hotel **15**	Number Sixteen **13**
The Cranley **7**	Regency Hotel **9**

KENSINGTON GARDENS

HYDE PARK CORNER

KNIGHTSBRIDGE

Kensington Rd.

Knightsbridge

KNIGHTSBRIDGE

Kinnerton St.

Lowndes Square

Wilton

Cres.

Belgrave Square

Rd.

Prince's Gardens

Enismore Gardens

Rutland Gate

Montpelier St.

Cheval Pl.

Brompton Rd.

Hans Cr.

Hans Rd.

Basil St.

Pavilion Road

Belgrave Pl.

Exhibition Rd.

Garden Mews

Brompton Square

Beauchamp Place

15

Sloane St.

Pont Street

Chesham Pl.

Chesham St.

Lyall St.

King's Rd.

Victoria & Albert Museum

Cromwell Rd.

Walton St.

16

Cadogan Lane

Cadogan Place

Egerton Gdns.

Cadogan Square

Pavilion Rd.

Thurloe Place

Thurloe

Thurloe Square

Brompton Rd.

Hasker St.

Milner St.

Cadogan Gdns.

Ellis St.

Eaton Terrace

Rd.

SOUTH KENSINGTON

Pelham St.

13

14

Pelham Crescent

Draycott Avenue

Cadogan St.

Draycott Place

SLOANE SQUARE

Bourne St.

BELGRAVIA

Onslow Square

Summer Pl.

Fulham Rd.

Ixworth Place

Elystan St.

Sloane Avenue

King's Rd.

Lower Sloane

Pimlico Rd.

Cale St.

Elystan Place

Astell St.

Sydney St.

CHELSEA

Chelsea Square

Dovehouse St.

King's Rd.

Chelsea Manor St.

Radnor Walk

Smith St.

Flood St.

Tedworth Square

Christchurch St.

Royal Hospital Rd.

West St.

Tite St.

Chelsea Bridge Rd.

RANELAGH GARDENS

Old Church St.

Glebe Place

Oakley St.

Rushmore Hotel **5**
Twenty Nevern Square **4**
The Vicarage Hotel **1**

| 0 | 1/4 mi |
| 0 | 1/4 km |

N

i Information
Tube stop

Hotels from Marylebone to Notting Hill

The Abbey Court **4**
Bryanston Court Hotel **12**
Byron Hotel **5**
Comfort Inn Notting Hill **2**
Dorset Square Hotel **17**
Durrants Hotel **14**
Fairways Hotel **8**
Gate Hotel **1**
Hart House Hotel **13**

Hall Pl.

Penfold St.

MARYLEBONE 17

BAKER STREET   Outer Circle

LISSON
GROVE

Marylebone Rd.

MARYLEBONE

Gloucester Pl.

Baker St.

Paddington St.

EDGEWARE ROAD 16

A40 (M)

Montague Pl.

Dorset St.

Seymour Pl.

Marylebone High St.

Bridge Rd.

PADDINGTON

Eastbourne Terr.

Paddington
Station

PADDINGTON
STATION

Praed St.

Sussex Gardens

Edgware Rd.

Blandford St.

Manchester St.

George St.

15

Wigmore St.

13   14

Upper Berkeley St.

BOND ST.

Westbourne Terr.

Craven Rd. Spring St.

8

7

9

Hyde Park St.

Connaught St.

Sussex Sq.

Seymour St.

Oxford St.

Duke St.

10

12

MARBLE ARCH

LANCASTER GATE 11

Bayswater Rd.

The Ring

North Ride

A40

Cumberland Gate

Speakers
Corner

North Audley St.

Park St.

Upper Brook St.

Grosvenor
Square

Marlborough
Gate

Victoria Gate

The Ring (West Carriage Dr.)

Upper Grosvenor St.

Park Ln.

Lancaster
Gate

HYDE PARK

MAYFAIR

Audley St.

Upper Grosvenor South

KENSINGTON
GARDENS

Nursery

The Long Water

Tea
House

Temple
Lodge

Serpentine Rd.

Serpentine
Gallery

The Serpentine

Rotten Row

HYDE PARK
CORNER

The Flower Walk

Albert Memorial

Coalbrookdale
Gate

Prince of Wales
Gate

South Carriage Dr.

Park
Cl.

Edinburgh
Gate

Albert
Gate

Grosvenor Cr.

Queen's
Gate

Alexandra
Gate

Kensington Gore

Knightsbridge

Ennismore
Gdns.

Brompton Rd.

KNIGHTSBRIDGE

Sloane St.

Wilton Pl.

Exhibition Rd.

Landmark London **16**
The Lennox **3**
Milestone Hotel **6**
Minotel Wigmore Court Hotel **15**
Mitre House Hotel **9**
Rhodes Hotel **10**
Royal Lancaster **11**
Stylotel **7**

0   1/4 mi

0   1/4 km

N

⊖ Tube stop

Byron Hotel
$$ Bayswater

The 45-room Byron occupies a Victorian house that's been thoroughly modernized but hasn't lost its traditional atmosphere. The guest rooms have ample closets, tile baths, and good lighting. Breakfast is served in a cheery dining room. The staff members are pleasant and helpful, and the hotel can provide child cots and help with special requirements for children's meals. Considering the amenities offered, this establishment offers an especially good value.

See map p. 120. 36–38 Queensborough Terrace (off Bayswater Road), W2 3SH. ☎ *020/7243-0987. Fax: 020/7792-1957.* www.capricornhotels.co.uk. *Tube: Queensway (then a 5-minute walk east on Bayswater Road and north on Queensborough Terrace). Rack rates: £120 ($240) double. English or continental breakfast included. AE, DC, MC, V.*

Cadogan Hotel
$$$$$ Chelsea

You feel transported back to the Victorian era at this beautiful 69-room hotel, with a small wood-paneled lobby and sumptuous drawing room (good for afternoon tea), close to all the exclusive Knightsbridge shops. The Cadogan (pronounced cah-*dug*-en) is the hotel where poet, playwright, and novelist Oscar Wilde was staying when he was arrested (Room 118 is the Oscar Wilde Room). The large guest rooms, many overlooking the Cadogan Place gardens, are quietly tasteful and splendidly comfortable, with large bathrooms. The sedate Edwardian restaurant is known for its excellent cuisine.

See map p. 118. 75 Sloane St. (near Sloane Square), SW1X 9SG. ☎ *800/260-8338 in the U.S. or 020/7235-7141. Fax: 020/7245-0994.* www.cadogan.com. *Tube: Sloane Square (then a 5-minute walk north on Sloane Street). Rack rates: £255–£355 ($510–$710) double. Rates don't include 17.5 percent VAT. AE, MC, V.*

Cartref House
$ Westminster and Victoria

Cartref House is among the top budget B&Bs in London. Each guest room is individually designed and comfortably furnished; some of the larger ones contain bunk beds, which makes them suitable for families. All have small private bathrooms. The English breakfast is hearty (but ends at 8:30 a.m.), and the place is remarkably well kept. There's no elevator, but guests don't seem to mind. Friendly, personal service makes this a winner.

See map p. 115. 108 and 129 Ebury St. (near Victoria Station), SW1W 9QD. ☎ *020/7730-6176. Fax: 020/7730-7338.* www.jamesandcartref.co.uk. *Tube: Victoria Station (then a 10-minute walk south on Buckingham Palace Road, west on Eccleston Street, and south on Ebury Street). Rack rates: £90 ($180) double. English breakfast included. AE, MC, V.*

Claverley Hotel
$$–$$$$ Knightsbridge

On a quiet Knightsbridge cul-de-sac a few blocks from Harrods, this cozy place is considered one of London's best B&Bs. The public rooms feature Georgian-era accessories, 19th-century oil portraits, elegant antiques, and leather-covered sofas. The 29 guest rooms are smart and cozy, with marble bathrooms with tubs and power showers. The price includes an excellent English breakfast.

See map p. 118. 13–14 Beaufort Gardens (off Brompton Road), SW3 1PS. ☎ *800/747-0398 in the U.S. or 020/7589-8541. Fax: 020/7584-3410.* www.claverleyhotel. co.uk. *Tube: Knightsbridge (then a 2-minute walk south past Harrods on Brompton Road to Beaufort Gardens). Rack rates: £149–£219 ($298–$438) double. English breakfast included. AE, DC, MC, V.*

Comfort Inn Notting Hill
$$ Notting Hill

You'll get a lower room rate at this chain-hotel franchise if you book directly with the hotel instead of through central reservations. Located on a quiet, pretty street off Notting Hill Gate, the Comfort Inn stretches across five terrace houses and has 64 fair-size rooms on the three upper floors. (There's an elevator.) Rooms have been redecorated with a nice traditional look and equipped with firm, new beds; a few newly redone rooms are on a charming interior courtyard. Standard amenities include dataports, coffeemakers, and hair dryers. The bathrooms are also newly renovated.

See map p. 120. 6–14 Pembridge Gardens, W2 4DU. ☎ *020/7229-6666. Fax: 020/7229-3333.* www.1th-hotels.com. *Tube: Notting Hill Gate (then a 2-minute walk north on Pembridge Gardens). Rack rates: £110 ($220) double. Continental breakfast included. AE, DC, MC, V.*

Covent Garden Hotel
$$$$$ Covent Garden

Created from an 1850s French hospital and dispensary, this boutique hotel surrounds guests in luxury. No two of the 50 guest rooms are alike. Many rooms have large windows with rooftop views. The décor is a lush mix of antiques and fine contemporary furniture, and the granite-tiled bathrooms with glass-walled showers and heated towel racks are among the best in London. The wood-paneled public rooms are just as impressive. On-site **Brasserie Max** serves up eclectic bistro food and is a chic place to lunch. If you don't get enough exercise touring London, you can keep in shape at the small gym on the premises.

See map p. 116. 10 Monmouth St. (near Covent Garden Market), WC2H 9BH. ☎ *800/553-6674 in the U.S. or 020/7806-1000. Fax: 020/7806-1100.* www.firmdale. com. *Tube: Leicester Square (then a 5-minute walk north on St. Martin's Lane, which becomes Monmouth Street). Rack rates: £225–£320 ($550–$640) double. Rates don't include 17.5 percent VAT. AE, DC, MC, V.*

The Cranley
$$$–$$$$ South Kensington

On a quiet street near South Kensington's museums, the Cranley occupies a quartet of restored 1875 town houses. Luxuriously appointed public rooms and 39 high-ceilinged, air-conditioned guest rooms — with original plasterwork, a blend of Victorian and contemporary furnishings, and up-to-the-minute, in-room technology — make this property a standout. The bathrooms are large and nicely finished, with tubs and showers. Rates include tea with scones in the afternoon and champagne and canapés in the evening.

See map p. 118. 10–12 Bina Gardens (off Brompton Road), SW5 0LA. ☎ *800/448-8355 in the U.S. or 020/7373-0123. Fax: 020/7373-9497.* www.thecranley.com. *Tube: Gloucester Road (then a 5-minute walk south on Gloucester Road, west on Brompton Road, and north on Bina Gardens). Rack rates: £160–£245 ($320–$490) double. AE, DC, MC, V.*

Dorset Square Hotel
$$$$–$$$$$ Marylebone

This sophisticated, 38-room, luxury boutique hotel occupies a beautifully restored Regency town house overlooking Dorset Square, a private garden surrounded by graceful buildings. Inside and out, this hotel is the epitome of traditional English style. Each guest room is unique, filled with a superlative mix of antiques, original oils, fine furniture, fresh flowers, and richly textured fabrics. The bathrooms are marble and mahogany. (Just remember that some of those enticing little toiletries aren't free.)

See map p. 120. 39–40 Dorset Square (just west of Regent's Park), NW1 6QN. ☎ *800/553-6674 in the U.S. or 020/7723-7874. Fax: 020/7724-3328.* www.dorsetsquare.co.uk. *Tube: Marylebone (then a 2-minute walk east on Melcombe to Dorset Square). Rack rates: £230–£270 ($460–$540) double. Rates don't include 17.5 percent VAT. AE, MC, V.*

Durrants Hotel
$$$ Marylebone

Opened in 1789 off Manchester Square, this 92-room hotel provides an atmospheric London retreat. The pine-and-mahogany-paneled public areas, including an 18th-century letter-writing room and a wonderful Georgian room that serves as a restaurant, are quintessentially English. The guest rooms are generously proportioned (for the most part) and nicely furnished, with decent-size bathrooms.

See map p. 120. George Street (across from the Wallace Collection), W1H 6BJ. ☎ *020/7935-8131. Fax: 020/7487-3510.* www.durrantshotel.co.uk. *Tube: Bond Street (then a 5-minute walk west on Oxford Street and north on Duke Street and Manchester Street). Rack rates: £195 ($390) double. AE, MC, V.*

Fairways Hotel
$ Paddington

This large, late-Georgian house from the 1820s is a real bargain. Stephen Adams, who took over the management from his parents (they ran the hotel for 25 years), made several improvements in 2002, laying new carpeting and redoing all the shared toilets and showers. All 17 rooms are different, the ones in back much quieter. Some of the private bathrooms are much smaller than others. Coffeemakers and hair dryers are in the rooms, but the phone is in the hallway and, to keep prices low, breakfast is not included in the room rate.

See map p. 120. 186 Sussex Gardens, W2 1TU. ☎ 020/7723-4871. Fax: 020/7723-4871. www.fairways-hotel.co.uk. Tube: Paddington (then a 5-minute walk). Rack rates: £60 ($120) double without bathroom, £70 ($140) double with bathroom. AE, DC, MC, V.

Fielding Hotel
$$ Covent Garden

Named for author Henry Fielding (famous for *The History of Tom Jones*), the Fielding is on a beautiful, old street (now pedestrian-only) lit by 19th-century gaslights and across from the Royal Opera House. The stairways are steep and narrow (the hotel has no elevator), and the 24 rather cramped guest rooms are undistinguished in décor, but they do have showers and toilets. Those quibbles aside, this quirky hotel is an excellent value. A small bar is on the premises, and the area is loaded with cafes, restaurants, and fabulous shopping.

See map p. 116. 4 Broad Court, Bow Street, WC2B 5QZ. ☎ 020/7836-8305. Fax: 020/7497-0064. www.the-fielding-hotel.co.uk. Tube: Covent Garden (then a 5-minute walk north on Long Acre and south on Bow Street). Rack rates: £105–£150 ($210–$300) double. AE, DC, MC, V.

41
$$$$ Westminster and Victoria

Overlooking Buckingham Palace Mews, this unique, 18-room boutique hotel is the epitome of luxury and offers superior personal service. The hotel lobby and breakfast room is an elegant conservatory that was once the waiting room for debutantes who were going to Buckingham Palace to be presented. Every detail in the beautifully furnished rooms, from the Frette sheets to the Penhaligon toiletries, is pure *luxe*. The staff here is wonderfully friendly.

See map p. 115. 41 Buckingham Palace Rd. (just north of Victoria Station), SW1W 0PS. ☎ 877/955-1515 in the U.S. or 020/7300-0041. Fax: 020/7300-0141. www.41hotel.com. Tube: Victoria (then a 5-minute walk northeast along Buckingham Palace Road). Rack rates: £219–£239 ($438–$478) double. Rates don't include 17.5 percent tax. Continental breakfast included. AE, MC, V.

The Gallery
$$–$$$ South Kensington

This relatively unknown 36-room hotel, located near the cultural and retail attractions in South Kensington and Knightsbridge, occupies two completely restored and converted Georgian residences. The elegant guest rooms are individually designed and include half-canopied beds and marble-tiled bathrooms. The lounge, with its rich mahogany paneling and moldings and deep colors, has the ambience of a private club. The overall décor is wonderfully Victorian, but every modern convenience is available, including Wi-Fi. Two of the suites have their own roof terraces.

See map p. 118. 8–10 Queensberry Place (opposite the Natural History Museum), SW7 2EA. ☎ *020/7915-0000. Fax: 020/7915-4400.* www.eeh.co.uk. *Tube: South Kensington (then a 5-minute walk west on Thurloe Street and Harrington Road and north on Queensberry Place). Rack rates: £145–£180 ($290–$360) double. Rates don't include 17.5 percent VAT. English breakfast included. AE, DC, MC, V.*

Gate Hotel
$ Notting Hill

This tiny, three-story building dates from the 1820s (when people were evidently much smaller), so the six color-coordinated guest rooms are cramped but atmospheric, and the stairs are steep. The Gate is one of only two hotels along the length of Portobello Road, famous for its antiques shops and Saturday bric-a-brac stalls. Kensington Gardens is a five-minute walk away.

See map p. 120. 6 Portobello Rd., W11 3DG. ☎ *020/7221-0707. Fax: 020/7221-9128.* www.gatehotel.co.uk. *Tube: Notting Hill Gate (then a 5-minute walk north on Pembridge Road and northwest on Portobello Road). Rack rates: £80–£90 ($160–$180) double. Continental breakfast included. MC, V.*

The Gore
$$$–$$$$$ South Kensington

If you dream of the days of Queen Victoria, you'll definitely appreciate the Victorian-era charm of the Gore, which has been in more or less continuous operation since 1892. On a busy road near Kensington Gardens and the Royal Albert Hall, the Gore is loaded with historic charm: walnut-and-mahogany paneling, oriental rugs, and 19th-century prints. Each of the 54 guest rooms is unique, filled with high-quality antiques and elegant furnishings, including old commodes that conceal the toilets.

See map p. 118. 189 Queen's Gate (south of Kensington Gardens), SW7 5EX. ☎ *800/ 637-7200 in the U.S. or 020/7584-6601. Fax: 020/7589-8127.* www.gorehotel.com. *Tube: Gloucester Road (then a 10-minute walk east on Cromwell Road and north on Queen's Gate). Rack rates: £255–£295 ($310–$590) double. Rates don't include 17.5 percent VAT. AE, DC, MC, V.*

Grange Strathmore Hotel
$$–$$$ South Kensington

Formerly the residence of the 14th earl of Strathmore, the late Queen Mum's father, this hotel overlooks a private garden square just minutes from the South Ken museums. Some of the guest rooms feature a high-ceilinged spaciousness rare in London hotels, and bathrooms with tubs and showers. Plenty of hand-carved rosewood furniture and well-chosen fabrics decorate the rooms. One drawback is that, on weekends, no general manager is on duty; also, service can sometimes be rather impersonal.

See map p. 118. 41 Queen's Gate Gardens (at the southeast corner of the gardens), SW7 5NB. ☎ 020/7584-0512. Fax: 020/7584-0246. www.grangehotels.com. *Tube: Gloucester Road (then a 2-minute walk north on Gloucester Road and east on Queen's Gate Gardens). Rack rates: £110–£180 ($220–$360) double. AE, MC, V.*

Harlingford Hotel
$–$$ Bloomsbury

In the heart of Bloomsbury, this wonderfully personable and immaculately maintained hotel occupies three 1820s town houses joined by an array of staircases (no elevators) and hallways. The 44 guest rooms are pleasantly comfy, some graced with floral prints and double-glazed windows to cut down on noise; the best rooms are on the second and third levels. The bathrooms are very small, however. The hotel has family rooms and can provide cots for children. Guests have use of the tennis courts in Cartwright Gardens.

See map p. 116. 61–63 Cartwright Gardens (north of Russell Square), WC1H 9EL. ☎ 020/7387-1551. Fax: 020/7387-4616. www.harlingfordhotel.com. *Tube: Russell Square (then a 10-minute walk northwest on Woburn Place, east on Tavistock Square, and north on Marchmont Street). Rack rates: £104 ($208) double. English breakfast included. AE, DC, MC, V.*

Hart House Hotel
$$ Marylebone

A Georgian town house built in 1782 and used by members of the French nobility during the French Revolution, Hart House is one of the most welcoming and professionally run B&Bs in London. It has retained its dignified entrance hall and polished paneling. The 16 rooms (all nonsmoking) are attractive and comfortable with small but immaculate bathrooms. Double-glazing on the windows screens out the traffic roar on Gloucester Place. Some very large rooms, perfect for families, have big bathtubs and showers, and the staff can help you arrange babysitting.

See map p. 120. 51 Gloucester Place, Portman Square (just north of Marble Arch), W1U 8JF. ☎ 020/7935-2288. Fax: 020/7935-8516. www.harthouse.co.uk. *Tube: Marble Arch (then a 5-minute walk north on Gloucester Place). Rack rates: £125 ($250) double. English breakfast included. AE, MC, V.*

Hazlitt's
$$$$–$$$$$ Soho

Built in 1718 (you may have guessed it from the name), this intimate, 23-room gem offers old-fashioned atmosphere and a hip Soho location. Recent restoration exposed original wood paneling and other features hidden for years, but the hotel still lacks an elevator. The charming Georgian-era guest rooms feature mahogany and pine furnishings and antiques, as well as lovely bathrooms, many with claw-foot tubs. The back rooms are quieter; the front rooms are lighter, but without the quieting effect of double-glazed windows, you do hear the street noise.

See map p. 116. 6 Frith St., Soho Square (just west of Charing Cross Road), W1D 3JA. ☎ *020/7434-1771. Fax: 020/7439-1524.* www.hazlitts.co.uk. *Tube: Tottenham Court Road (then a 10-minute walk west on Oxford Street and south on Soho Street to Frith Street at the south end of Soho Square). Rack rates: £205–£265 ($410–$530) double. Rates don't include 17.5 percent VAT. AE, DC, MC, V.*

Hotel La Place
$$ Marylebone

This desirable hotel, north of Oxford Street, caters to women traveling alone. The interior has been upgraded to boutique-hotel standards (although the exterior isn't especially impressive); the 21 moderate-size guest rooms are done in classic English style, with mahogany furnishings, brocades, TV armoires, and writing desks; you also find air-conditioning and free Wi-Fi. The bathrooms are as nice as the rooms. The hotel's **Jardin** is a chic, intimate wine bar/restaurant.

See map p. 116. 17 Nottingham Place (near the southwest corner of Regent's Park), W1M 3FF. ☎ *020/7486-2323. Fax: 020/7486-4335.* www.hotellaplace.com. *Tube: Baker Street (then a 5-minute walk east on Marylebone Road and south on Nottingham Place). Rack rates: £115–£145 ($230–$290) double. English breakfast included. AE, DC, MC, V.*

Hotel 167
$–$$ South Kensington

Hotel 167 attracts hip young visitors with its price, and business people with its central location (and the price doesn't hurt either). This hotel is bright and attractive, offering 16 comfortable guest rooms, each with a decent-size bathroom (some with showers, others with tubs). The rooms are furnished with a mix of fabrics and styles. Nearby Tube stations make the hotel convenient to the rest of London, and the busy neighborhood itself is fun to explore.

See map p. 118. 167 Old Brompton Rd., SW5 0AN. ☎ *020/7373-0672. Fax: 020/7373-3360.* www.hotel167.com. *Tube: South Kensington (then a 10-minute walk west on Old Brompton Road). Rack rates: £99–£110 ($198–$220) double. Continental breakfast included. AE, DC, MC, V.*

The Hoxton
$–$$ **Shoreditch**

This trendsetting "Urban Lodge" opened in 2007 and offers something quite unique for London: chic style at a cheap price. In fact, check its Web site because the Hoxton periodically holds incredible sales and you may be able to nab a room for as little as £1 ($2)! The rooms are comfortable, well-designed, and refreshingly free of froufrou. The beautifully tiled, shower-only bathrooms have every hotel in this price range beat by a mile. A simple bagged breakfast arrives at your room every morning, food and wine are sold in the lobby at supermarket prices, high-speed computers are on hand for the guests, and phone calls are incredibly cheap. In short, you'll find great value and no rip-offs. The trendy Shoreditch area is considered part of the East End of London.

See map p. 116. 81 Great Eastern St., EC2A 3HU. ☎ *020/7550-1000. Fax: 020/7550-1090.* www.hoxtonhotels.com. *Tube: Old Street (then a 5-minute walk north on Old Street, then turn right down Great Eastern Street). Rack rates: £59–£159 ($118–$318) double. Rates include continental breakfast. AE, MC, V.*

Imperial Hotel
$ **Bloomsbury**

The décor is dated and the exterior epitomizes the worst of 1960s architecture, but so what? The 448-room Imperial is a full-service hotel and a terrific value. Nine floors are guest rooms; the third floor is entirely nonsmoking. The hotel does plenty of tour-group business, but the rooms have stood up well to the traffic. They're all a decent size, with unusual triangular-shaped bay windows, good storage space, and workable bathrooms. Amenities include a restaurant, a late-hour Internet cafe, concierge, and room service.

See map p. 116. Russell Square, WC1B 5BB. ☎ *020/7278-7871. Fax: 020/7837-4653.* www.imperialhotels.co.uk. *Tube: Russell Square (the hotel is on the east side of the square). Rack rates: £99 ($198) double. English breakfast included. AE, DC, MC, V.*

Jenkins Hotel
$ **Bloomsbury**

This nonsmoking hotel offers a bit of Georgian charm; a great location near the British Museum and West End theaters; a nice, comfortable atmosphere; a full breakfast; and a low price. The 15 guest rooms are small, but all have private bathrooms. You don't find reception or sitting rooms, or even an elevator, but you can still settle in and feel at home. Although the hotel has no special facilities for kids, it welcomes children.

See map p. 116. 45 Cartwright Gardens (just south of Euston Station), WC1H 9EH. ☎ *020/7387-2067. Fax: 020/7383-3139.* www.jenkinshotel.demon.co.uk. *Tube: Euston Station (then a 5-minute walk east on Euston Road and south on Mabledon Place to the south end of Cartwright Gardens). Rack rates: £89 ($178) double. English breakfast included. MC, V.*

Kensington International Inn
$$ Earl's Court

This recently refurbished hotel on an elegant Victorian street near the Earl's Court Tube station has small rooms but a surprisingly chic contemporary décor that makes it stand out. All 60 rooms are done in pale, wheaty colors and have sleek, wooden headboards and furnishings. Bathrooms are small, too, with glass-walled showers. The hotel has a hip little bar, a conservatory lounge, and in-room amenities such as a trouser press, a coffeemaker, and a hair dryer. You may find a lower price on the hotel's Web site than the rack rates listed here.

See map p. 118. 4 Templeton Place, SW5 9LZ. ☎ *020/7370-4333. Fax: 020/7244-7873.* www.kensingtoninternationalinn.com. *Tube: Earl's Court (then a 3-minute walk along Trebovir Road and north on Templeton Place). Rack rates: £125 ($250) double. Continental breakfast included. MC, V.*

Landmark London
$$$–$$$$$ Marylebone

The finest Victorian railway hotel in England when it opened in 1899, the Landmark was recently restored to its former glory. The hotel sits in a great location, particularly if you're with kids, because Madame Tussaud's wax museum and Regents Park are only around the corner. Built around an eight-story atrium, the 299 rooms are among London's largest and feature marble bathrooms. The hotel offers every amenity, including babysitting, a large health club, and an indoor pool.

See map p. 120. 222 Marylebone Rd. (½ block from Madame Tussaud's), NW1 6JQ. ☎ *800/323-7500 in the U.S. or 020/7631-8000. Fax: 020/7631-8080.* www.landmark london.co.uk. *Tube: Marylebone (the hotel is just a few steps away). Rack rates: £155–£310 ($310–$620) double. Rates don't include 17.5 percent VAT. AE, DC, MC, V.*

Langham Hotel
$$$$$ Marylebone

A fabulous location at the head of Regent Street, ultra-comfy rooms, and superlative service make this newly refurbished grand hotel one of London's grandest places to stay. Guest rooms are stylish and quietly sumptuous with good-size bathrooms and luxury amenities. For an extra charge, you can get a room in the "Club" section, which includes breakfast and evening canapés. **Artesian,** right off the main lobby, is the hotel's glam cocktail bar. There's a wonderful gym, a big indoor pool, and a full-service spa. Book online and you'll pay far less than the published rack rate for a room.

See map p. 116. 1c Portland Place, London W1B 1JA. ☎ *020/7636-1000. Fax: 020/7323-2340.* www.langhamhotels.com. *Tube: Oxford Circus (then a 5-minute walk north on Regent Street). Rack rates: £350 ($700) double. AE, DC, MC, V.*

Lime Tree Hotel
$$ **Westminster and Victoria**

This attractive, brick-fronted town house is located near Buckingham Palace, Westminster Abbey, and the Houses of Parliament. It's nicely furnished, with deep cornices in the hall and statues and flowers in the alcoves up the stairs. The more expensive of the 26 rooms are quite luxurious, with swagged curtains, canopied beds, and pretty furniture; others are more simply furnished, but all are generally larger and have more amenities than you usually find in this price range. The bathrooms are small. The front rooms have small balconies overlooking Ebury Street; the rear rooms are quieter and look out over a small garden.

See map p. 115. 135–137 Ebury St. (near Victoria Station), SW1W 9RA. ☎ *020/7730-8191. Fax: 020/7730-7865.* www.limetreehotel.co.uk. *Tube: Victoria Station (then a 5-minute walk north on Grosvenor Gardens and south on Ebury Street). Rack rates: £110–£140 ($220–$280) double. English breakfast included. AE, DC, MC, V.*

London Bridge Hotel
$–$$$ **Southwark**

Quietly elegant and independently owned, the London Bridge Hotel occupies a prime South Bank location close to the famous bridge and all the South Bank attractions; just across the Thames is the Tower of London, and the City. Though not particularly large, the standard bedrooms here are smartly appointed and very comfortable. The hotel houses two good restaurants and a well-equipped gym.

See map p. 116. 8–18 London Bridge St., SE1 9SG. ☎ *020/7855-2200. Fax: 020/7855-2233.* www.londonbridgehotel.com. *Tube: London Bridge (the hotel is oposite the station's main entrance). Rack rates: £99–£199 ($98–$398) double. English breakfast included. AE, DC, MC, V.*

Luna & Simone Hotel
$ **Westminster and Victoria**

The outside of this big, stuccoed, family-run hotel gleams bright white, and all the guest rooms have been freshly renovated with private bathrooms installed. The 36 rooms vary widely in size, but with their pleasant décor and newly tiled bathrooms (all with showers), they beat all the dowdy, badly designed hotels and B&Bs for miles around. The reception area and smart-looking breakfast room (now totally nonsmoking) are also new. The look throughout is refreshingly light, simple, and modern.

See map p. 115. 47–49 Belgrave Rd., SW1V 2BB. ☎ *020/7834-5897. Fax: 020/7828-2474.* www.lunasimonehotel.com. *Tube: Victoria (then a 15-minute walk east along Belgrave Road; the hotel is just beyond Warwick Square). Rack rates: £70–£90 ($140–$180) double. English breakfast included. MC, V.*

Milestone Hotel
$$$$$ **South Kensington**

Service is what sets the Milestone apart from most of its high-toned, high-priced competitors. There's a butler on duty round-the-clock and two staff people for every guest. Add to that an unbeatable location right across from Kensington Gardens and Kensington Palace, and close to great Kensington High Street shopping and restaurants, and you can't go wrong. Each of the individually designed and decorated rooms have endless amenities, including free Wi-Fi or wired Internet and iPod docking stations. The gym is fitted out with one of London's few heated resistance pools. Look online for special rates.

See map p. 120. Kensington Court, London W8 5DL. ☎ *877/955-1515 in the U.S. or 020/7917-1000. Fax: 020/7917-1010.* www.milestonehotel.com. *Tube: High Street Kensington (then a 5-minute walk east on Kensington High Street and Kensington Road). Rack rates: £320–£345 ($640–$690). Rates don't include 17.5 percent VAT. AE, DC, MC, V.*

Minotel Wigmore Court Hotel
$ **Marylebone**

This appealing Georgian-era B&B lacks an elevator but rewards anyone who is willing to climb up to a fifth-floor room with a four-poster bed. The 18 rooms are decorated with a mix of traditional styles and contain coffeemakers and hair dryers. The quieter rooms at the back look over a mews. Guests can use the kitchen and laundry facilities, a big bonus normally restricted to budget B&Bs.

See map p. 120. 23 Gloucester Place, W1H 3PB. ☎ *020/7935-0928. Fax: 020/7487-4254.* www.wigmore-hotel.co.uk. *Tube: Marble Arch (then a 10-minute walk east on Marble Arch and north on Gloucester Place). Rack rates: £70 ($140) double without bathroom; £89 ($178) double with bathroom. English breakfast included. MC, V.*

Mitre House Hotel
$ **Paddington**

This fine, midsize hotel near Paddington Station stretches across four Georgian town houses and is kept in tiptop shape. The assortment of accommodations makes it great for families: two-bedroom family suites come with private bathrooms, and superior family suites that face quiet, leafy Talbot Square have toilets and tubs/showers off private corridors. All 69 rooms are above-average size for London; those at the back are quieter, though the view north across back alleys to Paddington isn't very inspiring. A pleasant lounge and bar, and even an elevator, are on-site.

See map p. 120. 178–184 Sussex Gardens, W2 1TU. ☎ *020/7723-8040. Fax: 020/7402-0990.* www.mitrehousehotel.com. *Tube: Lancaster Gate (a 5-minute walk north on Lancaster Terrace and east on Sussex Gardens). Rack rates: £90 ($180) double. English breakfast included. AE, DC, MC, V.*

The Montague
$$$$–$$$$$ Bloomsbury

For service and sheer sumptuousness, you won't find a better hotel anywhere in the vicinity of the British Museum — which happens to be right across the street from the Montague. Every room in this immaculately kept property has been individually decorated and features every amenity you can think of, from twice-daily maid service with evening turndown to luxuriously equipped bathrooms. The airy gardenside conservatory is a delightful spot for afternoon tea or a cocktail, and the **Chef's Table** restaurant is an enjoyable spot for lunch or dinner.

See map p. 116. 15 Montague St. (east side of the British Museum), WC1B 5BJ.
☎ *877/955-1515 in U.S. or 020/7637-1001. Fax: 020/7637-2516.* www.montague
hotel.com. *Tube: Russell Square (then a 5-minute walk south across Russell Square to Montague Street). Rack rates: £245–£290 ($490–$580) double. Rates don't include 17.5 percent VAT. AE, MC, V.*

Number Sixteen
$$$–$$$$ South Kensington

Gardeners will appreciate the award-winning gardens at this luxuriously appointed B&B in four early-Victorian town houses. The 40 guest rooms feature an eclectic mix of English antiques and modern paintings, and the bathrooms are large by London standards. The rooms look out over the private gardens of Sumner Place. On chilly days, you find a fire crackling in the drawing-room fireplace. Breakfast is served in the rooms, but if the weather's fine, you can have it in the garden and enjoy the fish pond and the bubbling fountain.

See map p. 118. 16 Sumner Place (north of Onslow Square), SW7 3EG. ☎ *800/592-5387 in the U.S. or 020/7589-5232. Fax: 020/7584-8615.* www.numbersixteen
hotel.co.uk. *Tube: South Kensington (then a 5-minute walk west on Brompton Road and south on Sumner Place). Rack rates: £150–£265 ($300–$530) double. Continental breakfast included. Rates don't include 17.5 percent VAT. AE, DC, MC, V.*

Park Lane Sheraton Hotel
$$$–$$$$ Mayfair

Sometimes called the "Iron Lady of Piccadilly" because it's so well built, this landmark hotel opened in 1927. Executive rooms and suites are decorated with a warm mix of classic English furnishings and have beautiful marble bathrooms. The price goes up according to location (particularly if it's a suite overlooking Green Park), size, and décor. Every conceivable amenity is available. The **Palm Court Lounge** (see Chapter 10) is a swank place for afternoon tea, and two restaurants are on the premises.

See map p. 116. Piccadilly (across from Green Park), W1Y 8BX. ☎ *800/325-3535 in the U.S. or 020/7499-6321. Fax: 020/7499-1965.* www.sheraton.com/parklane. *Tube: Green Park (then a 3-minute walk southwest along Piccadilly). Rack rates: £150–£250 ($300–$500) double. AE, DC, MC, V.*

Regency Hotel
$–$$$ South Kensington

This hotel occupies six refitted Victorian terrace houses. A Chippendale fireplace graces the lobby, and five Empire chandeliers suspended vertically, one on top of the other, hang in one of the stairwells. The 210 modern guest rooms are subdued and attractive, with good-size bathrooms. The one downside is that the air-conditioning system on the west side of the building can be pretty loud on hot summer nights. Guests can use the health club with steam rooms and saunas.

See map p. 118. 100 Queen's Gate (near Royal Albert Hall), SW7 5AG. ☎ *800/223-5652 in the U.S. or 020/7373-7878. Fax: 020/7370-9700.* www.regency-london.co.uk. *Tube: South Kensington (then a 3-minute walk west on Old Brompton Road to Queen's Gate). Rack rates: £99–£160 ($187–$320) double. Rates don't include 17.5 percent VAT. English breakfast included. AE, DC, MC, V.*

Rhodes Hotel
$ Paddington

The personable owner of the Rhodes recently spruced up the entire hotel, adding hand-painted, Greek-inspired murals to the public areas. Other improvements include air-conditioning in the main part of the hotel (though not in the annex, which is why rooms are cheaper there) and dataports for Internet access in all 18 guest rooms. The room décor is quite simple and comfortable; bathrooms are small but well kept. Room 220 has its own little private roof terrace, complete with table and chairs.

See map p. 120. 195 Sussex Gardens, W2 2RJ. ☎ *020/7262-0537. Fax: 020/7723-4054.* www.rhodeshotel.com. *Tube: Paddington (then a 5-minute walk south on Spring Street or London Street to Sussex Gardens). Rack rates: £70–£100 ($140–$200) double. Continental breakfast included. MC, V.*

Royal Lancaster
$–$$$$$ Bayswater

I happen to like big old hotels that keep themselves in good condition and retain a sense of friendly courtesy. The Royal Lancaster has been around for ages, and it's one of those hotels that have a loyal clientele. The hotel sits directly across from Hyde Park, and the airy city and park views from the upper floors are among the best in London. The rooms are decorated with a modern flair and have marble bathrooms, air-conditioning, and double-glazing to cut down on the traffic noise. You can usually find a room in every price range, but go for the higher floors with a park view if you can.

See map p. 120. Lancaster Terrace, W2 2TY. ☎ *020/7262-6737. Fax: 020/7724-3191.* www.royallancaster.com. *Tube: Lancaster Gate (the hotel is across from the station). Rack rates: £85–£257 ($170–$514) double. AE, MC, V.*

St. Margaret's Hotel
$ **Bloomsbury**

The welcome that you get here inspires devoted loyalty. Mrs. Marazzi is the second generation of her family to run this nonsmoking B&B, which rambles over four houses. The 64 rooms are simple and immaculate, and no two are alike. Only about 10 rooms have private bathrooms, but the Marazzis recently created some extra public bathrooms, so it's easy to survive the sharing experience. Some rooms look out onto the quiet communal garden that all the guests can use. Babysitting can be arranged.

See map p. 116. 26 Bedford Place, WC1B 5JL. ☎ **020/7636-4277.** *Fax: 020/7323-3066.* www.stmargaretshotel.co.uk. *Tube: Russell Square (then a 5-minute walk to Bedford Place on the south side of Russell Square). Rack rates: £68 ($136) double without bathroom, £95–£99 ($190–$198) double with bathroom. English breakfast included. MC, V.*

Stylotel
$ **Paddington**

Stylotel and B+B Belgravia (reviewed earlier in this chapter) prove that budget hotels don't have to be dull and conventional when it comes to interior design. Housed in two 19th-century town houses, this B&B features a small, modern lobby and small, modern guest rooms fitted out with aluminum wallcoverings, big mirrors, upholstered headboards, and one-piece prefabricated bathrooms with shower.

See map p. 120. 160–162 Sussex Gardens, W2 1UD. ☎ **020/7723-1026.** *Fax: 020/7262-2983.* www.stylotel.com. *Tube: Paddington (then a 5-minute walk south on Spring Street or London Street to Sussex Gardens). Rack rates: £78 ($156) double. Continental breakfast included. AE, DC, MC, V.*

Twenty Nevern Square
$$$ **Earl's Court**

This sumptuously refurbished boutique hotel in a Victorian town house overlooking Nevern Square shows off the gentrified side of Earl's Court. The look throughout is plush and glamorous, with great attention paid to detail. The 20 bedrooms are all individually designed with an emphasis on natural materials, such as linen, cotton, silk, and wood. The bathrooms are just as lovely. The hotel has its own bar and restaurant, **Café Twenty.** Book online and you'll get a much lower rate than the rack rate listed here.

See map p. 118. 20 Nevern Square, SW5 9PD. ☎ **020/7565-9555.** *Fax: 020/7565-9444.* www.twentynevernsquare.co.uk. *Tube: Earl's Court (then a 2-minute walk along Trebovir Road to Nevern Square). Rack rates: £175 ($350) double. Continental breakfast included. AE, MC, V.*

22 Jermyn Street
$$$$ St. James's

This chic 18-room boutique hotel near Piccadilly Circus is an Edwardian town house on an exclusive street where almost every shop has a *Royal Warrant* (the sign of official royal patronage). In the richly appointed guest rooms, contemporary décor and fabrics mix with antique furnishings to create a stylish and comfortable ambience. The granite bathrooms are just as nice. Many amenities and 24-hour room service are available.

See map p. 116. 22 Jermyn St. (just south of Piccadilly Circus), SW1Y 6HL. ☎ 800/ 682-7808 in the U.S. or 020/7734-2353. Fax: 020/7734-0750. www.22jermyn.com. *Tube: Piccadilly Circus (take Lower Regent Street exit; Jermyn Street is the first right outside the station). Rack rates: £220 ($440) double. AE, DC, MC, V.*

The Vicarage Hotel
$–$$ Kensington

The family-run Vicarage offers old-world English charm, hospitality, and a good value. The hotel is on a residential garden square close to High Street Kensington and Kensington Palace. The 18 guest rooms, individually furnished in Victorian style, can accommodate up to four; Room 19 on the top floor is particularly charming. Some of the double and twin rooms have small bathrooms. The hotel welcomes children and will arrange for babysitting; however, the hotel isn't really equipped to deal with the needs of the under-3 set. Many guests return here year after year.

See map p. 118. 10 Vicarage Gate (west of Kensington Gardens), W8 4AG. ☎ 020/ 7229-4030. Fax: 020/7792-5989. www.londonvicaragehotel.com. *Tube: Kensington High Street (then a 10-minute walk east on Kensington High Street and north on Kensington Church Street). Rack rates: £75–£85 ($150–$170) double without bathroom, £100–£110 ($200–$220) double with bathroom. English breakfast included. No credit cards.*

Winchester Hotel
$ Westminster and Victoria

One of the best choices along Belgrave Road, this 18-room hotel is owned and managed by Jimmy McGoldrick, who goes out of his way to make his customers happy. Guests have been returning for 20 years, and if you stay here you'll understand why. Jimmy's staff maintains an extremely high level of service and cleanliness. The recently refurbished guest rooms are comfortable and well decorated. Each room has a small private bathroom with a good shower. Guests are served a big English breakfast in a lovely and inviting room. A sleek modernity is displayed throughout — rare in small London hotels.

See map p. 115. 17 Belgrave Rd., SW1 1RB. ☎ 020/7828-2972. Fax: 020/7828-5191. www.winchester-hotel.net. *Tube: Victoria. Rack rates: £85 ($170) double. English breakfast included. No credit cards.*

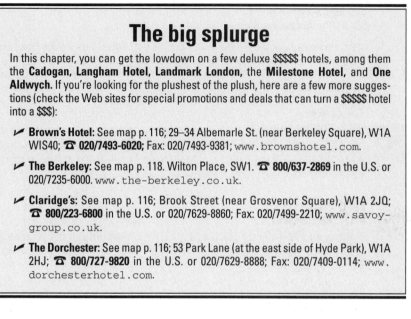

The big splurge

In this chapter, you can get the lowdown on a few deluxe $$$$$ hotels, among them the **Cadogan, Langham Hotel, Landmark London,** the **Milestone Hotel,** and **One Aldwych.** If you're looking for the plushest of the plush, here are a few more suggestions (check the Web sites for special promotions and deals that can turn a $$$$$ hotel into a $$$):

- ✔ **Brown's Hotel:** See map p. 116; 29–34 Albemarle St. (near Berkeley Square), W1A WIS40; ☎ **020/7493-6020;** Fax: 020/7493-9381; www.brownshotel.com.

- ✔ **The Berkeley:** See map p. 118. Wilton Place, SW1. ☎ **800/637-2869** in the U.S. or 020/7235-6000. www.the-berkeley.co.uk.

- ✔ **Claridge's:** See map p. 116; Brook Street (near Grosvenor Square), W1A 2JQ; ☎ **800/223-6800** in the U.S. or 020/7629-8860; Fax: 020/7499-2210; www.savoy-group.co.uk.

- ✔ **The Dorchester:** See map p. 116; 53 Park Lane (at the east side of Hyde Park), W1A 2HJ; ☎ **800/727-9820** in the U.S. or 020/7629-8888; Fax: 020/7409-0114; www.dorchesterhotel.com.

Runner-Up Hotels

Dukes Hotel
$$$$–$$$$$ St. James's

Dukes provides charm, style, and sophistication in a 1908 town house; babysitting is just one of its many amenities. *See map p. 116. 35 St. James's Place, SW1A 1NY.* ☎ *800/381-4702 in the U.S. or 020/7491-4840. Fax: 020/7493-1264.* www.dukeshotel.co.uk.

Ebury House
$ Westminster and Victoria

This B&B near Victoria Station offers clean, basic accommodations in a central location. *See map p. 115. 102 Ebury St., SW1W 9QD.* ☎ *020/7730-1350. Fax: 020/7259-0400.* www.belgraviarooms.com.

Goring Hotel
$$$–$$$$ Westminster and Victoria

The Goring has a great location, just behind Buckingham Palace, and top-notch service. This family-run property offers a particularly warm welcome to families. *See map p. 115. 15 Beeston Place, Grosvenor Gardens, SW1W 0JW.* ☎ *020/7396-9000. Fax: 020/7834-4393.* www.goringhotel.co.uk.

Grange Blooms Hotel
$$–$$$ **Bloomsbury**

With its cozy fireplace and period art, this 27-room hotel evokes a luxurious country-home atmosphere. *See map p. 116. 7 Montague St. (next to the British Museum), WC1B 5BP.* ☎ *020/7323-1717. Fax: 020/7636-6498.* www.grange hotels.com.

The Lennox
$$$ **Notting Hill**

Located in trendy Notting Hill Gate, this newly refurnished hotel has rooms large enough for families. *See map p. 120. 34 Pembridge Gardens, W2 4DX.* ☎ *020/7229-9977. Fax: 020/7727-4982.* www.thelennox.com.

Morgan Hotel
$$ **Bloomsbury**

Every room is different in this attractive, air-conditioned, 18th-century town-house hotel near the British Museum. *See map p. 116. 24 Bloomsbury St., WC1B 3QJ.* ☎ *020/7636-3735. Fax: 020/7636-3045.* www.morganhotel.co.uk.

One Aldwych
$$$$$ **The Strand**

Super-chic and super-comfortable, this high-style West End hotel is known for its innovative modern design. *See map p. 116. 1 Aldwych, WC2B 4RH.* ☎ *020/7300-1000. Fax: 020/7300-1001.* www.onealdwych.com.

Rushmore Hotel
$ **Earl's Court**

This gracious town-house hotel is comfortable and well designed, with many special decorative touches. *See map p. 118. 11 Trebovir Rd., SW5 9LS.* ☎ *020/7370-3839. Fax: 020/7370-0274.* www.rushmore-hotel.co.uk.

St. Martin's Lane
$$$$–$$$$$ **Piccadilly Circus**

Developed by hotelier Ian Schrager, St. Martin's Lane appeals to those into trendy high design. *See map p. 116. 45 St. Martin's Lane, WC2N 4HX.* ☎ *020/ 7300-5500. Fax: 020/7300-5501.* http://stmartinslane.com.

Index of Accommodations by Neighborhood

Bayswater
Byron Hotel ($$)
Royal Lancaster ($–$$$$$)

Belgravia
B+B Belgravia ($$)

Bloomsbury
Grange Blooms Hotel ($$–$$$)
Harlingford Hotel ($$)
Imperial Hotel ($)
Jenkins Hotel ($)
The Montague ($$$$–$$$$$)
Morgan Hotel ($$)
St. Margaret's Hotel ($)

Chelsea
Cadogan Hotel ($$$$$)

Covent Garden
Covent Garden Hotel ($$$$$)
Fielding Hotel ($$)

Earl's Court
Kensington International Inn ($$)
Rushmore Hotel ($)
Twenty Nevern Square ($$$)

Kensington
Avonmore Hotel ($)
The Vicarage Hotel ($–$$)

Knightsbridge
Claverley Hotel ($$–$$$$)

Marylebone
Bryanston Court Hotel ($$)
Dorset Square Hotel ($$$$–$$$$$)
Durrants Hotel ($$$)
Hart House Hotel ($$)
Hotel La Place ($$)
Landmark London ($$$–$$$$$)

Langham Hotel ($$$$$)
Minotel Wigmore Court Hotel ($)

Mayfair
Park Lane Sheraton Hotel ($$$–$$$$)

Notting Hill
The Abbey Court ($$–$$$$)
Comfort Inn Notting Hill ($$)
Gate Hotel ($)
The Lennox ($$$)

Paddington
Fairways Hotel ($)
Mitre House Hotel ($)
Rhodes Hotel ($)
Stylotel ($)

Piccadilly Circus
St. Martin's Lane ($$$$–$$$$$)

Shoreditch
The Hoxton ($–$$)

Soho
Hazlitt's ($$$$–$$$$$)

South Kensington
Aster House ($$$–$$$$)
Astons Apartments ($–$$)
The Cranley ($$$–$$$$)
The Gallery ($$–$$$)
The Gore ($$$–$$$$$)
Grange Strathmore Hotel ($$–$$$)
Hotel 167 ($–$$)
Milestone Hotel ($$$$$)
Number Sixteen ($$$–$$$$)
Regency Hotel ($–$$$)

St. James's
Dukes Hotel ($$$$–$$$$$)
22 Jermyn Street ($$$$)

Southwark
London Bridge Hotel ($–$$$)

The Strand
One Aldwych ($$$$$)

Westminster and Victoria
Cartref House ($)
Ebury House ($)
41 ($$$$)
Goring Hotel ($$$–$$$$)
Lime Tree Hotel ($$)
Luna & Simone Hotel ($)
Winchester Hotel ($)

Index of Accommodations by Price

$

Astons Apartments (South Kensington)
Avonmore Hotel (Kensington)
Cartref House (Westminster and Victoria)
Ebury House (Westminster and Victoria)
Fairways Hotel (Paddington)
Gate Hotel (Notting Hill)
Harlingford Hotel (Bloomsbury)
Hotel 167 (South Kensington)
The Hoxton (Shoreditch)
Imperial Hotel (Bloomsbury)
Jenkins Hotel (Bloomsbury)
London Bridge Hotel (Southwark)
Luna & Simone Hotel (Westminster and Victoria)
Minotel Wigmore Court Hotel (Marylebone)
Mitre House Hotel (Paddington)
Regency Hotel (South Kensington)
Rhodes Hotel (Paddington)
Royal Lancaster (Bayswater)
Rushmore Hotel (Earl's Court)
St. Margaret's Hotel (Bloomsbury)
Stylotel (Paddington)
The Vicarage Hotel (Kensington)
Winchester Hotel (Westminster and Victoria)

$$

The Abbey Court (Notting Hill)
Aster House (South Kensington)
Astons Apartments (South Kensington)
B+B Belgravia (Belgravia)
Bryanston Court Hotel (Marylebone)
Byron Hotel (Bayswater)
Claverley Hotel (Knightsbridge)
Comfort Inn Notting Hill (Notting Hill)
Fielding Hotel (Covent Garden)
The Gallery (South Kensington)
Grange Blooms Hotel (Bloomsbury)
Grange Strathmore Hotel (South Kensington)
Harlingford Hotel (Bloomsbury)
Hart House Hotel (Marylebone)
Hotel La Place (Marylebone)
Hotel 167 (South Kensington)
The Hoxton (Shoreditch)
Kensington International Inn (Earl's Court)
Lime Tree Hotel (Westminster and Victoria)
London Bridge Hotel (Southwark)
Morgan Hotel (Bloomsbury)
Royal Lancaster (Bayswater)
Regency Hotel (South Kensington)
The Vicarage Hotel (Kensington)

$$$

The Abbey Court (Notting Hill)
Aster House (South Kensington)
Claverley Hotel (Knightsbridge)
The Cranley (South Kensington)
Durrants Hotel (Marylebone)
The Gallery (South Kensington)
The Gore (South Kensington)
Goring Hotel (Westminster and Victoria)
Grange Blooms Hotel (Bloomsbury)

Grange Strathmore Hotel (South Kensington)
Landmark London (Marylebone)
London Bridge Hotel (Southwark)
Number Sixteen (South Kensington)
Park Lane Sheraton Hotel (Mayfair)
The Lennox (Notting Hill)
Regency Hotel (South Kensington)
Royal Lancaster (Bayswater)
Twenty Nevern Square (Earl's Court)

$$$$

The Abbey Court (Notting Hill)
Aster House (South Kensington)
Claverley Hotel (Knightsbridge)
The Cranley (South Kensington)
Dorset Square Hotel (Marylebone)
Dukes Hotel (St. James's)
41 (Westminster and Victoria)
The Gore (South Kensington)
Goring Hotel (Westminster and Victoria)
Hazlitt's (Soho)

Landmark London (Marylebone)
The Montague (Bloomsbury)
Number Sixteen (South Kensington)
Park Lane Sheraton Hotel (Mayfair)
Royal Lancaster (Bayswater)
St. Martin's Lane (Piccadilly Circus)
22 Jermyn Street (St. James's)

$$$$$

Cadogan Hotel (Chelsea)
Covent Garden Hotel (Covent Garden)
Dorset Square Hotel (Marylebone)
Dukes Hotel (St. James's)
The Gore (South Kensington)
Hazlitt's (Soho)
Landmark London (Marylebone)
Langham Hotel (Marylebone)
Milestone Hotel (South Kensington)
The Montague (Bloomsbury)
One Aldwych (The Strand)
Royal Lancaster (Bayswater)
St. Martin's Lane (Piccadilly Circus)

Chapter 10

Dining and Snacking in London

*L*ondon's dining scene now offers a vast array of culinary choices; more than 5,700 restaurants prepare the cuisines of more than 60 countries. But you can still find traditional English dishes in London: Yorkshire pudding, fish and chips, or *bangers and mash* (sausages and mashed potatoes). So if you want to sample the old cuisine, you won't be disappointed. This chapter explains what you need to know about new trends; traditional, modern, and ethnic cuisines; spots favored by locals; and finding a bargain. I list my favorite London dining spots, too.

For a glossary of English food terms, see the Cheat Sheet at the beginning of this book.

Getting the Dish on the Local Scene

London is now considered one of the food capitals of the world, and its restaurant scene is a volatile one. To be trendy and talked about, a London restaurant must have a celebrity owner, a celebrity chef, a solid reputation, a great view, a chic location, and/or an unmistakable ambience — and, of course, memorable food helps, too. But two trends are worth noting: The days of Sir Terence Conran's mega-eateries — places that held hundreds of diners — are pretty much over; and, in a city where even an ordinary meal can easily cost £25 ($50), Londoners are looking more and more toward ethnic foods and restaurants that don't charge exorbitant prices.

Multicultural London is always in the midst of culinary evolution. The local food horizon expanded as the postwar generation began to travel and experience new cuisines outside England, and as "exotic" foods and spices became more readily available in the English markets.

"Plain English cooking" —hearty, old-fashioned, and sometimes considered dull — is certainly still prevalent in London, and the style is even enjoying renewed interest and respect. The best traditional dishes — game, lamb, meat and fish pies, and roast beef with Yorkshire pudding — are readily available. Modern British cuisine takes old standards and deliciously reinvents them with foreign influences and ingredients, mostly from France (sauces), the Mediterranean (olive oil, oregano, and garlic), and northern Italy (pasta, polenta, and risotto). Besides Modern British, London foodies continue to favor classic French and Italian cuisines. (For more on English cooking, see Chapter 2.)

Indian cooking has been a favorite ethnic food for some time. In fact, curry is now considered a "national" dish. London is filled with Indian restaurants (about 1,500 of them) serving curries and dishes cooked in clay tandoori pots. *Balti,* a thick curry from Pakistan, is one of the more recent ethnic must-try dishes in London. Other new influences making their way into Modern British cooking come from Thailand and Morocco.

If you want to dine in a restaurant, reserving a table is always a good idea. At all but the smartest London restaurants, you can usually get a table on fairly short notice during the week, especially if you're willing to dine before 7 p.m. or after 9 p.m.

With the passage of the new nonsmoking ordinances of 2007, you can now be assured that your meal in any London restaurant and pub will be smoke-free.

Discovering the top dining areas

London offers a mouth-watering mix of restaurants; you can enjoy a wide variety of foods throughout the city. Soho and neighboring Covent Garden offer the most choices in the West End, with African, British, Caribbean, Eastern European, French, Italian, Japanese, Korean, Middle Eastern, Modern European, Mongolian, North American, South American, Spanish, Thai, Turkish, and vegetarian all represented. South Kensington makes up another eclectic grab bag of culinary choices.

Unlike some other large cities, ethnic restaurants aren't grouped together within specific areas of Central London. However, several Chinese restaurants are clustered along Lisle, Wardour, and Gerrard streets in Soho's Chinatown. And Notting Hill has long been a standby for low-price Indian and Caribbean restaurants.

Eating with the locals

Londoners, like the residents in any large city, have their favorite neighborhood eateries. Pubs, cafes, and wine bars are places where locals go for casual meals that aren't as expensive as restaurants.

Ordering up pub grub

If you're not into ethnic dining, then pubs are your best bet for getting a good meal for a low price. Until fairly recently, pub food was generally traditional and down to earth: meat pies and *mash* (mashed potatoes), fish and chips, *mixed grills* (sausages and a chop or cutlet), salads, sandwiches, and the famous *ploughman's lunch* (bread and cheese, or pâté). But lately, a multi-ethnic variety of current food faves has changed the cooking in many a pub kitchen, and you're now just as likely to encounter curries and kebabs as fish and chips. Pub food may be prepackaged and frozen and then microwaved. However, more and more pubs resemble casual restaurants. A new genre of pub restaurants exists called *gastropubs,* where the cooking is fresher, more adventurous, and better prepared than at traditional pubs.

Pubs are drop-in places, and finding a table at lunchtime isn't always easy. Pubs don't accept reservations. Usually, you order your food from the serving counter and your drinks from the bar, and then seat yourself. Sometimes you get table service. Pub grub is generally washed down with beer, the British national drink. Draft beer in Britain is served at room temperature, as are most soft drinks. Bottled imported beer, served cold, is generally available but more expensive.

Unless a pub has a special *children's certificate,* kids under 14 are allowed only into the gardens and separate family rooms. The legal drinking age in the United Kingdom is 18, although restaurants can serve beer or cider to kids over 16 who order a meal.

Wining and dining at wine bars

Londoners may love to knock back a pint of beer at their local pub, but when it comes to restaurant dining, wine is the favored accompaniment. You can get wine in a pub, but the choices will be limited. Wine bars, on the other hand, are dedicated to good food and good grape, most of it imported from France, Australia, and South America. Wine bars are more upscale than pubs. Like pubs, wine bars don't permit children under 14, except in gardens or family rooms. Be aware that a meal in a wine bar costs more than a similar meal in a pub.

Kicking back at cafes

London's cafes generally serve light, inexpensive food and offer limited menus. Most people enjoy a cup of coffee or pot of tea and a sandwich, but you'll also find pastas, salads, and burgers. The cakes and other sweets may tempt you, too.

Gays and lesbians on the lookout for low-priced meals in groovy gay-friendly environments flock to Soho's gay cafes and bars. These trendy hangouts serve good, reasonably priced meals and pay serious attention to décor.

Roast beef or royalty?

In a 2006 poll, adults in England, Scotland, Wales, and Northern Ireland were asked to come up with an icon that summed up "traditional England." The monarchy was the most popular choice at 48 percent. The runner-up was roast beef at 42 percent.

Trimming the Fat from Your Budget

If the thought of paying $50 for dinner tabs gives you heartburn, you can visit pubs, cafes, sandwich bars, and pizza places to get good, economical food. And, of course, you can find fast-food chains throughout the city. Another alternative: supermarkets, where you can buy take-away meals and dine in your hotel room or outdoors in one of London's beautiful parks. In addition, many of London's top restaurants offer *fixed-price meals* (also called *set-price* or *prix-fixe* meals), which allow you to order two to three courses from a limited menu for a set price that is cheaper than ordering the courses individually. Sometimes these bargains are called *pre-* or *post-theater menus,* and they're served only from about 5:30 to 7 p.m. and after 9:30 p.m. Wine is expensive, so forgo that if price is an issue. And try your splurge-dining at lunch, when prices are often one-third less than those at dinner and the food is the same. Remember that tap water (never iced) will be brought to your table only if you request it, and your glass will not be automatically refilled. If you order water, and don't specify tap water, you'll get bottled water (either still or "fizzy").

 Restaurants automatically add that annoying 17.5 percent value-added tax (VAT) to your tab. They may tack on a moderate cover charge for bread (even if you don't eat it), as well.

 Plenty of unwary tourists double-tip without realizing it. Some restaurants add a service charge to your bill and also have a tip area on the credit card receipt that you sign. Be aware that the words *service charge included* on a menu mean that a gratuity will automatically be added to your bill. When the bill arrives, you're not expected to leave any additional tip. If the menu says *service not included,* however, leave a tip of 10 percent to 15 percent for acceptable service.

 At the end of a meal, Americans ask for a "check," whereas Brits ask for the "bill."

London's Best Restaurants

As London is home to more than 5,700 restaurants, deciding which establishments to include in this chapter of my favorites was a monumental task. I try to cover as much of Central London as possible. If you want to get the flavor of merry old England, I include some of the oldest and most respected London restaurants serving traditional English food. For the more chic and trendy, I include restaurants that serve the best of Modern British cuisine, as well as hybrids of British/French and British/ Continental. For people on a budget — or those who just want to eat in a down-to-earth, amiable environment — I also review some of the best London pubs. All the establishments are easy to get to, and you can reach all of them by taking the Underground (Tube) system and perhaps walking a bit. For indexes of the restaurants by neighborhood, cuisine, and price, see the end of this chapter. For locations, refer to the maps in this chapter.

Each restaurant I review is given one to four dollar signs ($). The dollar signs indicate the average price of a meal, including an appetizer, entree, and nonalcoholic beverage. Table 10-1 lists the dollar amounts used for each dollar sign. Please bear in mind that if you order the most expensive entree and a bottle of wine, a $$ restaurant will become a $$$$ restaurant. On the other hand, if you order from a set-price menu, a $$$$ restaurant tab may dip down to $$.

Table 10-1	Key to Restaurant Dollar Signs
Dollar Sign(s)	*Price Range*
$	£13/$25 or less
$$	£13–£25/$26–$50
$$$	£26–£38/$51–$75
$$$$	£38/$75 and up

The Kid Friendly icon in front of a restaurant name indicates that the place is suitable for families with children. These restaurants welcome families and may offer a children's menu.

Note that restaurant prices in this chapter do not include the 17.5 percent value-added tax (VAT). Unfortunately, you can't avoid paying this extra expense.

The skinny on the beef

Sirloin, so the story goes, got its name from James I when he was a guest at Houghton Tower in Lancashire. When a succulent leg of beef was placed before him, he knighted it with his dagger, crying, "Arise, Sir Loin!"

Aubergine
$$$$ Chelsea FRENCH

You compete with celebrities, royalty, and commoners for the privilege of dining at this top-name restaurant, and you have to give your credit card number when booking and be prepared to pay £50 ($100) if you don't show. Every dish, from the fish and lighter Mediterranean-style choices to *assiette* of veal with watercress and artichokes, is a culinary achievement of the highest order, winning chef William Drabble a Michelin star. The celebrated cappuccino of white beans with grated truffle makes a perfect ending to a superb dining experience. Service is polished and efficient.

See map p. 152. 11 Park Walk, SW10. ☎ 020/7352-3449. Reservations essential. Tube: Sloane Square (then a 10-minute walk southwest on King's Road to Park Walk and Fulham Road; or bus 11, 19, 22, or 211 southwest on King's Road from the Tube station). Fixed-price menu: Lunch £34 ($68), dinner £64–£77 ($128–$154). AE, DC, MC, V. Open: Mon–Fri noon to 2:15 p.m., Mon–Sat 7–11 p.m.

Boxwood Café
$$$ Knightsbridge MODERN BRITISH

This may be the most stylish kid-friendly restaurant in London, but grown-ups will find plenty of comforting delights on the menu, too. Created by culinary superstar Gordon Ramsay, Boxwood Café is chic without being fussy, and the same goes for the food, which emphasizes fresh and healthy dishes ranging from fresh steamed fish to glazed pea-and-leek tart, roast chicken salad, wine-braised veal, and steaks.

See map p. 152. In the Berkeley Hotel, Wilton Place, SW1. ☎ 020/7235-1010. www.gordonramsay.com/boxwoodcafe. *Reservations recommended. Tube: Knightsbridge (then a 5-minute walk east on Brompton Road). Main courses: £9–£25 ($18–$50); fixed-price lunch £21 ($42); fixed-price dinner £55 ($110); children's menu £7.50 ($15). AE, DISC, MC, V. Open: Mon–Fri noon to 3 p.m., Sat–Sun noon to 4 p.m., daily 6–11 p.m.*

Brasserie St. Quentin
$$ South Kensington FRENCH

London's most authentic-looking French brasserie, St. Quentin attracts many people in the city's French community (a positive sign for a French restaurant outside of France). Mirrors and crystal chandeliers add a touch of elegance. The brasserie has excellent-value fixed-price meals, two or three courses, both at lunch and pre-theater. These menus offer a blend of classic and updated French fare, from shoulder of lamb with root vegetables to poached halibut, chicken breast with lemon and thyme, and fish soup. Vegetarian options include artichoke fondant with seasonal vegetables, spinach ravioli, and warm leek salad.

See map p. 152. 243 Brompton Rd., SW3. ☎ 020/7589-8005. www.brasserie stquentin.co.uk. *Reservations required. Tube: South Kensington (then a 5-minute walk east on Brompton Road). Main courses: £13–£24 ($26–$48); fixed-price menus (noon to 7:30 p.m.) £16–£18 ($32–$36). AE, DC, MC, V. Open: Daily noon to 3 p.m., Mon–Sat 6–11:30 p.m., Sun 6:30–10:30 p.m.*

Restaurants in and around the City

Mosaique **1**
Oxo Tower Brasserie **3**
Ye Olde Cheshire Cheese **2**

Canteen **6**
Dickens Inn by the Tower **5**
The Founders Arms **4**

Restaurants in Westminster and Victoria

Capri Sandwich Bar **3**
Ebury Wine Bar &
Restaurant **1**
Ken Lo's Memories
of China **2**
The Lanesborough **5**
Seafresh Fish
Restaurant **4**

Restaurants in the West End

Brown's Hotel **10**
Cafe in the Crypt **17**
Café Parlour at Sketch **9**
Cigala **32**
Claridge's **8**
Criterion Bar & Grill **20**
Ed's Easy Diner **25**
Food for thought **38**
Fortnum & Mason **13**
Fryer's Delight **33**
The Gay Hussar **24**
Giovanni's Sandwich Bar **3**
Golden Hind **6**
Gourmet Pizza Company **44**
Hard Rock Cafe **11**
Itsu **23**
The Ivy **29**
Joe Allen **41**
Langan's Bistro **4**
L'Osteria 57 **35**
Mash **7**
Mela **30**
Mildred's **22**
Moro **36**
Mosaique **34**
Muffinski's **19**
The Museum Tavern **31**
North Sea Fish Restaurant **2**
Pâtisserie Cappucetto **26**
Pâtisserie Deux Amis **1**
Pâtisserie Valerie **12, 27**
Porter's English Restaurant **39**
Pret à Manger **18**
Richoux **14**
Rock & Sole Plaice **37**
R.S. Hispaniola **43**
Rules **40**
Simpson's-in-the-Strand **42**
St. James's **13**
The Stockpot **16, 28**
Veeraswamy **15**
Wagamama Noodle Bar **21**

Restaurants from Knightsbridge to Earl's Court

Aubergine **2**

Boxwood Café **13**

Brasserie St. Quentin **8**

Chelsea Kitchen **7**

Harrods Georgian Restaurant **9**

Harvey Nichols **11**

Itsu **6**

Lanesborough **14**

Mona Lisa **3**

Noor Jahan **1**

KENSINGTON GARDENS

HYDE PARK CORNER

KNIGHTSBRIDGE

Kensington Rd.

Knightsbridge

KNIGHTSBRIDGE

Rd.

Prince's Gardens

Enismore Gardens

Rutland Gate

Montpelier St.

Cheval Pl.

Brompton Rd.

Hans Cr.

Hans Rd.

Basil St.

Pavilion Road

Sloane St.

Pont Street

Lowndes Square

Kinnerton St.

Wilton Cres.

Belgrave Square

Belgrave Pl.

Exhibition Rd.

Garden Mews

Brompton Square

Beauchamp Place

Walton St.

Cadogan Lane

Cadogan Place

Chesham St.

Chesham Pl.

Lyall St.

King's Rd.

Victoria & Albert Museum

Cromwell Rd.

Thurloe Place

Thurloe Square

Thurloe

Brompton Rd.

Egerton Gdns.

Hasker St.

Milner St.

Cadogan Square

Pavilion Rd.

Cadogan Gdns.

Ellis St.

Eaton Terrace

Bourne

SOUTH KENSINGTON

Pelham St.

Pelham Crescent

Draycott Avenue

Sloane Avenue

Cadogan St.

Draycott Place

SLOANE SQUARE

BELGRAVIA

Onslow Square

Sumner Pl.

Fulham Rd.

Ixworth Place

Elystan St.

Elystan Place

King's Rd.

Lower Sloane

Pimlico Rd.

Cale St.

Astell St.

CHELSEA

Smith St.

Chelsea Bridge Rd.

Chelsea Square

Dovehouse St.

Sydney St.

King's Rd.

Radnor Walk

Tedworth Square

Christchurch St.

Royal Hospital Rd.

West St.

RANELAGH GARDENS

Old Church St.

Glebe Place

Oakley St.

Flood St.

Chelsea Manor St.

Tite St.

0 — 1/4 mi
0 — 1/4 km

N

The Oratory **5**
Pig's Ear **4**
Richoux **10**
Zafferano **12**

(i) Information
⊖ Tube stop

Restaurants from Marylebone to Notting Hill

Clarke's **4**
Costas Fish Restaurant **2**
Geales **1**
Kensington Palace Orangery **3**
Langan's Bistro **7**

Maggie Jones's **5**
Pâtisserie Valerie **8**
Richoux **10**
Sea-Shell **6**
Suze in Mayfair **9**

Cafe in the Crypt
$ Piccadilly Circus and Leicester Square BRITISH

Eating in a crypt may not be everyone's idea of fun, but eating in this crypt — below St. Martin's-in-the-Fields church on Trafalgar Square — is an inexpensive London dining experience that you won't forget. The food is basic but good, served cafeteria-style. Choose from a big salad bar; traditional main courses, such as shepherd's pie; filled rolls; and hearty soups. One fixture is that most traditional of British desserts, *bread-and-butter pudding* (bread soaked in eggs and milk with currants or sultanas and then oven-baked). The cavernous, candlelit room with its stone pillars and gravestones is wonderfully atmospheric. This is also a good place to come for afternoon tea.

See map p. 150. St. Martin-in-the-Fields, Duncannon St., WC2. ☎ 020/7839-4342. Tube: Charing Cross (then a 3-minute walk west to Trafalgar Square). Main courses: £5.95–£7.50 ($12–$15); fixed-price meal £5.25 ($11), afternoon tea £4.95 ($10). No credit cards. Open: Mon–Sat 11:30 a.m.–7:30 p.m., Thurs–Sat 11:30 a.m.–10:15 p.m., Sun noon to 5 p.m.

Canteen
$–$$ Spitalfields TRADITIONAL BRITISH

Canteen looks so hip and modern you might expect some kind of flashy, faddy cuisine to be on the menu. Wrong. This is classic English cooking, almost like you would have gotten in a cafeteria 20 years ago. All-day breakfasts (including toasted crumpets), light dishes (like a leek-and-cheese tart), and sturdier main courses (rib-eye steak and chips) are available. You can even get a glass of Horlick's malted milk. This is great stop-in spot if you're prowling around the new Spitalfields Market in the East End.

See map p. 148. 2 Crispin Place (off Brushfield Street), E1. ☎ 0845/686-1122. www.canteen.co.uk. *Tube: Aldgate East (then a 10-minute walk north on Commercial Street and south on Shoreditch High Street). Main courses: £7–£12 ($14–$24). AE, MC, V. Open: Mon–Fri 11 a.m.–10 p.m., Sat–Sun 9 a.m.–10 p.m.*

Chelsea Kitchen
$ Chelsea INTERNATIONAL

A London institution, Chelsea Kitchen has been serving locals and drop-ins since 1961 and hasn't changed much since — except that now it's surrounded by a sea of trendy, expensive eateries. At this simple place with a dinerlike atmosphere, both the plates and the crowds move fast. Menu staples include leek-and-potato soup, chicken parmigiana, spaghetti Bolognese, omelets, burgers, goulash, and lamb chops. Kids enjoy the casual atmosphere and simple foods. Far from fancy, but still good.

See map p. 152. 98 King's Rd. (off Sloane Square), SW3. ☎ 020/7589-1330. Reservations recommended. Tube: Sloane Square (the restaurant is at the beginning of King's Road just west of the square). Main courses: £4–£7 ($8–$14); fixed-price menu £6–£7 ($12–$14). No credit cards. Open: Mon–Sat 8 a.m.–11:45 p.m., Sun 9 a.m.–11:45 p.m.

Cigala
$$ Bloomsbury SPANISH

This hip, clean-lined, Spanish-inspired restaurant serves great tapas. Order two or three tapas per person and then share. Some possibilities include *chorizo* (sausage with hot paprika sauce), oak-smoked cured beef, marinated sardines, wind-dried tuna, olives, and scrambled eggs with artichokes. At lunch or dinner, you may prefer to begin with something like grilled razor clams, and follow up with an entree of pork belly with beans. The vegetarian stew is bland and not particularly memorable, but the paella, which requires 30 minutes of preparation, is delectable.

See map p. 150. 54 Lamb's Conduit St., WC1N 3LW. ☎ 020/7405-1717. www.cigala. co.uk. *Tube: Holborn (then a 7-minute walk east on High Holborn and north on Red Lion Street, which becomes Lamb's Conduit when you cross Theobald's Road). Main courses: £11–£20 ($22–$40); tapas £2–£8 ($4–$16); fixed-price lunch Mon–Fri £16–£19 ($32–$38), fixed-price lunch Sun £11 ($22). AE, MC, V. Open: Mon–Fri noon to 10:45 p.m., Sat 12:30–10:45 p.m., Sun noon to 9:45 p.m.*

Clarke's
$$$ Notting Hill MODERN EUROPEAN

This bright modern restaurant, owned by chef Sally Clarke, has had a loyal following since opening in the 1980s. The menu changes daily but always emphasizes British produce and California-style charcoal-grilled foods with herbs and organically grown vegetables. A typical meal may include an appetizer of grilled goat cheese *crostini* with fresh tomato chutney; an entree of wild sea bass roasted with tarragon and lemon hollandaise; followed by an assortment of cheeses with oatmeal biscuits and celery, plus warm bitter chocolate pudding with whipped cream and raspberries. There's a fixed-price dinner menu.

See map p. 154. 124 Kensington Church St., W8. ☎ 020/7221-9225. Reservations essential. Tube: Notting Hill Gate (then a 5-minute walk south on Kensington Church Street). Main courses: Fixed-price lunch £14–£16 ($28–$32), fixed-price dinner £40–£50 ($80–$100). AE, DC, MC, V. Open: Mon–Fri 12:30–2 p.m., Tues–Sat 5:30–11:30 p.m.

Criterion Bar & Grill
$$–$$$ Piccadilly Circus and Leicester Square BRITISH/FRENCH

It's almost worth coming to the Criterion just to see its Byzantine palace interior with gold-vaulted ceiling. The food — a mixture of modern French and British standards — doesn't quite match the grandeur of the décor, but it's generally quite good. You can order Brit faves like haddock or sausages, or French faves like slow-roast duck with applesauce or steak au poivre. This place is smack-dab on Piccadilly Circus, so it's wonderfully convenient. The fixed-price lunches and dinners are a great deal.

See map p. 150. 224 Piccadilly, W1. ☎ 020/7930-0488. Reservations recommended. Tube: Piccadilly Circus (the restaurant is right on Piccadilly Circus). Main courses: £11–£23 ($22–$46); fixed-price lunch and pre-theater dinner 5:30–7 p.m. £15–£18 ($30–$36). AE, DC, MC, V. Open: Daily noon to 2:30 p.m., Mon–Sat 5:30–11:30 p.m.

Dickens Inn by the Tower
$-$$ The City   TRADITIONAL/MODERN BRITISH

This former spice warehouse is now a three-story restaurant with sweeping Thames and Tower Bridge views. The ground-floor Tavern Bar serves a variety of snacks, sandwiches, and traditional pub food. Pizza on the Dock, a floor above and a good spot for families, offers four sizes of pizza. Grill on the Dock, on the top floor, is a relatively formal dining room serving Modern British cuisine; specials include steaks and a variety of charcoal-grilled dishes.

See map p. 148. St. Katharine's Dock (near the Tower of London), E1. ☎ *020/7488-2208.* www.dickensinn.co.uk. *Reservations recommended. Tube: Tower Hill (then a 10-minute walk east on Tower Hill East and south on St. Katharine's Street to St. Katharine's Way). Main courses: Grill on the Dock £15–£21 ($30–$42); Tavern Bar £3.50–£7.50 ($7–$15); Pizza on the Dock £9–£15 ($18–$30). AE, DC, MC, V. Open: Grill on the Dock daily noon to 3 p.m. and 6:30–10:30 p.m.; Tavern Bar food served daily 11 a.m.–3 p.m.; Pizza on the Dock daily noon to 10 p.m.*

Ebury Wine Bar & Restaurant
$$ Westminster and Victoria   MODERN BRITISH/INTERNATIONAL

This popular wine bar offers a surprisingly good and varied menu and excellent wines. The narrow, woodsy, attractive interior is reminiscent of a Paris bistro. In addition to steaks, the oft-changing menu features traditional dishes and specials such as pork mignon with roasted sweet potato mash, and ostrich steak with balsamic cream sauce. It has added a bar menu, so you can also stop in for a lamb kebab, a club sandwich, or a burger.

See map p. 149. 139 Ebury St., SW1. ☎ *020/7730-5447.* www.eburywinebar.co.uk. *Reservations recommended. Tube: Victoria (then a 10-minute walk west on Belgrave Street and south on Ebury Street). Main courses: £10–£16 ($20–$32); fixed-price lunch and pre-theater dinner £14–£18 ($28–$36); bar menu £5–£8.50 ($10–$17). Cover: £2 ($4). AE, DC, MC, V. Open: Daily noon to 2:45 p.m. and 6–10 p.m.*

Ed's Easy Diner
$ Soho   NORTH AMERICAN

This replica of an old American diner, where customers perch on stools at a wraparound counter and listen to oldies blaring from the jukebox, is a safe bet for the kids. A bit more authentic than the version at the Pepsi Trocadero in Piccadilly Circus, this Ed's still attracts a fair share of teens. If you've a yen for cholesterol-laden food, chow down on Ed's big burgers with fries or onion rings, or giant kosher weenies slathered with cheddar cheese. On the lighter side, you can get a veggie burger, tuna salad, or a chicken Caesar salad.

See map p. 150. 12 Moor St. (off Cambridge Circus), W1. ☎ *020/7439-1955.* www.edseasydiner.co.uk. *Tube: Leicester Square (then a 5-minute walk north on Charing Cross Road and west on Moor Street). Main courses: £5–£8 ($10–$16). MC, V. Open: Mon–Thurs 11:30 a.m. to midnight, Fri and Sat 11:30 a.m.–1 a.m., Sun 11:30 a.m.–11:30 p.m.*

Food for Thought
$ Covent Garden   VEGETARIAN

Covent Garden offers a plethora of expensive restaurants for meat-eaters, so this old-fashioned basement hole-in-the-wall with cafeteria-style service is a pleasant and welcome alternative. The menu changes constantly, but the daily soup (such as carrot and fresh coriander) is always a treat, and the main courses can include a sweet and tangy Jamaican curry, Italian bean casserole, and cannelloni *ripieni* (stuffed with eggplant), as well as daily quiche and salad specials. The desserts — think apple-and-rhubarb crumble and fruit with yogurt — are simple and satisfying.

See map p. 150. 31 Neal St., WC2. ☎ *020/7836-0239. Reservations not accepted. Tube: Covent Garden (then a 2-minute walk north on Neal Street). Main courses: £4–£7 ($8–$14). No credit cards. Open: Mon–Sat noon to 8:30 p.m., Sun noon to 5 p.m.*

Fortnum & Mason
$$ St. James's   TRADITIONAL BRITISH

Fortnum & Mason, a posh, legendary London store that's a "purveyor to the queen" and famous for its food section (see Chapter 12), also has three restaurants. The mezzanine-level **Patio** is a good lunch spot, with a menu that offers an assortment of pricey sandwiches and main courses, including hot and cold pies (steak and kidney, curried fish and banana, chicken, and game) and *Welsh rarebit* (thick melted cheese poured over toast) prepared with Guinness stout. The lower-level **Fountain** offers breakfast and lunch, and the fourth-floor **St. James's** serves lunch and afternoon tea. The more well-heeled dine at St. James's, where the menu is traditionally British: For starters, try the *kipper* (smoked herring) mousse or potato and Stilton brûlée; main courses include pies and roast rib of Scottish beef. Although crowded with tourists, these three establishments remain pleasant places where you can get a good meal and a glimpse of the fading Empire. The Fountain and Patio are good places to dine with a family; ice-cream sundaes are a specialty.

See map p. 150. 181 Piccadilly, W1. ☎ *020/7734-8040. Reservations accepted for St. James's only. Tube: Piccadilly Circus (then a 5-minute walk west on Piccadilly). Main courses: Lunch £9–£24 ($18–$48); fixed-price menus £20–£37 ($40–$74). AE, DC, MC, V. Open: St. James's and the Patio Tues–Sat 9:30 a.m.–5:30 p.m., Fountain Mon–Sat 8:30 a.m.–7:45 p.m.*

The Founders Arms
$ South Bank   MODERN BRITISH

This modern pub/restaurant sits right on the Thames, a few minutes' walk east from the South Bank Centre or west from the new Tate Modern and Shakespeare's Globe. You can sit inside or out by the water. Although some British pub favorites such as *bangers and mash* (sausages and mashed potatoes), game pie, and fish and chips are available, other dishes are more ambitious. Pasta, fresh fish, and other daily specials are listed on a chalkboard. Or you can just get a sandwich.

See map p. 148. 52 Hopton St., SE1. ☎ 020/7928-1899. www.foundersarms. co.uk. *Tube: Waterloo (then a 10-minute walk north along the Thames Path in front of the National Theatre). Main courses: £7.50–£12 ($15–$24). AE, MC, V. Open: Mon–Thurs 10 a.m.–11 p.m., Fri 10 a.m. to midnight, Sat–Sun 9 a.m.–11 p.m.*

The Gay Hussar
$$–$$$ Soho   HUNGARIAN

The Gay Hussar is considered to be one of the best Hungarian restaurants outside Hungary. The restaurant serves undeniably authentic Hungarian comfort food: chilled wild-cherry soup, caraway potatoes, cabbage stuffed with minced veal and rice, tender chicken served in mild paprika sauce with cucumber salad and noodles, and, of course, veal goulash with egg dumplings. The portions are large, but try to save room for the poppyseed strudel or the walnut pancakes for dessert.

See map p. 150. 2 Greek St. (off Soho Square), W1. ☎ 020/7437-0973. www. gayhussar.co.uk. *Reservations recommended. Tube: Tottenham Court (then a 2-minute walk west on Oxford Street and south on Soho Street; Greek Street is at the southeast corner of Soho Square). Main courses: £9.50–£17 ($19–$34); fixed-price lunch menus £17–£19 ($34–$38). AE, DC, MC, V. Open: Mon–Sat 12:15–2:30 p.m. and 5:30–10:45 p.m.*

Gourmet Pizza Company
$ Southwark   PIZZA/PASTA

This large, family-friendly restaurant on the Thames inhabits what looks like a temporary building, but the location is great and it provides an economical meal if you're exploring the South Bank. You can choose from 20 varieties of pizza — everything from a B.L.T. to one with Cajun chicken and prawns. About half the choices are vegetarian. The crusts are light and crispy, and the toppings are fresh and flavorful. Pasta dishes are also available.

See map p. 150. Upper Ground, Gabriel's Wharf SE7. ☎ 020/7928-3188. Tube: Blackfriars (then a 10-minute walk across Blackfriars Bridge and west along the river). Main courses: Pizzas £6–£10 ($12–$20), pastas £8–£11 ($16–$22). AE, DC, MC, V. Open: Daily noon to 11:30 p.m.*

Hard Rock Cafe
$$ Mayfair   NORTH AMERICAN

This restaurant is one of a worldwide chain of rock-'n'-roll/American-road-side-diner-themed restaurants. Teens enjoy the rock memorabilia and loud music as well as the burgers and shakes. Tasty vegetarian dishes are available, too. The portions are generous, and main dishes include salad and fries or baked potato. Consider the homemade apple pie if you have room for dessert. Be prepared to stand in line on weekend evenings and pay fairly outrageous prices for the experience.

See map p. 150. 150 Old Park Lane, W1. ☎ *020/7629-0382.* www.hardrock.com. *Tube: Hyde Park Corner (take the Park Lane exit; Old Park Lane is just to the east of Park Lane). Main courses: £8.50–£15 ($17–$30). AE, MC, V. Open: Sun–Thurs 11:30 a.m. to midnight, Fri–Sat 11:30 a.m.–1 a.m.*

Itsu
$ Soho JAPANESE

Itsu is popular, and with good reason: It serves better-than-average Japanese food at bargain prices. The cool, colorful interior is always abuzz, and especially crowded at lunchtime. Sushi and pan-Asian dishes trundle past on a conveyer belt, so if something looks good, nab it. The seafood is always fresh; you can also get dishes like seared beef with a sweet dipping sauce. Another branch is located in Soho at 103 Wardour St., W1 (☎ **020/ 7479-4790**).

See map p. 150. 118 Draycott Ave., SW3. ☎ *020/7479-2400.* www.itsu.co.uk. *Tube: South Kensington (then a 5-minute walk east on Pelham Street to Brompton Road and Draycott Avenue). Main courses: £2–£7 ($4–$14). AE, DC, MC, V. Open: Mon–Sat noon to 11 p.m., Sun noon to 10 p.m.*

The Ivy
$$$–$$$$ Soho BRITISH/FRENCH

Are you looking for a hip place to dine after enjoying the theater? The Ivy, with its 1930s look, tiny bar, glamour-scene crowd, and later-than-usual hours, fits the bill. The cooking features skillful preparations of fresh ingredients, with such popular dishes as white asparagus with sea kale and truffle butter, roast chicken and stuffing, and roast beef and potatoes. You can also enjoy lamb sweetbreads with broad beans and peas in gravy, cod on saffron risotto, and traditional English desserts, such as sticky toffee and caramelized bread-and-butter pudding. You need to book as far in advance as possible for this top dining spot.

See map p. 150. 1–5 West St., WC2. ☎ *020/7836-4751.* www.the-ivy.co.uk. *Reservations required. Tube: Leicester Square (then a 5-minute walk north on Charing Cross Road; West Street is at the southeastern end of Cambridge Circus). Main courses: £10–£39 ($20–$78); fixed-price menu (Sat–Sun lunch) £22 ($44). AE, DC, MC, V. Open: Daily noon to 3 p.m. and 5:30 p.m. to midnight.*

Joe Allen
$$ Covent Garden NORTH AMERICAN

Joe Allen is a low-profile place on a back street in Covent Garden. Its crowded dining room with checkered tablecloths is the sort of place where actors like to come after a performance to scarf down chili con carne or gnaw on barbecued ribs. The dependable food includes American classics with some international twists, and the set menu is a real value: After a starter (maybe *smoked haddock vichyssoise,* a cold soup with fish), you can choose main courses such as pan-fried pork loin, Cajun chicken breast, and grilled lamb cutlets. If you're a tad homesick, try a burger, a brownie, and a Coke for consolation. Come before the show for the best prices; come after the show for potential star-gazing.

See map p. 150. 13 Exeter St., WC2. ☎ *020/7836-0651.* www.joeallenrestaurant. com. *Reservations recommended. Tube: Covent Garden (then a 5-minute walk south past the Market to Burleigh Street on the southeast corner of the Piazza and west on Exeter Street). Main courses: £9–£16 ($18–$32); fixed-price lunch (Mon–Fri noon to 3 p.m.) and pre-theater dinner (Mon–Sat 5–6:45 p.m.) £15–£17 ($30–$34), fixed-price Sun brunch £18–£20 ($36–$40). AE, MC, V. Open: Mon–Fri noon to 12:45 a.m., Sat 11:30 a.m.–12:45 a.m., Sun 11:30 a.m.–11:30 p.m.*

Ken Lo's Memories of China
$$$$ Westminster and Victoria   CHINESE

Founded by the late Ken Lo, author of more than 30 cookbooks and once the host of a TV cooking show, this restaurant is one of the better (and certainly one of the more expensive) pan-Chinese restaurants in London. The interior décor is appealingly minimalist, and the service is impeccable. Spanning broadly divergent regions of China, the ambitious menu features Cantonese quick-fried beef in oyster sauce, lobster with Szechuan pepper sauce, and "bang-bang chicken" (a Szechuan dish), among many others.

See map p. 149. 65–69 Ebury St. (near Victoria Station), SW1. ☎ *020/7730-7734.* www.memories-of-china.co.uk. *Reservations recommended. Tube: Victoria Station (then a 10-minute walk west on Belgrave Street and south on Ebury Street). Main courses: £12–£20 ($24–$40); fixed-price lunch £19–£22 ($38–$44), fixed-price dinner £30–£48 ($60–$96). AE, DC, MC, V. Open: Mon–Sat noon to 2:30 p.m., daily 7–11:15 p.m.*

Kensington Palace Orangery
$ Kensington   TRADITIONAL BRITISH/TEA/LIGHT LUNCH

Most folks come here for tea, which I highly recommend, but you can also get a light lunch. Dining in this vast, minimally decorated room where flowers grace the tables and a magnificent selection of desserts is on call, is quite pleasant. The meals are simple: a hearty ploughman's lunch of bread and cheese or fresh salads. But it's mostly afternoon tea that brings the crowds, and your tea can be as simple or extravagant as you wish. A kid's menu is available, too.

See map p. 154. Kensington Palace, Kensington Gardens, W8. ☎ *020/7376-0239. Tube: High Street Kensington (then a 10-minute walk east on Kensington High Street and north into Kensington Gardens; the Orangery is just beyond the palace). Main courses: £8–£12 ($16–$24); set tea £8–£17 ($16–$34). DC, MC, V. Open: Daily 10 a.m.–6 p.m., Nov–Feb until 5 p.m.*

Langan's Bistro
$$ Marylebone   BRITISH/FRENCH

The menu for this bistro is English with an underplayed (some may say underdeveloped) French influence. Behind a brightly colored storefront, the dining room is covered with clusters of Japanese parasols, rococo mirrors, paintings, and old photographs. Depending on the season, the fixed-price menu may start with goose liver parfait or smoked trout mousse and move on to steamed brill with lime and ginger sauce or coq au vin. The dessert extravaganza known as Mrs. Langan's Chocolate Pudding is a must for chocoholics.

See maps on p. 150 and 154. 26 Devonshire St., W1. ☎ *020/7935-4531.* www. langansrestaurants.co.uk. *Reservations recommended 3 days in advance. Tube: Regent's Park (then a 5-minute walk south on Portland Place and west on Devonshire Street). Main courses: Fixed-price menus £20–£22 ($40–$44). AE, DC, MC, V. Open: Mon–Fri 12:30–2:30 p.m., Mon–Sat 6:30–11 p.m.*

L'Osteria 57
$–$$ Holborn   ITALIAN

Here's a fine little Italian restaurant that most tourists never find. Locals in Holborn flock to it, especially at lunchtime, because the food is so good and so reasonably priced. All the classic Italian pasta dishes are here, including deliciously sauced spaghetti, linguine, tortellini, ravioli, tagliatelle, and risotto. Veal scaloppini, grilled chicken, and steak are available, as are fresh fish dishes and delicious pizza. The menu is small and everything on it is carefully prepared. The service is bright and friendly.

See map p. 150. 57 Gray's Inn Rd., WC1. ☎ *020/7404-1383. Reservations recommended. Tube: Chancery Lane (then a 5-minute walk north on Gray's Inn Road to Theobold's Road). Main courses: £5.50–£13 ($11–$26). AE, DC, MC, V. Open: Mon–Fri noon to 10:30 p.m.*

Maggie Jones's
$$–$$$ Kensington   TRADITIONAL BRITISH

At this tri-level restaurant with pine tables and tons of English country memorabilia, the all-British menu includes such traditional favorites as grilled leg of lamb chop with rosemary, grilled trout with almonds, steak-and-kidney and chicken-and-artichoke pies, and Maggie's famous fish. For dessert, try the bread-and-butter pudding. The cooking is reliable, but don't expect anything exceptional. By the way, the place was named for the late Princess Margaret, who used to eat here. It's packed every night.

See map p. 154. 6 Old Court Place (off Kensington Church Street), W8. ☎ *020/7937-6462. Reservations recommended. Tube: High Street Kensington (then a 5-minute walk east on Kensington High Street, north on Kensington Church Street, and east on Old Court Place). Main courses: £7–£20 ($14–$40); fixed-price Sun lunch £17 ($34). AE, DC, MC, V. Open: Daily 12:30–2:30 p.m. and 6:30–11 p.m.*

Mash
$$–$$$ Soho   MODERN BRITISH/MICROBREWERY

This microbrewery/cafe a few steps from Oxford Street has a bar (with good home brews and bar food) on the first floor and a gastropub-like restaurant with a full-view kitchen on the second. The menu is short and to the point: fresh fish, deluxe burgers, steaks, and a few pizzas. It can be a trend scene, which is all part of the fun, but the service isn't always up to snuff.

See maps on p. 150. 619–621 Great Portland St., W1. ☎ *020/7637-5555. Tube: Oxford Circus (then a 2-minute walk east on Oxford Street and north on Great Portland Street). Main courses: £9–£17 ($18–$34); fixed-price lunch £9.50 ($19), fixed-price dinner £26 ($52). AE, DC, MC, V. Open: Mon–Sat noon to 3 p.m. and 6–10:30 p.m.*

Mela
$–$$ Covent Garden   INDIAN

Mela claims to take its inspiration from a food stall favored by workers in Delhi, and lunch here is a fantastic deal: curry or dahl of the day, with bread, pickle, and chutney for under £3 ($6). Pay a little more, and you can build your own version of the meal with different breads and toppings. This is a great, inexpensive way for curry novices to give it a try — and see it being made in the open kitchen. But do come back in the evening for a proper go at the innovative Indian country cuisine. Early birds get three courses. Fixed-price sharers have ten dishes and accompaniments between them. The word *mela* means "fair," and Mela the restaurant does its best to create a festive atmosphere.

See map p. 150. 152–156 Shaftesbury Ave., WC2. ☎ *020/7836-8635.* www. melarestaurant.co.uk. *Tube: Leicester Square (then a 3-minute walk east on Shaftesbury Avenue). Main courses: £9–£15 ($18–$30); fixed-price lunch £3–£6 ($6–$12); pre-theater (5:30–7 p.m.) menu £11 ($22). AE, MC, V. Open: Mon–Sat noon to 11:30 p.m., Sun noon to 10:30 p.m.*

Mildred's
$$ Soho   VEGETARIAN

Considered by many to be London's best vegetarian restaurant, Mildred's is a busy, buzzy place. It isn't fancy but that only seems to add to the hip ambience. The menu always features a pasta of the day and a variety of robustly flavored offerings such as organic lentil casserole with roasted pumpkin and squash or sundried tomato, bean and tarragon sausages. Try the sweet potato fries as a side, and don't forget dessert.

See map p. 150. 45 Lexington St., W1. ☎ *020/7494-1634.* www.mildreds.co.uk. *Reservations not accepted. Tube: Piccadilly Circus (then a 5-minute walk). Main courses: £7–£8.50 ($14–$17). No credit cards. Open: Mon–Sat noon to 11 p.m.*

Mona Lisa
$–$$ Chelsea   ITALIAN

Make Mona Lisa your destination for lunch or dinner after walking the length of King's Road, one of London's great shopping streets (from Sloane Square, the walk takes about 30 minutes, or you can hop on a bus). A popular cafe by day, the place becomes a restaurant at night, although they serve many of the same dishes for lunch and dinner. Everything is home-made and fresh, and the ambience is informal and fun. The menu includes many fish dishes, including sea bass and Dover sole. Pasta da Vinci, a house specialty, is pasta cooked in a paper bag with a sauce of squid, mussels, and prawns. Salad lovers can try the Mona Lisa salad with mozzarella, tomatoes, crispy bacon, avocado, and basil.

See map p. 152. 417 King's Rd. (near Millman's Street, just south of Beauford Street), SW10. ☎ *020/7376-5447. Tube: Sloane Square (then bus 11, 22, or 211; or a 40-minute walk south on King's Road). Main courses: £5–£16 ($10–$32). MC, V. Open: Mon–Sat 7 a.m.–11 p.m., Sun 9 a.m.–5:30 p.m.*

Moro
$$–$$$ Clerkenwell   SPANISH/NORTH AFRICAN

Clerkenwell, on the fringes of the City, has become a very hip neighborhood in recent years, and award-winning Moro has become this unpretentious area's best haute spot. The décor is modern and minimalist, and the North African cuisine is earthy and powerful. The kitchen uses only the best ingredients, organic whenever possible, in its daily-changing menu. Highly recommended are the grilled asparagus with pine nut, egg and dill sauce (a seasonal spring dish); the charcoal-grilled lamb with cauliflower, chickpea, and coriander salad; and the wood-roasted pork with chard. For dessert, try one of the yummy house-specialty desserts: yogurt cake with pistachios or rosewater and cardamom ice cream.

See map p. 150. 34–36 Exmouth Market, EC1. ☎ *020/7833-8336. Reservations recommended. Tube: Farringdon (then a 5-minute walk north on Farringdon to Exmouth Market). Main courses: £17–£18 ($34–$36); tapas £5–£7 ($10–$14). AE, DC, MC, V. Open: Mon–Sat 12:30–2:30 p.m. and 7–10:30 p.m.*

Mosaique
$$ Holborn   MEDITERRANEAN

Tourists staying on the beaten track manage to never find this wonderful restaurant, but the people who work in the area know it well. The interior is bright and cheerful, with yellow walls and white tablecloths glowing under skylights. The menu choices feature dishes from all across the Mediterranean region, prepared with an assured hand. You can dine here on the *mezes* (small plates), such as grilled *halloumi* or *tabbouleh,* or feast on a lamb or chicken "shish" (as in "kebab"), served with vegetables and rice. Vegetarian choices include risotto primavera and vegetable moussaka. A jazz pianist adds to the ambience Wednesday through Saturday from 7:30 to 10:30 p.m.

See map p. 150. 73 Gray's Inn Rd., WC1. ☎ *020/7404-7553.* www.mosaique restaurant.co.uk. *Tube: Chancery Lane (then a 5-minute walk north on Gray's Inn Road). Main courses: £7.50–£11 ($15–$22); mezes £3–£5 ($6–$10); fixed-price lunch £8–£9 ($16–$18). AE, MC, V. Open: Mon–Fri noon to midnight, Sat 5 p.m. to midnight.*

The Museum Tavern
$ Bloomsbury   TRADITIONAL BRITISH

Across from the British Museum's front entrance, this ornate Victorian pub is a convenient spot for a hearty lunch after perusing the Parthenon sculptures. You order food at the counter and drinks at the bar and bring them to your table. Most of the main courses are traditional pub staples: meat pies (chicken and ham; steak and kidney; cottage), bangers and mash, fish and chips, salads, and lasagna. Traditional roasts are also served.

See map p. 150. 49 Great Russell St., WC1. ☎ *020/7242-8987. Tube: Russell Square (then a 5-minute walk south on Montgomery Street, along the west side of Russell Square, to Great Russell Street). Main courses: £4.95–£9.50 ($10–$19). AE, MC, V. Open: Mon–Sat 11 a.m.–11 p.m., Sun 11 a.m.–10:30 p.m. (food served daily to half-hour before closing).*

Noor Jahan
$$ South Kensington   INDIAN

Noor Jahan is a small, unpretentious neighborhood favorite in South Ken. The reliably good food includes moist and flavorful marinated chicken and lamb dishes cooked tandoori-style in a clay oven. If you want to try one of their tasty specialties, consider chicken *tikka,* a staple of northern India, or the *biriani* dishes — where chicken, lamb, or prawns are mixed with basmati rice, fried in *ghee* (thick, clarified butter), and served with a mixed vegetable curry. If you're unfamiliar with Indian food, the waiters will gladly explain the dishes.

See map p. 152. 2A Bina Gardens (off Old Brompton Road), SW5. ☎ *020/7373-6522. Reservations recommended. Tube: Gloucester Road (then a 5-minute walk south on Gloucester Road, west on Brompton Road, and north on Bina Gardens). Main courses: £4.50–£15 ($9–$30); fixed-price menu £19 ($38). AE, DC, MC, V. Open: Daily noon to 2:45 p.m. and 6–11:45 p.m.*

North Sea Fish Restaurant
$$ Bloomsbury   SEAFOOD

When they go to London, many people want to experience *real* fish and chips — not the generic frozen stuff that often passes for this traditional dish. Definitely try this unassuming chippie where the fish is *always* fresh. This restaurant, with its sepia prints and red velvet seats, is pleasant, comfortable, and popular with adults and kids. You may want to start with grilled fresh sardines or a fish cake before digging into a main course of cod or haddock. The fish is most often served battered and deep-fried, but you can also order it grilled. The chips are almost as good as the fish.

See map p. 150. 7–8 Leigh St. (off Cartwright Gardens), WC1. ☎ *020/7387-5892. Reservations recommended. Tube: Russell Square (then a 10-minute walk north on Marchmont Place and east on Leigh Street). Main courses: £8–£17 ($16–$34). AE, DC, MC, V. Open: Daily noon to 2:30 p.m., Mon–Sat 5:30–10:30 p.m.*

The Oratory
$$ South Kensington MODERN BRITISH

Named for the nearby Brompton Oratory, a famous late-19th-century Catholic church, and close to the Victoria & Albert Museum and Harrods shopping, this funky bistro serves some of the best and least expensive food in posh South Ken. The high-ceilinged room is decorated in what I call Modern Rococo, with enormous glass chandeliers, patterned walls and ceiling, and wooden tables with wrought-iron chairs. Note the daily specials on the chalkboard, especially any pasta dishes. The homemade fish cakes, roasted field mushroom risotto, and grilled calf's liver with bacon and deep-fried sage are all noteworthy. For dessert, the sticky toffee pudding with ice cream is a melt-in-the-mouth delight.

See map p. 152. 232 Brompton Rd., SW3. ☎ *020/7584-3493. Tube: South Kensington (then a 5-minute walk north on Brompton Road). Main courses: £7–£16 ($14–$32); fixed-price lunch specials £4–£7 ($8–$14). MC, V. Open: Daily noon to 11 p.m.*

Oxo Tower Brasserie
$$$ South Bank FRENCH/INTERNATIONAL

This stylish brasserie sits atop the landmark Oxo Tower on the South Bank. Although the brasserie is less elegant than the adjacent Oxo Tower Restaurant, its food is marvelous and costs about half of what you pay to dine on tablecloths. The superlative river-and-city views are just as sublime, so book in advance and insist on a window table. Recently the food has taken on more fusion elements but remains as good as ever. Order such tasty dishes as duck breast with pistachio and five-spice or turbot fillet with spiced crab and grapefruit. The fixed-price lunch and pre-theater menu make this brasserie an affordable extravagance.

See map p. 148. Oxo Tower Wharf, Barge House St., SE1. ☎ *020/7803-3888.* www.oxotower.co.uk. *Reservations essential at least 1 or 2 weeks in advance. Tube: Waterloo (the easiest foot route is to head north to the South Bank Centre and then follow the Thames pathway east to the Oxo Tower, about a 10-minute walk). Main courses: £14–£18 ($28–$36); fixed-price lunch and pre-theater menu (Mon–Fri) £17–£22 ($34–$44). AE, DC, MC, V. Open: Daily noon to 3:15 p.m., Mon–Sat 5:30–11 p.m., Sun 6–10 p.m.*

Pig's Ear
$-$$ Chelsea MODERN BRITISH

When a pub upgrades its food to restaurant standards, it becomes known as a gastropub. And Pig's Ear is one of the best and most reasonably priced gastropubs in London. If you're on a tight budget, eat in the bar downstairs; the seasonally adjusted menu has fewer choices, but the cooking is just as good (if not quite as elaborate) as in the dining room upstairs. Look for specialties like chilled pea and mint soup, crab salad on watermelon, and spicy potted shrimps.

See map p. 152. 35 Old Church St., SW3. ☎ *020/7352-2908. Reservations recommended on weekends. Tube: Sloane Square (then a 10-minute walk southwest on*

King's Road and south on Old Church Street). Main courses: £4–£20 ($8–$40). AE, MC, V. Open: Daily 12:30–3 p.m., 7–10:30 p.m.

Porter's English Restaurant
$$ Covent Garden   TRADITIONAL BRITISH

This comfortably informal restaurant specializes in English pies, including Old English fish pie; lamb and apricot; and steak, mushroom, and Guinness stout. Forgo appetizers because the main courses, accompanied by vegetables and side dishes, are generous. If pie isn't your thing, try the bangers and mash, grilled sirloin, or lamb steak. The desserts, including bread-and-butter pudding and *spotted dick* (suet with raisins), are served hot or cold, with whipped cream or custard. The casual atmosphere and kid's menu makes this a good spot for families. The fixed-price meals are good value in pricey Covent Garden.

See map p. 150. 17 Henrietta St., WC2. ☎ 020/7836-6466. www.porters.uk.com. *Reservations recommended. Tube: Covent Garden (then a 5-minute walk south on James Street; Henrietta Street is at the southwest corner behind Covent Garden Market). Main courses: £11–£19 ($22–$38); fixed-price lunch and pre-theater menu £12 ($24), fixed-price dinner £22 ($44). AE, DC, MC, V. Open: Mon–Sat noon to 11:30 p.m., Sun noon to 10:30 p.m.*

R.S. Hispaniola
$$$ The Strand   BRITISH/FRENCH

This former passenger boat is permanently moored in the Thames and provides good food and spectacular views of the river traffic. The menu changes often, with a variety of sturdy and generally well-prepared dishes, such as pork tenderloin with apple and sage puree, rack of lamb, poached halibut, and several vegetarian dishes. The place can be fun and romantic — live music is played most nights. This is also an unusual spot for afternoon tea.

See map p. 150. River Thames, Victoria Embankment, Charing Cross, WC2. ☎ 020/7839-3011. Reservations recommended. Tube: Embankment (the restaurant is a few steps from the station). Main courses: £15–£20 ($30–$40); fixed-price lunch and dinner £23–£25 ($46–$48); afternoon tea £18 ($36). AE, DC, MC, V. Open: Daily noon to 3 p.m. and 6:30–11 p.m. Closed Dec 24–Jan 4.

Rules
$$–$$$$ Covent Garden   TRADITIONAL BRITISH

If you want to eat classic British cuisine in a memorable (nay, venerable) setting, put on something dressy and head for Maiden Lane. Founded in 1798, Rules is London's oldest restaurant, with two centuries' worth of prints, cartoons, and paintings decorating its walls. If you're game for game, go for it because that's what Rules is famous for. On the menu, you may find roast loin of Wiltshire rabbit, Irish sirloin steak with béarnaise sauce, or Gloucestershire pork chops with crackling and chutney. The food is delicious — traditional yet innovative, until you get to the puddings (desserts), which are a mix of nursery and dinner-dance classics. In recent years, the restaurant has added fish and a few vegetarian dishes for those diners not keen on game.

See map p. 150. 35 Maiden Lane, WC2. ☎ *020/7836-5314.* www.rules.co.uk. *Reservations recommended. Tube: Covent Garden (then a 5-minute walk south on James Street to Southampton Street behind Covent Garden Market and west on Maiden Lane). Main courses: £16–£21 ($32–$42); fixed-price post-theater menu (Mon–Thurs 10–11:30 p.m.) £19 ($38). AE, DC, MC, V. Open: Mon–Sat noon to 11:45 p.m., Sun noon to 10:45 p.m.*

Simpson's-in-the-Strand
$$$ The Strand   TRADITIONAL/MODERN BRITISH

Simpson's, in this location since 1848, is — or used to be — a London institution serving the best of traditional English food. Lately, however, sloppy service and indifferent cooking have made dining here a hit-or-miss experience. You still find the largest array of roasts in London: sirloin of beef, saddle of mutton with red-currant jelly, and Aylesbury duckling. (Remember to tip the tail-coated carver.) For a pudding (dessert course), you may want to order treacle roll and custard or Stilton with vintage port. A smart-casual dress code is in effect (leave your tennis shoes and jeans in your hotel room).

See map p. 150. 100 The Strand (next to the Savoy Hotel), WC2. ☎ *020/7836-9112. Reservations recommended. Tube: Charing Cross (then a 5-minute walk east along The Strand). Main courses: £16–£25 ($32–$50); fixed-price menus (Mon–Fri 5–6:45 p.m.) £24–£28 ($48–$56). AE, DC, MC, V. Open: Mon–Fri 7:15–10:30 a.m., daily 12:15–2:30 p.m. and 5–10:45 p.m.*

The Stockpot
$ Piccadilly Circus and Leicester Square   BRITISH/CONTINENTAL

Now here's a dining bargain! This simple bi-level restaurant in the heart of the West End doesn't offer refined cooking, but the food is filling and the price is right — making it a good spot for families. You can find such staples as minestrone soup, spaghetti Bolognese (the eternal favorite), braised lamb, and apple crumble on the fixed-price daily menu. (During peak dining hours, you may have to share a table with other guests.) Always reliable, and one of the few bargain dining spots left in London. Another branch is located in Soho at 18 Old Compton St., W1 (☎ **020/7287-1066**).

See map p. 150. 38 Panton St. (off Haymarket, opposite the Comedy Theatre), SW1. ☎ *020/7839-5142. Tube: Piccadilly Circus (then a 5-minute walk south on Haymarket and east on Panton Street). Main courses: £3.40–£5.50 ($6.80–$11); fixed-price menu £4.95–£6.50 ($10–$13). No credit cards. Open: Mon–Sat 11:30 a.m.–11:30 p.m., Sun noon to 10 p.m.*

Suze in Mayfair
$–$$ Mayfair   PACIFIC RIM

For relaxed, charming, bistrolike ambience in Mayfair, check out Suze. The food is Australasian with some international crossovers and is always simple and well prepared. Try the succulent New Zealand green-tipped mussels, a house specialty, or a New Zealand meat or fish pie. You can also get New Zealand rack of lamb. You can choose from several sharing platters: Italian antipasti, vegetarian, Greek, seafood, and cheese. A must-have dessert is Pavlova, a light meringue covered with kiwi, strawberries, passion fruit, and mangoes. And, of course, you can get a fine glass of Australian wine.

See map p. 154. 41 North Audley St., W1. ☎ *020/7491-3237.* www.suzeinmayfair. com. *Reservations recommended. Tube: Marble Arch (then a 5-minute walk east on Oxford Street and south on North Audley Street). Main courses: £6.50–£17 ($13–$34); platters to share £5–£13 ($10–$26). AE, DC, MC, V. Open: Mon–Sat 11 a.m.–11 p.m.*

Veeraswamy
$$–$$$$ **Piccadilly Circus & Leicester Square   INDIAN**

Established in 1926 by a general and an Indian princess, Veeraswamy claims to be the oldest Indian restaurant in London. Nowadays, it's very hip and resolutely upscale, painted in vibrant colors, with frosted-glass panels dividing up the sections and ultramodern furniture. For starters, the stir-fried mussels with coconut and Kerala spices are sublime. For an exotic and only mildly hot choice, try the shanks of lamb curried in bone stock and spices. Unless you're in the mood to splurge, this isn't the place to sample lots of different dishes. Go for a great-value fixed-price menu and enjoy the best of new Indian cuisine.

See map p. 150. 99–101 Regent St., W1. ☎ *020/7734-1401.* www.veeraswamy.com. *Tube: Piccadilly Circus (then a 2-minute walk along Regent Street to the restaurant, just off Swallow Street). Reservations recommended. Main courses: £14–£27 ($28–$54); fixed-price lunch and post-theater menu £16–£20 ($34–$40), fixed-price Sun menu £20 ($40). AE, DC, MC, V. Open: Mon–Sat 12:30–2:30 p.m. and 5:30–10:30 p.m., Sun 12:30–2:30 p.m. and 6–10:30 p.m.*

Wagamama Noodle Bar
$–$$ **Soho   JAPANESE**

Try this trendsetting noodle bar, modeled after the ramen shops of Japan, if you're exploring Soho and want a delicious, nutritious meal. You enter along a stark, glowing hall with a busy open kitchen and descend to a large open room with communal tables. The specialties are *ramen,* Chinese-style thread noodles served in soups with various toppings, and the fat, white noodles called *udon.* You can also order various rice dishes, vegetarian dishes, dumplings, vegetable and chicken skewers, and tempura. Your order is sent via radio signal to the kitchen and arrives the moment it's ready, which means that not everyone in a group is served at the same time. You may have to stand in line to get in, but it's worth the wait. Teens especially love the loud, hip, casual atmosphere. Several branches of Wagamamas are scattered around London, including a new one on the river beneath Royal Festival Hall on the South Bank.

See map p. 150. 10A Lexington St., W1. ☎ *020/7292-0990.* www.wagamama.com. *Reservations not accepted. Tube: Piccadilly Circus (then a 5-minute walk north on*

Shaftesbury Avenue and Windmill Street, which becomes Lexington Street). Main courses: £6–£10 ($12–$20). MC, V. Open: Mon–Sat noon to 11 p.m., Sun noon to 10 p.m.

Ye Olde Cheshire Cheese
$$ The City   TRADITIONAL BRITISH

Opened as a tavern in 1667 and a one-time haunt of Samuel Johnson, Charles Dickens, and Fleet Street newspaper scandalmongers, Ye Olde Cheshire Cheese is London's most famous chophouse and a wonderfully atmospheric place to dine. The place contains six bars and two dining rooms (reserve a table in The Chop Room for the most traditional dining experience) and is perennially popular with families and tourists looking for some Olde London atmosphere. The house specialties include Ye Famous Pudding (steak, kidney, mushrooms, and game), Scottish roast beef with Yorkshire pudding and horseradish sauce, and fish and chips. If those choices repulse the kids, they can choose sandwiches or salads.

See map p. 148. Wine Office Court, 145 Fleet St., EC4. ☎ *020/7353-6170. Tube: Blackfriars (then a 10-minute walk north on New Bridge Street and west on Fleet Street). Main courses: £8–£10 ($16–$20). AE, DC, MC, V. Open: Mon–Sat noon to 9:30 p.m., Sun noon to 2:30 p.m.; drinks and bar snacks daily noon to 10 p.m.*

Zafferano
$$$$ Knightsbridge   ITALIAN

At Zafferano, you find the best Italian food in London, served in a quietly elegant, attitude-free restaurant. The semolina pastas are perfectly cooked and come with various additions. The main courses, such as roast rabbit with Parma ham and polenta, charcoal-grilled chicken, and tuna with arugula and tomato salad, are deliciously simple and tender. For dessert, try the pear and almond tart with mascarpone ice cream.

See map p. 152. 15 Lowndes St., SW1. ☎ *020/7235-5800.* www.zafferano restaurant.com. *Reservations required. Tube: Knightsbridge (then a 5-minute walk south on Lowndes Street, 2 streets east of Sloane Street). Main courses: Fixed-price lunch £26–£35 ($52–$70), fixed-price dinner £30–£45 ($60–$90). AE, MC, V. Open: Daily noon to 2:30 p.m. and 7–11 p.m.*

Dining and Snacking on the Go

Londoners have a somewhat traditional outlook on food and meals. You won't see many adults in London eating on the street or having a bite while traveling the Tube. It's mostly tourists carrying those Starbucks cups. And you don't find street vendors peddling hot dogs and other foods from carts (although you may see a fast-food van or two near major attractions). Even the most frenetic Londoner likes to eat a proper, civilized "sit-down" meal. So what's a too-rushed tourist to do? To help you enjoy snacks and light meals the London way, I offer some interesting alternatives to fast-food restaurants.

Sandwich bars

Sandwiches are an English invention (supposedly of the Earl of Sandwich), and sandwich bars are a faster and cheaper alternative to sit-down restaurants and pubs. Most open early for breakfast and close in the afternoon. You can usually eat at a counter or in booths, or you can take your sandwich and go to the nearest park for an alfresco lunch. The bars sell coffee, tea, and nonalcoholic beverages.

 American visitors are sometimes confused by the way the English name their sandwiches. In general, the Brits use the word *mayonnaise* the way that Americans use *salad. Tuna mayonnaise* or *egg mayonnaise* simply means "tuna salad" or "egg salad." The word *salad* is used in Britain to denote that lettuce and tomato have been added to a sandwich, as in "chicken with salad."

The following sandwich bars are worth a bite:

> ✔ Near Victoria Station, **Capri Sandwich Bar** (see map p. 149; 16 Lower Belgrave Rd., NW1; ☎ 020/7834-1989; Tube: Victoria) serves an imaginative variety of sandwiches. The bar is open Monday through Friday 7:30 a.m. to 3:30 p.m.

> ✔ If you're in the vicinity of Euston Station, try the unpretentious but cheerful **Giovanni's Sandwich Bar** (see map p. 150; 152 North Gower St., at Euston Road; ☎ 020/7383-0531; Tube: Euston), open Monday through Friday 7 a.m. to 3 p.m.

 The best sandwich shops in Central London are the **Pret à Manger** chain stores, which offer fresh, inventive, healthy sandwiches and fast counter service. A convenient West End branch is located at 77–78 St. Martin's Lane, WC2 (see map p. 150; ☎ 020/7379-5335; Tube: Leicester Square). It's open Monday through Thursday 7:30 a.m. to 9 p.m., Friday 7:30 a.m. to 11 p.m., Saturday 9 a.m. to 11 p.m., and Sunday 9 a.m. to 9 p.m. You'll find Pret à Manger all over the city.

Fish and chips

The English call a fish and chips place a *chippie.* At some chippies, the food is wonderful; at others, it's hideous. At the good places (the only ones that I recommend), the fish (usually cod, haddock, or plaice) is fresh, the batter crisp, and the fries *(chips)* hand-cut. You can get tartar sauce, but the British also like to splash their fish and chips with malt vinegar. Prices for fish have gone up considerably, so fish and chips are no longer the bargain they used to be.

 The following restaurants all have sit-down and *takeaway* (takeout) service and welcome families with kids. Also see the **North Sea Fish Restaurant** in the section "London's Best Restaurants," earlier in this chapter.

✔ **Costas Fish Restaurant** (see map p. 154; 18 Hillgate St., W8; ☎ 020/ 7727-4310; Tube: Notting Hill Gate) is open Tuesday through Saturday noon to 2:30 p.m. and 5:30 to 10:30 p.m.

✔ **Fryer's Delight** (see map p. 150; 19 Theobald's Rd., WC1; ☎ 020/ 7405-4114; Tube: Chancery Lane or Holborn) is across from the Holborn Police Station. A plate of cod and chips costs $4.95 ($9.90); takeaway is also available. The Formica-clad chippie is open Monday through Saturday noon to 10 p.m. The fish is fried in beef fat here; other options include pastries and pies.

✔ **Geales** (see map p. 154; 2 Farmer St., W8; ☎ 020/7727-7969; Tube: Notting Hill Gate) is open Tuesday through Saturday noon to 3 p.m. and 6 to 10:30 p.m.

✔ **Golden Hind** (see map p. 150; 73 Marylebone Lane, W1; ☎ 020/7486-3644; Tube: Baker Street or Bond Street) is a few blocks south of Madame Tussaud's. This bargain chippie has an average meal cost of $6 ($12); hours are Monday through Friday noon to 3 p.m. and Monday through Saturday 6 to 10 p.m.

✔ **Rock & Sole Plaice** (see map p. 150; 47 Endell St., WC2; ☎ 020/ 7836-3785; Tube: Covent Garden) offers all-day takeaway service, as well as a place to sit down and eat amid the bustle of the Covent Garden Piazza (you can get a table on the lower level). Because of its location, this chippie crowds with theatergoers in the evening. You pay at least $8 ($16) for a meal. It's open Monday through Saturday 11:30 a.m. to 10:30 p.m. and Sunday noon to 10 p.m.

✔ **Seafresh Fish Restaurant** (see map p. 149; 80–81 Wilton Rd., SW1; ☎ 020/7828-0747; Tube: Victoria) offers a good cod fillet and great chips for about $8.50 ($17). It's open Monday through Friday noon to 3 p.m. and 5 to 10:30 p.m.

✔ **Sea-Shell** (see map p. 154; 49–51 Lisson Grove, NW1; ☎ 020/7723-8703; Tube: Marylebone) is within easy walking distance west of Madame Tussaud's and is considered one of the best chippies in London. Main courses range from $7 ($14) to $16 ($32); average cost for fish and chips is about $9 ($18). It's open Monday through Friday noon to 2:30 p.m. and 5 to 10:30 p.m., Saturday noon to 10:30 p.m.

Costas Fish Restaurant and **Geales** are both good choices if you've been poking around the antiques and whatnot stands along Portobello Road.

Department store restaurants

If you're in the midst of a shopping spree and don't want to be distracted, you can easily grab a bite at one of the many department store restaurants. These eateries are convenient, but they aren't necessarily cheap; see the restaurant entry for Fortnum & Mason in the section "London's Best Restaurants," earlier in this chapter. A new trend among high-end boutiques is to have a fancy little cafe or coffee bar right on the premises.

Never too latte: London's coffee bars

It had to happen sooner or later, and frankly I'm glad it did because finding a good cup of coffee in London wasn't always the easiest thing to do. But now **Starbucks** has opened branches all over the city, offering nice places to sit down and have a latte, cappuccino, or "regular" cup of joe. Starbucks also sells pastries and sandwiches.

Here are some more department-store possibilities:

✔ **Harrods** (see map p. 152; 87–135 Brompton Rd., SW1; ☎ 020/7730-1234; Tube: Knightsbridge), in addition to its ice cream parlor and awe-inspiring Food Hall, offers its **Famous Deli Counter,** where you can perch on stools (no reservations) and pay too much for what's called "traditional Jewish food" but often isn't. It's open Monday through Saturday 10 a.m. to 6 p.m.

✔ **Harvey Nichols** (109–125 Knightsbridge, SW7; ☎ 020/7235-5250; Tube: Knightsbridge) is another Knightsbridge emporium with a restaurant, the **Fifth Floor at Harvey Nichols** (see map p. 152). It's open Monday through Friday noon to 3 p.m. and 5:30 to 10 p.m., but eating here is pretty expensive. A better bet is the cafe, also on the fifth floor, where you can get a cup of tea and a salad or light meal; it's open Monday through Saturday 10 a.m. to 11 p.m. and Sunday 10 a.m. to 6 p.m. Like Harrods, Harvey Nichols has a fabulous food emporium where you can buy now and eat later.

Treating Yourself to Tea

The stereotype is true: Brits do drink tea, though consumption is dropping because of the new emphasis on coffee. Teatime is traditionally from about 3:30 to 5 p.m. Your afternoon tea can be a lavish affair served by a black-coated waiter in a posh hotel lobby, or a quick cup with a slice of cake or a sandwich at a corner tea shop or *patisserie* (a bakery where you can sit down or get pastries to take away). Tea may be served fast-food-style in paper cups, home-style in mugs, or more elegantly on bone china.

So what exactly, you ask, is the difference between afternoon tea and high tea?

✔ **Afternoon tea** is tea with cakes, scones, sandwiches, or all of them, served between 3 and 5 p.m. It's a pre-dinner ritual.

✔ **High tea,** served from about 5 to 6 p.m., is a more of a light supper followed by dessert and tea.

Casual tea rooms and patisseries

In the following comfortable neighborhood tearooms and patisseries, you can get a good cup of tea, along with a scone or other pastry or a plate of tea sandwiches, for about £4 to £10 ($8–$20):

✔ **Café Parlour at Sketch** (see map p. 150; 9 Conduit St., W1; ☎ 0870/777-4488; www.sketch.uk.com; Tube: Oxford Circus) offers superb pastries and cakes in a room that makes up the patisserie component of the ultrahip Sketch, a gastro-empire founded by Pierre Gagnaire. You can also get breakfast and lunch. Worth a visit just to see the loos. Hours are Monday through Friday 8 a.m. to 11 p.m., Saturday 10 a.m. to 11 p.m.

✔ **Muffinski's** (see map p. 150; 5 King St., WC2; ☎ 020/7379-1525; Tube: Leicester Square) offers great homemade muffins, including low-fat, organic, and vegetarian. Hours are Monday through Friday 8 a.m. to 7 p.m., Saturday 9 a.m. to 7 p.m., and Sunday 10 a.m. to 6 p.m.

✔ **Pâtisserie Cappucetto** (see map p. 150; 8 Moor St., W1; ☎ 020/7437-9472; Tube: Leicester Square) serves breakfast, sandwiches, soups, and superb desserts Monday through Thursday 8 a.m. to 11:30 p.m. and Friday and Saturday 8 a.m. to 12:30 a.m.

✔ **Pâtisserie Deux Amis** (see map p. 150; 63 Judd St., WC1; ☎ 020/7383-7029; Tube: Russell Square) is a good choice for a quick bite. Hours are Monday through Saturday 9 a.m. to 5:30 p.m. and Sunday 9 a.m. to 1:30 p.m.

✔ **Pâtisserie Valerie** (see map p. 150; 44 Old Compton St., W1; ☎ 020/7437-3466; www.patisserie-valerie.co.uk; Tube: Leicester Square or Tottenham Court Road) has been around since 1926 and serves a mouthwatering array of pastries, but expect to stand in line night or day. Hours are Monday through Friday 7:30 a.m. to 8 p.m., Saturday 8 a.m. to 6:30 p.m., and Sunday 9 a.m. to 6 p.m.

Pâtisserie Valerie also has other branches throughout London. One is at 105 Marylebone High St., W1 (see map p. 154; ☎ 020/7935-6240; Tube: Bond Street or Baker Street); another is right on Piccadilly at 162 Piccadilly, W1 (see map p. 150; ☎ 020/7491-1717; Tube: Green Park). The Marylebone branch is open Monday through Saturday 7:30 a.m. to 6 p.m., and Sunday 9 a.m. to 6 p.m. The Piccadilly branch is open Monday through Friday, 7:30 a.m. to 7:30 p.m., Saturdays from 8 a.m. to 8 p.m., and Sundays from 9 a.m. to 7 p.m.

✔ **Richoux** has three old-fashioned tearooms in choice London locations. They serve food all day long, and they're kind to your budget. The locations are **Richoux-Knightsbridge** (see map p. 152; 215 Brompton Rd., SW3; ☎ 020/7823-9971; Tube: Knightsbridge), **Richoux-Mayfair** (see map p. 154; 41a South Audley St., W1; ☎ 020/7629-5228; Tube: Bond St. or Green Park), and **Richoux-Piccadilly** (see map p. 150; 172 Piccadilly, W1; ☎ 020/7493-2204; Tube: Piccadilly Circus). All locations keep basically the same hours:

Monday through Saturday 8 a.m. to 11 p.m. (the Mayfair branch is open until 9 p.m.), Sunday 9 a.m. to 11 p.m. (the Mayfair branch is open until 9 p.m.). The Web site for all locations is www.richoux.co.uk.

Elegant spots for high tea

A traditional afternoon English tea has cakes, sandwiches, and scones with clotted cream and jam, and is taken in a posh hotel or restaurant. These rather lavish affairs are ridiculously expensive but memorable. At any one of the following places, you can get a proper traditional afternoon or high tea, sometimes with strawberries and champagne. Also check out the less expensive and atmospheric Café in the Crypt beneath St. Martin-in-the-Fields church, the Kensington Palace Orangery, and the R.S. *Hispaniola* docked on the Thames (all are reviewed earlier in this chapter). *Note:* When you take tea at any of the following tony spots, a smart-casual dress code is in effect — tennis shoes and jeans are inappropriate.

✔ **Brown's Hotel** (see map p. 151; Albemarle Street, W1; ☎ 020/7493-6020; www.brownshotel.com; Tube: Green Park): This hotel's English Tea Room serves a superlative and very pricey tea from 3 to 6 p.m. (Sat–Sun from 2 p.m.) for £33 to £45 ($66–$90). Reservations are highly recommended.

✔ **Claridge's** (see map p. 150; Brook St., W1; ☎ 020/7629-8860; www.claridges.co.uk; Tube: Bond Street): Claridge's serves a glamorous and expensive tea daily from 3 to 5:30 p.m. for £31 to £38 ($62–$76). Reservations are a good idea.

✔ **Fortnum & Mason** (see map p. 150; 181 Piccadilly, W1; ☎ 020/7734-8040; Tube: Piccadilly Circus): Fortnum & Mason serves afternoon and high tea in the **St. James's Restaurant** Monday through Saturday from 3 to 5:30 p.m. for £24 to £34 ($48–$68). Reservations aren't necessary.

✔ **Georgian Restaurant** (see map p. 152; 87–135 Brompton Rd., SW1; ☎ 02/07225-6800; Tube: Knightsbridge): On the fourth floor of Harrods, the Georgian Restaurant serves afternoon and high tea Monday through Saturday from 3:45 to 5:30 p.m. Afternoon tea costs £20 ($40) per person, and you don't need reservations.

✔ **The Lanesborough Hotel** (see map p. 152; Hyde Park Corner, SW1; ☎ 020/7259-5599; Tube: Hyde Park Corner) requires reservations for high tea daily 3:30 to 6 p.m. and costs £31 to £39 ($62–$78).

Planning a Picnic

London may not be the perfect city for picnics. Rain can quickly put a damper on a picnic hamper, and nothing is quite as unappetizing as a wet sandwich. But on days when the weather cooperates, nothing is more enjoyable than packing up some sandwiches and heading to a special spot to eat outdoors.

Glean your picnic pickings from supermarkets, delis, and sandwich shops (see "Sandwich bars," earlier in this chapter), or drop in at the legendary and far more expensive food halls at **Fortnum & Mason** or **Harrods. Marks & Spencer** also has a food hall. In neighborhoods outside the West End (South Kensington or Marylebone, for example), you can go into any supermarket and find packaged sandwiches, crisps (potato chips), fresh fruit, and drinks.

In the West End, the **Embankment Gardens** is a pretty picnic spot, looking out on the Thames. This flower-filled strip of green is next to the Embankment Tube station, below the Savoy hotel. You have to sit on benches instead of the grass, and the traffic noise along the Embankment can be annoying, but it's still a nice place to know about. Sandwich shops and takeaway food shops are clustered around the Embankment Tube station.

Kensington Gardens (see Chapter 11) offers vast green lawns, frolicsome fountains, Kensington Palace, and the famous statue of Peter Pan. This spot is a favorite with children of all ages. The park is close to all the great museums in South Ken. Adjacent **Hyde Park** is another lovely picnic site, particularly along the shores of Serpentine Lake. You can buy sandwiches and snacks at the Dell Restaurant (see Chapter 11) at the east end of the lake. In summer, bandstand concerts are given in the park.

The royal parks — **Green Park** and **St. James's Park** — are more sedate. You can choose to picnic on a lovely knoll and gaze upon Buckingham Palace.

Looking for an urban space that's good for people-watching and has great views across the river? Picnic on the **South Bank** of the Thames, along the riverside promenade close to Royal Festival Hall and the National Theatre.

Index of Restaurants by Neighborhood

Bloomsbury
Cigala (Spanish, $$)
Giovanni's Sandwich Bar (Sandwich Bars, $)
The Museum Tavern (Traditional British, $)
North Sea Fish Restaurant (Fish and Chips/Seafood, $$)

Chelsea
Aubergine (French, $$$$)
Chelsea Kitchen (International, $)
Harvey Nichols (Food Halls, $$)
Mona Lisa (Italian, $–$$)
Pig's Ear (Modern British, $–$$)

The City
Dickens Inn by the Tower (Traditional/Modern British, $–$$)
Ye Olde Cheshire Cheese (Traditional British, $$)

Clerkenwell
Moro (Spanish/North African, $$–$$$)

Covent Garden
Food for Thought (Vegetarian, $)
Joe Allen (North American, $$)
Mela (Indian, $–$$)
Porter's English Restaurant
(Traditional British, $$)
Rules (Traditional British, $$–$$$$)

Holborn
Fryer's Delight (Fish and Chips, $)
L'Osteria 57 (Italian, $–$$)
Mosaique (Mediterranean, $$)

Kensington
Kensington Palace Orangery
(Traditional British/Tea/Light Lunch, $)
Maggie Jones's (Traditional British,
$$–$$$)

Knightsbridge
Boxwood Café (Modern British, $$$)
Harrods (Food Halls/Tea/Patisseries/
Traditional British, $$)
Richoux (Tea/Patisseries, $)
Zafferano (Italian, $$$$)

Marylebone
Golden Hind (Fish and Chips, $)
Langan's Bistro (British/French, $$)
Pâtisserie Valerie (Tea/Patisseries, $)
Sea-Shell (Fish and Chips, $)

Mayfair
Brown's Hotel (Tea/Patisseries,
$$$–$$$$)
Café Parlour at Sketch (Tea/
Patisseries, $)
Claridge's (Tea/Patisseries, $$$)
Hard Rock Cafe (North American, $$)
The Lanesborough (Tea/Patisseries,
$$$–$$$$)
Richoux (Tea/Patisseries, $)
Suze in Mayfair (Pacific Rim, $–$$)

Notting Hill
Clarke's (Modern European, $$$)
Costas Fish Restaurant (Fish and
Chips, $)
Geales (Fish and Chips, $)
Seafresh Fish Restaurant (Fish and
Chips, $)

Piccadilly Circus and Leicester Square
Cafe in the Crypt (Traditional
British, $)
Criterion Bar & Grill (British/French,
$$–$$$)
Pret à Manger (Sandwich Bars, $)
Richoux (Tea/Patisseries, $)
The Stockpot (British/Continental, $)
Veeraswamy (Indian, $$–$$$$)

Soho
Ed's Easy Diner (North American, $)
The Gay Hussar (Hungarian, $$–$$$)
The Ivy (British/French, $$$–$$$$)
Itsu (Japanese, $)
Mash (Modern British/
Microbrewery, $–$$$)
Mildred's (Vegetarian, $$)
Muffinski's (Tea/Patisseries, $)
Pâtisserie Cappucetto (Soho, $)
Pâtisserie Deux Amis (Tea/
Patisseries, $)
Rock & Sole Plaice (Fish and Chips, $)
Wagamama Noodle Bar (Japanese, $–$$)

South Bank
The Founders Arms (Modern British, $)
Oxo Tower Brasserie
(French/International, $$$)

South Kensington
Brasserie St. Quentin (French, $$)
Noor Jahan (Indian, $$)
The Oratory (Modern British, $$)

Southwark
Gourmet Pizza Company (Pizza/
Pasta, $)

St. James's
Fortnum & Mason (Food Halls/Tea/
Patisseries/Traditional British, $$)
Gourmet Pizza Company (Pizza/
Pasta, $)

Spitalfields
Canteen (Traditional British, $–$$)

The Strand
R.S. *Hispaniola* (British/French, $$$)
Simpson's-in-the-Strand
(Traditional/Modern British, $$$)

Westminster and Victoria
Capri Sandwich Bar (Sandwich Bar, $)
Ebury Wine Bar & Restaurant
(British/International, $$)
Ken Lo's Memories of China
(Chinese, $$$$)

Index of Restaurants by Cuisine

British/Continental
The Stockpot (Piccadilly Circus and
Leicester Square, $)

British/French
Criterion Bar & Grill (Piccadilly Circus
and Leicester Square, $$–$$$)
The Ivy (Soho, $$$–$$$$)
Langan's Bistro (Marylebone, $$)
R.S. *Hispaniola* (The Strand, $$$)

British (Modern)
Boxwood Café (Knightsbridge, $$$)
Dickens Inn by the Tower
(The City, $–$$)
Ebury Wine Bar & Restaurant
(Westminster and Victoria, $$)
The Founders Arms (South Bank, $)
Mash (Modern British/Microbrewery,
$–$$$)
The Oratory (South Kensington, $$)
Pig's Ear (Chelsea, $–$$)
Simpson's-in-the-Strand (The
Strand, $$$)

British (Traditional)
Cafe in the Crypt (Piccadilly Circus and
Leicester Square, $)
Canteen (Spitalfields, $–$$)

Dickens Inn by the Tower (The City,
$–$$)
Fortnum & Mason (St. James's, $$)
Harrods (Knightsbridge, $$)
Kensington Palace Orangery
(Kensington, $)
Maggie Jones's (Kensington, $$–$$$)
The Museum Tavern (Bloomsbury, $)
Porter's English Restaurant (Covent
Garden, $$)
Rules (Covent Garden, $$–$$$$)
Simpson's-in-the-Strand (The Strand,
$$$)
Ye Olde Cheshire Cheese (The City, $$)

Chinese
Ken Lo's Memories of China
(Westminster and Victoria, $$$$)

Fish and Chips
Costas Fish Restaurant (Notting Hill, $)
Fryer's Delight (Holborn, $)
Geales (Notting Hill, $)
Golden Hind (Marylebone, $)
North Sea Fish Restaurant
(Bloomsbury, $$)
Rock & Sole Plaice (Soho, $)
Seafresh Fish Restaurant
(Notting Hill, $)
Sea-Shell (Marylebone, $)

Food Halls
Fortnum & Mason (St. James's, $$)
Harrods (Knightsbridge, $$)
Harvey Nichols (Chelsea, $$)

French
Aubergine (Chelsea, $$$$)
Brasserie St. Quentin (South
Kensington, $$)
Oxo Tower Brasserie (South Bank, $$$)

Hungarian
The Gay Hussar (Soho, $$–$$$)

Indian
Mela (Covent Garden, $–$$)
Noor Jahan (South Kensington, $$)
Veeraswamy (Piccadilly Circus and
Leicester Square, $$–$$$$)

International
Chelsea Kitchen (Chelsea, $)
Ebury Wine Bar & Restaurant
(Westminster and Victoria, $$)
Oxo Tower Brasserie (South Bank, $$$)

Italian
L'Osteria 57 (Italian, $–$$)
Mona Lisa (Chelsea, $–$$)
Zafferano (Knightsbridge, $$$$)

Japanese
Itsu (Soho, $)
Wagamama Noodle Bar (Soho, $–$$)

Mediterranean
Mosaique (Holborn, $$)

Modern European
Clarke's (Notting Hill, $$$)

North African
Moro (Clerkenwell, $$–$$$)

North American
Ed's Easy Diner (Soho, $)
Hard Rock Cafe (Mayfair, $$)
Joe Allen (Covent Garden, $$)

Pacific Rim
Suze in Mayfair (Mayfair, $–$$)

Pizza/Pasta
Gourmet Pizza Company
(Southwark, $)

Sandwich Bars
Capri Sandwich Bar (Westminster and
Victoria, $)
Giovanni's Sandwich Bar
(Bloomsbury, $)
Pret à Manger (Piccadilly Circus and
Leicester Square, $)

Seafood
North Sea Fish Restaurant
(Bloomsbury, $$)

Spanish
Cigala (Bloomsbury, $$)
Moro (Clerkenwell, $$–$$$)

Tea/Patisseries
Brown's Hotel (Mayfair, $$$–$$$$)
Café Parlour at Sketch (Mayfair, $)
Claridge's (Mayfair, $$$)
Fortnum & Mason (St. James's, $$)
Harrods (Knightsbridge, $$)
Kensington Palace Orangery ($)
The Lanesborough (Mayfair, $$$–$$$$)
Muffinski's (Soho, $)
Pâtisserie Cappucetto (Soho, $)
Pâtisserie Deux Amis (Soho, $)
Pâtisserie Valerie (Marylebone, $)
Richoux (Knightsbridge, Mayfair,
Piccadilly Circus and Leicester
Square, $)

Vegetarian
Food for Thought (Covent Garden, $)
Mildred's (Soho, $$)

Index of Restaurants by Price

$

Cafe in the Crypt (Traditional British, Piccadilly Circus and Leicester Square)

Café Parlour at Sketch (Tea/Patisseries, Mayfair)

Canteen (Traditional British, Spitalfields)

Capri Sandwich Bar (Sandwich Bar, Westminster and Victoria)

Chelsea Kitchen (International, Chelsea)

Costas Fish Restaurant (Fish and Chips, Notting Hill)

Dickens Inn by the Tower (Traditional/Modern British, The City)

Ed's Easy Diner (North American, Soho)

Food for Thought (Vegetarian, Covent Garden)

The Founders Arms (Modern British, South Bank)

Fryer's Delight (Fish and Chips, Holborn)

Geales (Fish and Chips, Notting Hill)

Giovanni's Sandwich Bar (Sandwich Bars, Bloomsbury)

Golden Hind (Fish and Chips, Marylebone)

Gourmet Pizza Company (Pizza/Pasta, Southwark)

Itsu (Japanese, Soho)

Kensington Palace Orangery (Traditional British/Tea/Light Lunch)

L'Osteria 57 (Italian, Holborn)

Mela (Indian, Covent Garden)

Mona Lisa (Italian, Chelsea)

Muffinski's (Tea/Patisseries, Soho)

The Museum Tavern (Traditional British, Bloomsbury)

Pâtisserie Cappucetto (Tea/Patisseries, Soho)

Pâtisserie Deux Amis (Tea/Patisseries, Soho)

Pâtisserie Valerie (Tea/Patisseries, Marylebone)

Pig's Ear (Modern British, Chelsea)

Pret à Manger (Sandwich Bars, Piccadilly Circus and Leicester Square)

Richoux (Tea/Patisseries, Knightsbridge, Mayfair, Piccadilly Circus and Leicester Square)

Rock & Sole Plaice (Fish and Chips, Soho)

Seafresh Fish Restaurant (Fish and Chips, Notting Hill)

Sea-Shell (Fish and Chips, Marylebone)

The Stockpot (British/Continental, Piccadilly Circus and Leicester Square)

Suze in Mayfair (Pacific Rim, Mayfair)

Wagamama Noodle Bar (Japanese, Soho)

$$

Brasserie St. Quentin (French, South Kensington)

Canteen (Traditional British, Spitalfields)

Cigala (Spanish, Bloomsbury)

Criterion Bar & Grill (British/French, Piccadilly Circus and Leicester Square)

Dickens Inn by the Tower (Traditional/Modern British, The City)

Ebury Wine Bar & Restaurant (Modern British/International, Westminster and Victoria)

Fortnum & Mason (Food Halls/Tea/Patisseries/Traditional British, St. James's)

The Gay Hussar (Hungarian, Soho)

Hard Rock Cafe (North American, Mayfair)

Harrods (Food Halls/Tea/Patisseries/Traditional British, Knightsbridge)

Harvey Nichols (Food Halls, Chelsea)

Joe Allen (North American, Covent Garden)

Langan's Bistro (British/French, Marylebone)

L'Osteria 57 (Italian, Holborn)

Maggie Jones's (Traditional British, Kensington)

Mash (Modern British/Microbrewery, Soho)

Mela (Indian, Covent Garden)

Mildred's (Vegetarian, Soho)
Mona Lisa (Italian, Chelsea)
Moro (North African/Spanish, Clerkenwell)
Mosaique (Mediterranean, Holborn)
Noor Jahan (Indian, South Kensington)
North Sea Fish Restaurant (Fish and Chips/Seafood, Bloomsbury)
The Oratory (Modern British, South Kensington)
Pig's Ear (Modern British, Chelsea)
Porter's English Restaurant (Traditional British, Covent Garden)
Rules (Traditional British, Covent Garden)
Suze in Mayfair (Pacific Rim, Mayfair)
Veeraswamy (Indian, Piccadilly Circus and Leicester Square)
Wagamama Noodle Bar (Japanese, Soho)
Ye Olde Cheshire Cheese (Traditional British, The City)

$$$

Boxwood Café (Modern British, Knightsbridge)
Brown's Hotel (Tea/Patisseries, Mayfair)
Claridge's (Tea/Patisseries, Mayfair)
Clarke's (Modern European, Notting Hill)
Criterion Bar & Grill (British/French, Piccadilly Circus and Leicester Square)
The Gay Hussar (Hungarian, Soho)
The Ivy (British/French, Soho)

The Lanesborough (Tea/Patisseries, Mayfair)
Maggie Jones's (Traditional British, Kensington)
Mash (Modern British/Microbrewery, Soho)
Moro (North African/Spanish, Clerkenwell)
Oxo Tower Brasserie (French/International, South Bank)
R.S. *Hispaniola* (British/French, The Strand)
Rules (Traditional British, Covent Garden)
Simpson's-in-the-Strand (Traditional/Modern British, The Strand)
Veeraswamy (Indian, Piccadilly Circus and Leicester Square)

$$$$

Aubergine (French, Chelsea)
The Ivy (British/French, Soho)
Brown's Hotel (Tea/Patisseries, Mayfair)
Ken Lo's Memories of China (Chinese, Westminster and Victoria)
The Lanesborough (Tea/Patisseries, Mayfair)
Rules (Traditional British, Covent Garden)
Veeraswamy (Indian, Piccadilly Circus and Leicester Square)
Zafferano (Italian, Knightsbridge)

Part IV
Exploring London

The 5th Wave   By Rich Tennant

"Now THAT was a great meal! Beautiful presentation, an imaginative use of ingredients, and a sauce with nuance and depth. The British really know how to make a 'Happy Meal.'"

In this part . . .

Ready to hit the streets? Raring to go? Turn to Chapter 11 for descriptions of London's top sights — along with directions, opening hours, and admission prices; you can also find my rundown of additional sights to see, all of them intriguing and worth exploring. In Chapter 11, I also tell you about the best options for guided tours of London by bus, by boat, and on foot.

Check out Chapter 12 for some great tips on how to make the most of your shopping in London, as well as specific stores to visit. Chapter 13 gives you four suggested London itineraries — sightseeing strategies to help you enjoy the city on a *realistic* schedule. Finally, in Chapter 14, I send you on your way to six fascinating places that you can explore on day trips. I think you'll love each and every one of them.

Chapter 11

Discovering London's Top Attractions

In This Chapter

▶ Reviewing London's top attractions

▶ Finding sights and activities for history buffs, art lovers, bookworms, kids, gardeners, and others

▶ Visiting royal palaces and castles

▶ Focusing on Greenwich, home of the prime meridian

▶ Listing London's sights by neighborhood and type

---

*H*ere's the big question: What do you want to see and enjoy while you're in London? The possibilities are endless: fabulous museums, royal palaces, important historic sites, beautiful parks and gardens, and grand churches. In this chapter, I give you the information that you need to make your itinerary fit your interests, time, and energy level.

To help you find your way around London, you may want to go beyond my directions in this chapter and get yourself a *London A–Z* map. Even Londoners use this comprehensive street gazette, which comes in many different formats and can be found at just about every bookstore and news kiosk in London.

I arrange the top sights in this chapter alphabetically. For locations, see the "London's Top Sights" map on p. 186. Following the must-see list are more top attractions grouped together by type. For the locations of these sights, turn to the "More London Sights" map on p. 210. To help you pull together your itinerary, see the end of this chapter, where I index all the top attractions by neighborhood and type. (For useful information about planning workable itineraries based on the length of your trip, turn to Chapter 13.)

London's top museums are spectacular treasure-troves — and they're all absolutely free. To save money on transportation costs, buy one of the single-day or multiday Travelcards I describe in Chapter 8.

London's Top Sights

British Airways London
   Eye **23**
British Museum **13**
Buckingham Palace **10**
Covent Garden Market
   and Piazza **14**
Green Park **9**
Houses of Parliament
   and Big Ben **22**
Hyde Park **3**
Kensington Gardens **5**
Kensington Palace **4**
Leicester Square **15**
London Zoo **1**
Madame Tussaud's **2**
National Gallery **18**

National Portrait
   Gallery **16**
Natural History
   Museum **6**
Piccadilly Circus **12**
Science Museum **7**
St. James's Park **11**
St. Martin-in-the-Fields **17**
St. Paul's Cathedral **25**
Tate Britain **21**
Tate Modern **24**
Tower of London **26**
Trafalgar Square **19**
Victoria & Albert
   Museum **8**
Westminster Abbey **20**

The Top Attractions from A to Z

British Airways London Eye
South Bank

As a piece of fast-track engineering, the 400-foot-high London Eye observation wheel is impressive. Each glass-sided elliptical module holds about 25 passengers, with enough space so you can move about freely. Although most people stand the entire time, you can sit on the available bench if you prefer. Lasting about 30 minutes (equivalent to one rotation), the ride (or *flight,* as they call it) is remarkably smooth — even on windy days riders don't feel any nerve-twittering shakes. As long as the weather is good, the wheel provides unrivaled views of London.

For the London Eye, you may want to reserve your place (with a specific entry time) before you arrive; if you're ticketless, you can line up for a ticket at the office right behind the wheel, but you may have to wait an hour or more before you can get on the wheel.

See map p. 186. Bridge Road, SE1 (beside Westminster Bridge). ☎ **0870/500-0600.** www.londoneye.com. *Tube: Westminster (then a 5-minute walk south across Westminster Bridge) or Waterloo (then a 3-minute walk west along the riverside promenade). Admission: £15 ($30) adults, £11 ($22) seniors, £7.50 ($15) children under 16; advance credit card booking fee 50p ($1). Open: June–Sept daily from 9 a.m.; Oct–May daily from 10 a.m.; last admission varies seasonally.*

British Museum
Bloomsbury

The British Museum ranks as the most visited attraction in London, with a splendid, wide-ranging collection of treasures from around the world.

Wandering through the museum's 94 galleries (see the "British Museum" map on p. 189), you can't help but be struck by humanity's enduring creative spirit. Permanent displays of antiquities from Egypt, Western Asia, Greece, and Rome are on view, as well as prehistoric and Romano-British, Medieval, Renaissance, Modern, and Oriental collections.

In November 2000, the museum's **Great Court** reopened with a glass-and-steel roof designed by Lord Norman Foster. Inaccessible to the general public for 150 years, the Great Court is now the museum's new central axis. In the center, you find a circular building completed in 1857 that once served as the museum's famous **Reading Room.** Completely restored, it now houses computer terminals where visitors can access images and information about the museum's vast collections.

The most famous of the museum's countless treasures are the superb **Parthenon Sculptures** brought to England in 1801 by the seventh Lord Elgin. These marble sculptures once adorned the Parthenon in Athens, and Greece wants them returned.

The British Museum

Upper Floors

Main Floor

Lower Floor

Montague Place Entrance

Main Entrance
Great Russell Street

Reading Room

Great Court

Restaurant

Clore Education Centre

Ford Centre for Young Visitors

ⓘ Information
⊠ Elevator/Lift
▦ Stairs

HIGHLIGHTS
Egyptian Mummies 5
Great Court 4
Lindow Man 6
Parthenon Sculptures 1
Reading Room 3
Rosetta Stone 2
Sutton Hoo Treasure 7

To enhance your enjoyment and understanding of the Parthenon Sculptures, pick up one of the sound guides available right outside Room 18 on the first floor, where the sculptures are exhibited; the guide costs £3.50 ($7).

Other famous treasures in the museum include the **Rosetta Stone,** which enabled archaeologists to decipher Egyptian hieroglyphics; the **Sutton Hoo Treasure,** an Anglo-Saxon burial ship, believed to be the tomb of a 7th-century East Anglian king; and **Lindow Man,** a well-preserved ancient corpse found in a bog. The museum's ethnography collections are filled with marvelous curiosities: everything from a pair of polar-bear slacks worn by Eskimos to a Hawaiian god with a mohawk haircut, found by Captain Cook and shipped back to London.

Give yourself at least three unhurried hours in the museum. You can avoid big crowds by going on a weekday morning. If you have only limited time for the British Museum, consider taking one of the 90-minute highlight tours offered daily at 10:30 a.m., 1 p.m., and 3 p.m.; these tours cost £8 ($16). You can rent audio tours, which also cover museum highlights, for £3.50 ($7). You can get tickets and information for guided tours and audio tours at the information desk in the Great Court.

See map p. 186. Great Russell Street, WC1, between Bloomsbury Street and Montgomery Street. ☎ *020/7323-8000.* www.thebritishmuseum.ac.uk. *Tube: Russell Square (then a 5-minute walk south on Montgomery Street, along the west side of Russell Square, to the museum entrance on Great Russell Street). Admission: Free. Open: Sat–Wed 10 a.m.–5:30 p.m., Thurs–Fri 10 a.m.–8:30 p.m.; closed Jan 1, Good Friday (Fri before Easter), and Dec 24–26. Most of the museum has wheelchair access via elevators; call for entrance information.*

Buckingham Palace
St. James's

Since 1837, when Victoria ascended the throne, all the majesty, scandal, intrigue, triumph, tragedy, power, wealth, and tradition associated with the British monarchy has been hidden behind the monumental facade of Buckingham Palace, the reigning monarch's London residence.

An impressive early-18th-century pile, the palace was rebuilt in 1825 and further modified in 1913. From August through September, when the royal family isn't in residence, you can buy a ticket to get a glimpse of the impressive staterooms used by Elizabeth II and the other royals. You don't get a guided palace tour; instead, you can wander at your own pace through 19 rooms (including the Throne Room and the vast ballroom built by Queen Victoria), most of them baroque, filled with some fine artwork. In these rooms, the queen receives guests on official occasions. You leave through the gardens where the queen holds her famous garden parties each summer. Budget about two hours for your visit.

Throughout the year, you can visit the **Royal Mews,** one of the finest working stables in existence, where the magnificent Gold State Coach, used in every coronation since 1831, and other royal conveyances are housed (and horses stabled). The **Queen's Gallery,** which features changing exhibits of works from the Royal Collection, went through a refurbishment and reopened for the queen's Golden Jubilee in June 2002. The palace lies between Green Park and St. James's Park, described later in this chapter.

You can buy admission tickets for Buckingham Palace by calling ☎ **020/ 7766-7303.** Green Park also houses a ticket office, open daily July 29 to October 1; the office opens at 9 a.m. and closes at 4 p.m. or when the last ticket has been sold. Keep in mind that every visitor gets a specific time for entry into the palace, which is why phoning ahead for tickets is smart. All phone-charged tickets cost an additional £1 ($2); at the ticket booth, special rates are available for seniors, kids under 17, and families.

See map p. 186. Buckingham Palace Road, SW1. Palace Visitor Office, Royal Mews, and Queen's Gallery ☎ 020/7839-1377 (9:30 a.m.–5:30 p.m.) or 020/7799-2331 (24-hour recorded info). www.royal.gov.uk. *Tube: St. James's Park (then a 10-minute walk north on Queen Anne's Gate and west on Birdcage Walk to Buckingham Gate) or Green Park (walk directly south through the park). Admission (includes audio guide): Palace £15 ($30) adults, £14 ($28) seniors, £8.50 ($17) children under 17, £39 ($78) families (2 adults and 3 children under 17); Royal Mews £7 ($14) adults, £6 ($12) seniors, £4.50 ($9) children, £19 ($38) families; Queen's Gallery £8 ($16) adults, £7 ($14) seniors, £4 ($8) children. Discounted tickets good for all attractions available on some days. Open: Palace late Aug–late Sept daily 9:45 a.m.–6 p.m. (last admittance 5:30 p.m.); Royal Mews Mar–Oct Sat–Thurs 11 a.m.–4 p.m. (last admission 3:15 p.m.), Aug–Sept daily 10 a.m.–5 p.m. (last admission 4:15 p.m.); Queen's Gallery daily 10 a.m.–5:30 p.m. (last admittance 4:30 p.m.). Royal Mews and Queen's Gallery closed Dec 25–26. Visitors with disabilities must prebook for palace visits; Royal Mews and Queen's Gallery are wheelchair accessible.*

Changing of the Guard at Buckingham Palace
St. James's

Free of charge, you can stand outside Buckingham Palace and watch the Foot Guards of the Household Division of the Army, the queen's personal guard, carry out the Changing of the Guard. The Old Guard forms in the palace forecourt before going off duty and handing everything over to the New Guard, which leaves Wellington Barracks at precisely 11:27 a.m. and marches to the palace via Birdcage Walk, usually accompanied by a band. The guard consists of 3 officers and 40 men, but this number decreases when the queen is away. The entire ceremony takes around 40 minutes. If you can't find a spot at the front of the railings of Buckingham Palace, you can see pretty well from the Victoria Memorial in front of the palace.

The pageantry of the Changing of the Guard is no longer a daily occurrence. The event takes place at 11:30 a.m. daily May to July but only on alternate days at other times of the year. To avoid disappointment, make sure to call ahead or check the Web site.

Buckingham Palace Road, SW1. ☎ 020/7321-2233. www.royal.gov.uk. *Tube: St. James's Park (then a 10-minute walk north on Queen Anne's Gate and west on Birdcage Walk to Buckingham Gate) or Green Park (then walk directly south through the park). Admission: Free.*

Covent Garden Market and Piazza
Covent Garden

In 1970, the old, noisy, bustling public market where vendors hawked everything under the sun moved out of Covent Garden and the area became the site of London's earliest and most successful urban recycling effort. The market buildings now house dozens of enticing shops and eating and drinking places. The wrought-iron stalls in the former Flower Market are loaded with vendors. The piazza in front may be the most popular public gathering place outside of Trafalgar Square; the space is always "heaving," as the Brits say. Covent Garden is also the home of the **Royal Opera House** (see Chapter 15) and the excellent **Transport Museum** (see the "Places that please kids" section, later in this chapter).

See map p. 186. Tube: Covent Garden (when you come out of the Tube stop, you're in Covent Garden; the market and piazza are a 1-minute walk south in a pedestrian-only zone).

Houses of Parliament and Big Ben
Westminster

The **Houses of Parliament,** situated along the Thames, house the landmark clock tower containing **Big Ben,** the biggest bell in the booming hourly chime that Londoners have been hearing for nearly 150 years. Designed by Sir Charles Barry and A. W. N. Pugin, the Parliament's impressive Victorian buildings were completed in 1857. Covering approximately 8 acres, they occupy the site of an 11th-century palace of Edward the Confessor.

At one end (Old Palace Yard) you find the **Jewel House,** built in 1366 and once the treasury house of Edward III, who reigned from 1327 to 1377. The best overall view of the Houses of Parliament is from Westminster Bridge, but if you prefer, you can sit in the **Stranger's Gallery** to hear a Parliamentary debate.

More guard changing

If you miss the Changing of the Guard or the event doesn't take place on the day of your visit, you can still get an eyeful of London pageantry by attending the **Mounted Guard Changing Ceremony** at the Horse Guards Building in Whitehall. These are the same guards as the ones at Buckingham Palace, only on horseback. The ceremony takes place daily Monday through Saturday at 11 a.m. and Sunday at 10 a.m. You don't need a ticket, but arrive early for a good view. To get there, take the Tube to Charing Cross and walk south from Trafalgar Square along Whitehall (about a five-minute walk); the Horse Guards Building will be on your right.

Big Ben tolls for thee

"Big Ben" isn't the name of the clock tower or its clock. It's the name of the largest bell that you hear booming in that famous hourly chime. Some people believe that the bell was named after Sir Benjamin Hall, the commissioner of works when the bell was hung in 1859. Others maintain that Big Ben was named for a champion prizefighter of the time, Ben Gaunt.

The 5-ton clock mechanism housed in the 316-foot tower kept ticking until 1976, when it succumbed to "metal fatigue" and had to be repaired. At night, new energy-efficient lighting now gives the illuminated clock faces a greenish tinge. The light at the very top is lit when Parliament is in session.

Trivia buffs will be interested to know that the minute hands on each of the tower's four clocks are as large as a double-decker bus. For information on touring the tower holding Big Ben, which you can do only if you write for tickets three months in advance, go to www.parliament.uk.

Previously, overseas visitors had to go through an elaborate procedure weeks in advance of their trip in order to tour the Houses of Parliament. Now, however, 75-minute guided tours are available in August and September. The tours cost £7 ($14) for adults, and you probably want to book your ticket in advance. You can reserve by phone at ☎ **0870/906-3773** or order tickets online at www.firstcalltickets.com. You can also buy tickets at the kiosk in Westminster Hall (at the Houses of Parliament). For the rest of the year, the procedure for getting a tour is much more difficult. If you're interested, you can find details on the Web at www.parliament.uk.

See map p. 186. Bridge Street and Parliament Square, SW1. ☎ 020/7219-4272. Tube: Westminster (you can see the clock tower with Big Ben directly across Bridge Street when you exit the Tube). Admission: Free; for tickets, join the line at St. Stephen's entrance. Open: Stranger's Gallery House of Commons Mon 2:30–10:30 p.m., Tues–Wed 11:30 a.m.–7:30 p.m., Thurs 11:30 a.m.–6:30 p.m., most Fri 9:30 a.m.–3 p.m.; House of Lords Mon–Wed 2:30–10 p.m., Thurs 10 a.m.–7:30 p.m. Parliament isn't in session late July–mid-Oct or on weekends. Guided tours: Aug Mon–Tues and Fri–Sat 9:15 a.m.–4:30 p.m., Wed–Thurs 1:15–4:30 p.m.; Sept Mon and Fri–Sat 9:15 a.m.–4:30 p.m., Tues–Thurs 1:15–4:30 p.m.

Hyde Park
Westminster

Once the private hunting domain of Henry VIII, Hyde Park is one of the largest urban parks in the world. With adjoining Kensington Gardens, it offers 630 acres of lushly landscaped lawns, magnificent flower beds,

Fountain for Diana

The **Diana, Princess of Wales Memorial Fountain** is Hyde Park's newest attraction. Made of Cornish granite, the fountain aims to reflect Diana's life through its design. From its highest point, water flows in two directions, falling in cascades, swirls, and bubbles before meeting in a calm pool at the bottom. Three bridges where you can cross the water and go right to the heart of the fountain are meant to reflect Diana's openness.

Ironically, the fountain was plagued with problems after it was opened by the queen in 2004. Visitors slipped on the granite and at one point the fountain malfunctioned and flooded Hyde Park. It is now functioning properly and open daily from 10 a.m. Knightsbridge is the nearest Tube stop. Diana fans will also want to visit the new **Diana: A Princess Remembered** exhibit at Kensington Palace.

avenues of trees, and a 41-acre lake known as the **Serpentine,** where you can row and sail model boats. **Rotten Row,** the park's famous 300-year-old riding track, was the country's first public road to be lit at night. At the northeastern tip, near Marble Arch, **Speakers' Corner** is a famous Sunday-morning venting spot for anyone who wants to climb up on a soapbox. Free band concerts are held in the park's band shell on Sundays and Bank Holidays May to August, and the **Dell Restaurant** (☎ **020/7706-0464**), at the east end of the Serpentine, offers cafeteria-style food and drinks Monday through Friday 10 a.m. to 4 p.m. in winter (to 5 p.m. on weekends) and 10 a.m. to 6 p.m. in summer (to 7 p.m. on weekends). The park is a pleasant place for an hour's stroll, but staying longer is always tempting.

See map p. 186. Bounded by Knightsbridge to the south, Bayswater Road to the north, and Park Lane to the east. ☎ *020/7298-2100.* www.royalparks.org.uk. *Tube: Marble Arch or Lancaster Gate on the north side (the park is directly across Bayswater Road) or Hyde Park Corner in the southeast corner of the park. Open: Daily dawn to midnight.*

Kensington Gardens
Kensington

Kensington Gardens adjoins Hyde Park west of the lake known as the Serpentine. Children especially love the famous bronze statue of **Peter Pan,** located north of the Serpentine Bridge. Commissioned in 1912 by Peter Pan's creator, J. M. Barrie, the statue marks the spot where Peter Pan in the book *Peter Pan in Kensington Gardens* entered the gardens to get to his home on Serpentine Island.

The park is also home to the **Albert Memorial,** an ornate neo-Gothic memorial honoring Queen Victoria's husband, Prince Albert; the lovely **Italian Gardens;** and the free **Serpentine Gallery** (☎ **020/7298-1515**), which has a reputation for showing cutting-edge art and is open daily (except Dec 24–27 and Jan 1) 10 a.m. to 6 p.m. The **Princess Diana**

Memorial Playground is in the northwest corner of the park. If the weather is fine, give yourself enough time for a leisurely stroll — at least a couple of hours.

See map p. 186. Bounded by Kensington Palace Gardens and Palace Green on the west, Bayswater Road on the north, Kensington Road and Kensington Gore on the south. ☎ 020/7298-2100. www.royalparks.org.uk. *Tube: High Street Kensington (then a 10-minute walk east on Kensington High Street) or Queensway (which is directly across from the northwest corner of the park). Open: Daily dawn to midnight.*

Kensington Palace
Kensington Gardens

Kensington Palace was used as a royal residence until 1760. Victoria was born in this palace, and it was here, in 1837 when she was 18 years old, that she was awakened from her slumbers and informed that she was the new queen of England (and could move to the grander Buckingham Palace). One wing of Kensington Palace (not open to visitors) was Princess Diana's London home after her divorce from Prince Charles. The palace was also home to Princess Margaret, who died in 2002, and remains the home of other "grace and favor" royals and dependents (the Crown provides them with free housing). Visitors can visit the **State Apartments,** several interesting exhibits relating to the history of the palace, and see some of Diana's dresses in the new **Diana: A Princess Remembered** exhibit. The freshly restored **King's Apartment** features a magnificent collection of Old Masters. Give yourself about 1½ hours to view the palace.

For a pleasant and not-too-expensive tea or snack after visiting Kensington Palace, stop in at **The Orangery** (☎ 020/7376-0239) in the gardens adjacent to the palace. (For more information, see Chapter 10.)

See map p. 186. The Broad Walk, Kensington Gardens, W8. ☎ 0870/751-5170. www.hrp.org.uk. *Tube: Queensway on the north side (then a 10-minute walk south through the park) or High Street Kensington on the southwest side (then a 10-minute walk through the park). Open: Daily 10 a.m.–6 p.m. (last admission 5 p.m.). Admission: £12 ($24) adults, £10 ($20) seniors and students, £6 ($12) children 5–15, £33 ($66) families (2 adults and 2 children). Wheelchair accessible, despite some stairs; call first.*

Leicester Square
Leicester Square

Leicester (pronounced *les*-ter) Square is a crowded place with a big-city buzz. Mimes, singers, and street entertainers of all kinds vie for attention. Once a dueling ground, the square is now a pedestrian zone and the heart of West End entertainment. You can find a half-price ticket booth (no phone) for theater, opera, and dance at the south end of the square (see Chapter 15). In the square's center, surrounded by movie theaters and restaurants, is **Leicester Square Gardens,** a small grassy park with four corner gates named for William Hogarth, Sir Joshua Reynolds, John Hunter, and Sir Isaac Newton, all of whom once lived or worked in the area. You also find statues of William Shakespeare and Charlie Chaplin, a bow to theater and cinema. You probably won't want to linger long, but just walking through the square can be fun. If you're traveling with kids, keep in mind this area is one place with a restroom (coin-operated).

See map p. 186. Tube: Leicester Square (take the Leicester Square exit and you're in the pedestrian-only zone that leads to the square).

London Zoo
Marylebone

The 36-acre London Zoo is Britain's largest, and has recently created a series of new habitats and exhibits. The best attractions are **B.U.G.S.** (insects of every description), **Gorilla Kingdom** (with a colony of Western lowland gorillas), the **Clore Rainforest Lookout** (South American monkeys, birds, and vertebrates), **Komodo Dragons,** and **Into Africa** (zebras, giraffes, okapi, red river hogs). The **Children's Zoo,** with interactive exhibits placed at low height, is designed for 4- to 8-year-olds. Many families budget almost an entire day for the zoo; I recommend that you give it at least three hours.

A fun way to arrive at the London Zoo is by water. The **London Waterbus Co.** (☎ 020/7482-2660; www.londonwaterbus.com) operates single and return trips in snug, converted canal boats along the Regent's Canal from Warwick Crescent in Little Venice to Camden Lock Market. Take the Tube to Warwick Avenue and walk south across Regent's Canal, and then you can see the moorings. Trips from both locks depart daily 10 a.m. to 5 p.m. The round-trip fare costs £8.40 ($11) for adults, £5.40 ($11) for seniors and children.

See map p. 186. At the north end of Regent's Park, NW1. ☎ *020/7722-3333.* www.londonzoo.co.uk. *Tube: Regent's Park (then a 30-minute walk north through the park; or take bus C2 from tube north on Albany Street to Delaney Street, a 10-minute walk) or Camden Town (then a 12-minute walk south on Parkway, following the signs). Admission: £15 ($30) adults; £13 ($26) seniors, students, and the disabled; £11 ($22) children 3–15; £49 ($98) families (2 adults and 2 children). Open: Early Mar–late Oct daily 10 a.m.–5:30 p.m.; late Oct–early Mar daily 10 a.m.–4 p.m.; closed Dec 25.*

Madame Tussaud's
Marylebone

Madame Tussaud's wax museum is a world-famous tourist attraction and a fun spot for older kids. The question is: Do you want to pay the exorbitant admission and devote time to see a collection of lifelike figures? (If you do go in, you need at least 2 hours to see everything.) The original moldings of members of the French court, to whom Madame Tussaud had direct access (literally, because she made molds of their heads after they were guillotined during the French Revolution), are undeniably fascinating. And animatronic gadgetry makes the **Spirit of London** theme ride fun. But **Chamber Live** (formerly called the Chamber of Horrors) is definitely for the ghoulish and unsuitable for kids under 12. The **Blush** exhibit features screen faves like Brad Pitt, Samuel L. Jackson, and Daniel Radcliffe of the Harry Potter series. Next door, the former London Planetarium has been remade into the **Stardome,** and now features a special-effects show about the stars on earth rather than those in the heavens.

Go early to beat the crowds; better still, reserve tickets one day in advance, and go straight to the head of the line. You can order tickets by phone or online.

See map p. 186. Marylebone Road, NW1. ☎ *020/7935-6861 or 0870/400-3000 for advance reservations with credit card.* www.madametussauds.com. *Tube: Baker Street (then a 2-minute walk east on Marylebone Road). Admission: £20 ($40) adults, £16 ($32) children under 16; children under 4 not admitted. Combination tickets (including the British Airways London Eye): £29 ($58) adults, £20 ($40) children under 16. Open: Daily 9 a.m.–5:30 p.m. Wheelchair accessible via elevators, but call first because only 3 chair-users are allowed in at a time.*

National Gallery
St. James's

If you're passionate about great art, you'll think that the National Gallery is paradise. This museum houses one of the world's most comprehensive collections of British and European paintings. All the major schools from the 13th century to the 20th century are represented, but the Italians get the lion's share of wall space, with works by artists such as Botticelli, Leonardo da Vinci, and Raphael. The French Impressionist and post-Impressionist works by Cézanne, Degas, Manet, Monet, Seurat, and van Gogh are splendid. And because you're on English soil, check out at least a few of Turner's stunning seascapes, Constable's landscapes, and Reynolds's society portraits. And you won't want to miss the Rembrandts. Budget at least two hours to enjoy the gallery. The second floor has a good restaurant for lunch, tea, or snacks.

To make the most of your time at the gallery, pick up a portable audio-tour guide. The guides are free but a security deposit is required.

See map p. 186. Trafalgar Square, WC2. ☎ *020/7747-2885.* www.national gallery.org.uk. *Tube: Charing Cross (then a 2-minute walk north across Trafalgar Square). Admission: Free, but special exhibits may require paying a fee, usually around £8 ($16). Open: Thurs–Tues 10 a.m.–6 p.m., Wed 10 a.m.–9 p.m.; closed Jan 1, Dec 24–26. The entire museum is wheelchair accessible.*

National Portrait Gallery
St. James's

What do these people all have in common: Sir Walter Raleigh, Shakespeare (wearing a gold earring), Queen Elizabeth I, the Brontë sisters, Winston Churchill, Oscar Wilde, Noël Coward, Mick Jagger, and Princess Di? You can find portraits of them, as well as nearly every other famous English face, at the National Portrait Gallery. The portraits are arranged in

Queen Mum memorials

In 2000, the National Portrait Gallery commissioned a royal family portrait to celebrate the Queen Mother's 100th birthday. Artist John Wonnacott painted a canvas that portrays Queen Elizabeth, Prince Phillip, Prince Charles, Prince William, and Prince Harry in conversation with the Queen Mother in the White Drawing Room in Buckingham Palace. (Interestingly, Prince William — Charles's firstborn and, thus, the second in line to the throne — dominates the picture.) The much-loved Queen Mum died in 2002, and plans are now afoot to erect a bronze statue of her to stand beneath a sculpture of her husband, King George VI, off the Mall. Artist Philip Jackson's representation of the royal matriarch as a younger woman is scheduled to be unveiled in mid-2008.

chronological order. The earliest portraits are in the **Tudor Gallery;** the latest (such as Dame Helen Mirren) are on the first floor. Plan on spending at least two hours, but getting sidetracked here is easy, so you may want more time. On the top floor, the **Portrait Restaurant & Bar** looks out over the rooftops of the West End.

See map p. 186. St. Martin's Place (off Trafalgar Square behind the National Gallery), WC2. ☎ *020/7306-0055.* www.npg.org.uk. *Tube: Leicester Square (then a 2-minute walk south on Charing Cross Road). Admission: Free; audio tour £2 ($4). Open: Sat–Wed 10 a.m.–6 p.m., Thurs–Fri 10 a.m.–9 p.m. All but the landing galleries are wheelchair accessible; call first for entry instructions.*

Natural History Museum
South Kensington

Filled with magnificent specimens and exciting displays relating to natural history, this museum houses the national collections of living and fossilized plants, animals, and minerals. The most popular attraction in this enormous Victorian Era museum is the huge **Dinosaurs** exhibit, with 14 complete skeletons, two creepy animatronic raptors, and a full-size, robotic *T. rex* guarding a fresh kill. Kids also love the bug-filled **Creepy Crawlies.** The sparkling gems and crystals in the **Mineral Gallery** literally dazzle, and in the **Meteorite Pavilion,** you can see fragments of rock that crashed into the earth from the farthest reaches of the galaxy. The intriguing **Darwin Centre** showcases the private collection of Charles Darwin, father of evolutionary theory, and houses the museum's huge collection of preserved specimens. The museum offers enough to keep you occupied for at least two hours.

See map p. 186. Cromwell Road, SW7. ☎ *020/7942-5000.* www.nhm.ac.uk. *Tube: South Kensington (the Tube station is on the corner of Cromwell Road and Exhibition Road, at the corner of the museum). Admission: Free. Open: Daily 10 a.m.–5:50 p.m. Nearly all the galleries are flat or ramped for wheelchair users; call for instructions on entering the building.*

Piccadilly Circus
Piccadilly Circus

Nearly everyone who visits London wants to see Piccadilly Circus, which marks the beginning of the West End. Piccadilly Circus, along with neighboring Leicester Square, is London's equivalent to New York's Times Square. Around the landmark statue of Eros, jostling crowds pack the pavements and an international group of teens heads for the **Pepsi Trocadero,** the area's mega-entertainment center (see "Activities for teens," later in this chapter). Regent Street at the west side of the circus and Piccadilly at the south end are major shopping streets (see Chapter 12). Piccadilly, traditionally the western road out of London, was named for the *picadil*, a ruffled collar created by a 17th-century tailor named Robert Baker.

See map p. 186. Tube: Piccadilly Circus.

Science Museum
South Kensington

The Science Museum is a popular tourist attraction that showcases the history and development of science, medicine, and technology. The fascinating displays include the Apollo 10 space module, an 1813 steam locomotive, Fox Talbot's first camera, and Edison's original phonograph. The **Wellcome Wing** is devoted to contemporary science and has an **IMAX 3-D theater.** Interactive displays tickle the brains of 7- to 12-year-olds, and the **Garden Galleries** provide construction areas, sound-and-light shows, and games for younger kids. Give yourself at least two hours.

See map p. 186. Exhibition Road, London SW7. ☎ ***020/7942-4454.*** www.science museum.org.uk. *Tube: South Kensington (a signposted exit in the Underground station goes directly to the museum). Admission: Museum free; IMAX £8 ($16) adults, £6 ($12) seniors and children 5–15. To book IMAX tickets in advance, call* ☎ *0870/ 870-4868. Open: Daily 10 a.m.–6 p.m.; closed Dec 24–26. All galleries are wheelchair accessible.*

St. James's Park and Green Park
St. James's

Henry VIII acquired these two adjoining royal parks in the early 16th century and today they flank Buckingham Palace. St James's Park, the prettier of the two, was landscaped in 1827 by John Nash in a picturesque English style with an ornamental lake and promenades. Major ceremonial occasions are held in the **Mall,** a processional route between the palace and Whitehall and Horse Guards Parade. **St. James's Palace,** the former London abode of Prince Charles and his two sons, and adjacent **Clarence House,** residence of the Queen Mum until her death in 2002 and now the London home of Prince Charles, are between the Mall and **Pall Mall** (pronounced *pell mell*), a broad avenue running from Trafalgar Square to St. James's Palace. **Clarence House** is now open to visitors in August and

Green with envy

Green Park is called Green Park because it's the only royal park without any flower beds. Why? A popular story has it that one day, as Charles II was walking through the park with his entourage, he announced that he was going to pick a flower and give it to the most beautiful lady present. This lady happened to be a milkmaid and not Queen Catherine, his wife. The queen was livid and ordered that all flowers be removed from the park (a horticultural version of "Off with their heads!").

September, daily from 10 a.m. to 5:30 p.m. Admission is £7.50 ($15) for adults and seniors, and £4 ($8) for children 5 to 15.

See map p. 186. Bounded by Piccadilly to the north, Regent Street to the east, Birdcage Walk and Buckingham Palace Road to the south, and Grosvenor Place to the west. ☎ *020/7930-1793.* www.royalparks.org.uk. *Tube: Green Park (the Tube station is right at the northeast corner of Green Park) or St. James's Park (then a 5-minute walk north on Queen Anne's Gate to Birdcage Walk, the southern perimeter of St. James's Park). Open: Daily dawn to dusk.*

St. Paul's Cathedral
The City

After the Great Fire of 1666 destroyed the city's old cathedral, the great architect Christopher Wren was called upon to design St. Paul's, a huge and harmonious Renaissance-leaning-toward-baroque building (see the "St. Paul's Cathedral" map on p. 202). During World War II, Nazi bombing raids wiped out the surrounding area but spared the cathedral, so Wren's masterpiece, capped by the most-famous dome in London, rises majestically above a crowded sea of undistinguished office buildings. Grinling Gibbons carved the exceptionally beautiful choir stalls, the only impressive artwork inside.

Christopher Wren is buried in the **crypt,** and his epitaph, on the floor below the dome, reads LECTOR, SI MONUMENTUM REQUIRIS, CIRCUMSPICE ("Reader, if you seek his monument, look around you"). His companions in the crypt include two of Britain's famed national heroes: the duke of Wellington, who defeated Napoleon at Waterloo, and Admiral Lord Nelson, who took down the French at Trafalgar during the same war. But many people want to see St. Paul's simply because Lady Diana Spencer wed Prince Charles here in what was billed as "the fairy-tale wedding of the century."

You can climb up to the **Whispering Gallery** for a bit of acoustical fun or gasp your way up to the very top for a breathtaking view of London. You can see the entire cathedral in an hour or less.

St. Paul's is now linked to the Tate Modern on the South Bank by the pedestrian-only **Millennium Bridge,** designed by Lord Norman Foster.

See map p. 186. St. Paul's Churchyard, Ludgate Hill, EC4. ☎ *020/7246-8348.* www. stpauls.co.uk. *Tube: St. Paul's (then a 5-minute walk west on Ludgate to the cathedral entrance on St. Paul's Churchyard). Admission: £10 ($20) adults, £8.50 ($17) seniors and students, £3.50 ($7) children. Tours: Guided tours (11 a.m., 11:30 a.m., 1:30 p.m., and 2 p.m.) and audio tours £3.50 ($7) adults, £3 ($6) seniors and students, £2 ($4) children under 10. Open: Mon–Sat 8:30 a.m.–4 p.m.; no sightseeing on Sun (services only). The cathedral is wheelchair accessible by the service entrance near the North Transept; ring the bell for assistance.*

Tate Britain
Pimlico

The Tate Gallery took this new name to distinguish it from its new counterpart, Tate Modern, which opened in May 2000 and is devoted to International Modernism. Tate Britain retains the older (pre-20th-century) collections of exclusively British art plus works by major British stars like David Hockney and experimental works by Brits and foreigners living in Britain. Among the masterpieces on display in a host of newly refurbished galleries are dreamy works by the British pre-Raphaelites, the celestial visions of William Blake, bawdy satirical works by William Hogarth, genteel portraits by Sir Joshua Reynolds, pastoral landscapes by John Constable, and the shimmering seascapes of J. M. W. Turner. The collection is hung thematically rather than chronologically. Plan on spending at least two hours here. The gallery has a well-regarded restaurant and a cafe on the lower level.

See map p. 186. Millbank, Pimlico SW1. ☎ *020/7887-8888.* www.tate.org.uk. *Tube: Pimlico (then a 10-minute walk south on Vauxhall Bridge Road to the river and north on Millbank to the museum entrance). Bus: For a more scenic route, take bus 77A, which runs south along The Strand and Whitehall to the museum entrance on Millbank. Admission: Free; varying admission fees for special exhibits. Tours: Audio tours £3 ($6). Open: Daily 10 a.m.–5:50 p.m. Most of the galleries are wheelchair accessible, but call first for details on entry.*

Inter-Tate travel

From Millbank Pier, on the river just outside Tate Britain, a ferry service links the Tate Britain and the Tate Modern. Vessels operated by Thames Clippers make the run between Millbank Pier and Bankside Pier, with one additional stop at Waterloo Pier, in case you want to take a spin on the British Airways London Eye. A one-way fare costs £4.30 ($8.60) for adults, free for children under 16 with an adult; if you have a Travelcard, you get one-third off the price. For more information, contact **Transport for London** (☎ **020/7222-1234;** www.tfl.gov.uk).

St. Paul's Cathedral

All Souls' Chapel **2**
American Memorial Chapter **8**
Anglican Martyr's Chapel **6**
Chapel of St. Michael
 & St. George **14**
Dean's Staircase **15**
Entrance to Crypt
 (Wren's grave) **11**
Font **5**

High Altar **7**
Lady Chapel **9**
Nelson Monument **12**
Pulpit **10**
St. Dunstan's Chapel **3**
Staircase to Library, Whispering
 Gallery & Dome **13**
Wellington Monument **4**
West Doorway **1**

Tate Modern
South Bank

The former Bankside Power Station is the setting for the fabulous Tate Modern, which opened in May 2000. Considered one of the top modern art museums in the world, it houses the Tate's collection of international 20th-century art, displaying major works by some of the most influential artists of this century: Frances Bacon, Salvador Dalí, Marcel Duchamp, Henri Matisse, Henry Moore, and Pablo Picasso among them. A gallery for the 21st-century collection exhibits contemporary art. Fans of contemporary art and architecture shouldn't miss this new star on the London art scene. Plan on spending at least two hours. The museum is now linked to St. Paul's Cathedral by the pedestrian-only **Millennium Bridge,** designed by Lord Norman Foster.

See map p. 186. 25 Sumner Street, SE1. ☎ *020/7887-8888.* www.tate.org.uk. *Tube: Southwark (then a 10-minute walk north along Blackfriars Road and east along the riverside promenade) or Blackfriars (then a 10-minute walk south across*

Blackfriars Bridge). Admission: Free; varying admission fees for special exhibits. Tours: Free, hourly 11 a.m.–3 p.m. Open: Sun–Thurs 10 a.m.–6 p.m., Fri–Sat 10 a.m.–10 p.m.; closed Jan 1 and Dec 24–26.

Tower of London
The City

The Tower of London offers enough to keep you captivated for a good three to four hours, but make sure that you save time for the **Crown Jewels,** which include the largest diamond in the world (the 530-carat Star of Africa) and other breathtaking gems set into royal robes, swords, scepters, and crowns.

The Tower of London (see the "Tower of London" map on p. 204) is the city's best-known and oldest historic site. In 1066, William the Conqueror built the tower, which served as his fortress and later as a prison, holding famous captives, such as Sir Walter Raleigh and Princess Elizabeth I. Anne Boleyn and Catherine Howard (two of the eight wives of Henry VIII), the nine-day queen Lady Jane Grey, and Sir Thomas More were among those unlucky souls who got their heads chopped off on **Tower Green.** According to Shakespeare, the two little princes (the sons of Edward IV) were murdered in the **Bloody Tower** by henchmen of Richard III — but the story is controversial among modern historians.

You can attend the nightly **Ceremony of the Keys,** the ceremonial locking-up of the Tower by the Yeoman Warders. For free tickets, write to the Ceremony of the Keys, Queen's House, HM Tower of London, London EC3N 4AB, and request a specific date, but also list three alternate dates. At least six weeks' notice is required. You must enclose an International Reply Coupon and a self-addressed stamped envelope (British stamps only), or two International Reply Coupons with all requests and list the names and addresses of all visitors. If you have a ticket, a Yeoman Warder will admit you at 9:35 p.m.

In the bad old days, important prisoners often arrived at the tower by boat. You can, too. **Catamaran Cruisers** (☎ **020/7925-2215;** www.catamarancruisers.co.uk) provides daily ferry service between Embankment Pier (Tube: Embankment) and Tower Pier. A one-way ticket for the 30-minute trip is ₤5.50 ($11) adults and ₤2.75 ($5.50) children under 16. **City Cruises** (☎ **020/7740-0400;** www.citycruises.com) makes the journey to the Tower of London from Westminster Pier approximately every 40 minutes from 10:10 a.m. to 5:50 p.m. for ₤5.60 ($11).

See map p. 186. Tower Hill, EC3. ☎ 020/7709-0765. www.hrp.org.uk. Tube: Tower Hill (then a 5-minute walk west and south on Tower Hill). Bus: You can take the eastbound bus 25 from Marble Arch, Oxford Circus, or St. Paul's; it stops at Tower Hill, north of the entrance. Admission: £16 ($32) adults, £12 ($24) seniors and students, £10 ($20) children 5–15, £45 ($90) families (2 adults and 3 children). Tours: The Yeoman Warders (also known as Beefeaters) give free 1-hour guided tours of the entire compound every half-hour, starting at 9:30 a.m. (Sun 10 a.m.) from the Middle Tower near the main entrance. The last guided walk starts about 3:30 p.m. in summer or 2:30 p.m. in winter; weather permitting. Open: Mar–Oct Tues–Sat 9 a.m.–6 p.m., Sun–Mon

The Tower of London

Beauchamp Tower **11**
Bell Tower **3**
Bloody Tower **7**
Bowyer Tower (torture chamber) **14**
Brick Tower **15**
Broad Arrow Tower **18**
Byward Tower **2**
Chapel Royal of St. Peter ad Vincula **8**
Constable Tower **17**
Cradle Tower **21**
Develin Tower **23**
Devereux Tower **12**

Flint Tower **13**
Jewel House (entrance) **9**
Lanthorn Tower **20**
Martin Tower **16**
Middle Tower **1**
Salt Tower **19**
Site of Scaffold **10**
St. Thomas's Tower **5**
Traitor's Gate **4**
Wakefield Tower **6**
Well Tower **22**

10 a.m.–6 p.m.; Nov–Feb Tues–Sat 9 a.m.–4 p.m., Sun–Mon 10 a.m.–5 p.m. (last admission 1 hour before closing); closed Jan 1 and Dec 24–26. Wheelchair access onto the grounds is available, but many of the historic buildings can't accommodate wheelchairs.

Trafalgar Square
St. James's

Until very recently, Trafalgar Square was an island in the midst of a roaringly busy traffic interchange surrounded by historic buildings, such as

St. Martin-in-the-Fields church and the National Gallery. Then, after a major urban redesign, it reopened in 2003 with one side attached to the steps of the National Gallery, so visitors can easily get to the square without crossing any streets at all. Besides being a major tourist attraction, Trafalgar Square is the site of many large gatherings, such as political demonstrations and holiday celebrations. The square honors military hero Horatio Viscount Nelson (1758–1805), who lost his life at the 1805 Battle of Trafalgar against the French. **Nelson's Column,** with fountains and four bronze lions at its base, rises 145 feet above the square. At the top, a 14-foot-high statue of Nelson (5'4" tall in real life) looks commandingly toward **Admiralty Arch,** passed through by state and royal processions between Buckingham Palace and St. Paul's Cathedral. You don't need more than a few minutes to take in the square.

The neoclassical church on the northeast corner of Trafalgar Square was the precursor for dozens of similar-looking churches throughout colonial New England. Designed by James Gibbs, a disciple of Christopher Wren, **St. Martin-in-the-Fields** (see map on p. ###; ☎ 020/7930-0089) was completed in 1726; the 185-foot spire was added about 100 years later. The **Academy of St. Martin-in-the-Fields,** a famous music ensemble, frequently performs here. Lunchtime concerts are held on Monday, Tuesday, and Friday at 1 p.m., and evening concerts are held Thursday through Saturday at 7:30 p.m. Concert tickets cost £6 to £15 ($12–$30). For reservations by credit card, call ☎ 020/7839-8362. The church is open Monday through Saturday 10 a.m. to 6 p.m. and Sunday noon to 6 p.m.; admission is free.

Café-in-the-Crypt (☎ 020/7839-4342), one of the West End's most pleasant restaurants, is in the crypt of St. Martin-in-the-Fields (see Chapter 10 for the restaurant review). The busy crypt also contains the **London Brass Rubbing Centre** (☎ 020/7437-6023), which provides paper, metallic waxes, and instructions on how to rub your own replica of historic brasses. Prices range from £3 to £15 ($6–$30). This activity is a great diversion for kids 10 and up. The center is open Monday through Saturday 10 a.m. to 6 p.m. and Sunday noon to 6 p.m.

See map p. 186. Bounded on the north by Trafalgar, on the west by Cockspur Street, and on the east by Whitehall. Tube: Charing Cross (the Underground station has an exit to the square).

Birds and Beefeaters

Huge black ravens hop around the grounds of the Tower of London. An old legend says that the British Commonwealth will end when the ravens leave the tower. Their wings have been clipped as a precaution, and in 2006, during the avian flu scare, the Tower ravens were put in quarantine. The ancient, all-male order of Yeomen Warders, more familiarly known as the Beefeaters, installed its first woman member in 2006.

Victoria & Albert Museum
South Kensington

The Victoria & Albert (known as the V&A) is the national museum of art and design. In the 145 galleries, filled with fine and decorative arts from around the world, you find superbly decorated period rooms, a fashion collection spanning 400 years of European designs, Raphael's designs for tapestries in the Sistine Chapel, the Silver Galleries, and the largest assemblages of Renaissance sculpture outside Italy and of Indian art outside India. The Canon Photography Gallery shows works by celebrated photographers. In November 2001, the museum opened its spectacular new British Galleries. Allow at least two hours just to cover the basics.

See map p. 186. Cromwell Road, SW7. ☎ *020/7942-2000.* www.vam.ac.uk. *Tube: South Kensington (the museum is across from the Underground station). Admission: Free. Open: Thurs–Tues 10 a.m.–5:45 p.m., Wed 10 a.m.–10 p.m.; closed Dec 24–26. The museum is wheelchair accessible (only about 5 percent of the exhibits include steps).*

Westminster Abbey
Westminster

The Gothic and grand Westminster Abbey (see the "Westminster Abbey" map on p. 207) is one of London's most important historic sites. The present abbey dates mostly from the 13th and 14th centuries, but a church has been on this site for more than a thousand years. Since 1066, when William the Conqueror became the first English monarch to be crowned here, every successive British sovereign except for two (Edward V and Edward VIII) has sat on the **Coronation Chair** to receive the crown and scepter. In the **Royal Chapels,** you can see the **chapel of Henry VII,** with its delicate fan vaulting, and the **tomb of Queen Elizabeth I,** who was buried in the same vault as her Catholic half-sister, Mary I, and not far from her rival, Mary Queen of Scots. In **Poets' Corner,** some of England's greatest writers (including Geoffrey Chaucer, Charles Dickens, and Thomas Hardy) are interred or memorialized. Other points of interest include the College Garden, cloisters, chapter house, and the Undercroft Museum, which contains the Pyx Chamber with its display of *church plate* (the silver owned by the church). In September 1997, the abbey served as the site of Princess Diana's funeral, and in 2002, the funeral service for the Queen Mother was held here. The abbey is within walking distance of the Houses of Parliament.

See map p. 186. Broad Sanctuary, SW1. ☎ *020/7222-7110.* www.westminster-abbey.org. *Tube: Westminster (then a 3-minute walk west following Parliament Square to Broad Sanctuary). Bus: The 77A going south along The Strand, Whitehall, and Millbank stops near the Houses of Parliament, near the Abbey. Admission: £10 ($20) adults; £7 ($14) seniors, students, and children 11–16; £24 ($48) families (2 adults and 2 children). Guided tours: Led by an Abbey Verger £5 ($10); tickets for tours at Enquiry Desk in the Abbey; audio tours £4 ($8); call for times. Open: Cathedral Mon–Sat 9:30 a.m.–3:45 p.m., no sightseeing on Sun (services only); College Garden Apr–Sept 10 a.m.–6 p.m., Oct–Mar 10 a.m.–4 p.m. You can use ramped wheelchair access through the Cloisters; ring the bell for assistance.*

Westminster Abbey

Bookshop **16**

Chapel of St. John the Baptist **6**

Chapel of St. John the Evangelist **5**

Chapter House **14**

Henry V's Chantry **8**

Poets' Corner **13**

Royal Air Force Chapel **11**

St. Andrew's Chapel **3**

St. Edward's Chapel
(Coronation Chair) **7**

St. George's Chapel **1**

St. Michael's Chapel **4**

Tomb of Mary I &
Elizabeth I **9**

Tomb of Henry VII **10**

Tomb of Mary,
Queen of Scots **12**

Tomb of the Unknown Warrior/
Memorial to Churchill **2**

Undercroft Museum and
Pyx Chamber **15**

Finding More Cool Things to See and Do

If you think you've "done" London because you've marveled at Westminster Abbey, seen where the queen lives, toured the Tower of London, and feasted your eyes on the masterpieces in the British Museum, think again. London is teeming with more sightseeing possibilities: glorious gardens, magnificent mansions, singular museums, ancient corners, historic churches, and many themed attractions that fill you in on the history and flavor of majestic London Town. In the following sections,

A window on Oscar Wilde's window

In 1995, 100 years after Oscar Wilde was tried for "gross indecency" and sentenced to two years' hard labor in Reading Gaol, the Church of England finally recognized his immortal genius with a memorial window at Westminster Abbey. But because his name is nowhere to be seen in the abbey, the blue window with its abstract design is the kind of dubious honor that would no doubt provoke a witty quip from the great playwright. Maybe something like, "Clear glass wasn't good enough for me; it had to be stained."

I highlight a few more of the many activities that may tickle your fancy and organize them by categories of interest. (For locations, see the "More London Sights" map on p. 210.)

In the following sections, I also cover four major attractions just outside Central London and easily accessible by Tube or train — **Hampstead Heath, Hampton Court Palace,** the **Royal Botanic Gardens** at Kew, and **Windsor Castle.** You can spend the better part of a day visiting any one of these sights — all are well worth your time — before returning to Central London in time for a play or concert in the evening.

The following sights are fully or partially wheelchair accessible; visitors with disabilities should call the attraction to find out about special entrances, ramps, and elevator locations:

- Bank of England Museum
- British Library Exhibition Galleries
- Chelsea Physic Garden
- Courtauld Gallery
- Design Museum
- Hampton Court
- Imperial War Museum
- London Aquarium
- London Dungeon
- London Transport Museum
- Museum of Childhood
- Museum of London
- Regent's Park
- Royal Academy of Arts

- ✔ Royal Botanic Gardens (Kew Gardens)
- ✔ Tower Bridge Experience
- ✔ Wallace Collection

Sights for history buffs

You can't escape history in London. The past is woven into the very fabric of the city, and it's why many visitors want to come here. The "history" contained in the sights in this section is as old as Rome, as new as the current prime minister, and as dramatic as the events of World War II.

Churchill Museum and Cabinet War Rooms
Westminster

You can almost hear the air-raid sirens. In this 21-room underground bunker, Prime Minister Winston Churchill and his War Cabinet planned out the military campaigns of World War II. The site has been meticulously preserved, right down to the nightshirt and cigar waiting by Churchill's bed. The Churchill Museum, dedicated to the life of Sir Winston Churchill, is a permanent exhibition within the Cabinet War Rooms. Give yourself at least an hour to explore the site.

See map p. 210. Clive Steps, King Charles Street, SW1. ☎ *020/7930-6961.* http://cwr.iwm.org.uk. *Tube: Westminster (then a 10-minute walk west, staying on the north side of the street, to Parliament Street; turn right to reach King Charles Street). Admission: £11 ($22) adults, £9 ($18) seniors and students, free for children under 16; a free self-guided audio tour comes with your ticket. Open: Daily 9:30 a.m.–6 p.m. (last admission 5 p.m.). Closed Dec 24–26.*

Imperial War Museum
Lambeth

The former insane asylum known as Bedlam is now devoted to the insanity of war. You can see a wide range of weapons and historic equipment, including a Battle of Britain Spitfire, a German one-man submarine, a Mark V tank, and a rifle once carried by Lawrence of Arabia. Other exhibits include coded messages, forged documents, espionage equipment from World War I to the present, and multimedia presentations about the Blitz and trench warfare. The Holocaust Gallery documents one of history's darkest episodes through film, photos, and artifacts, many shown for the first time. Enough history is on display to keep you occupied for a couple of hours.

See map p. 210. Lambeth Road, SE1. ☎ *020/7416-5320.* www.iwm.org.uk. *Tube: Lambeth North (then a 10-minute walk south on Kennington, south of Westminster Bridge Road, and east on Lambeth Road). Admission: Free. Open: Daily 10 a.m.–6 p.m. Closed Dec 24–26.*

More London Sights

Admiral Lord Nelson &
George IV statues **36**
Apsley House **3**
Bank of England Museum **22**
Benjamin Franklin House **34**
British Library Exhibition
Centre **15**
Carlyle's House **6**
Charles Dickens Museum **16**
Charles I equestrian statue **37**
Chelsea Physic Garden **7**
Churchill Museum & Cabinet
War Rooms **39**
Church of St. Bartholomew
the Great **25**
Church of St. Stephen
Walbrook **20**
Courtauld Gallery **32**
Design Museum **52**

Dr. Johnson's House **28**
Duke of York
Monument **13**
Edward VII statue **11**
Gilbert Collection **32**
Golden Hinde **47**
Henry VIII Gateway **26**
Hermitage Rooms **32**
H.M.S. Belfast **50**
Imperial War Museum **55**
James II and George
Washington statues **33**
London Aquarium **44**
London Dungeon **49**
London Transport
Museum **31**
The Monument **18**
Museum of Childhood **17**
Museum of London **24**

Old Operating Theatre
Museum & Herb Garret **53**
Oliver Cromwell and
Charles I statues **42**
Pepsi Trocadero **14**
Peter Pan statue **4**
Prince Albert Memorial **5**
Prince Albert Statue **27**
Queen Boudicca statue **43**
Regent's Park **1**
Royal Academy of Arts **9**
Saatchi Gallery **8**
Shakespeare's Globe
Theatre & Exhibition **46**
Sir John Soane's Museum **30**
Somerset House **32**
Southbank Centre **45**
Southwark Cathedral **48**

continued below

King's Cross
Station — **KING'S CROSS
ST. PANCRAS**
York Way
Caledonian Rd.
ISL
15
Euston Rd.
King's Cross Rd.
Grays Inn Rd.
Judd St.
**ST.
PANCRAS**
**Coram's
Fields**
Bernard St.
Guilford St.
16
Moburn Pl.
Russell
Sq.
Southampton Row
Montague Pl.
RUSSELL SQUARE
Theobalds Rd.

**British
Museum**
Bloomsbury
High
Holborn
Kingsway
HOLBORN
Hatton Gdn.
Holborn
27 **26**
**COVENT
GARDEN**
COVENT GARDEN
Aldwych
30
29 **28**
Fetter Ln.
Farringdon St.
Via.
Leicester
Square
31
Strand
Law Courts
TEMPLE
**BLACKFRIARS
STATION**
**CHANCERY
LANE**
THE CITY
**St. Paul's †
Cathedral**
21
Cheapside
Cornhill
19 **20**
Cannon St.
32
LEICESTER SQUARE
Victoria Embankment
Blackfriars
Bridge
3 **34 35**
EMBANKMENT
River Thames
Waterloo Bridge
Stamford St.
45
**Trafalgar
Square**
Whitehall
38
Whitehall
WESTMINSTER
39
40
43
42
44
41
**Houses of
Parliament**
Westminster
Abbey
BARBICAN
**The Barbican
Centre**
25
24
23
MOORGATE
London Wall
ST. PAUL'S
Bank of **22**
England
Stock Exchange
Leadenhall St.
Grace.
Upper Thames St.
**CANNON ST.
STATION**
Lower
Thames St.
Millennium
Bridge
Southwark
Bridge
Globe Theatre **46**
Tate Modern
BANKSIDE
Southwark St.
48
53
54
SOUTH BANK
Union St.
SOUTHWARK
**THE
BOROUGH**
BOROUGH
The Cut
**WATERLOO
STATION**
York Rd.
Waterloo Rd.
Blackfriars Rd.
**LAMBETH
NORTH**
Westminster Bridge Rd.
Borough Rd.
Lambeth Palace Rd.
St. George's Rd.
55
Lambeth
Bridge
Lambeth Rd.
**WEST-
MINSTER**
LAMBETH
Lambeth Rd.
Kennington Rd.
**ELEPHANT & CASTLE
(BAKERLOO)**
**ELEPHANT
& CASTLE**
New Kent Rd.
NEWINGTON
Borough Rd.
Southwark Bridge Rd.
London Rd.
Kennington Causeway
Harper Rd.
Great Dover St.
WALWORTH
Walworth Rd.
Tower Bridge Rd.
Grange Rd.
Abbey St.
Druid St.
Jamaica Rd.
Tate Britain
Millbank
Vauxhall
Bridge
VAUXHALL
Albert Embankment
Kennington Ln.
Harleyford Rd.
KENNINGTON
Kennington Park Rd.
KENNINGTON
OVAL
VAUXHALL

**LIVERPOOL ST.
STATION**
Beech St.
Aldersgate St.
Moorgate
Liverpool St.
Station
Commercial St.
Brick Ln.
Bishopsgate
Hounsditch
ALDGATE
Houndsditch
**THE
EAST
END**
Mansell St.
Leman St.
Dock St.
Minories
**TOWER
HILL**
Byward St.
**Tower of
London**
WAPPING
Tower
Bridge East
Tower
Bridge
MONUMENT
Lower Thames St.
**London
Bridge**
49
**LONDON
BRIDGE**
50
51
**London
City Hall**
Tooley St.
Thomas St.
Bermondsey St.
Long Ln.
DOCKLANDS
52

Spencer House **10**
St. Botolph's **23**
St. Dunstan's-in-the-West **29**
St. George the Martyr Church **54**
St. Margaret's Westminster **41**
St. Martin-in-the-Fields **35**
St. Mary-le-Bow **21**
Temple of Mithras **19**
10 Downing Street **38**
Tower Bridge Exhibition **51**
Victims of the Crimean
War Statue **12**
Wallace Collection **2**
Winston Churchill and
Abraham Lincoln statues **40**

Museum of London
The City

The Museum of London is the most comprehensive city museum anywhere in the world. Located in the original square-mile Londinium of the Romans and overlooking the city's Roman and medieval walls, the museum includes archaeological finds; paintings and prints; social, industrial, and historical artifacts; and costumes, maps, and models to recount the city's history from prehistoric times to today. Of special interest is the gilt-and-scarlet **Lord Mayor's Coach,** built in 1757 and weighing 3 tons. A major new expansion of the ground floor galleries (which span the centuries from the Great Fire of 1666 to modern multicultural London) got under way in 2007. Give yourself at least an hour to skim through the engaging collections.

See map p. 210. 150 London Wall (in the Barbican district near St. Paul's Cathedral), EC2. ☎ *0870/444-3853.* www.museumoflondon.org.uk. *Tube: St. Paul's (then a 10-minute walk north on St. Martin Le Grand and Aldersgate). Admission: Free. Open: Mon–Sat 10 a.m.–5:50 p.m., Sun noon to 5:50 p.m. Closed Dec 24–26 and Jan 1.*

10 Downing Street
St. James's

The prime minister's residence is a place on many visitors' "must-see" lists, so I'm sorry to tell you that there's nothing to see except a heavily guarded gate. By peering through the gate, you can get a glimpse, on the right side, of No. 10, the official residence of the British PM since 1732. In 2007, the sizeable Blair family (Tony, Cherie, and four kids) moved out and the new prime minister, Gordon Brown, moved in. The chancellor of the exchequer resides at No. 11, and No. 12 serves as the office of the chief government whip, responsible for maintaining discipline and cooperation in the vociferous House of Commons. These three small brick terrace houses, built on a cul-de-sac in 1680, stand in sharp contrast to the enormous 19th-century offices lining Whitehall, the government quarter around Downing Street.

See map p. 210. 10 Downing St., SW1. Tube: Westminster (then a 5-minute walk north on Parliament Street and Whitehall).

Attractions for art lovers

In addition to visiting the great art museums described in "London's Top Sights," earlier in this chapter, you may want to check out some of the city's smaller galleries.

Royal Academy of Arts
St. James's

Housed in 18th-century Burlington House, the site of Britain's first art school, the Royal Academy presents major exhibits throughout the year and mounts a renowned (and usually jam-packed) Summer Exhibition

From Blair to Brown: A new prime minister takes the reins

Of course, London gossip swirls around 10 Downing Street, just as it does around Buckingham Palace. After Tony Blair's position on the Iraq War cost his New Labour Party one-third of their seats in 2005, he announced that he would not run for a fourth term, and in 2007 he stepped down and handed over the reins of power to Gordon Brown, a Scotsman who had served as Blair's chancellor of the exchequer.

Unlike the voluble Blair, Brown is something of an enigma to the British public. Born in 1951 in Glasgow, he earned a PhD in history at the University of Edinburgh (and is only one of four prime ministers not to attend Oxford University or Cambridge University). During a school rugby match he was kicked in the head and suffered a detached retina that left him blind in his left eye. Later, the same symptoms threatened the vision in his right eye, but several surgeries saved his sight. After working as a lecturer in politics and a journalist, Brown was elected to Parliament in 1983. After the sudden death of Labour leader John Smith in 1994, Brown was regarded as a potential party leader, but he did not contest the leadership when Tony Blair became the favorite.

It has long been rumored that a deal was struck between Blair and Brown in which Blair promised to give Brown control of economic policy in return for Brown not standing against him in the leadership election. In public, the two remained mostly united but there have been many reports of serious rifts between them.

The new resident of 10 Downing Street has been careful not to suggest that there will be any changes in the key areas of Blair's social policy or any radical changes in New Labour itself. Since taking office, he has promoted the idea of creating several "eco-towns" with affordable, environmentally friendly housing, and proposed tighter coastal security controls after the thwarted terrorist attacks of 2007. The new prime minister is married to Sarah Macauley, a public relations executive, and has two sons, one of whom was diagnosed in 2006 with cystic fibrosis.

of juried works from around the United Kingdom. Give yourself about an hour.

See map p. 210. Burlington House, Piccadilly, W1. ☎ 020/7300-8000. www.royal academy.org.uk. *Tube: Piccadilly Circus (then a 5-minute walk down Piccadilly; the Academy is on the north side of the street just before the Burlington Arcade). Admission: Varies according to exhibit but usually £10 ($20) adults, £8 ($16) seniors, £3 ($6) children. Open: Sat–Thurs 10 a.m.–6 p.m. (last admission 5:30 p.m.), Fri 10 a.m.–10 p.m.*

Saatchi Gallery
Chelsea

Ex-adman Charles Saatchi has amassed one of the world's largest independent collections of contemporary British and international art. His gallery shows pieces from the permanent collection, as well as changing international exhibits. Regardless of what you think of the sometimes controversial works on display — many of them vapid, self-serving, and silly — the gallery remains a showcase for the art trends of the second. At press time, the gallery was moving to a new location in Chelsea and was due to reopen in 2008. Phone number and hours of operation may change.

See map p. 210. Duke of York's HQ, Sloane Sq. ☎ *020/7825-2363.* www.saatchi-gallery.co.uk. *Tube: Sloane Square (then a 3-minute walk down King's Road to Duke of York's HQ). Admission: Free. Open: Sun–Thurs 10 a.m.–8 p.m., Fri–Sat 10 a.m.–10 p.m.*

Somerset House
The Strand

The late Queen Mother once remarked how sad it was that the courtyard at Somerset House had become an Inland Revenue car park. It was just the spur that the long-running campaign needed to open up the 1,000-room civil service palace, designed by Sir William Chambers (1724–1796), to the public. The government moved its workers out and the Heritage Lottery Fund coughed up the millions needed to restore the buildings, the courtyard with its dancing fountains, and the river terrace (open daily 8 a.m. to 10 p.m., weather permitting) that's now the home of a great summer cafe. A heady mix of high culture and street entertainment, the "new" Somerset House is home to three noteworthy art collections. Each gallery charges an admission fee of £5 ($10) for adults, £4 ($8) for seniors; children under 18 enter free. The three galleries are all open daily from 10 a.m. to 6 p.m.

The **Courtauld Gallery** (☎ 020/7848-2526) has been in Somerset House since 1989. Impressionist and post-Impressionist paintings are still the gallery's main strength. Major works include Manet's *Bar at the Folies Bergères;* Monet's *Banks of the Seine at Argenteuil; Lady with Parasol* by Degas; *La Loge* by Renoir; Van Gogh's *Self-Portrait with Bandaged Ear;* and several Cézannes, including *The Card Players.* But you'll find work by most great names (many by Rubens), right up to modern greats Ben Nicholson, Graham Sutherland, and Larry Rivers. Free admission on Mondays, 10 a.m. to 2 p.m.

The **Gilbert Collection** (☎ 020/7420-9400), in the South Building, showcases the glittering gold, silver, and mosaics that were valued at £75 million when Arthur Gilbert donated the 800-piece collection to the nation in 1996. Some objects came from Princess Diana's old home, Althorp.

The last and perhaps most extraordinary of the treasures of Somerset House are the **Hermitage Rooms** (☎ 020/7845-4630). This offshoot of the State Hermitage Museum in St. Petersburg exhibits pieces from the Russian Imperial collections in changing shows.

See map p. 210. Strand, WC2. ☎ *020/7845-4600.* www.somerset-house.org.uk. *Tube: Temple (then a 5-minute walk north on Arundel Street and west on The Strand). Admission: Somerset House free; separate admissions for the galleries. Open: Courtyard 7:30 a.m.–11 p.m. (until 7 p.m. in winter); galleries daily 10 a.m.–6 p.m. (last admittance 45 minutes to 1 hour earlier). Closed Jan 1 and Dec 24–26.*

Wallace Collection
Marylebone

The palatial town house of the late Lady Wallace is the setting for a spectacular collection of art, ornaments, and armaments. You can enjoy outstanding French works by the likes of Watteau and Fragonard, as well as masterpieces from the Dutch (Frans Hals and Rembrandt), English, Spanish, and Italian schools. Decorative art from 18th-century France and European and Asian weapons are also on display. Give yourself at least an hour. The courtyard, with its new glass roof, is a pleasant spot for lunch or tea.

See map p. 210. Hertford House, Manchester Square, W1. ☎ *020/7563-9500.* www.wallacecollection.org. *Tube: Baker Street (then a 10-minute walk south on Baker Street to the museum entrance on the north side of Manchester Square). Admission: Free. Open: Daily 10 a.m.–5 p.m.*

Literary landmarks

Writers have been drawn to London for centuries and have left their literary imprints all over this vast metropolis. Listed in this section are some of the unique places associated with writers who lived in London, as well as one of the world's great storehouses of literary treasures.

British Library Exhibition Centre
Marylebone

The venerable British Library moved to this new building in 1998 and displays some of the world's most famous books, maps, manuscripts, and documents in a series of special galleries. This is where you can see a copy of the Magna Carta, Shakespeare's first folio, and handwritten manuscripts by authors such as Jane Austen, Charlotte Brontë, and Thomas Hardy. Just as fascinating are the audio recordings that let you hear the voices of Virginia Woolf and William Butler Yeats among others reading from their own works. Give this sight at least an hour; allow more time if you love literature or literary history.

See map p. 210. Euston Road, NW1. ☎ *020/7412-7332.* www.bl.uk. *Tube: King's Cross/St. Pancras (then a 5-minute walk west on Euston; the museum entrance is just beyond Midland Road). Admission: Free. Tours: Mon, Wed, Fri 3 p.m., Sat 10:30 a.m. and 3 p.m., Sun 11:30 a.m. and 3 p.m.; £6 ($12) adults, £4.50 ($9) seniors, students, and children. Open: Mon–Sat 9:30 a.m.–6 p.m. (Tues until 8 p.m.), Sun 11 a.m.–5 p.m.*

Carlyle's House
Chelsea

Thomas Carlyle (author of *The French Revolution* and many other rarely read books) and his witty wife, Jane (a noted letter writer), lived in this pretty 1708 Queen Anne terrace house from 1834 to 1881. Furnished as it was during their residence, the house is an accurate representation of middle-class Victorian domestic life. Carlyle's "soundproof" study in the skylit attic is filled with memorabilia — his books, a letter from Benjamin

Disraeli, personal effects, a writing chair, and even his death mask. You can browse through the house in about a half-hour.

See map p. 210. 24 Cheyne Row, SW3. ☎ 020/7352-7087. Tube: Sloane Square (then a 20-minute walk south on Lower Sloane Street and Hospital Road to Cheyne Walk and north on Cheyne Row; or from Sloane Square, take bus 11, 19, or 22). Admission: £4.50 ($9) adults, £2.30 ($4.60) children. Open: Mid-Mar–late Oct Wed–Fri 2–5 p.m., Sat–Sun 11 a.m.–5 p.m.

The Charles Dickens Museum
Bloomsbury

Charles Dickens lived in many places, but he and his family called this Bloomsbury house home from 1837 to 1839. Here, the great author penned *The Pickwick Papers, Oliver Twist,* and *Nicholas Nickleby,* the poignant and famous portrayals of Victorian England. The museum contains the world's most comprehensive Dickens library, portraits, illustrations, and rooms furnished exactly as they were in Dickens's time. You can see everything in a half-hour, but allow more time if you're a Dickens fanatic.

See map p. 210. 48 Doughty St., WC1. ☎ 020/7405-2127. www.dickensmuseum. com. Tube: Russell Square (then a 10-minute walk up Guilford Street and turn right on Doughty Street; the museum is on the east side of the street). Admission: £5 ($10) adults, £4 ($8) seniors, £3 ($6) children. Open: Mon–Sat 10 a.m.–5 p.m., Sun 11 a.m.–5 p.m.

Dr. Johnson's House
Holborn

Hidden away in a tiny square north of Fleet Street is the Queen Anne house where Dr. Samuel Johnson, best known as the lexicographer who compiled one of the first dictionaries of the English language, lived (quite humbly) from 1748 to 1759. A copy of the original dictionary is on display, along with Johnson memorabilia. The restored 17th-century house is close to Ye Olde Cheshire Cheese pub (see Chapter 10), a favorite haunt of the good doctor, who was celebrated as a storyteller of the first order. You can see everything on view here in less than half an hour.

See map p. 210. 17 Gough Square, EC4. ☎ 020/7353-3745. www.drjohnsons house.org. Tube: Temple (then a 10-minute walk north on Arundel Street to Fleet Street and east on Fleet Street to Dunstan's Court; Gough Square is to one side of Dunstan's Court). Admission: £4.50 ($9) adults, £3.50 ($7) seniors and students. Open: Mon–Sat 11 a.m.–5:30 p.m. (Oct–Apr until 5 p.m.).

All manner of intriguing museums

London's museums are surprisingly varied in their scope and substance. In addition to all the great art museums that you can read about in the "Attractions for art lovers" section, earlier in this chapter, the city has museums dedicated to architecture, design, transportation, medicine, and money.

Benjamin Franklin's London abode

A signer of the Declaration of Independence, Benjamin Franklin (1706–1790) was as American as they come. As a writer, he coined such famous aphorisms as "A penny saved is a penny earned." Franklin was also an inventor, and St. Paul's Cathedral in London was the first public building in the world to get one of his new lightning rods. As a statesman, Franklin resided in London between 1757 and 1775, and his "genteel lodgings," on Craven Street near Charing Cross Station, served as the first de facto American embassy after Independence. The **Benjamin Franklin House** (see map on p. 210; 36 Craven St., WC2N; ☎ **020/7930-9121**), the only Franklin house remaining in the world today, opened to the public in 2006 (the 300th anniversary of Franklin's birth). Visitors can now enjoy a 45-minute tour led by a costumed guide. Tours take place Wednesday through Sunday at noon, 1 p.m., 2 p.m., 3:15 p.m., and 4:15 p.m. and cost £7 ($14) for adults (free for children under 16). You can find more information and book a tour online at www.rsa.org.uk/franklin.

Bank of England Museum
The City

Devoted capitalists enjoy the Bank of England Museum, housed in the enormous Bank of England building. The museum chronicles changes in the banking industry since the Bank of England's beginnings in 1694, when funds were needed to finance the war against France's Louis XIV. On display are documents from famous customers (including George Washington), gold bullion, bank notes (forged and real), and coins. Interactive video displays present information about today's high-tech world of finance and a reconstructed 18th-century Banking Hall. You can see it all in less than an hour.

See map p. 210. Bartholomew Lane, EC2. ☎ *020/7601-5545.* www.bankofengland. co.uk. *Tube: Bank (then a 5-minute walk east on Threadneedle Street; turn left on Bartholomew's Lane for the museum entrance). Admission: Free. Open: Mon–Fri 10 a.m.–5 p.m.*

Design Museum
South Bank

If you're a design enthusiast — or want to see how commercial design affects our everyday lives — check out this museum in the hot "new" Butler's Wharf area east of Tower Bridge. You can find classical, kitsch, modern, surreal, and innovative — from Corbusier chairs to the Coke bottle — all chronicled here. Plus, you get to see some great river views. Plan to spend at least an hour.

See map p. 210. Butlers Wharf, Shad Thames, SE1. ☎ *0870/909-1909.* www.design museum.org. *Tube: Tower Hill (then a 10-minute walk across Tower Bridge to Butler's Wharf east of the bridge on the South Bank; or London Bridge, then a*

10-minute walk east along The Queen's Walk beside the Thames). Admission: £7 ($14) adults, £4 ($8) seniors, children under 12 free. Open: Daily 10 a.m.–5:45 p.m.

Geffrye Museum
Shoreditch

The Geffrye is one of London's most interesting and charming small museums, but it's off the beaten tourist track in East London and consequently overlooked by many visitors. In a chronological sequence of meticulously recreated period rooms, the museum displays the furniture and domestic interiors of the urban middle classes in London from Tudor times up to the present day. Each room has an audio component that allows you to hear extracts of books, newspapers, or letters written during the period. Set in beautiful 18th-century buildings that were once the almshouses of the Ironmongers' Company, the museum has a nice cafe for lunch or tea. Allow about an hour to see everything.

Kingsland Road (just north of Old Street), Shoreditch, E2. ☎ 020/7739-9893. www. geffrye-museum.org.uk. *Tube: Old Street (then a 10-minute walk east along Old Street and north on Kingsland Road). Admission: Free. Open: Tues–Sat 10 a.m.–5:45 p.m., Sun noon to 5 p.m.*

Old Operating Theatre Museum & Herb Garret
South Bank

The Old Operating Theatre isn't for the faint of heart. The roof garret of the church of St. Thomas, once attached to St. Thomas's Hospital, contains Britain's oldest operating theater (from 1822), where students could witness surgical procedures on poor (literally and figuratively) patients. You'll shudder over the collection of mid-19th-century "state-of-the-art" medical instruments, including amputation saws. The theater was in use long before the advent of anesthesia in 1846. Prior to that time, if a patient had a limb amputated, only a blindfold and a bottle of liquor were provided (and you thought *your* healthcare was bad). The herb garret was used for the storage and curing of medicinal herbs.

See map p. 210. 9A St. Thomas St., SE1. ☎ 020/7955-4791. www.thegarret. org.uk. *Tube: London Bridge (then a 5-minute walk east on St. Thomas Street). Admission: £5.25 ($11) adults, £4.25 ($8.50) seniors, £3 ($6) children under 16. Open: Daily 10 a.m.–5 p.m.; closed Dec 15–Jan 5.*

Sir John Soane's Museum
Holborn

The house of Sir John Soane (1753–1837), architect of the Bank of England, is an eccentric cache of ancient sculpture, artifacts, and art mixed in with odd architectural perspectives, fool-the-eye mirrors, flying arches, and domes. This captivating Holborn attraction is rarely crowded, which makes spending an hour even more of a treat. The oldest piece in the house is the 3,300-year-old sarcophagus of Pharaoh Seti I. Top prize in the picture gallery goes to William Hogarth's satirical and sometimes bawdy series from *The Rake's Progress*. On the first Tuesday of every month, the house is open in the evening and illuminated by candlelight.

See map p. 210. 13 Lincoln's Inn Fields, WC2. ☎ *020/7405-2107.* www.soane.org. *Tube: Holborn (then a 5-minute walk south on Kingsway to Lincoln's Inn Fields; the museum entrance is on the north side of the street). Admission: Free (£5/$10 on first Tues evening of each month). Guided tours (Sat 11 a.m.): £5 ($10). Open: Tues–Sat 10 a.m.–5 p.m., first Tues of every month 6–9 p.m.*

Activities for teens

If you have teens in tow, you may wonder where to take them so that they won't feel as though their interests are being completely ignored. The choices in this section — all places where local London teens hang out — provide a few screams, a wonderland of games, and some really loud music.

London Dungeon
South Bank

Don't bring young children here unless you want to pay for therapy, but teens seem to love the grisly re-creations of medieval torture and executions presented at this house of horrors. You find a scream (literally) around every corner. Amid the tolling bells, dripping water, and caged rats, you can face Jack the Ripper or witness a simulated burning at the stake. It's ghoulishly expensive, but some think it's more fun than Madame Tussaud's. Prices vary according to date and time of entry; you'll save by booking online.

See map p. 210. 28–34 Tooley St., SE1. ☎ *020/7403-7221.* www.thedungeons.com. *Tube: London Bridge (the exhibit is across from the station). Admission: £10–£20 ($20–$40) adults, £10–£16 ($20–$32) seniors, students, and children under 15; children 14 and under must be accompanied by an adult (not recommended for young children). Open: Apr–Sept daily 10 a.m.–6:30 p.m. (last admission 5:30 p.m.); Oct–Mar daily 10 a.m.–5:30 p.m. (last admission 4:30 p.m.). Closed Dec 25.*

Pepsi Trocadero
Piccadilly Circus

This "total entertainment complex" is right on Piccadilly Circus. The lead attraction is **Segaworld,** which offers various rides, including Max Drop, the world's first indoor freefall ride (don't eat for at least an hour before), and 400 ear-splitting, eye-popping video games and simulators. Theme restaurants include the ersatz **Rainforest Cafe** (which doesn't pretend its proceeds go to support the rain forests and has what may be the worst food in London) and the 1950s-style **Ed's Easy Diner** (see my review in Chapter 10). Plan to spend some time, because the Pepsi Trocadero is designed and packaged in such a way that after you're in, finding your way out again seems to take forever.

See map p. 210. Piccadilly Circus. www.londontrocadero.com. *Tube: Piccadilly Circus (then a 1-minute walk to the northeast side). Admission: Segaworld is free, but games and rides cost £2–£5 ($4–$10). Open: Sun–Thurs 10 a.m. to midnight, Fri–Sat 10 a.m.–1 a.m.*

Places that please kids

The little(r) ones probably won't have much interest in London's art museums and historic buildings. But the city offers all kinds of diversions for preteens, including a museum crammed with antique toys and attractions related to the sea, the stars, and the subway (Tube).

London Aquarium
South Bank

London's subterranean aquarium, located right beside the British Airways London Eye, may be a bit disappointing if you've been to any of the great aquariums in North America, and the admission prices have shot up so much that you may want to think twice about visiting. That said, children enjoy observing its more than 350 species of fish and aquatic invertebrates, including sharks, graceful stingrays, man-eating piranhas, and sea scorpions. Exhibits, some in floor-to-ceiling tanks, re-create marine habitats from around the world. Plan on spending at least an hour here — more if you can't pull the kids away, or you want to get your money's worth.

See map p. 210. Bridge Road (beside Westminster Bridge), SE1. ☎ *020/7967-8000.* www.londonaquarium.co.uk. *Tube: Waterloo (then a 5-minute walk west along the river). Admission: £13 ($26) adults, £11 ($22) seniors and students, £10 ($20) children 3–16, £29 ($58) families (2 adults and 2 children). Open: Daily 10 a.m.–6 p.m. (last admission 5 p.m.). Closed Dec 25.*

London Transport Museum
Covent Garden

Housed in a splendid Victorian building (once the Flower Market at Covent Garden) that recently received a complete interior overhaul, this museum chronicles the development of the city's famous Underground and double-decker red bus system. A fabulous collection of historic vehicles, including a horse-drawn bus, and London's first trolley bus, are on display. Several KidZones offer interactive exhibits that enable younger visitors to operate the controls of a Tube train, get their tickets punched, and play with touch-screen technology. After two hours, you may have to drag them away.

See map p. 210. The Piazza, WC2. ☎ *020/7379-6344.* www.ltmuseum.co.uk. *Tube: Covent Garden (then a 2-minute walk west to the Piazza; the museum is in the southeast corner). Admission: £8 ($16) adults, £6.50 ($7) seniors, free for children under 16. Open: Daily 10 a.m.–6 p.m.(last admission at 5:15 p.m.).*

Museum of Childhood
Bethnal Green

A branch of the Victoria & Albert Museum, this museum specializes in toys from the past and present. You can find a staggering collection of dolls, many with elaborate period costumes, and fully furnished dollhouses ranging from simple cottages to miniature mansions. Optical toys, marionettes, puppets, tin soldiers, war toys, toy trains and aircraft, and a display of clothing and furniture relating to the social history of childhood make this museum an enchanting place to invest a couple of hours. Oh, how times — and toys — have changed.

See map p. 210. Cambridge Heath Rd., E2. ☎ *020/8980-2415.* www.vam.ac.uk/moc. *Tube: Bethnal Green (then a 5-minute walk north on Cambridge Heath Road to the museum entrance on the east side of the street). Admission: Free. Open: Daily 10 a.m.–5:45 p.m.*

To see or not to see: Shakespearean sights

If you don't have time to visit Stratford-upon-Avon (see Chapter 14), where the great poet and dramatist William Shakespeare was born and died, you can visit two Shakespeare-associated sights on London's South Bank.

Shakespeare's Globe Theatre
South Bank

A guided tour of this full-size replica of Shakespeare's Globe Theatre and its workshops, all located just east of the original site, will transport you to the days of Shakespeare and Elizabethan theater: what audiences were like, the rivalry among the theaters, the cruel bear-baiting shows, and the notorious Southwark Stews (a nearby area where prostitutes plied their trade). Watching a Shakespeare play from one of the benches in this roof-less "wooden O" is a memorable experience, though the hard benches can be rough on the backside. See Chapter 15 for details on obtaining tickets for one of the performances, presented mid-April through early October.

If you plan to see a Shakespeare play at the Globe, you can have a snack, tea, or a full meal in the theater itself. You don't need to make reservations at **The Globe Café**; it's open daily mid-April through early October 10 a.m. to 11 p.m. and mid-October through mid-April 10 a.m. to 6 p.m. Make reservations ahead for lunch or dinner at **The Globe Restaurant** (☎ **020/7928-9444**), open daily noon to 2:30 p.m. and 6 to 11 p.m.

See map p. 210. New Globe Walk (just west of Southwark Bridge), SE1. ☎ *020/ 7902-1500.* www.shakespeares-globe.org. *Tube: Mansion House (then a 10-minute walk across Southwark Bridge; the theater is visible on the west side along the river). Tours: £9 ($18) adults, £7.50 ($15) seniors and students, £6.50 ($13) children, £20 ($40) families (2 adults and 3 children). Open: Mid-Oct–mid-Apr daily 10 a.m.–5 p.m., mid-Apr–mid-Oct (performance season) daily 9 a.m. to noon.*

Southwark Cathedral
South Bank

Chaucer and Shakespeare both worshiped at Southwark Cathedral. London's second-oldest church after Westminster Abbey, Southwark (pronounced *suth*-ick) Cathedral is in what was London's first theater district (as well as a church-sanctioned center of prostitution). Although the cathedral was partially rebuilt in 1890, a great deal of history is associated with this 15th-century church. In under 30 minutes, you can see the entire site, including the Shakespeare memorial window and a 13th-century wooden effigy of a knight. Lunchtime concerts are regularly given on Monday and Tuesday; call for exact times and schedules.

See map p. 210. Montague Close (just west of London Bridge), SE1. ☎ 020/7367-6700. Tube: London Bridge (then a 5-minute walk across London Bridge Road to Cathedral Street). Admission: Free, but a £3 ($6) donation is suggested. Open: Mon–Fri 7:30 a.m.–6 p.m., Sat–Sun 8:30 a.m.–6 p.m.

Ships ahoy! Nautical London

The River Thames, London's watery artery to the English Channel, is full of all kinds of watercraft. This section details two intriguing ships that you can visit. I also tell you about touring the Thames by boat in the "Seeing London by Guided Tour" section, later in this chapter.

Golden Hinde
South Bank

A full-scale reconstruction of Sir Francis Drake's 16th-century flagship, complete with a crew dressed in Tudor costumes, the *Golden Hinde* was built in Devon but launched in San Francisco in 1973 to commemorate Drake's claiming of California for Queen Elizabeth I. Like the original, this ship circumnavigated the globe, sailing more than 140,000 miles before becoming a permanent floating museum in 1996. A self-guided tour of the fully rigged ship, once the home to 20 officers and gentlemen and between 40 to 60 crew members, takes about a half-hour.

See map p. 210. St. Mary Overie Dock, Cathedral Street (west of London Bridge), SE1. ☎ 08700/118-700. www.goldenhinde.org. Tube: London Bridge (then a 5-minute walk west on Bedale and Cathedral streets). Admission: £4.50 ($9) adults, £3.50 ($7) seniors, £2.50 ($5) children, £15 ($30) families (2 adults and 2 children). Open: Mon–Fri 11 a.m.–5:30 p.m., Sat–Sun 10 a.m.–5:30 p.m.; may be closed for educational events.

H.M.S. Belfast
South Bank

The *Belfast,* a huge Royal Navy cruiser built in 1938 and used in World War II, is now moored in the Thames near London Bridge, opposite the Tower of London. Tours of this floating 10,500-ton museum allow visitors to see all seven decks. On-ship exhibits are devoted to the history of the ship and the Royal Navy. You and your kids can witness a re-created surface battle. Plan to spend about 90 minutes.

See map p. 210. Morgan's Lane, Tooley Street (between Tower Bridge and London Bridge), SE1. ☎ 020/7940-6300. http://hmsbelfast.iwm.org.uk. Tube: London Bridge (then a 10-minute walk north across Tooley Street and north on Hays Lane toward the entrance on the river). Admission: £10 ($20) adults, £6.15 ($12) seniors and students, free for children under 16. Open: Mar–Oct daily 10 a.m.–6 p.m.; Nov–Feb daily 10 a.m.–5 p.m. (last admission 45 minutes before closing).

Architectural highlights and stately homes

Stepping into one of London's great mansions, you can see what life lived on a grand scale was really like. The capital is also full of intriguing monuments, including one called, simply, The Monument, and famous bridges, such as Tower Bridge, which you can visit high above the Thames.

Apsley House
St. James's

Once known as Number One London because it was the first house past the tollgate into London, this magnificent neoclassical mansion, designed by Robert Adam and built between 1771 and 1778, was the London residence of the first duke of Wellington. The last great London town house, Apsley contains original collections that are mostly intact. After his phenomenal military career, which included defeating Napoleon at Waterloo in 1815, the duke was one of the most popular men in England. Apsley House, with its sumptuous interiors and treasure-trove of paintings, china, swords, and military honors, reflects the first duke's position as the most powerful commander in Europe. A free audio guide explains it all on a self-guided tour that lasts about an hour. The family is still in residence, although you never see them.

See map p. 210. Hyde Park Corner, W1. ☎ *020/7499-5676. Tube: Hyde Park Corner (Exit 3 brings you up next to the house). Admission: £5.30 ($11) adults, £4 ($8) seniors, £2.70 ($5.40) children. Open: Tues–Sun 11 a.m.–5 p.m. (Nov–Mar until 4 p.m.). Closed Dec 24–26, Jan 1, Good Friday (Fri before Easter), and May 1.*

The Monument
The City

This 202-foot-high Doric column was designed by Sir Christopher Wren and commemorates the Great Fire of 1662, which allegedly began in nearby Pudding Lane and swept through London. The Monument is the tallest isolated stone column in the world — you'll know just how tall if you climb the 311 steps to the viewing platform at the top. *Note:* The Monument is closed for repair and not scheduled to reopen until late 2008.

See map p. 210. Monument Street (just north of London Bridge), EC3. ☎ *020/ 7626-2717.* www.themonument.info. *Tube: Monument (you get out right across the street). Admission: £6 ($12) adults, £4.50 ($9) seniors and students, £3 ($6) children. Open: Daily Apr–Sept 10 a.m.–6:30 p.m., Oct–Mar 9:30 a.m.–6 p.m. (last admission 45 minutes before closing).*

Spencer House
St. James's

The late Princess Diana is probably the most famous member of the Spencer family, but she never lived in her family's ancestral London home, built for the first Earl Spencer in 1766. The house, one of London's most beautiful private palaces, hasn't been a private residence since 1927. Brilliantly restored and opened as a museum in 1990, its rooms are filled with period furniture and art loans from Queen Elizabeth, the Tate Britain, and the Victoria & Albert Museum. Guided tours (the only way to see the place) take about an hour and are limited to groups of 20.

See map p. 210. 27 St. James's Place, SW1. ☎ **020/7514-1958.** www.spencer house.co.uk. *Tube: Green Park (then a 5-minute walk south on Queen's Walk to St. James's Place on your left). Admission: £9 ($18) adults, £7 ($14) seniors and students. Children under 10 not admitted. Open: Sun 10:30 a.m.–4:45 p.m. Closed Jan and Aug.*

Tower Bridge Exhibition
South Bank

Step inside Tower Bridge and find out why, how, and when this famous drawbridge with its pinnacled towers was built and how the mechanism for raising the bridge for ship traffic actually works. The spectacular views up and down the Thames from the bridge's glass-enclosed walkways double the value of this attraction.

See map p. 210. North Pier, Tower Bridge, SE1. ☎ **020/7403-3761.** www.tower bridge.org.uk. *Tube: Tower Hill (then a 10-minute walk south to the north pier of Tower Bridge). Admission: £6 ($12) adults, £4.50 ($9) seniors and students, £3 ($6) children 5–15. Open: Daily Oct–Mar 9:30 a.m.–6 p.m., Apr–Sept 10 a.m.–6:30 p.m. (last admission 75 minutes before closing). Closed Dec 25–26.*

Parks and gardens

Part of London's charm comes from its giant green parks, small neighborhood squares, and special gardens. You never have to feel oppressed by too much brick and concrete in this city. If the mood strikes, you may want to visit one of the lovely spots in this section.

Chelsea Physic Garden
Chelsea

Hidden behind high brick walls, the Chelsea Physic Garden is the second-oldest surviving botanical garden in England and one of London's most beautiful places. The garden, containing more than 7,000 exotic herbs, shrubs, trees, and flowers, plus England's earliest rock garden, was

---

For fans of Princess Di

If you're a true Princess Diana fan, note that she's buried on a picturesque island on the Oval Lake at **Althorp,** the Spencer family estate in Northamptonshire. The grounds are open for a limited time each year from July through September, but you can view the island from across the lake only. Admission costs £12 ($24) adults, £10 ($20) seniors, £6 ($12) children, and £30 ($60) families (two adults and two children). The charge includes admission to the Diana Museum set up by her brother, Earl Spencer. The museum contains an exhibit celebrating Diana's childhood, her royal wedding (including her famous wedding gown), and her charitable works. You can book your tickets in advance by calling ☎ **0870/167-9000.** You can also buy day-of tickets at the Gate House or online at www.althorp.com.

founded in 1673 by the Worshipful Society of Apothecaries to develop medicinal and commercial plant species. Cotton seeds from this garden launched an industry in the new colony of Georgia. The garden is small enough (3½ acres) to wander through in less than an hour, but budget some more time if you love plants. Drop by the nice teahouse on the premises for a spot of tea.

See map p. 210. Swan Walk, 66 Royal Hospital Rd., SW3. ☎ 020/7352-5646. www. chelseaphysicgarden.co.uk. *Tube: Sloane Square (then a 15-minute walk south on Lower Sloane Street and west to the end of Royal Hospital Road). Bus: Southbound bus 11, 19, or 22 from Sloane Square. Admission: £7 ($14) adults, £4 ($8) students and children 5–15. Open: Apr–Oct Wed noon to dusk, Thurs–Fri noon to 5 p.m., Sun noon to 6 p.m.*

Regent's Park
Marylebone

Regent's Park spans 400 acres of green, mostly open parkland fringed by imposing Regency terraces. The park is the home of the **London Zoo** (described under "London's Top Sights," earlier in this chapter). People come here to play soccer, cricket, tennis, and softball; boat on the lake; visit **Queen Mary's Rose Garden** (which includes an outdoor theater — see Chapter 15); and let their kids have fun at the many playgrounds. The park offers summer lunch and evening bandstand concerts, as well as puppet shows and other children's activities on weekdays throughout August. The northernmost section of the park rises to the summit of **Primrose Hill,** which provides fine views of Westminster and the City. The restrooms by Chester Gate, on the east side of the park, offer facilities for persons with disabilities.

See map p. 210. Just north of Marylebone Road and surrounded by the Outer Circle road. ☎ 020/7486-7905, or 020/7486-2431 *for advance booking for Open Air Theatre (operating late May–early Sept).* www.royalparks.org.uk *and* www.open airtheatre.org. *Tube: Regent's Park or Baker Street (then a 5-minute walk north to the south end of the park). Open: Daily 5 a.m. to dusk.*

Royal Botanic Gardens
Kew

Located 9 miles southwest of Central London, the **Royal Botanic Gardens** at Kew — more familiarly known as Kew Gardens — are a gift to garden lovers. A trip to Kew takes the better part of a day to allow for travel time and garden strolling, but the enjoyment of the experience is well worth the time investment. On display in the 300-acre gardens is a marvelous array of specimens first planted in the 17th and 18th centuries. Orchids and palms are nurtured in the Victorian glass pavilion hothouse. The site contains a lake, aquatic gardens, a Chinese pagoda, and even a royal palace. **Kew Palace,** smallest and loveliest of the former royal compounds, where King George III went insane and where Queen Charlotte died in 1818, is open from April through September. **Queen Charlotte's Cottage** (not open to the public) served as the mad king's summer retreat. A sightseeing bus called **Kew Explorer** makes a complete circuit of the gardens (with hop-on/hop-off service) and costs £3.50 ($7) for adults, and £1 ($2) for children.

Tired of the Tube? Why not take a boat to Kew Gardens? April to late September, vessels operated by the **Westminster Passenger Service Association** (☎ 020/7930-2062; www.wpsa.co.uk) leave from Westminster Pier daily at 10:30 a.m., 11 a.m., and 2 p.m. Round-trip fare for the 90-minute journey costs £17 ($34) adults, £11 ($22) seniors, £8.25 ($17) children, and £41 ($82) families (two adults and two children). The last boat from Kew usually departs around 5.30 p.m. (depending on the tide).

Kew. ☎ *020/8332-5622.* www.kew.org. *Tube: Kew Gardens (then a 10-minute walk west on Broomfield Street to the Victoria Gate entrance on Kew Road). Admission: £12 ($24) adults, £10 ($20) seniors and students, free for children 5–16. Tours: Mar–Nov free 1-hour tours daily at 11 a.m. and 2 p.m. Open: Gardens daily 9:30 a.m.–5:30 p.m.(summer until 6:30 p.m., winter until 4:15 p.m.); glass pavilion closes 1 hour before gardens; Kew Palace Apr–Sept 9:30 a.m.–4:15 p.m. Closed Dec 25 and Jan 1.*

A quaint village just a Tube ride away

The London that you see today was once a series of separate villages. The nearby village of Hampstead, with its adjacent heath land, still retains its rural charm and makes for an excellent mini day trip.

Hampstead and Hampstead Heath

Although only 15 minutes by Tube from Central London, **Hampstead** maintains its old-world charm. It's filled with Regency and Georgian houses (many set in lovely gardens) favored by artists and writers, from Keats to John le Carré. **Flask Walk,** the village's pedestrian mall, provides an eclectic assemblage of historic pubs, shops, and chic boutiques. The village itself has a lot of old alleys, steps, courts, and groves just begging to be explored.

Adjacent **Hampstead Heath** is 800 acres of high parkland offering an opportunity for picnicking, swimming, and fishing. On a clear day, you can see St. Paul's Cathedral and even the hills of Kent. An excursion here takes up at least a half-day or more.

See map p. 227. Tube: Hampstead (the Tube stop is 1 minute from Flask Walk) or Hampstead Heath (Parliament Hill, right behind the Tube stop, leads up into the park itself).

Kenwood House

This lovely neoclassical villa sits on the shore of Kenwood Lake in the northern section of Hampstead Heath. The villa was remodeled in the 1760s by Robert Adam. Inside, you find a small but impressive collection of paintings (with works by Gainsborough, Rembrandt, Reynolds, Turner, and Vermeer) and jewelry. You can get something to eat in the cafeteria in the former coach house. For an enjoyable summer outdoor concert experience, visit the Kenwood Lakeside concert (see Chapter 15).

Hampstead Lane (Hampstead), NW3. ☎ *020/8348-1286. Tube: Archway (then bus 210 west along Highgate and Hampstead Lane). Admission: Free. Open: Apr–Oct daily 11 a.m.–6 p.m.; Nov–Mar daily 11 a.m.–4 p.m.*

Hampstead

Royal castles and palaces

Everyone wants to see Buckingham Palace, the queen's London residence. But another royal residence, accessible year-round, awaits in nearby Windsor. Just as memorable is Hampton Court, another great royal compound from the time of Henry VIII.

Hampton Court Palace

In 1514, Cardinal Wolsey began building the splendid Tudor Hampton Court in East Moseley, Surrey, 13 miles west of London on the north side of the Thames. Henry VIII nabbed Hampton Court for himself and made it a royal residence, which it remained until 1760. The **Anne Boleyn Gate,** with its 16th-century astronomical clock, and the **Great Hall,** with its hammer-beam ceiling, are remnants from Hampton Court's Tudor days. Later, the palace was much altered by Sir Christopher Wren for William and Mary. Wren also designed the famous **Maze,** where visitors can wander in dizzy confusion. Inside the enormous palace are various state apartments and private rooms, including the **King's Dressing Room** and Tudor kitchens, and containing wooden carvings by Grinling Gibbons, Italian paintings, and guides dressed in period costumes. The manicured Thamesside gardens are lovely. You find a cafe and restaurant on the grounds. You need a full day for this excursion.

Hampton Court, East Moseley, Surrey. ☎ *0870/752-7777.* www.hrp.org.uk. *Train: Frequent trains from Waterloo Station make the half-hour trip to Hampton Court Station; the round-trip fare costs about £5 ($10). Admission: £13 ($26) adults, £11 ($21) seniors and students, £6.50 ($13) children 5–15. Open: Apr–Oct daily 10 a.m.–6 p.m.; Nov–Feb daily 10 a.m.–4:30 p.m. Closed Jan 1 and Dec 24–26.*

Windsor Castle

Windsor is one of the queen's official residences. The castle, with its imposing skyline of towers and battlements rising from the center of the 4,800-acre Great Park, is located in Windsor, Berkshire, 20 miles from the center of London. Royals have used the castle as a residence since its construction by William the Conqueror approximately 900 years ago. The **State Apartments** that are open to visitors range from the intimate chambers of Charles II to the enormous Waterloo Chamber, built to commemorate the victory over Napoleon in 1815. All apartments are furnished with important works of art from the Royal Collection. **Queen Mary's Dollhouse,** designed by Sir Edwin Lutyens as a present for Queen Mary in 1921, is a marvelous palace in miniature. **St. George's Chapel,** a Gothic masterpiece of the 14th century, is the burial place of ten monarchs and the home of the Order of the Garter.

April through June, the **Changing of the Guard** takes place Monday through Saturday at 11 a.m. (on alternate days the rest of the year). From

Ghost palace

So many people, from staff to visitors, have reported encounters with Catherine Howard's ghost in the "haunted gallery" at Hampton Court that psychologists from the University of Hertfordshire conducted an investigation to see if they could find a scientific explanation for the phenomenon. Not surprisingly, the results were inconclusive. Catherine, the fifth wife of King Henry VIII, was locked up in Hampton Court prior to her beheading for adultery in 1542. One day, she supposedly escaped and in desperation ran along the 40-foot gallery to pound on the King's door and beg for mercy. Sightings in this gallery of a running, screaming apparition have been reported for centuries.

the ramparts of Windsor, you can look down on the playing fields of **Eton College,** where aristocrats have been sending their boys for generations. All the royals attend the famous school in the charming town of **Eton** across the Thames Bridge. Give yourself a full day for this excursion.

Windsor. ☎ *01753/831118.* www.royal.gov.uk. *Train: Trains leave every half-hour from Waterloo Station for the 50-minute trip (the stop is Windsor and Eton); the round-trip fare costs approx £8 ($16). Admission: £14 ($28) adults, £13 ($26) seniors and students, £8 ($16) children under 17, £37 ($74) families (2 adults and 3 children). Open: Mar–Oct daily 9:45 a.m.–5:15 p.m. (last entry 4 p.m.); Nov–Feb daily 9:45 a.m.–4:15 p.m. (last entry 3 p.m.); closed Jan 1, Mar 28, June 16, and Dec 25–26.*

Greenwich: The center of time and space

Time is of the essence in Greenwich, a town and borough of Greater London, about 4 miles east of the City. The world's clocks are set according to Greenwich mean time, and visitors from around the globe flock here to stand on the **prime meridian,** the line from which the world's longitude is measured. The historic buildings in Greenwich are important enough that UNESCO has listed them as a World Heritage Site. Greenwich offers enough to keep you fully occupied for a full day, and it makes a great outing for kids.

The most interesting route to get to Greenwich is by Docklands Light Rail from Tower Hill Gateway, which takes you past Canary Wharf and all the new Docklands development. The one-way fare costs £4 ($8). Take the train to Island Gardens, the last stop, and then walk through the foot tunnel beneath the Thames to Greenwich. You come out next to the *Cutty Sark.* You can also take the Jubilee Underground line to Greenwich North and then bus 188 to the *Cutty Sark.* **Thames River Services** (☎ 020/ 7930-4097) runs a year-round fleet of boats from Westminster Pier to Greenwich Pier. A round-trip ticket costs £10 ($20) adults, £26 ($52) for families (two adults and two children).

All the attractions in Greenwich are clearly signposted, and you can reach them on foot. The Greenwich Tourist Information Centre (Pepys House, Cutty Sark Gardens; ☎ 0870/608-2000) is open daily 10 a.m. to 5 p.m. The center offers 1½- to 2-hour walking tours (at 12:15 p.m. and 2:15 p.m.) of the town's major sights for £4 ($8). Reservations aren't necessary, but you may want to call first to make sure that the schedule hasn't changed.

Cutty Sark

The majestic *Cutty Sark,* berthed on the river Thames, is the last of the tea-clipper sailing ships. It was launched in 1869 and first used for the lucrative China Sea tea trade. Later, the ship carried wool from Australia and after that (up until the end of World War II) served as a training ship. The ship had been closed for restoration when a fire struck on May 21, 2007, causing major damage. It is scheduled to reopen in late 2008. Until that time, you can visit an adjacent exhibition that details the history of the *Cutty Sark* and the work that's being done to save it.

Cutty Sark Visitor Centre, King William Walk. ☎ *020/8858-3445.* www.cutty
sark.org.uk. *Admission: £2 ($4) per person. Open: Daily 11 a.m.–5 p.m. Closed
Dec 24–26.*

National Maritime Museum

The paintings of ships are boring, but the National Maritime Museum also
displays sailing crafts and models and an extensive exhibit on Lord Nelson,
which includes hundreds of his personal artifacts (including the coat that
he was wearing when he was shot at the Battle of Trafalgar). New galleries
with interactive technology explore modern maritime issues. You can sail
through in about a half-hour. There's a nice cafe for lunch or a snack.

In Greenwich Park. ☎ *020/8312-6608.* www.nmm.ac.uk. *Admission: Free. Open:
Daily 10 a.m.–5 p.m. (June–Sept until 6 p.m.).*

Queen's House

Adjacent to the National Maritime Museum, you can find the splendidly
restored Queen's House, designed by Inigo Jones in 1616 and later used as
a model for the White House. The house, the first classical building in
England, was commissioned by Anne of Denmark, the wife of James I, and
completed in 1635 (with later modifications). You can visit the royal apartments on a self-guided tour that takes about a half-hour. You may catch a
special exhibit being held here.

In Greenwich Park. ☎ *020/8312-6608.* www.nmm.ac.uk. *Admission: Free. Open:
Daily 10 a.m.–5 p.m.*

Royal Naval College

Near the *Cutty Sark,* the Royal Naval College occupies the site of Greenwich
Palace, which stood here from 1422 to 1620 and was the birthplace of Henry
VIII, Mary I, and Elizabeth I. Badly damaged by Cromwell's troops during
the English Civil War, the palace was later torn down, and in 1696 a naval
hospital for retired seamen was erected in its place. The Thames-side buildings, designed by Sir Christopher Wren, became the Naval College in 1873
and are today a UNESCO-designated World Heritage Site. The only rooms
open to visitors are the chapel and the imposing **Great Hall** with its daz-
zling painted ceiling. The body of Lord Nelson lay in state here in 1805.

King William Walk. ☎ *020/8858-2154.* www.oldroyalnavalcollege.org.
Admission: Free. Open: Daily 10 a.m.–5 p.m.

Royal Observatory Greenwich

Huff your way up the hill from Queen's House (see listing above) in
Greenwich Great Park to explore the Royal Observatory, where you can
straddle the **prime meridian** (longitude 0 degrees), the center of time and
space. The Observatory reopened in 2007 after a spectacular £15 million
($30 million) redevelopment. Interactive exhibits in the new **Weller**

Astronomy Galleries explain how stars and planets are born and help unravel the mysteries of the universe. The Star Life planetarium show in the new, state-of-the-art Peter Harrison Planetarium explores the night sky and how stars are born, grow up, grow old, and die. Shows are hosted by real astronomers, who are available to answer questions after the main program (children must be 7 years or older). Also look for the collection of original 18th-century chronometers (marked H1, H2, H3, and H4), beautiful instruments that were developed to help mariners chart longitude by time instead of by the stars.

In Greenwich Park. ☎ *020/8312-8565.* www.nmm.ac.uk/astronomy. *Admission: Observatory free; planetarium adults £6 ($12); planetarium seniors, students, and children (no children under 7 permitted) £4 ($8). Open: Daily 10 a.m.–5 p.m. (June–Sept until 6 p.m.); planetarium shows Mon–Fri 1 p.m., 2 p.m., 3 p.m., 4 p.m., Sat–Sun additional shows at 11 a.m. and noon.*

Seeing London by Guided Tour

When it comes to London sightseeing tours, you're limited only by your imagination, stamina, and budget. You can tour London with an experienced guide by bus, by boat, or on foot.

Bus tours

Original London Sightseeing Tours (☎ 020/8877-1722; www.theoriginal tour.com) maintains a fleet of double-decker buses (many of them open on top) and offers hop-on/hop-off service at more than 90 boarding points around the city and includes a 50-minute river cruise. You can choose from four tour routes. The **Original London Sightseeing Tour** lasts 90 minutes and passes every major sight in Central London and the South Bank; the tour starts from Piccadilly Circus (Tube: Piccadilly Circus) outside the Planet Hollywood restaurant on Coventry Street and departs every few minutes daily from 9 a.m. to 6 p.m. (to 9 p.m. in summer). You don't have to book any of the sightseeing tours in advance; you can pay on the bus. A ticket good for 24 hours on all routes costs £19 ($38) for adults and £12 ($24) for children under 16. For more information or to book discounted tickets online, check out the Web site.

The **Big Bus Company** (☎ 020/7233-9533; www.bigbus.co.uk) leaves from Green Park, Victoria, and Marble Arch daily, from 8:30 a.m. to 7 p.m. (4:30 p.m. in winter) on three different routes that take anywhere from 1½ to 2½ hours. Tickets include a river cruise and walking tours, and cost £20 ($40) for adults and £10 ($20) for children ages 5 to 15. Valid for 24 hours, they let you hop on and off at 54 locations. Big Bus often has special offers, too, throwing in cheap theater tickets, fast-entry to popular attractions, and so on.

Another tour company with many guided excursions is **Golden Tours** (4 Fountain Square, 123–151 Buckingham Palace Rd.; ☎ 800/456-6303 in the U.S. or 020/7233-7030; www.goldentours.co.uk). Its buses are comfy and have restrooms, and the certified guides have a certifiable sense of humor. The daily **Historic & Modern London** tour is a full-day outing that includes the West End, Westminster Abbey, the Changing of the Guard (at Buckingham Palace or Horse Guards Parade), the City of London, St. Paul's Cathedral, the Tower of London, and a cruise from the Tower down to Charing Cross Pier; the price includes a pub lunch and all admissions. This tour costs £72 ($144) for adults, £69 ($138) for seniors and students, and £62 ($124) for kids under 16. Tours depart from the office at Buckingham Palace Road (Tube: Victoria) and other points in Central London. You can book your tickets directly or online, or you can ask your hotel concierge to do it two days in advance.

Boat tours

A cruise down the majestic Thames is a marvelous way to take in the city's sights. Sightseeing boats regularly ply the river between Westminster and the Tower of London; some continue downstream to Greenwich (site of the prime meridian, *Cutty Sark,* and Old Royal Observatory) and upstream to Kew Gardens and Hampton Court. The main departure points along the Thames are at **Westminster Pier** (Tube: Westminster), **Waterloo Pier** (Tube: Waterloo), **Embankment Pier** (Tube: Embankment), **Tower Pier** (Tube: Tower Hill), and **Greenwich Pier** (Tube: Greenwich).

Transport for London (☎ 020/7222-1234; www.tfl.gov.uk) runs a fleet of commuter and sightseeing boats on the Thames from Westminster Pier to Greenwich. An all-day hop-on/hop-off River Rover ticket costs £11 ($22) adults, £27 ($54) for families (two adults and two children). You can buy tickets at Westminster, Waterloo, Tower, or City piers.

Daily from March through November and on weekends the rest of the year, Bateaux London/**Catamaran Cruisers** (☎ 020/7695-1800; www.catamarancruisers.co.uk) offers a one-hour circular cruise from Westminster Pier (Tube: Westminster) that passes most of London's major monuments and stops at Festival Pier, Bankside Pier, London Bridge City Pier, and St. Katharine's Pier (hop-on/hop-off service). All the boats provide live commentary and have a fully licensed bar. The cruise costs £10 ($20) for adults, £4.75 ($9.50) for children, and £23 ($46) for families (two adults and three children).

The same company offers a **daily lunch cruise** departing at 12:30 p.m. that costs £24 ($48) for adults, £13 ($26) for children. A **nightly dinner cruise** leaves at 7:15 p.m. and returns at 9:45 p.m. The cruise, which includes a two- to four-course dinner with live music and after-dinner dancing, costs £69 to £105 ($138–$210) per person, depending on the various add-ons that you choose. A two-hour **Sunday jazz lunch cruise** departs at 12:30 p.m. and costs £40 to £55 ($80–$110) per person. Advance reservations are required for all tours, and a smart-casual dress code applies (no sweatpants or running shoes). All cruises depart from Embankment Pier.

An amphibious tour

London Duck Tours (☎ 020/7928-3132; www.londonducktours.co.uk) has adapted several World War II amphibious troop carriers, known as DUKWs, to civilian comfort levels and painted them bright yellow. It runs 80-minute road-and-river trips. Tours start behind County Hall (site of the British Airways London Eye giant observation wheel). It picks up passengers on Chicheley Street (Tube: Westminster, then walk across Westminster Bridge), then rumbles through Westminster and up to Piccadilly, gathering bemused stares as it passes many of London's major tourist sites. Then the vehicle splashes into the Thames at Vauxhall for a 30-minute cruise as far as the Houses of Parliament. The tours cost £18 ($36) for adults, £14 ($28) for seniors, and £12 ($24) for children.

Walking tours

A walking tour is an affordable way to see London from street level in the company of a knowledgeable guide. This type of tour is great for history, literature, and architecture buffs, and older kids generally have a good time, as well. The weekly events listings in *Time Out* magazine, available at every news agent in London, include dozens of intriguing walks; a walk happens every day.

The Original London Walks, P.O. Box 1708, London NW6 4LW (☎ 020/7624-3978; www.walks.com), offers a terrific array of tours, including **Jack the Ripper's London, Christopher Wren's London, Oscar Wilde's London,** and **The Beatles' Magical Mystery Tour.** Guides lead different walks every day of the week, rain or shine; tours last about two hours and begin and end near Underground stations. You don't need to make advance reservations. Call for schedules and departure points. A London Walk costs £6 ($12) for adults and £5 ($10) for seniors and students with ID; kids under 15 can tour for free if accompanied by a parent.

If you want to follow detailed strolls on your own, check out the 11 tours offered in *Frommer's Memorable Walks in London* (Wiley Publishing, Inc.).

Index of Top Attractions by Neighborhood

St. Paul's Cathedral
Tower of London

Covent Garden
Covent Garden Market and Piazza
London Transport Museum

Greenwich
Cutty Sark
National Maritime Museum
Prime Meridian
Queen's House
Royal Naval College
Royal Observatory Greenwich

Hampstead
Hampstead Heath
Kenwood House

Hampton Court
Hampton Court Palace

Holborn
Dr. Johnson's House
Sir John Soane's Museum

Kensington and South Kensington
Kensington Gardens
Kensington Palace
Natural History Museum
Science Museum
Victoria & Albert Museum

Lambeth
Imperial War Museum

Kew
Royal Botanic Gardens

Marylebone
British Library Exhibition Centre
London Zoo
Madame Tussaud's
Regent's Park
Wallace Collection

Piccadilly Circus and Leicester Square
Leicester Square
Pepsi Trocadero
Piccadilly Circus

Pimlico
Tate Britain

Shoreditch
Geffrye Museum

South Bank
British Airways London Eye
Design Museum
Golden Hinde
H.M.S. *Belfast*
London Aquarium
London Dungeon
Old Operating Theatre Museum &
Herb Garret
Shakespeare's Globe Theatre
Southwark Cathedral
Tate Modern
Tower Bridge Exhibition

St. James's
Apsley House
Buckingham Palace
Changing of the Guard at
Buckingham Palace
National Gallery
National Portrait Gallery
Royal Academy of Arts
Spencer House
St. James's Park and Green Park
St. Martin-in-the-Fields
10 Downing Street
Trafalgar Square

The Strand
Benjamin Franklin House
Somerset House (Courtauld Gallery,
Gilbert Collection, and Hermitage
Rooms)

Westminster
Churchill Museum and Cabinet
War Rooms
Houses of Parliament and Big Ben
Hyde Park
Westminster Abbey

Windsor
Windsor Castle

Index of Attractions by Type

Art Galleries
Kenwood House
National Gallery
National Portrait Gallery
Royal Academy of Arts
Saatchi Gallery
Somerset House (Courtauld Gallery,
Gilbert Collection, and Hermitage
Rooms)
Tate Britain
Tate Modern
Wallace Collection

Churches
St. Martin-in-the-Fields
St. Paul's Cathedral
Southwark Cathedral
Westminster Abbey

Entertainment Venues and Themed Attractions
British Airways London Eye
Cutty Sark
Golden Hinde
H.M.S. *Belfast*
London Aquarium
London Dungeon
Madame Tussaud's
Pepsi Trocadero
Shakespeare's Globe Theatre
Tower Bridge Exhibition

Historic Houses and Buildings
Apsley House
Benjamin Franklin House
Carlyle's House
Charles Dickens Museum
Churchill Museum and Cabinet
War Rooms
Dr. Johnson's House
Houses of Parliament and Big Ben
Kenwood House
The Monument
Old Operating Theatre Museum &
Herb Garret
Queen's House
Royal Naval College
Royal Observatory Greenwich
Sir John Soane's Museum
Spencer House
10 Downing Street
Tower of London

Museums
Bank of England Museum
British Library Exhibition Centre
British Museum
Design Museum
Geffrye Museum
Imperial War Museum
London Transport Museum
Madame Tussaud's
Museum of Childhood
Museum of London
National Maritime Museum
Natural History Museum
Science Museum
Tate Britain
Tate Modern
Victoria & Albert Museum

Palaces and Castles
Buckingham Palace
Changing of the Guard at
Buckingham Palace

Hampton Court Palace
Kensington Palace
Queen's House
Tower of London
Windsor Castle

Parks, Gardens, and the Zoo
Chelsea Physic Garden
Hampstead Heath
Hyde Park
Kensington Gardens

London Zoo
Regent's Park
Royal Botanic Gardens
St. James's Park and Green Park

Squares
Covent Garden Market and Piazza
Leicester Square
Piccadilly Circus
Trafalgar Square

Chapter 12

Shopping the Local Stores

. . . .

In This Chapter

▶ Getting your VAT refund
▶ Taking your purchases through Customs
▶ Visiting the big department stores
▶ Shopping Knightsbridge and the West End

. . . .

*L*ondon is one of the world's great shopping meccas. If shopping is on your agenda, you can find any item that you're looking for. But you won't find many bargains, except during the department stores' big sales in January and July.

Surveying the Shopping Scene

You get the best values on goods that are manufactured in England. Items from the Body Shop, Filofax, or Dr. Martens cost less than they do abroad, though with the current strength of the pound they might not be such a bargain. Other potentially good values include woolens and cashmeres, English brands of bone china, English toiletries, antiques, used silver, old maps and engravings, and rare books. You can also do well with French products.

You may be surprised — and perhaps disappointed — at the number of big U.S. chains (called *multiples* in the U.K.) that have opened stores in London. But in addition to the familiar chains and mega-stores, London is still the home of hundreds of small, unique specialty shops and boutiques to delight the eye and empty the wallet.

Normal shopping hours are Monday through Saturday 10 a.m. to 5:30 p.m., with a late closing (7 p.m. or 8 p.m.) on Wednesday or Thursday. The law allows stores to be open for six hours on Sunday, usually 11 a.m. to 5 p.m.

If you're a truly dedicated shopper, check out *Suzy Gershman's Born to Shop London* (Wiley Publishing, Inc.). This comprehensive guide introduces you to just about every worthwhile shop and shopping experience in London.

Table 12-1 lists conversions for U.S. and U.K. sizes.

Table 12-1	The Right Fit: Size Conversions		
U.S.	**U.K.**	**U.S.**	**U.K.**
Women's Clothes		**Women's Shoes**	
8	10	4½	3
10	12	5½	4
12	14	6½	5
14	16	7½	6
16	18	8½	7
18	20	9½	8
Men's Clothes/Shirts		**Men's Shoes**	
Sizes are the same		7	6
		8	7
		9	8
		10	9
		11	10
		12	11

Getting the VAT back

You have to pay a 17.5 percent value-added tax (VAT) in London and throughout the United Kingdom on every retail item except books and children's clothing. Anyone who isn't a resident of the European Union can get a VAT refund, but every store requires a minimum purchase to qualify. The exact amount varies from store to store, but the minimum amount is never less than £50 ($100) and may be as high as £100 ($200) at a store like Harrods. But qualifying for a tax refund is far easier in Britain than in almost any other country in the European Union.

VAT isn't charged on goods shipped out of the country, no matter how much you spend, although books are exempt. You can avoid VAT and the hassle of lugging large packages back with you by having London stores ship your purchases for you; many are happy to do so. However, shipping charges can *double* the cost of your purchase, and you may also have to pay U.S. duties when the goods arrive. Instead of using this costly strategy, consider paying for excess baggage (rates vary with the airlines) when you fly home.

Saving on the London sales

Traditionally, London stores hold sales in January and July. In recent times, the July sales have begun in June or earlier. The January sale is the main event, and it generally starts after the first week (when round-trip airfares are low).

The January sale at Harrods is the most famous, but nearly every other store has a big sale at the same time. Discounts usually range from 25 percent to 50 percent at the major stores, such as Harrods and Selfridges. At Harrods, you can find the best buys on the store's logo souvenirs, English china, and English designer brands, such as Jaeger.

To get a VAT refund, you must get a VAT refund form from the retailer, and the retailer must complete the form at the time of purchase. Don't leave the store without a completed refund form. Don't let any merchant tell you that you can get refund forms at the airport.

You can get back about 15 percent of the 17.5 percent VAT that you pay on your purchases. (You can't get back the entire amount.) To obtain your refund, follow these steps:

1. **Ask the store whether it does VAT refunds and how much the minimum purchase is.**

2. **If you've spent the minimum amount, ask for the VAT refund paperwork.**

   The retailer must fill out a portion.

3. **Fill out your portion of the form (name and address).**

4. **Present the form — along with the goods — at the Cash VAT Refund counter at the airport.**

You may be required to show the goods at your time of departure, so don't pack them in your checked luggage; put them in your carryon instead.

After the paperwork is stamped, you have two choices:

- ✔ You can mail in the papers and receive your refund in a British check (no!) or a credit card refund (yes!).

- ✔ You can go directly to the Cash VAT Refund counter at the airport and get your refund in cash.

If you're traveling from London to other countries in the European Union, don't apply for your VAT refund at the London airport. Apply for all your VAT refunds at one time at your final destination, prior to departure from the European Union.

Getting your goodies through Customs

The U.S. Customs authority doesn't impose limits on how much loot U.S. citizens can bring home from a trip abroad, but it does put limits on how much they can bring back for free. You may bring home $800 worth of goods duty-free if you've been out of the country at least 48 hours and haven't used the exemption in the past 30 days. Here's some additional information about the limit and Customs law:

✔ You can bring back not more than 1 liter of an alcoholic beverage (you must be over 21 to carry any alcohol).

✔ You can carry up to 200 cigarettes and 100 cigars.

✔ Antiques more than 100 years old and works of art are exempt from the $800 limit, as is anything that you mail home from abroad.

✔ You may mail up to $200 worth of goods to yourself (marked "For Personal Use") and up to $100 worth to others (marked "Unsolicited Gift") once each day, as long as the package doesn't include alcohol or tobacco products.

✔ You have to pay an import duty on anything over these limits — a flat rate of 10 percent duty on the next $1,000 worth of purchases.

Be sure to have your receipts with you. For more specific guidance, contact the **U.S. Customs Service** (P.O. Box 7407, Washington, DC 20044; ☎ **202-927-6724;** www.cbp.gov) and request the free pamphlet "Know Before You Go." Or check out the details and order online at the Customs Department Web site.

Returning Canadian citizens are allowed a C$300 exemption and can bring back, free of duty, 200 cigarettes, 2.2 pounds of tobacco, 40 imperial ounces (1.2 quarts) of liquor, and 50 cigars. Declare all valuables that you're taking with you to the United Kingdom, such as expensive cameras, on the Y-38 Form before you leave Canada. For a clear summary of Canadian rules, write for the booklet "I Declare," issued by **Revenue Canada** (2265 St. Laurent Blvd., Ottawa K1G 4KE; ☎ **800-461-9999** or 613-993-0534; www.cbsa-asfc.gc.ca).

Returning Australian citizens have a duty-free allowance of A$400 (A$200 for children under 18). Citizens can bring home, free of duty, 250 cigarettes or 250 grams of loose tobacco, and 1.125 liters of alcohol. Australian citizens who plan to return home with valuable goods that they already own (for example, foreign-made cameras) need to file Form B263 before leaving Australia. For more information, contact **Australian Customs Services** (GPO Box 8, Sydney NSW 2001; ☎ **1300/363-263;** www.customs.gov.au).

The duty-free allowance for New Zealand citizens is NZ$700. Citizens over 17 can bring in up to 200 cigarettes, 50 cigars, or 250 grams of tobacco, or a mix of all three if the combined weight doesn't exceed 250 grams; plus 4.5 liters of beer and wine, or 1.125 liters of liquor. To avoid paying duty on goods that you already own (cameras and the like), fill out a certificate of export before you leave New Zealand, listing the valuables that you're taking out of the country. For more information, contact **New Zealand Customs** (The Customhouse, 17–21 Whitmore St., Box 2218, Wellington; ☎ **04/473-6099** or 0800/428-786; www.customs.govt.nz).

Checking Out the Big Names

London is full of department stores. Some, like world-famous Harrods, may be familiar to you. Others, like Harvey Nichols, may be pleasant surprises. Each of these established department stores has its own style and personality.

Fenwick of Bond Street
Mayfair

Fenwick of Bond Street is a high-style women's fashion store. Fenwick (pronounced _fen_-ick) was founded in 1891 and offers an impressive collection of designer women's wear, ranging from moderately priced ready-to-wear items to more expensive designer fashions. Fenwick also sells an array of lingerie in all price ranges.

See map p. 250. 63 New Bond St., W1. ☎ _020/7629-9161._ www.fenwick.co.uk. _Tube: Bond Street. Open: Mon–Tues and Thurs–Sat 10 a.m.–6:30 p.m. and Wed 10 a.m.–8 p.m._

Fortnum & Mason
St. James's

Fortnum & Mason holds two _Royal Warrants_ (a form of official patronage that the store can use in its advertising) and serves as the queen's London grocer. Amid a setting of deep-red carpets and crystal chandeliers, you can find everything from pâté de foie gras to Campbell's soup. The grocery department carries the finest foods from around the world, and on the other floors, you can find bone china, crystal, leather, antiques, and stationery departments. Dining choices include **Patio, St. James's,** and **The Fountain** (see Chapter 10).

See map p. 250. 181 Piccadilly, W1. ☎ _020/7734-8040._ www.fortnumandmason.com. _Tube: Piccadilly Circus. Open: Mon–Sat 10 a.m.–6:30 p.m._

Harrods
Knightsbridge

Harrods may be the most famous department store in the world, but I've always found its merchandise to be pretty dull stuff. Carrying one of the coveted green plastic Harrods bags that you get with your purchase can provide you with a sense of accomplishment, though. The store's 300

Harrods loses Royal Warrants

The London gossip columns were ablaze early in 2000 when Prince Philip withdrew his *Royal Warrant* (a sign of official royal patronage) from Harrods, claiming that the royal household just didn't use the store as much as it used to. Harrods just happens to be owned by Mohamed Al Fayed, father of Dodi Al Fayed, who was killed with Princess Diana in that famous car crash. The elder Mr. Al Fayed, an Egyptian who's been denied U.K. citizenship, has made some startling allegations against the House of Windsor, claiming that the deaths of Diana and his son were not accidental. Could that be the real reason that Harrods is now warrant-less?

departments offer an enormous range and variety of merchandise. Best of all are the Food Halls, stocked with a huge variety of foods and several cafes. Believe it or not, you may not be admitted if you're wearing inappropriate clothing or your belly button is showing.

See map p. 247. 87–135 Brompton Rd., SW1. ☎ *020/7730-1234.* www.harrods.com. *Tube: Knightsbridge. Open: Mon–Sat 10 a.m.–7 p.m.*

Harvey Nichols
Knightsbridge

Harvey Nichols, the late Princess Diana's favorite store, has its own gourmet food hall and fancy restaurant, the **Fifth Floor,** and is crammed with designer home furnishings, gifts, and fashions. Women's clothing is the largest segment of its business, a familiar fact to those fans of the 1990s British TV series *Absolutely Fabulous.* Harvey Nicks, as it's called, doesn't compete with Harrods because the former features a much more upmarket, fashionable image.

See map p. 247. 109–125 Knightsbridge, SW1. ☎ *020/7235-5000.* www.harvey nichols.com. *Tube: Knightsbridge. Open: Mon, Tues, and Sat 10 a.m.–7 p.m., Wed–Fri 10 a.m.–8 p.m., and Sun noon to 6 p.m.*

Liberty
Mayfair

Liberty provides six floors of fashion, china, home furnishings, upholstery fabrics, scarves, ties, luggage, and gifts. The store is best known for its Liberty Prints — fine quality fabrics, typically in floral patterns. These distinctive fabrics are highly sought after by interior decorators because they add an unmistakable touch of England to any room décor. A Liberty tie makes a great gift for your guy back home.

See map p. 250. 214–220 Regent St., W1. ☎ *020/7734-1234.* www.liberty.co.uk. *Tube: Oxford Circus. Open: Mon–Wed 10 a.m.–6:30 p.m, Thurs 10 a.m.–8 p.m., Fri–Sat 10 a.m.–7 p.m., Sun noon to 6 p.m.*

Marks & Spencer
Mayfair

Marks & Spencer is a private-label department store that offers basics of all kinds. The merchandise at both locations is high quality and has in recent years moved way beyond the store's trademark conservative image.

See map p. 250. 458 Oxford St., W1 (☎ 020/7935-7954; Tube: Marble Arch) and 173 Oxford St., W1 (☎ 020/7437-7722; Tube: Oxford Circus). www.marksand spencer.com. *Open: Mon–Fri 9 a.m.–8 p.m., Sat 9 a.m.–7:30 p.m., and Sun noon to 6 p.m.*

Selfridges
Mayfair

Selfridges is one of the largest department stores in Europe. The store has been redone to attract upscale customers, but its vast size provides room for less-expensive, mass-marketed lines as well. More than 500 divisions sell everything, from artificial flowers to groceries. The Miss Selfridge boutique, on one side of the store near the cosmetics department, features teen fashions, hotshot clothes, accessories, makeup, and moderately priced, cutting-edge fashions. While on this side of the store, you can visit the cafe.

See map p. 250. 400 Oxford St., W1. ☎ 020/7629-1234. www.selfridges.com. *Tube: Bond Street or Marble Arch. Open: Mon–Wed 10 a.m.–7 p.m., Thurs–Fri 10 a.m.–8 p.m., Sat 9:30 a.m.–7 p.m., and Sun 11:30 a.m.–6 p.m.*

Shopping the Street Markets

Markets make for fun shopping because you never know what you may find. Adventurous shoppers who like to browse and dawdle can really enjoy themselves at the places listed in this section.

Finding a drugstore

The English refer to a drugstore as a *chemist's shop*. All over London, you can find **Boots the Chemist** stores. In terms of size and convenience, the best one is just across from Harrods (72 Brompton Rd., SW3; ☎ 020/7589-6557; Tube: Knightsbridge). In addition to medicine, Boots sells film, pantyhose (called *tights*), sandwiches, and all of life's little necessities. The store is open Monday through Friday 8:30 a.m. to 7 p.m. and Saturday 9 a.m. to 7 p.m. One of the most centrally located chemists is **Bliss the Chemist** (5 Marble Arch, W1; ☎ 020/7723-6116; Tube: Marble Arch), open daily 9 a.m. to midnight. **Zafash Pharmacy** (233–235 Old Brompton Rd., SW5 ☎ 020/7373-2798; Tube: Earl's Court) is London's only 24-hour pharmacy.

Brick Lane and Spitalfields Markets

On Sundays between 8 a.m. and 2 p.m., **Brick Lane Market** (Cheshire Street and Sclater Street, E1; ☎ 020/7377-8963; Tube: Liverpool Street) is lined with hundreds of stalls, with clothing, fabrics, bric-a-brac, leather goods, antiques, and furniture all being traded. You may encounter some worthwhile bargains here, and you can check out the great Bangladeshi restaurants along the Lane.

Nearby **Spitalfields Market** (Commercial Street, E1; no phone; www. visitspitalfields.com; Tube: Liverpool Street), housed in a late-19th-century market building, has undergone a complete transformation and is now a trendy new gathering spot where you'll find great Italian/French breads, German cheesecakes and organic food, together with gifts, clothing, crafts and knickknacks. The food court, where most world cuisines are represented (including Chinese, West Indian, and Hungarian) is among the best of any London market. The market is open Monday through Friday 11 a.m. to 3:30 p.m., and Sunday 10 a.m. to 3 p.m.

Camden Market

Vying with Portobello Road for the title of London's most popular market, Camden actually boasts a number of distinct markets, which combine to give the visitor a great day out and bargains galore. Some areas are open Thursday to Saturday; others operate weekends only. The best of the many markets in Camden is the **Stables Market** (no phone; Tube: Camden Town), housed in a historic horse stable dating back to 1854 and offering an impressive array of fashion ranging from Goth, fetish, and cyberpunk to vintage, retro, and secondhand, plus stalls selling everything from secondhand records to leather goods, antiques, and other accessories. In addition to the markets, Camden High Street has some of the trendiest fashion boutiques in London.

Chelsea Antiques Market and Antiquarius

In a rambling old building, the **Chelsea Antiques Market** (253 King's Rd., SW3; ☎ 020/7352-5689; Tube: Sloane Square) offers endless bric-a-brac browsing possibilities. You can search out old or rare books at this market. You'll probably run across Staffordshire dogs, shaving mugs, Edwardian buckles and clasps, ivory-handled razors, old velours, lace gowns, and wooden tea caddies — and that's just the beginning. The market is closed on Sunday.

Another good market is **Antiquarius** (131–141 King's Rd., SW3; ☎ 020/7351-5353; Tube: Sloane Square), where more than 120 dealers offer specialized merchandise — usually of the small, domestic variety, such as antique and period jewelry, porcelain, silver, first-edition books, boxes, clocks, prints, and paintings. The shops and booths are generally open Monday through Saturday from 10 a.m. to 6 p.m.

Covent Garden Market

The **Covent Garden Market** (☎ 020/7836-9136; www.coventgarden market.co.uk; Tube: Covent Garden) includes retail stores and two different markets (the kind with open-air stalls), open daily 9 a.m. to 5 p.m.:

- Traders sell all kinds of goods at the busy **Apple Market** (no phone). Much of the merchandise is what the English call *collectible nostalgia,* which includes glassware and ceramics, leather goods, toys, clothes, hats, and jewelry. Antiques dealers predominate on Mondays.

- **Jubilee Market** (☎ 020/7836-2139), at the backside of Covent Garden, is a bit more downscale, where you can find cheap clothes and books. Some of London's best shopping can be found at the restored hall on The Piazza and at specialty shops in the area.

Petticoat Lane Market

Over 400 years old and still going strong, **Petticoat Lane** (☎ 020/7377-8963; Tube: Liverpool Street) is one of the East End's biggest and most famous markets, with over a thousand stalls. Taking up an area in and around Middlesex Street and Wentworth Street, E1, it's open Monday through Friday from 10 a.m. to 2:30 p.m. and Sunday from 9 a.m. to 2 p.m. Sunday is the best day for bargains on fashions, Asian fabrics, textiles, and jewelry. Haggling is a prerequisite.

Portobello Market

Kensington Church Street dead-ends at the Notting Hill Gate Tube station, which is the jumping-off point for **Portobello Market** (no phone; www.portobelloroad.co.uk; Tube: Notting Hill Gate), the famous London street market along Portobello Road. Portobello (market and road) is a magnet for collectors of virtually anything from precious junk to precious antiques. The market is generally open Saturday 6 a.m. to 5 p.m. You may find that perfect Regency commode that you've always wanted or a piece of Art Deco jewelry. But mixed in with the good stuff is an abundance of overpriced junk. Now that everything's been discovered and designated "collectible," the prices are often too high.

The Portobello Market on a busy Saturday is prime pickpocketing territory. Keep an eye or a hand on your wallet or purse.

If you want to check out the shops along Portobello Road, you may want to visit during the week, when approximately 90 antiques and art shops are open and the street market is closed. Weekdays are a better time for serious collectors to shop, because they get more attention from dealers who aren't distracted by the throngs of shoppers.

Discovering the Best Shopping Neighborhoods

London's two major shopping areas are Knightsbridge and the West End. You can find some of London's most famous and most impressive stores along several key streets in these two areas. You also can find all the department stores listed in the "Checking Out the Big Names" section, earlier in this chapter.

Knightsbridge: Home of Harrods

The home of department stores Harrods and Harvey Nichols, Knightsbridge is the second most famous of London's retail districts. (See the "Shopping in Knightsbridge and Chelsea" map on p. 247.)

Brompton Road (home to Harrods) runs southwest from the Knightsbridge Tube stop. Beauchamp Place (pronounced *beech*-um), one of the streets running south from Brompton Road, is only 1 block long, but it's full of the kinds of trendy, upscale shops where young British aristocrats buy their clothing for "the season." In the 1980s, the future Princess Diana and other young bluebloods and yuppies were dubbed "the Sloane Rangers" because this area near Sloane Square was their favorite shopping grounds (and Range Rovers their favorite cars). Cheval Place, running parallel to Brompton Road to the north, is lined with designer resale shops. Sloane Street, where you can find plenty of fashion boutiques, runs south from the Knightsbridge Tube stop to Sloane Square and the beginning of Chelsea.

The **Map House of London** (54 Beauchamp Place, SW3; ☎ 020/7589-4325; www.themaphouse.com; Tube: Knightsbridge) is an ideal place to find a sophisticated souvenir, maybe an antique map, an engraving, or an old print of London; a century-old original engraving can cost as little as £15 ($30).

Chelsea: The young and the antique

Chelsea is famous for **King's Road** (Tube: Sloane Square). This is the area's main street and, along with Carnaby Street, is branded in Londoner's minds (those over 50, that is) as the street of the Swinging Sixties. It's still swinging today, especially on a Saturday, when you can hardly find room to walk. About one-third of King's Road is devoted to antiques markets and *multi-stores* (large or small groups of indoor stands, stalls, and booths within one enclosure); another third houses design trade showrooms and stores of household wares; and the remaining third stays faithful to the area's teenybopper roots. King's Road begins on the west side of the Sloane Square Tube stop.

A Chelsea emporium founded in 1877, **Peter Jones** (Sloane Square, SW1; ☎ 020/7730-3434; www.peterjones.co.uk; Tube: Sloane Square) is known for household goods, household fabrics and trims, china, glass, soft furnishings, and linens. The linen department is one of the best in London. **Lush** (123 King's Rd., SW3; www.lush.com; Tube: Sloane Square)

Shopping in Knightsbridge and Chelsea

Antiquarius **6**
Boots The Chemist **2**
Chelsea Antiques Market **7**
Harrods **3**
Harvey Nichols **1**
Lush **8**
Map House of London **4**
Peter Jones **5**

is an aromatherapy bath and body shop where handmade soaps are cut from blocks, like cheese, and potential gifts include fizzing bath bombs. The other branches are in Covent Garden, Oxford Street, Kensington High Street, and Carnaby Street. You may also want to check out the **Chelsea Antiques Market** and **Antiquarius.** (See the "Shopping the Street Markets" section, earlier in this chapter.)

Kensington: Street chic

You can reach Kensington, west of Knightsbridge, by taking the Tube to **High Street Kensington,** the area's preeminent shopping street. Many of this neighborhood's retail shops cater to street-chic teens. Several chain stores are here as well.

Kensington Church Street, running north to Notting Hill, is one of the city's main shopping avenues for antiques, selling everything from antique furniture to Impressionist paintings.

The **Children's Book Centre** (237 Kensington High St., W8; ☎ 020/ 7937-7497; Tube: High Street Kensington) is the best place in London to go for children's books. Fiction is arranged according to age, up to 16. The center also sells videos and toys for kids.

Holborn: Heigh-ho, Silver!

Don't let the slightly out-of-the-way Holborn location, or the facade's lack of charm, put you off visiting the **London Silver Vaults** (Chancery House, 53–63 Chancery Lane, WC2; ☎ 020/7242-3844; www.thesilver vaults.com; Tube: Chancery Lane). Downstairs are the real vaults — 40 in all — filled with a staggering collection of old and new silver and silver plate, plus a collection of jewelry.

The West End: More famous shopping streets and stores

See the "Shopping in the West End" map on p. 250 for locations of the West End stores that I describe in the following sections. The key shopping areas in the West End are

- ✔ **Piccadilly** for older, established department stores

- ✔ **Jermyn Street** for traditional English luxury goods

- ✔ **Regent Street** for fancier shops and more upscale department stores and specialty dealers

- ✔ **Oxford Street** for affordable shopping

- ✔ **Bond Street** for chic, upscale fashion boutiques

- ✔ **St. Martin's Court** (between Charing Cross Road and St. Martin's Lane) for prints, posters, and books

- ✔ **Covent Garden** for all-purpose shopping, often with a hipper edge

Around Piccadilly Circus: A bit of everything

Many consider **Piccadilly Circus** the center of London. For the best shopping in this area, head south from the Piccadilly Tube stop along Piccadilly (the street) or northwest along Regent Street. The following list gives you some of the most renowned stores around Piccadilly Circus:

- ✔ **Burberry** (18–22 Haymarket, SW1; ☎ 020/7930-3343; www.burberry.com; Tube: Piccadilly Circus) sells those famous raincoats, plus top-quality men's shirts, sportswear, knitwear, and accessories.

- ✔ **Hatchards** (187 Piccadilly, W1; ☎ 020/7439-9921; www.hatchards.co.uk; Tube: Piccadilly Circus) was established in 1797 and is London's most historic and atmospheric bookstore.

- ✔ **Virgin Megastore** (1 Piccadilly Circus, W1; ☎ 020/7439-2500; Tube: Piccadilly Circus) is one of the largest music outlets in Europe. This store is practically a tourist attraction in its own right.

Jermyn Street: Traditional luxury

Two-block-long **Jermyn Street** lies a block south of Piccadilly between St. James's Street and Duke Street. Many of the posh men's haberdashers and toiletry shops along this street have been doing business for centuries and cater to the royals. They include the following shops:

- ✔ **Farlows** (9 Pall Mall, SW1; ☎ 020/7839-2423; www.farlows.co.uk; Tube: Piccadilly Circus) is famous for fishing and shooting equipment and classic country clothing.

- ✔ **Floris** (89 Jermyn St., SW1; ☎ 020/7930-2885; www.florislondon.com; Tube: Piccadilly Circus) is a small, mahogany-clad store that's been selling its own line of soaps and perfumes since 1851.

- ✔ **Hilditch & Key** (73 Jermyn St., SW1; ☎ 020/7930-5336; www.hilditchandkey.co.uk; Tube: Piccadilly Circus) has been selling perhaps the finest men's shirts in the world for more than a century. These quality goods are 100 percent cotton, cut by hand, and sport buttons fashioned from real shell.

- ✔ **Taylor of Old Bond Street** (74 Jermyn St., SW1; ☎ 020/7930-5544; www.tayloroldbondst.co.uk; Tube: Piccadilly Circus) was established in 1954 and is devoted to the shaving and personal hygiene needs of men. The store offers the world's finest collection of shaving brushes, razors, and combs, plus soaps and hair lotions.

Regent Street: Upscale specialties

Regent Street begins in a grand, sweeping curve on the west side of Piccadilly Circus and heads north to intersect with Oxford Street. This majestic thoroughfare is lined with upscale department stores and specialty boutiques. The **Burlington Arcade** is a must-see if you're in this area. This famous glass-roofed Regency passage, running from Piccadilly to Burlington Gardens, is lit by wrought-iron lamps and decorated with

Shopping in the West End

Anything Left Handed **24**
The Body Shop **6**
Burberry **12**
Burlington Arcade **14**
Charbonnel et Walker **15**
Church's **4**
Covent Garden Market **36**
Culpeper the Herbalist **38**
Davies Mews **5**
Dr. Martens
    Department Store **34**
Dress Circle **29**
Farlows **20**
Fenwick of Bond Street **7**
The Filofax Centre **10**
Floris **21**
Fortnum & Mason **16**
Hamleys **11**
Hatchards **17**
Hilditch & Key **19**
The Irish Shop **35**
Liberty **9**
London Silver Vaults **39**
Marks & Spencer **1, 8**
MDC Classic Music **32**
Murder One **25**
Neal's Yard Remedies **28**
Penhaligon's **37**
Royal Doulton Regent Street **13**
Scotch House **23**
Selfridges **2**
Silver Moon
    Women's Bookshop **27**
Stanfords **31**
Taylor of Old Bond Street **18**
The Tea House **33**
Tower Records **22**
Vivienne Westwood **3**
W & G Foyle, Ltd. **26**
Waterstone's **30**

clusters of ferns and flowers. The arcade is lined with intriguing shops and boutiques. (See the "Shopping in the West End" map on p. 250 for locations of all the stores that I describe in this section.)

Savile Row, synonymous with hand-tailored men's suits, lies a block west of Regent Street. Its once-countercultural counterpart — in the early Beatles years — is **Carnaby Street,** now making a comeback after years as a depressing street of souvenir shops; Carnaby Street is a block east of Regent Street. **Royal Doulton Regent Street** (154 Regent St., W1; ☎ 020/7734-3184; Tube: Piccadilly Circus or Oxford Circus) carries English bone china, including Minton, Royal Crown Derby, and Royal Doulton. (The Jan and July sales are excellent.) **Scotch House** (84–86 Regent St., W1; ☎ 020/7734-0203; Tube: Piccadilly Circus) is known globally for its selection of cashmere and wool knitwear for men, women, and children; the store also sells tartan garments and accessories, as well as Scottish tweed classics.

If you're left-handed, you're in luck at **Anything Left-Handed** (57 Brewer St., off Regent Street, W1; ☎ 020/7437-3910; www.anythingleft-handed.co.uk; Tube: Piccadilly Circus). This unique store sells practical items — everything from scissors to corkscrews — for the southpaws in the world.

Hamleys (188–196 Regent St., W1; ☎ 020/7494-2000; www.hamleys.com; Tube: Piccadilly Circus), the finest toy shop in the world, stocks more than 35,000 toys and games on seven floors of fun and magic. You can get everything, from cuddly stuffed animals and dolls to radio-controlled cars, train sets, model kits, board games, outdoor toys, and computer games.

Oxford Street: Affordable big names

You may want to begin your shopping adventure on Oxford Street, getting out at the Oxford Circus, Bond Street, or Tottenham Court Road Tube stop. Oxford Street is more affordable than Regent Street (which you can read about in the preceding section) — not as grand, but offering a good variety and quantity of stylish merchandise. (See the "Shopping in the West End" map on p. 250 for the locations of all the stores that I describe in this section.)

If you're a chronic organizer who can't live without your Filofax, head immediately for **The Filofax Centre** (21 Conduit St., W1; ☎ 020/7499-0457; www.filofax.com; Tube: Oxford Circus). At this store on Conduit Street, which leads west from Regency Street, you can find the entire range of inserts and books at prices that are lower than they are outside of the United Kingdom.

The Body Shop stores are based in the United Kingdom but are now all over the world; however, prices at the London branches are much lower. You can stock up on their politically and environmentally correct beauty, bath, and aromatherapy products (375 Oxford St., W1; ☎ 020/7409-7868; www.thebodyshop.com; Tube: Bond Street). You can find other branches in every shopping zone in London.

Bond Street: Designer chic

Bond Street, running parallel to Regent Street on the west and connecting Piccadilly with Oxford Street, is home to all the hot international designers and is London's answer to New York's Fifth Avenue. Bond Street is divided into New (the northern section) and Old (the southern section). Very expensive fashion boutiques line Bond Street and the adjacent streets. **Davies Street,** running south from outside the Bond Street Tube station, is just one of the area's choicer streets; **Davies Mews** is an upscale shopping zone noted for its antiques dealers. You can access the area from the north by the Bond Street Tube stop and from the south by Green Park. (See the "Shopping in the West End" map on p. 250 for the locations of the stores that I describe in this section.)

Vivienne Westwood (6 Davies St., W1; ☎ 020/7629-3757; www.vivienne westwood.co.uk; Tube: Bond Street) is one of the hottest British designers for women. This flagship store carries a full range of jackets, skirts, trousers, blouses, dresses, and evening dresses. **Church's** (133 New Bond St., W1; ☎ 020/7493-1474; Tube: Bond Street) sells classy shoes easily recognized by the fashion elite. Chocolate connoisseurs should visit **Charbonnel et Walker** (1 The Royal Arcade, 28 Old Bond St., W1; ☎ 020/7491-0939; www.charbonnel.co.uk; Tube: Green Park), famous for its hot chocolate (buy it by the tin) and strawberries-and-cream chocolates.

Around Leicester Square: Music and memorabilia

Leicester Square itself boasts only giant movie palaces and touristy restaurants (and a reduced-price ticket booth). But the streets around Leicester Square are filled with shops selling rare books, prints, and posters, some relating to the performing arts. (See the "Shopping in the West End" map on p. 250 for the locations of the stores that I describe in this section.)

The Leicester Square shops include the following:

- ✔ **Dress Circle** (57–59 Monmouth St., WC2; ☎ 020/7240-2227; www.dresscircle.co.uk; Tube: Leicester Square) specializes in show-business memorabilia for all West End and Broadway shows.

- ✔ **MDC Classic Music** (31–32 St. Martin's Lane, WC2; ☎ 020/7240-0270; www.mdcmusic.co.uk; Tube: Leicester Square), sitting right next to the English National Opera, specializes in opera recordings; you receive expert knowledge and personal service from the staff.

- ✔ **Stanfords** (12–14 Long Acre, WC2; ☎ 020/7836-1321; www.stanfords.co.uk; Tube: Leicester Square) was established in 1852, and is the world's largest map shop (many of its maps, which include worldwide touring and survey maps, are unavailable elsewhere). Stanfords is also London's best travel bookstore.

Charing Cross Road: A book lover's delight

Charing Cross Road is a book lover's paradise because of its vast number of bookstores, selling both new and old volumes. Many of these places sell maps and guides, too, including the tourist's necessity, *London A–Z. Remember:* no added 17.5 percent VAT charge on books. Some of the most fascinating bookstores include the following (for locations, see the "Shopping in the West End" map on p. 250):

✔ **Murder One** (76–78 Charing Cross Rd., WC2; ☎ 020/7734-3483; www.murderone.co.uk; Tube: Leicester Square) specializes in crime, romance, science fiction, and horror books. Crime and science fiction magazines, some obscure, are also available.

✔ **W & G Foyle, Ltd.** (113–119 Charing Cross Rd., WC2; ☎ 020/7440-3225; www.foyles.co.uk; Tube: Tottenham Court Road) claims to be the world's largest bookstore, with an impressive array of hardcovers and paperbacks, as well as travel maps, records, videotapes, and sheet music. **Silver Moon** (☎ 020/7440-1562), London's preeminent women's dealer, operates a boutique in Foyles.

✔ **Waterstone's** (121 Charing Cross Rd.; ☎ 020/7434-4291; www.waterstones.com; Tube: Tottenham Court Road) is a U.K. chain with branches all over London. You can find the latest releases and well-stocked sections of books currently in print.

Covent Garden: Something for everyone

Try to save some of your shopping energy for Covent Garden, home of what may be the most famous "market" in all of England: the **Covent Garden Market.** (See the "Shopping the Street Markets" section, earlier in this chapter.)

Excellent English soaps, toiletries, and aromatherapy goods, as well as herbal goods, are available throughout the market and surrounding streets, including at the following shops (for locations, see the "Shopping in the West End" map on p. 250):

✔ **Culpeper the Herbalist** (8 The Market, Covent Garden, WC2; ☎ 020/7379-6698; www.culpeper.co.uk; Tube: Covent Garden) sells food, bath, and aromatherapy products, as well as dream pillows, candles, sachets, and that popular favorite: the battery-operated aromatherapy fan.

✔ **Neal's Yard Remedies** (15 Neal's Yard, off Shorts Garden, WC2; ☎ 020/7379-7222; http://remedies.nealsyardremedies.com; Tube: Covent Garden) is noted the world over for its all-natural, herbal-based bath, beauty, and aromatherapy products in cobalt-blue bottles.

✔ **Penhaligon's** (41 Wellington St., WC2; ☎ 020/7836-2150; www.penhaligons.co.uk; Tube: Covent Garden) is an exclusive-line of Victorian perfumery dedicated to good grooming. Choose from a large selection of perfumes, after-shaves, soaps, candles, and bath oils for women and men.

Also in Covent Garden, you can find **Dr. Martens Department Store** (1–4 King St., WC2; ☎ **020/7497-1460;** www.drmartens.com; Tube: Covent Garden), the flagship for internationally famous "Doc Marts" shoes. Prices are better here than they are in the States.

Farther along, at 14 King St., is **The Irish Shop** (☎ **020/7379-3625;** Tube: Covent Garden), which sells a wide variety of articles shipped directly from Ireland, including colorful knitwear, traditional Irish linens, hand-knitted Aran fisherman's sweaters, and Celtic jewelry.

And you can finish off at **The Tea House** (15A Neal St., WC2; ☎ **020/ 7240-7539;** Tube: Covent Garden), which sells everything associated with tea, tea drinking, and teatime.

Index of Stores by Merchandise

Antiques
Antiquarius (Chelsea)
Chelsea Antiques Market (Chelsea)
Map House of London
(Knightsbridge)

Bath and hygiene products
The Body Shop (Mayfair)
Culpeper the Herbalist (Covent Garden)
Floris (St. James's)
Lush (Chelsea)
Neal's Yard Remedies (Covent Garden)
Penhaligon's (Covent Garden)
Taylor of Old Bond Street (St. James's)

Books and maps
Children's Book Centre (Kensington)
Hatchards (St. James's)
Murder One (Soho)
Silver Moon Women's Bookshop (Soho)
Stanfords (Covent Garden)
W & G Foyle, Ltd. (Soho)
Waterstone's (Soho)

Candy
Charbonnel et Walker (Mayfair)

Clothing
Burberry (St. James's)
Hilditch & Key (St. James's)
Scotch House (St. James's)
Vivienne Westwood (Mayfair)

Department stores
Fenwick of Bond Street (Mayfair)
Fortnum & Mason (St. James's)
Harrods (Knightsbridge)
Harvey Nichols (Knightsbridge)
Liberty (Mayfair)
Marks & Spencer (Mayfair)
Selfridges (Mayfair)

Drugstores (chemists)
Bliss the Chemist (Bayswater)
Boots the Chemist (Knightsbridge)
Zafash Pharmacy (South Kensington)

Housewares and china
Peter Jones (Chelsea)
Royal Doulton Regent Street (St. James's)

Markets
Antiquarius (Chelsea)
Brick Lane Market (Shoreditch)
Chelsea Antiques Market (Chelsea)
Covent Garden Market (Covent Garden)

Petticoat Lane (East End)
Portobello Market (Notting Hill)
Spitalfields Market (Shoreditch)
Stables Market (Camden)

Miscellaneous
Anything Left-Handed (Soho)
Dress Circle (Soho)
The Filofax Centre (Covent Garden)
The Irish Shop (Covent Garden)
The Tea House (Covent Garden)

Music
MDC Classic Music (Covent Garden)
Virgin Megastore (St. James's)

Shoes
Church's (Bond Street)
Dr. Martens Department Store
(Covent Garden)

Silver
London Silver Vaults (Holborn)

Sporting goods
Farlows (St. James's)

Toys
Hamleys (St. James's)

Chapter 13

Following an Itinerary: Four Great Options

In This Chapter
▶ Seeing London on a reasonable schedule
▶ Planning fun itineraries for trips lasting three to seven days
▶ Visiting London with kids

*E*very London visitor has to face one problem: how to see as much as possible in a limited amount of time. You're lucky if you have an entire week or more. But what if you have only three or five days at your disposal? What if you're bringing the family along? These questions are what this chapter is all about. If you budget your time wisely and choose your sights carefully, you can make the most of a limited schedule or a trip with the kids.

This chapter offers four easy-to-do suggested daily itineraries. The first itinerary covers the big sights. The next two are a little more adventurous. The itinerary for families first addresses the top spots and then heads to family-friendly destinations just outside the city.

For complete descriptions of the sights, plus exact street addresses, open hours, and admission prices, see Chapter 11, unless I give you a different chapter to check out.

London in Three Days

Three days doesn't seem like a very long time. But in that short period, you can hit most of the key sights in London for a memorable trip.

Start **Day 1** with a visit to majestic **Westminster Abbey,** visiting the Royal Tombs and Poets' Corner. Afterward, because they're right next door, stroll around the **Houses of Parliament.** Unless you queue up to hear a debate or take one of the guided tours, available from August through September, you won't be able to get inside, but you can enjoy a great riverside view from Westminster Bridge. On the opposite side of the Thames is the **British Airways London Eye,** a 450-foot-high observation wheel. Reserve in advance for the trip up and over London; otherwise, you may spend at least a half-hour in line for a ticket and another hour before your scheduled "flight." You're not far from **Tate Britain,** so if you're in the mood to look at great English art, head over to Pimlico. Renting a self-guided audio tour is a great way to enhance your appreciation of the museum. Later in the afternoon, explore **Piccadilly Circus,** the teeming epicenter of London's West End. You find great shopping on Regent Street, Piccadilly, and Jermyn Street (see Chapter 12 for shopping). If you haven't already reserved a seat for a **West End show,** you may want to stop by the half-price ticket booth in **Leicester Square** to see what's available (see Chapter 15 for info on theaters). Have dinner in Soho before the show (see Chapter 10 for restaurants).

Greet **Day 2** with a walk through **Green Park.** You're on your way to **Buckingham Palace** to witness the pageantry of the **Changing of the Guard** (check beforehand to make sure that it's taking place that day). If you're visiting during August or September, you can tour the State Rooms of Buckingham Palace. Reserve tickets in advance, so you know your specific entry time; otherwise, you may have to wait in line for an hour or more to get in. If you're not touring the palace itself, visit the **Royal Mews.** From Buckingham Palace, you can stroll down the Mall, through **St. James's Park,** passing **Clarence House,** where the Queen Mother lived until her death in 2002, and **St. James's Palace,** once the London home of Prince Charles and his two sons, William and Harry.

Trafalgar Square, London's grandest and certainly most famous plaza, is your next stop. You can have lunch or tea at the **National Gallery's restaurant** or at **Café-in-the-Crypt** in St. Martin-in-the-Fields church on the east side of the square (see Chapter 10 for more on these restaurants). Spend your afternoon viewing the treasures of the **National Gallery.** Renting one of the self-guided audio tours will help you to home in on the most important paintings in the collection. After dinner in the Covent Garden area or on a Thames River cruise, head to one of the bars, pubs, or clubs that I describe in Chapter 16.

On **Day 3,** arrive as early as you can at the **Tower of London** and immediately join one of the one-hour guided tours led by the Beefeaters. Later, you can explore the precincts on your own, making certain you allot enough time to see the **Crown Jewels.** From the Tower, head over to nearby **St. Paul's Cathedral,** which you can see in about a half-hour.

The **British Museum,** your next stop, has enough to keep you occupied for several days; if you want to see only the highlights, allow yourself a minimum of two hours. Finish off your afternoon in Knightsbridge at **Harrods** (see Chapter 12), the most famous department store in London and, perhaps, the world. Knightsbridge and adjacent South Kensington offer innumerable dining options (see Chapter 10).

London in Five Days

This section assumes that you've already followed the suggested itineraries for your first three days (see the preceding section).

Day 4 begins at the **National Portrait Gallery,** where you can find the likeness of just about every famous British person you've ever heard of. Renting one of the self-guided audio tours is a good idea. From the portrait gallery, you can easily walk to **Covent Garden Market** (see Chapter 12). Scores of interesting shops are in and around the market, and **Covent Garden Piazza,** a lively hub filled with restaurants, makes a perfect spot for lunch. Spend your afternoon strolling in **Kensington Gardens** and visiting **Kensington Palace,** once the London home of Princess Diana. Then go for a traditional English dinner at **Rules,** London's oldest restaurant, or **Simpson's-in-the-Strand** (see Chapter 10). Are you up for a play or a concert tonight? If so, check your theater options in Chapter 15.

Day 5 begins with a morning at the museum of your choice. Choosing among the three major South Kensington museums — the **Natural History Museum,** the **Science Museum,** and the **Victoria & Albert Museum** — is entirely a matter of taste. If you like modern art, the new **Tate Modern** on the South Bank is the place to spend your morning. In the afternoon, expand your horizon with a short trip outside the city. The **Royal Botanic Gardens** at Kew, **Hampton Court, Windsor Palace, Hampstead Heath,** and **Greenwich** aren't terribly far away; the trips to reach them take anywhere from 20 minutes to an hour. You can be back in London in time for dinner.

London in Seven Days

How time flies! By now, if you follow the suggested itineraries for the last five days (see the preceding two sections), you've seen most of the major sights in London.

On **Day 6,** you're ready for a day trip. Riding in one of Britain's sleek new trains is terrific fun. The only problem is that you have to decide where you want to go. In Chapter 14, I give you the lowdown on six places, each remarkable in its own way. Do you want to see Shakespeare's birthplace in **Stratford-upon-Avon** or the famous prehistoric stone circle called **Stonehenge?** Do you want to spend a day by the seaside in **Brighton** or strolling around ancient **Canterbury** with its mighty cathedral? Perhaps you want to head to **Bath** to discover its splendid Georgian crescents, or **York** to explore the venerable York Minster. You can reach most of these places in 90 minutes or less.

Day 7 is your last day in London, and you'll want it to be special. In the morning, visit **Madame Tussaud's** wax museum or one of the museums that you haven't yet seen. Afterward, stroll through **Hyde Park** and stop at **Apsley House,** the London home of the first duke of Wellington. This house gives you a glimpse of what life was like inside one of London's great private palaces. If it's Sunday, you may instead want to visit **Spencer House,** the family home of the late Princess Diana. You can also do some last-minute shopping, if you prefer. Check out London's various shopping neighborhoods in Chapter 12, and then make your way to the major shopping arteries: Knightsbridge, Oxford Street, Bond Street, King's Road in Chelsea, or Regent Street. A traditional afternoon tea at one of London's great hotels (see Chapter 10) makes a delightful end to the afternoon. After that? You've booked theater tickets, haven't you?

London with Kids

So you want to spend five days in London and bring along your kids? No problem. I have a few suggestions to keep you *and* your kids excited and entertained. (For tips on traveling with kids, see Chapter 6.)

Don't schedule too much on **Day 1.** Exercise helps ward off jet lag. After sitting in a plane for several hours, the best option may be to take smaller children to one of London's great parks, so they can run and let off steam. Depending on where your hotel is located, your destination may be **Hyde Park, Kensington Gardens, Green Park, St. James's Park,** or **Regent's Park.** If you're traveling with teens, you may want to introduce them to the city by taking a stroll through London's four royal parks, following the **Princess Diana Commemorative Walk** (see p. 102).

You can begin more focused sightseeing on **Day 2.** Consider a guided bus tour that helps orient everyone and gives you at least a glimpse of all the major sights. Several outfits provide tours on double-decker buses — always a treat for kids — and one company offers a wonderful road and river trip on amphibious vehicles. After the tour, make the **British Airways London Eye** your first stop. Reserve your ticket beforehand to avoid waiting in a long line. Afterward, cross Westminster Bridge and stroll over to view the **Houses of Parliament** and **Big Ben** (if you're lucky, the clock will strike the hour while you're in the vicinity). And because it's close at hand, use this opportunity to visit **Westminster Abbey.** Younger children may not get much out of the place, but you will. Later in the afternoon, take a boat ride down the Thames to the **Tower of London;** you can board the boat at Westminster Pier near the Houses of Parliament. When you're inside the Tower, hook up with one of the Beefeater tours. If you're with a kid ages 10 to 17, you may want to have dinner at the **Hard Rock Cafe** in Mayfair (see Chapter 10).

Begin **Day 3** at the **Natural History Museum** in South Kensington, where the dinosaur exhibit with a ferocious animatronic *T. rex* captures the imaginations of both young and old(er). If your child's a budding Einstein, the **Science Museum** with its many hands-on, interactive exhibits may be a better choice. Afterward, if you have small children in tow, stroll over to **Kensington Gardens** for a look at the famous statue of

Peter Pan. The new **Princess Diana Memorial Playground** in the north-west corner of Kensington Gardens enchants little ones. You can have lunch in **The Orangery** of adjacent Kensington Palace or make your way to **Café-in-the-Crypt** (see Chapter 10) in St. Martin-in-the-Fields church in Trafalgar Square; you find a brass-rubbing center in the church, too. If you're with a teen, you may want to spend the morning or afternoon in **Madame Tussaud's** wax museum or the **London Dungeon;** just keep in mind that young children may find some of the gorier exhibits frightening. In the evening, older kids and teens may also enjoy one of the West End's razzmatazz musicals. If dinner and a play for just the grown-ups sounds good, you can get a baby sitter for the little ones (see the Quick Concierge, at the end of this book, for a reputable service).

Organizing your time

You can make the most of your visit to London if you organize your days efficiently and with common sense. Disorganized travelers waste a lot of time, show up at the museum on the day it's closed, and end up in the nether regions of Tooting Bec because they hopped on the wrong Underground line. Don't assume that every museum or site is open every day, all day. Take a moment to look at the details that I provide for each attraction in Chapter 11. And carry a copy of *London A–Z*.

An average top sight takes about two hours to visit, after you're actually inside. Some (Buckingham Palace and the Royal Mews) take more; others (Westminster Abbey and St. Paul's) take less. But other variables enter in: whether you're taking a guided tour (usually about an hour to an hour and a half, no matter where), whether you have kids in tow, or whether lines move slowly due to the crowds of visitors. Predicting how much time you'll spend at a major attraction, such as the British Museum and the National Gallery, is difficult. But as a general rule, you can do about three or four sights in a day if you're pushing yourself, fewer if you're not.

Many of London's major sights are concentrated in specific areas, so walking is the best way to see several sights in a short period of time. To cover larger areas, I recommend that you take the fast and convenient Underground.

Try to hit the very top sights on your list early in the day, preferably when they open, or late in the afternoon. Visit the places that are really important to you when you're feeling fresh and when they're less crowded. I mean, in particular, Buckingham Palace (when it's open to the public during Aug and Sept), the Tower of London, Westminster Abbey, and Madame Tussaud's. Westminster Abbey, to cite just one example, can receive upwards of 15,000 visitors per day!

Unless you have adrenaline to spare, try to unwind a little before you begin your round of after-dark diversions. You may need some downtime between the end of your sightseeing day and the beginning of your evening activities. I suggest that you head back to your hotel to take a shower or bath, to curl up with a novel or the evening paper for an hour, or maybe to catch a quick snooze to recharge your batteries. Then it's back to those perennially fascinating London streets.

Make **Day 4** a day trip to **Brighton** on the Sussex coast (see Chapter 14). The quick trip takes less than an hour. After you arrive, you can visit the **Royal Pavilion** and take the kids over to **Palace Pier,** a spot filled with games and souvenir stands. If the weather's warm, you can rent a deck chair and sit on the beach. Brighton is a fun place just to stroll around, with plenty to keep you and the family entertained.

On **Day 5,** head out to **Hampton Court Palace,** another quick train ride of less than an hour. Hampton Court offers much to explore, so give your-self at least four hours. Small children may not get much out of the visit, but they'll probably be intrigued by the staff wearing period costumes. You can eat on the premises. Save the best part for last: The famous maze in the gardens brings out the kid in everyone. Finally, return to London for a good night's rest before flying out the next morning.

Chapter 14

Going Beyond London: Six Great Day Trips

. . . .

In This Chapter

▶ Taking the best day trips from London

▶ Getting there and back

▶ Deciding what to see and do after you arrive

▶ Choosing where to eat and where to stay

. . . .

*E*ngland is a relatively small country. You can visit countless places on one-day side trips from London.

In Chapter 11, I describe the easiest side trips from London: **Kew Gardens, Hampton Court Palace, Windsor Palace,** and **Greenwich.** In this chapter, I venture out to some of England's most popular, impressive, and famous places: Bath, Brighton, Canterbury, Stratford-upon-Avon, Stonehenge, and York. By train, you can get to all these sites in two hours or less from London (see the "Day Trips from London" map on p. 264).

By Train or by Car: Weighing the Options

Because of England's small size and easy-access train and road networks, this country is a joy to explore.

For all the trips in this chapter, I'd recommend that you take the train instead of renting and driving a car. From London, you can reach Bath, Brighton, and Canterbury in 90 minutes or less by train. The train trip to Stratford-upon-Avon or to Salisbury (the closest large town to Stonehenge) takes about two hours. A trip to York will take about two hours. At each of these places, the attractions are within walking distance of the train station. The one exception is Stonehenge, which you can reach by public bus from Salisbury. If you get an early start, you can explore any one of these places, have lunch, and still get back to London in time for dinner.

Day Trips from London

The following sections help you decide whether train travel or auto-motion is for you.

Taking the train

If you plan to travel around England by train, get a **BritRail pass** *before* you arrive (they're not available in the U.K.) from **Rail Europe** (☎ 877/272-7245 in the U.S. or 800/361-7245 in Canada; www.raileurope.com). Rail Europe only sells to North Americans and quotes prices in U.S. dollars. You cannot buy Rail Europe passes outside of North America. The **London Plus Pass** gets you to three of the towns in this chapter — Brighton, Canterbury, and Salisbury (plus Windsor, which you can read about in Chapter 11) — but not to Bath, Stratford-upon-Avon, or York. Trains offer first-class and standard-class seating — first-class cars are less crowded, and the seats are roomier and more comfy. Because the train trips to the destinations in this chapter aren't very long, standard-class may be fine for most travelers. For 2 days of travel in an 8-day period, the pass costs $113 first class, $74 standard class; for 4 days in an 8-day period, it costs $187 first class, $140 standard class; and for 7 days of travel in a 15-day period, it costs $249 first class, $187 standard class. See Rail Europe's Web site for more information on the London Plus and other BritRail passes.

National train schedules, routes, and fares can be found online at www.nationalrail.co.uk, or by calling ☎ 0845/484-950.

Taking a car: Driving on the left, passing on the right

I always suggest that people visiting London travel by train instead of driving. Much of your car trip will be on motorways without much scenery, so what's the point? Then, when you arrive, you have to find parking (generally outside the historic city center); if you arrive by train, however, you can easily walk to the center of town from the train station (or take a cab if you have mobility issues). The historic towns of England are compact and centralized — you won't necessarily need a car to get from point A to point B.

Before you even consider renting a car, ask yourself whether you're comfortable driving with a steering wheel on the right-hand side of the vehicle while shifting with your left hand (you can get an automatic, but it costs considerably more). *Remember:* You must drive on the left and pass on the right.

Although the car rental market in Britain is highly competitive, renting a car here costs more than back home — unless you can find a special promotional offer from an airline or a car rental agency. Most U.K. car rental agencies accept valid foreign driver's licenses. In most cases, you must be 23 years old (21 in some instances), no older than 70, and have had your driver's license for more than a year.

You can often get a discount on car rental rates if you reserve 48 hours in advance through the toll-free reservations offices. Weekly rentals are almost always less expensive than daily rates. And the rate, of course, depends on the size of the vehicle.

When you make your reservation, ask whether the quoted price includes the 17.5 percent VAT and unlimited mileage. Then find out whether personal accident insurance (PAI), collision-damage waiver (CDW), and any other insurance options are included. If they aren't a part of the deal, which they usually aren't, be sure to ask how much they cost. When you drive in any foreign country (or anywhere, for that matter), arrange for as much coverage as possible.

 Some credit card companies offer the collision-damage waiver and other types of insurance for free if you use that card to pay for the rental. If you're planning to rent a car, check with your credit card company to see what's covered, or you may end up paying for coverage you already have.

Bath: Hot Mineral Springs and Cool Georgian Magnificence

Bath, 185km (115 miles) west of London, is a beautiful spa town on the Avon River (see the "Bath" map on p. 267). Since the days of the ancient Celts — and later the Romans — Bath has been famous for its hot mineral springs. In 1702, Queen Anne frequented the soothing, sulfurous waters and transformed Bath into a spa for the elite. Aristocrats, socialites, social climbers, and flamboyant dandies, such as Beau Nash, have added to the spa's fashionable and fascinating history. The great author Jane Austen used Bath as an upwardly genteel setting for her class-conscious plots.

Today, the spa is a grand legacy from the Georgian era, graced with beautiful curving *crescents* (a row of houses built in a long curving line) and classically inspired buildings of honey-colored stone. Must-sees are the **Roman Baths Museum** and adjoining **Pump Room** (where visitors can continue the long tradition of sipping water while listening to music), the adjacent **Abbey,** and the **Assembly Rooms** (once used for balls and gaming).

Getting there

Trains for Bath leave from London's Paddington Station every hour; the trip takes about 90 minutes. The standard return (round-trip) fare costs £35 ($70). For schedules, go to www.nationalrail.co.uk, or call ☎ 0845/484-950. By car, take the M4 to Junction 18 and then drive a few miles south on A46.

Bath

Information ⓘ
Church ✝

ROYAL VICTORIA PARK

Royal Crescent ❶

Methodist Chapel ✝

Brock St.

CRESCENT GARDENS

Royal Ave.

Gravel Walk

Gay St.

Bennett St.

Lansdown Rd.

Paragon St.

Guinea Ln.

St. John's Rd.

River Avon

❷ ❸ Alfred St.

Bartlett St.

George St.

Milsom St.

Broad St.

Northgate St.

❹

Old King St.

John St.

Bristol Rd.

Charlotte St.

❺

Barton St.

Quiet St.

Queen

Green St.

New Bond St.

Pulteney Bridge ❼

Argyle St.

❻

❽

Beaufort Sq.

Trim

Monmouth St.

Charles St.

Saw Close

Upper Borough Walls

Union Passage

Union St.

Bridge St.

High St.

Grand Parade

James St. West

Westgate St.

Cheap St.

Orange Grove ⓘ

❾

PARADE GARDENS

Midland Bridge Rd.

Green Park Rd.

GREEN PARK

Bath St.

York St.

❿

Church St.

⓫

Stall St.

Orchard St.

⓬ Henry St.

Pierrepont St.

Avon St.

St. James Parade

Southgate St.

Manvers St.

River Avon

Dorchester St.

Churchill Bridge

Train Station

Claverton St.

ATTRACTIONS ●
Assembly Rooms and
  Fashion Museum **3**
Bath Abbey **9**
The Circus **2**
Jane Austen Centre **4**
North Parade **11**
Pulteney Bridge **8**
Queen Square **5**
Roman Baths Museum
  and Pump Room **10**
Royal Crescent **1**
South Parade **12**
HOTEL ■ / RESTAURANT ◆
Kennard Hotel **6**
No. 5 Bistro **7**

0   100 mi
0   100 km

SCOTLAND

North Sea

Irish Sea

ENGLAND

WALES   London ✪

Bath

English Channel

0   300 ft
0   100 meters

N

Finding information and taking a tour

Bath's Tourist Information Centre (☎ 01225/477-761; www.visitbath.
co.uk), located in the center of town on the square in front of Bath
Abbey, is open Monday through Saturday 9:30 a.m. to 5 p.m. (until 6 p.m.
in the summer) and Sunday 10 a.m. to 4 p.m. The Centre provides **free
guided walks** that leave from outside the **Pump Room** Sunday through
Friday at 10:30 a.m. and 2 p.m. and Saturday at 10:30 a.m. Additional
walks are offered at 7 p.m. on Tuesday, Friday, and Saturday from May
through September.

One-hour, open-top **bus tours** with audio commentary are presented by
City Sightseeing (☎ 01871/666-0000) at a cost of £10 ($20) for adults,
£8 ($16) for seniors and students, and £4.50 ($9) for children. Tours
depart from the bus station every 15 minutes in summer; otherwise,
they leave hourly. Tickets are valid all day, and you can get off and on to
explore places along the route.

Seeing the sights

The Romans — who arrived in A.D. 75 — built the huge bath-and-temple
complex at the center of the **Roman Baths Museum** (☎ 01225/477-785;
www.romanbaths.co.uk) beside Bath Abbey. When visitors enter, they
receive a portable self-guided audio tour keyed to everything on display,
including the original Roman baths and heating system; the audio tour is
fun, informative, and very well done. Admission costs £11 ($22) for adults,
with discounts for seniors, students, children, and families. The museum
is open daily March through June, September, and October 9 a.m. to
5 p.m.; July and August 9 a.m. to 9 p.m.; January through February and
November through December 9:30 a.m. to 4:30 p.m. (closed Dec 25–26).

Overlooking the Roman baths is the late-18th-century **Pump Room**
(☎ 01225/477-7785), where the fashionable assembled to sip the reputedly health-promoting water. You're welcome to taste it for yourself (your
ticket to the Roman Baths Museum entitles you to one free glass of mineral
water in the Pump Room). Admission is free. In the Pump Room, you can
enjoy *elevenses* (morning tea), lunch, or afternoon tea to a background of
live music. Main courses cost £11 to £15 ($22–$30); afternoon tea goes for
£16 ($32). The Pump Room is open Monday through Saturday 9:30 a.m. to
5 p.m. (until 10 p.m. July–Aug) and Sunday 10:30 a.m. to 4:30 p.m.

Step inside **Bath Abbey** (☎ 01225/422-462; www.bathabbey.org) and
view the graceful fan vaulting, the great East Window, and the ironically
simple memorial to Beau Nash, the most flamboyant of the dandies who
frequented Bath in its heyday. Admission is by a suggested donation of
£2.50 ($5). April through October, the abbey is open Monday through
Saturday 9 a.m. to 6 p.m. (to 4:30 p.m. Nov–Mar); year-round, it's open
Sunday 1 to 2:30 p.m. and 4:30 to 5:30 p.m.

Another classic building worth visiting is the **Assembly Rooms** (Bennett
Street; ☎ 01225/477-789), the site of all the grand balls and social climb-
ing in 18th-century Bath. Entrance is free unless you want to visit the

excellent **Fashion Museum** (☎ **01225/477-173**; www.fashionmuseum. co.uk) that is part of the complex. Admission for the museum costs £6.75 ($14) adults; £5.75 ($12) seniors, students, and children 6 to 18. The museum is open daily 11 a.m. to 4 p.m. (to 5 p.m. Mar–Oct); the Assembly Rooms are open when not in use.

Bath's newest attraction, the **Jane Austen Centre** (40 Gay St.; ☎ **01225/ 443-000;** www.janeausten.co.uk), is located in a Georgian town house on an elegant street where Austen once lived. Exhibits and a video convey a sense of what life in Bath was like during the Regency period; all in all, though, this museum is a bit of a bore to all but the most avid Austen fans. Admission costs £6.50 ($13). The center is open daily 10 a.m. to 5 p.m. (Sun from 10:30 a.m.). Afternoon tea is served in the Regency tearooms for £6.95 ($14).

Bath is a wonderful walking town, filled with beautiful squares and sweeping residential crescents. Stroll along the **North Parade** and the **South Parade, Queen Square,** and **The Circus** and be sure to have a look at the **Royal Crescent,** a magnificent, curving row of 30 town houses designed in 1767 by John Wood the Younger. Regarded as the epitome of England's *Palladian style* (a classical style incorporating elements from ancient Greek and Roman buildings), the Royal Crescent is now designated a UNESCO World Heritage site. **No. 1 Royal Crescent** (☎ **01225/428-126**) is a gorgeously restored 18th-century house with period furnishings. Admission costs £5 ($10). The house is open mid-February through October, Tuesday through Sunday 10:30 a.m. to 5 p.m. (to 4 p.m. in Nov).

Pulteney Bridge, built in 1770, spans the River Avon a few blocks south of the Assembly Rooms. The bridge is one of the few in Europe lined with shops and restaurants.

Dining locally

A popular French eatery in Bath's city center is **No. 5 Bistro** (5 Argyle St.; ☎ **01225/444-499**). The chef at this pleasant restaurant produces mouth-watering dishes that may include baked ricotta with olive, spinach, and sun-dried tomato soufflé; Provençal fish soup; pan-fried pepper steak; or vegetarian dishes, such as roasted stuffed peppers and vegetable gratin. Main courses cost £14 to £17 ($28–$34). The bistro, open daily noon to 2:30 p.m. and 6:30 to 10:30 p.m., accepts American Express, MasterCard, and Visa.

Spending the night

If you want to spend the night in Bath, try the **Kennard Hotel** (11 Henrietta St.; ☎ **01225/310-472;** fax: 01225/460-054; www.kennard. co.uk). On the east side of Pulteney Bridge, within walking distance of everything in Bath, this elegant hotel with 13 guest rooms occupies a beautifully restored 1794 Georgian town house. The rates are £98 to £118 ($196–$236) for a double, breakfast included. The hotel accepts American Express, MasterCard, and Visa.

Brighton: Fun beside the Seaside

On the Sussex coast, a mere 80km (50 miles) south of London, Brighton is England's most famous, and probably most popular, seaside town (see the "Brighton" map on p. 271). Brighton was a small fishing village until the Prince Regent, who would become George IV, became enamored with the place and had the incredible Royal Pavilion built. Where royalty moves, fashion follows, and Brighton eventually became one of Europe's most fashionable towns. The lovely Georgian terraces that you see everywhere date from this period. Later in the 19th century, when breathing sea air was prescribed as a cure-all for everything from depression to tuberculosis, the Victorians descended in hordes. Today, Brighton is a commuter suburb of London and a popular place for conventions and romantic weekend getaways. Gays and lesbians are very much a part of the local and visitor scene.

Brighton is a compact town, and the easiest way to get around is on foot. Forget about that frantic need for sightseeing and relax. Relaxation is what Brighton is all about. This place is for leisurely strolling, either in the town or along the seaside promenades. The town is small enough so you won't get lost and large enough to offer some good cultural diversions.

Getting there

More than 40 trains a day leave from London's Victoria Station for Brighton. The trip takes about an hour. If you travel off-peak (after 9:30 a.m.), a cheap *day-return* (round-trip) ticket costs about £18 ($36). For schedules, go to www.nationalrail.co.uk, or call ☎ 0845/484-950. If you're driving, the M23 from Central London leads to Brighton. The drive typically takes about an hour, but if roads are clogged, it may take twice as long.

Finding information

Brighton's **Visitor Information Centre** (Royal Pavilion Shop, 4–5 Pavilion Buildings; ☎ 0906/711-2255; www.visitbrighton.com), in the Royal Pavilion, is about a ten-minute walk south from the train station. The center is a good place to pick up info on current events and a Gay Information Sheet listing gay guesthouses, pubs, and clubs. If you fall in love with Brighton and decide to stay overnight, you can reserve a room through this office. The center is open daily from 9:30 a.m. to 5 p.m.

Seeing the sights

Brighton's one must-see attraction is the **Royal Pavilion** (☎ 01273/290-900; www.royalpavilion.org.uk), set in a small landscaped park bounded by North Street, Church Street, Olde Steine, and New Road. The pavilion is one of the most extraordinary palaces in Europe. John Nash redesigned the original farmhouse and villa on this site for George IV (when the king was still Prince Regent), who lived here with his mistress, Lady Conyngham, until 1827.

Brighton

ATTRACTIONS ●
Brighton Museum
& Art Gallery **1**
Palace Pier **4**
Royal Pavilion and Queen
Adelaide Tea Room **3**

HOTEL ■
Hotel du Vin & Bistro **2**

RESTAURANTS ◆
Strand Restaurant **5**
Terre à Terre **6**

The exterior, as crazily wonderful as anything King Ludwig of Bavaria dreamed up, is an Indian fantasy of turrets and minarets. The interior, decorated in a Chinese style, is fantastically extravagant. The king's brother, William IV, and Queen Victoria later used the pavilion. Admission, which includes an audio guide, costs £7.70 ($15) adults, £5.10 ($10) seniors and students, £5.90 ($12) children under 16, and £21 ($42) for families (two adults and two children). The pavilion is open daily October through May 10 a.m. to 5 p.m. and June through September 9:30 a.m. to 5:45 p.m.

Before you leave the pavilion, consider having lunch or a *cream tea* (tea and scones served with clotted cream and strawberry preserves) in the restored **Queen Adelaide Tea Room** (☎ **01723/292-736**), open daily 10:30 a.m. to 4:30 p.m. (to 5 p.m. in summer). Queen Adelaide, who used this suite in 1830, didn't appreciate the epicurean tastes of her husband, George IV. Dismissing his renowned French chefs, she reverted back to

British cuisine so dreary that Lord Dudley complained "you now get cold pâté and hot champagne." The lunch selections and cream teas range from £7 to £13 ($14–$26).

Close to the Royal Pavilion, on Church Street, you find the small **Brighton Museum & Art Gallery** (☎ 01273/292-882), with some interesting collections of Art Nouveau and Art Deco furniture, glass, and ceramics, plus a Fashion Gallery. Reopened in 2002 after a major refurbishment, it's a good place to wile away an hour. Admission is free, and it's open Tuesday 10 a.m. to 7 p.m., Wednesday through Saturday from 10 a.m. to 5 p.m., Sunday 2 to 5 p.m. (closed Dec 24–26 and Jan 1).

The town's famous amusement area, **Palace Pier,** jutting out into the sea just south of the Royal Pavilion, was built in the late 19th century. Today the pier is rather tacky but worth visiting nonetheless. At night, all lit up with twinkling lights, this place is almost irresistible. Spend half an hour, but don't expect to find much more than junk food, kiddie rides, and arcade games. The more famous West Pier, now over 130 years old and gradually sinking into the sea, isn't open to the public.

Brighton and neighboring Hove stretch out along the English Channel. The entire **seafront** is a pebbly public beach used for swimming and sunning. Promenades for strolling are all along the seafront. If you're into sunbathing *au naturel,* Brighton has the only nude beach in England, about a mile west of Brighton Pier. You'll recognize it when you get there.

Dining locally

One of the hippest (and friendliest) places for dining is the bow-fronted **Strand Restaurant** (6 Little East St.; ☎ 01273/747-096; www.thestrand brighton.co.uk), which serves Modern British cuisine with an emphasis on fish. The ever-changing menu may include herby homemade vegetable soup, followed by chicken breast with creamy mushrooms; homemade fish cakes; or basil, leek, and parmesan risotto. Main courses cost £8 to £10 ($16–$20). The restaurant is open Monday and Tuesday 6 p.m. to midnight, Wednesday through Saturday noon to midnight. It accepts American Express, Diners Club, MasterCard, and Visa.

For a new outlook on vegetarian food, try **Terre à Terre** (71 East St.; ☎ 01273/729-051; www.terreaterre.co.uk). Considered the best vegetarian restaurant in England, perhaps in all Europe, this place elevates meatless cuisine to an art form. The food is impeccably fresh and beautifully presented. You can eat your way through the menu with the Terre à Tapas, a superb selection of all their best dishes, big enough for two. Main courses cost £13 to £15 ($26–$30). The restaurant is open Tuesday 6:30 to 10:30 p.m., and Wednesday through Sunday noon to 10:30 p.m. Reservations are essential on weekends. The restaurant accepts Diners Club, MasterCard, and Visa.

Spending the night

A sophisticated new addition to Brighton's hotel scene, the ultrastylish **Hotel du Vin & Bistro** (Ship Street; ☎ 01273/718-588; fax: 01273/718-599; www.hotelduvin.com) occupies a set of Mock Tudor and Gothic Revival buildings a stone's throw from the seafront. This is Brighton's most unique contemporary hotel, with an impressive three-story lobby, a signature French bistro, and 37 cool, uncluttered, and very comfortable bedrooms featuring marvelous beds with fine Egyptian linens, deep soaker tubs, and power showers. Rack rates for a double room with breakfast range from £145 to £250 ($290–$500). The hotel accepts all major credit cards.

Canterbury: Tales from the Great Cathedral

Magnificent **Canterbury Cathedral** is one of the glories of England. For nearly 400 years, the devout, in search of miracles, salvation, and a bit of adventure, trekked to the cathedral's shrine of Thomas à Becket, Archbishop of Canterbury, who was murdered in 1170 by henchmen of Henry II. Along the way, they spun the yarns found in Chaucer's *The Canterbury Tales.* (The pilgrims didn't stop coming until Henry VIII had the shrine destroyed in 1538.) Modern pilgrims, today called day-trippers, continue to pour into the Kentish city of Canterbury on the River Stour, 100km (62 miles) east of London (see "Canterbury" map on p. 274). They come to see the cathedral, of course, but also to visit the host of small museums and to enjoy the picturesque town surrounding it.

Getting there

Canterbury has two train stations, Canterbury East and Canterbury West, and you can easily walk to the city center from either one. From London's Victoria Station, trains run about every half-hour to Canterbury East. Hourly trains from London's Charing Cross stop at Canterbury West. The journey takes 90 minutes and costs about £18 ($36) for a cheap *day-return* (round-trip) ticket. For schedules, go to www.nationalrail.co.uk, or call ☎ 0845/484-950. To drive from London, take the A2 and then the M2; Canterbury is signposted all the way. The city center is closed to cars, but several parking areas are close to the cathedral.

Finding information and taking a tour

The **Visitors Information Centre** (12–13 Sun St.; ☎ 01227/378100; www.canterbury.co.uk), opposite Christchurch Gate at the entrance to the cathedral precincts, is open Easter through October, Monday through Saturday 9:30 a.m. to 5 p.m. and Sunday 10 a.m. to 4 p.m.; the rest of the year, the center is open Monday through Saturday 10 a.m. to 4 p.m. At the Centre, you can buy tickets for daily guided-tour walks of the city and cathedral at 2 p.m. (additional walks in July and Aug, Mon–Sat 11:30 a.m.). The tour costs £4.50 ($9) adults, £4 ($8) seniors and students, £3 ($6) for children under 12, and £15 ($30) families (two adults and two children).

Canterbury

ATTRACTIONS ●
Canterbury Cathedral **2**
The Canterbury Tales **4**
King's School **1**
Roman Museum **5**
St. Augustine's Abbey **6**
St. Martin's Church **7**
HOTEL ■ / **RESTAURANT** ◆
Cathedral Gate Hotel **3**
Michael Caines Restaurant **8**

Canterbury Historic River Tours (Weavers House, 1 St. Peter's St.;
☎ 07790/534-744; www.canterburyrivertours.co.uk) offers half-
hour boat trips on the Stour River with a commentary on the history of
the buildings that you pass. April through September, river conditions
permitting, boats depart daily every 15 to 20 minutes from 10 a.m. to
5 p.m. Tickets cost £6 ($12) adults, £5 ($10) seniors and students, £4
($8) children, and £17 ($34) for families (two adults and two children).
Umbrellas are available in case of rain. The boats leave from behind the
15th-century Weavers House (access via the Weavers restaurant garden).

Seeing the sights

Make your first stop the imposing **Canterbury Cathedral** (11 The
Precincts; ☎ 01227/762-862; www.canterbury-cathedral.org), a
magnificent structure that was the first major expression of the Gothic
style in England. The crypt dates from about 1100, and the cathedral
itself (rebuilt after a fire) dates from the 13th century, with a bell tower
added in the 15th century.

Although Henry VIII destroyed Becket's shrine, its site is still marked in the Trinity Chapel near the high altar. Noteworthy features of the cathedral include a number of panels of rare stained glass and the medieval royal tombs of Henry IV and Edward the Black Prince. Admission costs £6.50 ($13) adults; £5 ($10) seniors, students, and children. The cathedral is open Monday through Saturday 9 a.m. to 5 p.m. (until 6 p.m. in summer), and Sunday 12:30 to 4:30 p.m.; closed to sightseeing during services.

As you stroll the cathedral grounds, you may encounter flocks of well-behaved boys and girls wearing blazers and ties: They attend **King's School,** the oldest public school in England, housed in several fine medieval buildings north of the cathedral.

Off High Street, near the cathedral, is the entertaining exhibition known as **The Canterbury Tales** (23 St. Margaret's St.; ☎ **01227/454-888;** www.canterburytales.org.uk), where the pilgrimages of Chaucerian England are re-created in tableaux. On audio headsets, you can hear five of Chaucer's *Canterbury Tales* and the story of the murder of St. Thomas à Becket. Give yourself 45 minutes to an hour to see and hear the entire show. Admission costs £7.50 ($15) adults, £6.50 ($13) seniors and students, £5.50 ($11) children 5 to 15. The attraction is open daily 10 a.m. to 4:30 p.m. (9:30 a.m.–5 p.m. in summer).

Two millennia ago, the conquering Romans were living in Canterbury, which they called *Cantuaria.* Their daily lives are chronicled in the small but fascinating **Roman Museum** (☎ **01227/785-575**), in the excavated Roman levels of the city between the cathedral and High Street on Butchery Lane. Admission costs £3.10 ($6.20) adults; £1.90 ($3.80) seniors, students, and children. The museum is open Monday through Saturday 10 a.m. to 5 p.m. (also Sun 1:30–5 p.m. June–Oct).

Although the cathedral gets the lion's share of attention in Canterbury, another Christian site predates it by about 600 years. Set in a spacious park, about a ten-minute walk east from the center of town, you find the atmospheric ruins of **St. Augustine's Abbey** (Longport; ☎ **01227/767-345**), founded in A.D. 598 and one of the oldest Anglo-Saxon monastic sites in the country. This UNESCO World Heritage site offers interactive audio tours. Admission costs £4 ($8) adults, £3 ($6) seniors and students, and £2 ($4) children. The site is open April through June Wednesday through Sunday 10 a.m. to 5 p.m.; July and August daily 10 a.m. to 6 p.m.; September through March Sundays 11 a.m. to 5 p.m.

Trek another five minutes east from St. Augustine's Abbey to visit the oldest parish church in England. **St. Martin's Church** (North Holmes Road; ☎ **01227/459-482**), founded by Queen Bertha (the French wife of Saxon King Ethelbert), was already in existence when Augustine arrived from Rome to convert the natives in A.D. 597. Admission is free, and the church is open daily 9 a.m. to 5 p.m.

Dining locally

One of the best dining spots in Canterbury is **Michael Caines Restaurant,** located in the newly refurbished Abode (High Street; ☎ **01227/766-266**). You can choose from a selection of simple but imaginatively conceived dishes and seasonal specialties. Reservations are recommended. Main courses go for £14 to £20 ($28–$40). You can dine on more traditional pub fare in the Tavern, where prices run from £8 to £15 ($16–$30).The restaurant accepts American Express, Diners Club, MasterCard, and Visa. It's open daily for breakfast, lunch, and dinner.

Spending the night

If you're planning an overnight stay in Canterbury and want, like the pilgrims of yore, to stay near the cathedral, you can't get any closer than the **Cathedral Gate Hotel** (36 Burgate; ☎ **01227/464-381**; fax: 01227/462-800; www.cathgate.co.uk). Dating from 1438, the 27-room hotel adjoins Christchurch Gate and overlooks the Buttermarket. The guest rooms are comfortable and modestly furnished, with sloping floors, massive oak beams, and winding corridors — what else would you expect from a hotel built more than 500 years ago? With the cheapest rooms, you'll be sharing a bathroom. Rates are £40 to £98 ($80–$196) for a double, continental breakfast included. The hotel accepts American Express, Diners Club, MasterCard, and Visa.

Stratford-upon-Avon: In the Footsteps of the Bard

Stratford-upon-Avon (see the "Stratford-upon-Avon" map on p. 277) is a shrine to the world's greatest playwright, William Shakespeare, who was born, lived much of his life, and is buried in this market town on the Avon River, 146km (91 miles) northwest of London. In summer, crowds of international tourists overrun Stratford, which aggressively hustles its Shakespeare connection.

Stratford is comprised of many Elizabethan and Jacobean buildings, but it's not really a quaint village anymore. If you're arriving by train, your first glimpse will be of a vast parking lot across from the station. Don't let this sight put you off. The charms of Stratford haven't been completely lost — it still has lots of lovely corners to discover. Besides the literary pilgrimage sights, the top draw in Stratford is the **Royal Shakespeare Theatre,** where Britain's foremost actors perform.

Getting there

Direct trains leave frequently from London's Paddington Station; the journey takes two hours and costs £25 ($50) for a standard-class off-peak (after 9:30 a.m.) round-trip ticket. For schedules, go to www.national rail.co.uk, or call ☎ **0845/484-950.** To drive from London, take the M40 toward Oxford and continue to Stratford-upon-Avon on the A34.

Stratford-upon-Avon

ATTRACTIONS ●
Anne Hathaway's Cottage **11**
Hall's Croft **12**
Holy Trinity Church **13**
Mary Arden's House &
    Shakespeare Countryside Museum **1**
New Place/Nash's House **10**
Royal Shakespeare Theatre **9**
Shakespeare Centre **3**
Shakespeare's Birthplace **4**
Shakesperience **5**

HOTELS ■ / RESTAURANTS ◆
Hathaway Tea Rooms & Bakery **7**
Mercure Shakespeare Hotel Stratford **8**
The Oppo **6**
The Payton **2**

Finding information and taking a tour

Stratford's **Tourist Information Centre** (Bridgefoot; ☎ **0870/160-7930;**
www.shakespeare-country.co.uk) provides information and maps of
the town and its major sites. Easter through October, the center is open
Monday through Saturday 9 a.m. to 6 p.m. (until 5 p.m. in winter) and
Sunday 11 a.m. to 5 p.m. (10:30 a.m.–4:30 p.m. in winter).

Bus tours of Stratford, provided by **City Sightseeing** (☎
01708/866-000), leave from outside the tourist office. Open-top, double-
decker buses depart every 15 minutes daily 9:30 a.m. to 4:30 p.m. in
summer (until 3:30 p.m. the rest of the year). You can take the one-
hour ride without stops or get off and on at any or all of the town's five
Shakespeare properties, including Mary Arden's House in Wilmcote (see
the following section). The tour ticket is valid all day but doesn't include
admission into any of the houses. The tours cost £9 ($18) adults, £7
($14) seniors and students, and £4 ($8) children under 12. You can buy
your ticket on the bus.

Seeing the sights

You can buy a combination ticket at your first stop that gets you
into the five sites administered by the Shakespeare Birthplace Trust:
**Shakespeare's Birthplace, Anne Hathaway's Cottage, New Place/
Nash's House, Mary Arden's House,** and **Hall's Croft.** The ticket costs
£14 ($28) adults, £12 ($24) seniors and students, £6.50 ($13) children,
and £29 ($58) families (two adults and three children). Purchase a
reduced-price ticket if you only want to visit the three sites in town.

A logical place to begin your tour is **Shakespeare's Birthplace** (Henley
Street; ☎ **01789/204-016;** www.shakespeare.org.uk), where the bard,
son of a glover and wool merchant, first saw the light of day on April 23,
1564. You enter through the modern **Shakespeare Centre,** where you
can spend a few minutes browsing the exhibits that illustrate his life and
times. The house, filled with Shakespeare memorabilia, is actually two
16th-century half-timbered houses joined together. His father's shop was
on one side, and the family residence was on the other. After visiting the
bedroom where wee Willie was (probably) born, the Elizabethan kitchen,
and other rooms, you can walk through the garden. Admission costs £7
($14) adults, £6 ($12) seniors and students, £2.60 ($5.20) children, and
£17 ($34) families (two adults and three children). Shakespeare's
Birthplace is open daily April through May and September through
October 10 a.m. to 5 p.m. (Sun from 10:30 a.m.); June through August 9
a.m. to 5 p.m. (Sun from 9:30 a.m.); and November through March 10
a.m. to 4 p.m. (Sun from 10:30 a.m.). It's closed December 24 to 26.

To visit **Anne Hathaway's Cottage** (Cottage Lane, Shottery [about a mile
south of Stratford]; ☎ **01789/292-100**), take a bus from Bridge Street
or, better still, walk there along the well-marked country path from
Evesham Place. Anne Hathaway, who came from a family of yeomen
farmers, lived in this lovely thatched cottage before she married

18-year-old Shakespeare (a May-December marriage, as Anne was 25). Many original 16th-century furnishings, including the *courting settle* (a type of bench that courting couples often sat on), are preserved inside the house, which was occupied by Anne's ancestors until 1892. Before leaving, be sure to stroll through the beautiful garden and orchard. Admission costs £5.50 ($11) adults, £4.50 ($9) seniors and students, £2 ($4) children, and £13 ($26) families (two adults and three children). The cottage is open daily April through May and September through October 9:30 a.m. to 5 p.m. (Sun from 10 a.m.); June through August 9 a.m. to 5 p.m. (Sun from 9:30 a.m.); and November through March 10 a.m. to 4 p.m. (Sun from 10:30 a.m.). The cottage is closed January 1, Good Friday (the Friday before Easter), and December 24 to 26.

Shakespeare retired in 1610 to **New Place** (Chapel Street; ☎ **01789/ 204-016**). By that time, he was a relatively prosperous man whose plays had been seen by Queen Elizabeth. New Place was a Stratford house that he'd purchased a few years earlier and where he would die in 1616. The house was later torn down and, today, only the gardens remain. To reach the site from his birthplace, walk east on Henley Street and south on High Street, which becomes Chapel Street. Visitors enter through **Nash's House,** which belonged to Thomas Nash, husband of Shakespeare's granddaughter. The house contains 16th-century period rooms and an exhibit illustrating the history of Stratford. Adjoining the house is a knot garden landscaped in an Elizabethan style. Admission costs £3.75 ($7.50) adults, £3 ($6) seniors and students, £1.75 ($3.50) children, and £10 ($20) families (two adults and three children). Hours are daily April through May and September through October 11 a.m. to 5 p.m.; June through August 9:30 a.m. to 5 p.m. (Sun from 10 a.m.); and November through March 11 a.m. to 4 p.m.

Shakespeare's daughter, Susanna, probably lived with her husband, Dr. John Hall, in **Hall's Croft** (Old Town; ☎ **01789/292-107**), a magnificent Tudor house with a walled garden. From New Place, continue south on Chapel and Church streets and turn east on Old Town to reach Hall's Croft. The house is furnished in the style of a middle-class 17th-century home. On view are exhibits illustrating the theory and practice of medicine in Dr. Hall's time. Hours and admission are the same as for Nash's House (see the preceding paragraph).

Shakespeare died on his birthday, at age 52, and was buried in **Holy Trinity Church** (Old Town; ☎ **01789/266-316;** www.stratford-upon-avon.org), a beautiful parish church beside the Avon River. His wife, Anne, his daughter Susanna, and Susanna's husband, John Hall, lie beside him in front of the altar. A bust of the immortal bard looks down upon the gravesite. I find it a bit odd that the inscription on the tomb of the man who wrote some of the world's most enduring lines is little more than doggerel, ending with "and curst be he who moves my bones." Obviously William Shakespeare didn't want to leave Stratford — ever. Admission to the church is free, but a small donation (£1.50/$3) is requested to see Shakespeare's tomb. March and October, you can visit the church Monday through Saturday 9 a.m. to 5 p.m., April through

September from 8:30 a.m. to 6 p.m., November through February 9 a.m. to 4 p.m.; year-round, the church is open Sunday 12:30 to 5 p.m. It's closed December 24 to 26, January 1, and Easter.

About 5km (3 ½ miles) north of Stratford on the A34 (Birmingham) road is **Mary Arden's House & Shakespeare Countryside Museum** (Wilmcote; ☎ 01789/204-016), the last of the five Shakespeare shrines. For more than 200 years, Palmers Farm, a Tudor farmstead with an old stone dovecote and outbuildings, was identified as the girlhood home of Mary Arden, Shakespeare's mother. Recent evidence revealed, however, that Mary Arden actually lived in the house next door, at Glebe Farm. In 2000, the house at Glebe Farm was officially re-designated as the Mary Arden House. Dating from 1514, the house contains country furniture and domestic utensils; in the barns, stable, cowshed, and farmyard, you find an extensive collection of farming implements illustrating life and work in the local countryside from Shakespeare's time to the present. Admission costs £6 ($12) adults, £5 ($10) seniors and students, £2.50 ($5) children, and £15 ($30) families (two adults and three children). Hours are November through March and September through October 10 a.m. to 4 p.m. (Sun from 10:30 a.m.); April through May 10 a.m. to 5 p.m. (Sun from 10:30 a.m.); and June through August 9:30 a.m. to 5 p.m. (Sun from 10 a.m.).

Seeing a play at the Royal Shakespeare Theatre

The **Royal Shakespeare Theatre** (Waterside; ☎ 01789/295-623; www. rsc.org.uk) is the home of the **Royal Shakespeare Company (RSC)**, which typically stages five Shakespeare plays during a season, running from November through September (for current offerings, and to book tickets online, visit its Web site). A few tickets are always held for sale on the day of a performance, but if you wait until you arrive in Stratford, you may not be able to get a good seat. The box office is open Monday through Saturday 9:30 a.m. to 8 p.m. but closes at 6 p.m. on days when no performances are on the schedule. Tickets cost £8 to £46 ($16–$92). *Note:* The main RSC theatre is closed for restoration from 2007 to 2010; in the meantime, performances will be held at the Swan and Courtyard theatres.

Stratford's newest attraction, **Shakespearience** (Waterside Theatre, Waterside; ☎ 01789/290-111; www.shakespearience.co.uk), presents the life and works of Shakespeare in a unique way, using show technology and special effects. The show includes information about the Bard of Stratford and dramatic highlights from nine of his best-loved plays. Tickets cost £7.25 ($15) adults; £6.25 ($13) seniors, students, and children under 12; and £24 ($48) families (two adults and two children). Shows begin daily at 10:30 a.m. and end at 5 p.m. (4 p.m. in winter).

Dining locally

If you want to have lunch or afternoon tea in enjoyably old-fashioned surroundings, try **Hathaway Tea Rooms & Bakery** (19 High St.; ☎ 01789/292-404; www.hathawaytearooms.co.uk). The tearooms are on the second floor of a building that dates from 1610. Cream tea comes with homemade fruit scones, clotted cream, and jam, and high tea includes a variety of sandwiches. You can also get an English breakfast and light meals throughout the day. Main courses run from £6 to £8 ($12–$16); cream teas cost £5.20 ($10); and high teas cost £7 ($14). There's a kids' menu for £5 ($10). Credit cards are not accepted. The tearooms are open daily 9 a.m. to 5:30 p.m.

The Oppo (13 Sheep St.; ☎ **01789/269-980;** www.theoppo.co.uk), housed in a 16th-century building in the heart of Stratford, offers a historic setting and a mix of traditional and Modern British cuisine. Reservations are recommended. Main courses run from £9 to £18 ($18–$36). The restaurant accepts MasterCard and Visa, and it's open daily noon to 2 p.m. and 5 to 11 p.m.

Spending the night

During the long theater season, reserve in advance if you're planning to sleep, perchance to dream, in Stratford. However, the **Tourist Information Centre** (Bridgefoot; ☎ **0870/160-7930**) can help you find accommodations.

Mercure Shakespeare Hotel Stratford (Chapel Street; ☎ **01789/294-499;** fax: 01789/415-411; www.mercure.com) successfully blends old and new. Parts of this centrally located hotel date from 1635 and preserve the original Tudor Era beams and stone floor, but all 74 rooms were completely refurbished in 2005 in a comfortably elegant and traditional style. The rooms come with a host of modern amenities, and all the bathrooms have bathtubs with showers. Rack rates for a double with English breakfast range from £90 to £190 ($180–$380). The hotel accepts all major credit cards.

The Payton (6 St. John St.; ☎/fax **01789/266-442;** www.payton.co.uk), a Georgian-era town house B&B, is located on a quiet side street that's just a three-minute walk from the town center. The five en-suite guest rooms are clean, comfortable, and charming. A double room with private shower and English breakfast costs £70 to £75 ($140–$150). The Payton accepts MasterCard and Visa.

Salisbury and Stonehenge: Steeples and Standing Stones

The tall, slender spire of Salisbury Cathedral rises up from the plains of Wiltshire like a finger pointing toward the heavens. Salisbury (see the "Salisbury" map on p. 282), or *New Sarum* as it was once called, lies in the valley of the Avon River, 145km (90 miles) southwest of London. Filled with Tudor inns and tearooms and dominated by its beautiful cathedral, this old market town is often overlooked by visitors eager to see Stonehenge, about 15km (9 miles) away.

Salisbury

A360	
Churchill Way West	Bus Depot
St. Paul's Rd.	Castle St.
A36	Albany Rd.
	Council House
Train Station	A36
	Bedwin St. Bourne Hill
	Post Office
Fisherton St.	Endless St. Rollestone St.
The Maltings Shopping Centre	Salt Ln.
	St. Edmunds Ch. St.
St. Thomas Church	Greencroft St.
Crane Bridge Rd.	Winchester St.
QUEEN ELIZABETH GARDENS	Cross Keys Shopping Centre
	Bridge St.
	New Canal
	Milford St.
Crane St.	Catherine St.
	Old George Hall
	New St.
	Ivy St.
0 400 ft	Trinity St. Barnard St.
0 100 m	Lowe Ln.
N	Stann St.
	St. Anne's Gate
ATTRACTIONS ●	North Walk
Salisbury Cathedral **5**	West Walk
HOTELS ■	Bishops Walk
Macdonald White Hart Hotel **4**	St. Martin's Church
Red Lion Hotel **3**	Blackfriars Way
RESTAURANTS ◆	A36
Harper's Restaurant **2**	Exeter St. Friary Ln.
One Minster Street **1**	CHURCHILL GARDENS
	Carmelite Way
	Harnham's Gate
	Churchill Way South
	✝ Church
	ⓘ Information

Getting there

From London's Waterloo Station, trains run hourly to Salisbury; the journey takes about 90 minutes and costs about £25 ($50) for an off-peak (after 9:30 a.m.) round-trip ticket. For schedules, go to www.nationalrail.co.uk, or call ☎ **0845/484-950.** If you're driving from London, head west on the M3 to the end of the run, continuing the rest of the way on the A30.

Finding information

Salisbury's **Tourist Information Centre** is on Fish Row (☎ **01722/ 334-956;** www.visitsalisbury.com) and is open Monday through Saturday 9:30 a.m. to 5:30 p.m. (June–Sept until 6 p.m.; Sun May–Sept 10:30 a.m.–4:30 p.m.).

Seeing the sights

Visitors eager to see Stonehenge often overlook the lovely old market town of Salisbury, but I suggest that you try to spend a bit of time wandering through Salisbury Cathedral.

Salisbury

Despite an ill-conceived renovation in the 18th century, the 13th-century structure of **Salisbury Cathedral** (The Close; ☎ 01722/555-120; www. salisburycathedral.org.uk) remains the best example in England of Early English and Perpendicular Gothic style. The 123-meter (404-foot) spire is the tallest in the country. The beautiful 13th-century, octagonal **chapter house** possesses one of the four surviving original texts of the Magna Carta. Adding to the serene beauty of the cathedral are the cloisters and an exceptionally large **close,** comprising about 75 buildings. The suggested donation for admission is £5 ($10) for adults, £4.25 ($8.50) seniors and students, £3 ($6) for children, and £12 ($24) for families. The cathedral is open daily from 7:15 a.m. to 6:15 p.m. (June–Aug until 7:15 p.m).

Wilton House (☎ 01722/746-720; www.wiltonhouse.co.uk), in the town of Wilton, 5km (3 miles) west of Salisbury on the A30, is one of England's great country estates. The home of the earls of Pembroke, the house is noted for its 17th-century staterooms by the celebrated architect Inigo Jones. Shakespeare's troupe is believed to have entertained here. Several centuries later in this house, General Eisenhower and his advisers made preparations for the D-day landings at Normandy. Beautifully maintained furnishings and paintings by Brueghel, Reynolds, Rubens, and Van Dyck fill the house. You can visit a reconstructed Tudor kitchen and Victorian laundry, plus the Wareham Bears, a collection of some 200 miniature dressed teddy bears. The 21-acre grounds include rose and water gardens, riverside and woodland walks, and a huge adventure playground for children. Admission costs £12 ($24) adults, £9.75 ($20) seniors, £6.50 ($13) children 5 to 15, and £30 ($60) families (two adults and two children). Mid-April through October, the house and grounds are open daily April through September from 10:30 a.m. to 5:30 p.m. (last admission 4:30 p.m.; occasional closings). If you don't have a car, you can take the bus that stops on New Canal, a ten-minute walk north of Salisbury train station; check with the tourist office for schedules and to be certain that the house is open that day.

Stonehenge

About 15km (9 miles) north of Salisbury, at the junction of the A303 and the A344/A360, you find one of the world's most renowned prehistoric sites and one of England's most popular attractions, the prehistoric stone circle known as **Stonehenge** (☎ 01980/624-715; www. stonehenge.co.uk). If you're not driving, hop on one of the **Wilts & Dorset** (☎ 01202/673-555; www.wdbus.co.uk) buses that depart from the Salisbury train station daily between 11 a.m. and 2 p.m.; the trip takes about 40 minutes, and the round-trip fare costs about £7 ($14). The crowds can be overwhelming as the day wears on, so arrive as early as possible.

Stonehenge is a stone circle of megalithic pillars and lintels built on the flat Salisbury Plain. Archaeological dating has shown that the site was built in stages from 5,000 to 3,500 years ago. Many visitors to Stonehenge are disappointed to find that the standing stones aren't as enormous as they envisioned and are now surrounded by a barrier that keeps sightseers 15m (50 feet) from the stones. Keep in mind, however, that many of the stones, which weigh several tons, were mined and moved from distant quarries in a time before forklifts, trucks, and dynamite.

Stonehenge was a shrine and/or ceremonial gathering place of some kind. The old belief that Stonehenge was built by the Druids has been discredited (it's probably older than the Celtic Druids). A popular theory is that the site was an astronomical observatory, because it's aligned to the summer solstice and can accurately predict eclipses based on the placement of the stones. But in an age when experts think they know everything, Stonehenge still keeps its tantalizing mysteries to itself. Recent archaeological evidence has uncovered another ceremonial avenue and leads experts to speculate that Stonehenge was an important burial place. Admission costs £6.30 ($13) adults, £4.70 ($9.40) seniors and students, and £3.10 ($6.20) children. The site is open daily from March 16 through May, and September through October 15 9:30 a.m. to 6 p.m.; June through August 9 a.m. to 7 p.m.; and October 16 to March 15 9:30 a.m. to 4 p.m.

Dining locally

Looking for simple, healthy, homemade food? Go to **Harper's Restaurant** (7–9 Ox Row, Market Square; ☎ **01722/333-118**). You can order from two menus, one featuring cost-conscious, bistro-style platters and the other a longer menu with all-vegetarian pasta dishes. Main courses cost £7.50 to £14 ($15–$28), and fixed-price meals are £8.50 ($17) at lunch and £11 ($22) at dinner. The restaurant accepts American Express, MasterCard, and Visa. It's open Monday through Saturday noon to 2 p.m. and 6:30 to 9:30 p.m., plus Sundays in summer from 6 to 9 p.m.

One Minster Street (1 Minster St.; ☎ **01722/322-024**) is the new name for a creaky-timbered, wonderfully atmospheric, 1320 chophouse and pub that used to be called the Haunch of Venison. The menu at the third-floor restaurant features some good dishes, including many traditional favorites. Main courses go for £7.50 to £15 ($15–$30).It accepts American Express, MasterCard, and Visa. Do check out the ancient pub rooms (still called the Haunch of Venison), even if you don't dine here. The pub is open Monday through Saturday 11 a.m. to 11 p.m., Sunday noon to 10:30 p.m.

Spending the night

A Salisbury landmark since Georgian times, the **Mercure White Hart Hotel** (1 St. John St.; ☎ **01722/327478**; www.mercure-uk.com) was totally renovated in 2007. The hotel offers accommodations in the older section of the building or in a new motel-like section in the rear. A good restaurant is on-site. Rates start at £90 to £160 ($180–$320) for a double. The hotel accepts American Express, MasterCard, and Visa.

Atmosphere fills every nook and cranny of the **Red Lion Hotel** (Milford Street; ☎ **01722/323-334**; www.the-redlion.co.uk), founded more than 750 years ago. The cozy lounge is a popular spot for tea, and, in good weather, the vine-covered courtyard is a pleasant place for drinks. Although now part of the Best Western chain, the hotel has maintained its own venerable identity. Each guest room is uniquely furnished, some with fireplaces and four-poster beds. Double rooms with breakfast cost £90 to £110 ($180–$220). The hotel accepts American Express, Diners Club, MasterCard, and Visa.

York: Ancient Walls and Snickelways

York is only 314km (195 miles) north of London, close enough for a day trip but worlds apart in character. York (see the "York" map on p. 286) is the capital of the North and one of England's most historic cities. Under the Romans, who built a major fort here, the city was known as *Eboracum*. For hundreds of years after that, York was a thriving Viking settlement called *Jorvik*. And finally, after the Norman Conquest, it became *York,* queen of the North. Interesting museums, historic buildings of all kinds, good hotels, excellent shops, and fine restaurants make York a popular tourist city, and rightly so. Enormous York Minster, the largest Gothic structure north of the Alps, dominates the city. And, amazingly, the old town's 800-year-old walls and fortified gateways still girdle the old town center. Soak up the city's history while exploring its maze of ancient streets and *snickelways* (hidden alleyways); you can get everywhere on foot and see many attractions in just a day.

Getting there

To make York work as a day trip, you need to take one of the fast, direct trains from London's King's Cross Station that will get you there in two hours. The round-trip fare costs £75 ($150), but much lower fares are usually available. For train schedules and information, call National Rail Enquiries at ☎ **08457/484-950** or visit www.nationalrail.com. The train station is a five-minute walk from York's historic center.

If you need a taxi, contact **Station Taxis** (☎ **01904/623-332**).

York

| Church |
| Information |

0 ——— 400 ft
0 ——— 100 m

St. Mary's
Maygate
Bootham
Gillygate
Lord Mayor's Walk
Monk-gate

Theatre Royal

St. Olave

York City Art Gallery

Treasurer's House

St. Michael-le-Belfry

Goodramgate

Aldwark

Scarborough Bridge

River Ouse

Duncombe Pl.

Dean Court Hotel

Stonegate

War Memorial

Leeman Road

Station Road

Lendal Bridge

Coney St.

St. Helen

St. Sampson's Square

Parliament St.

The Stonebow

City Wall

Train Station

All Saints

North St.

Tanner Row

Piccadilly

Walmgate

Toft Green

Micklegate

Trinity Lane

Arts Centre

St. Martin

Ouse Bridge

Castlegate

St. Mary

R. Foss

Queen Street

Priory St.

South Esplanade

River Ouse

Tower Street

City Wall

Victor St.

Kyme St.

Skeldergate

Skeldergate Bridge

Clementhorpe

ATTRACTIONS ●
Jorvik Viking Centre **12**
Merchant Adventurers' Hall **10**
National Railway Museum **1**
The Shambles **9**
Treasurer's House **5**
York Castle Museum **13**
York City Art Gallery **3**
York Minster **6**
Yorkshire Museum **4**

HOTELS ■
The Bar Convent **14**
The Grange **2**

RESTAURANTS ◆
Betty's **8**
The Blue Bicycle **11**
Harkers **7**

Finding information and taking a tour

At both of the following places, you can get an inexpensive guidebook with a map, book a room, and obtain information on guided tours:

✔ A convenient branch of the **Tourist Information Centre** (no phone) is right in the train station. The office is open Monday through Saturday from 9 a.m. to 5 p.m. (until 6 p.m. in summer) and Sunday from 10 a.m. to 4 p.m. (until 5 p.m. in summer).

✔ The main **Tourist Information Centre,** De Grey Rooms, Exhibition Square (☎ **01904/550-099;** www.visityork.org), near York Minster, has the same open hours as the train station branch.

More guided tours are offered in York than in just about any other city in England, excluding London. You can explore the city by foot, bus, or boat. If you're staying overnight, see my list of evening Ghost Walks at the end of the chapter. Here are some of your daytime options:

✔ The **York Association of Voluntary Guides** (☎ **01904/640-780;** www.york.touristguides.btinternet.co.uk) presents free two-hour guided tours of the city. The tours depart daily at 10:15 a.m. year-round from Exhibition Square in the city center. Additional tours start at 2:15 p.m. and 6:45 p.m. in summer. You don't need to make a reservation; just show up.

✔ During the summer, you can hire a **horse-drawn carriage** in front of the Dean Court Hotel near York Minster. A 15-minute ride around the cathedral *close* (the walled precinct surrounding the cathedral) costs £3.50 ($7) for adults and £2.50 ($5) for children.

✔ Departing from the pier below Lendal Bridge, **York Boat** (☎ **01904/ 647-204;** www.yorkboat.co.uk) provides a 45-minute tour with live commentary that nicely complements a walking tour. From mid-February through November, at least four boats depart each day; you can buy your ticket onboard. The tour costs £7 ($14) for adults, £6 ($12) for seniors, £3.50 ($7) for children 5 to 15, and £20 ($40) for families (two adults, three children).

✔ **City Sightseeing** (☎ **01904/625-618**) runs open-top, double-decker tour buses on a circuit of all the main sights in York (one hour total). The ticket, valid all day so you can hop on and off as you want, costs £9 ($18) for adults, £7 ($14) for seniors and students, £4 ($8) for children 5 to 15, and £20 ($40) for families (two adults, two children). The buses run year-round from about 9:30 a.m. to 5 p.m.; you can get on at the train station and buy your ticket from the driver.

Seeing the sights

York is a delightful city to explore, with its old streets, lanes, snickel-ways, and many tourist attractions. You'll find more to do here than you could ever fit into a one-day excursion, so be selective and keep a map with you, because you can easily get lost on the city's medieval streets. (*Note:* I list the attractions in order of their overall interest.)

Awesome **York Minster** (Minster Yard; ☎ **01904/557-216;** www.yorkminster.org), the largest Gothic cathedral in northern Europe, was built between 1220 and 1472. Architecturally, it spans the entire range of Gothic style: Early English (1220–1260), Decorated (1280–1350), and Perpendicular (1361–1472).

York Minster

Chapter House **8**	Great West Window **1**
Choir Screen **6**	Jesse Window **3**
Entrance to Crypt, Undercroft, and Treasury **4**	Nave **2**
Five Sisters' Window **7**	Rose Window **5**

The chief cathedral in the north of England, York Minster (see the "York Minster" map above) contains half of all the medieval stained glass in the country. The **Five Sisters' Window** from 1260 is the oldest complete window in the Minster. (*Minster,* by the way, means a church, usually with cathedral status, attached to a monastery.) The **Great West Window,** painted in 1338 and set in heart-shaped tracery, is known as the "Heart of Yorkshire." Above the south door, a magnificent **Rose Window** (1500) commemorates the union of the royal houses of Lancaster and York. Painted in 1310, the **Jesse Window** in the south nave depicts Jesus's family tree. The Minster's Decorated Gothic **nave** (the main central space in the interior), begun in 1291 and finished in the 1350s, is one of Europe's widest. A 15th-century **Choir Screen** decorated with statues of 15 kings of England separates the nave from the choir. In the south transept, you can descend into the **Undercroft,** where excavations have revealed the Roman basilica (an assembly hall, not a Christian church) that stood here nearly 2,000 years ago. You can take a well-designed "time walk" to see Roman, Anglo-Saxon, and Norman remains. The walk leads to the 12th-century **Crypt** and the **Treasury,** where silver plate and other church treasures are on display. From the nave, a separate entrance leads to the 13th-century **Chapter House,** filled with fine stone carvings and medieval glass. You can also ascend the minster's soaring tower for a bird's-eye view of York and the surrounding region. Give yourself at least an hour to see everything in the cathedral. Admission to the Minster, undercroft, treasury, crypt, and tower is £9 ($18) for adults, £7.50 ($15) for seniors and students, and £3 ($6) for children. The Minster is open Monday to Saturday from 9 a.m. to 5 p.m., Sunday from noon to 3:45 p.m.

In Minster Yard you'll find the **Treasurer's House** (☎ 01904/624-247), an elegant town house that was originally the home of the treasurer of York Minster. Built in 1620, the house was extensively remodeled during the Victorian Era by an eccentric Yorkshireman who cared so passionately about interior décor that he threatened to return to haunt the place if anyone ever moved any of his furniture. As the furniture hasn't been moved, the house features beautiful period rooms with collections of 17th- and 18th-century furniture, glass, clocks, and china. You can see the entire collection in about 30 minutes. Stroll through the pretty walled garden, even if you don't visit the house. The tearoom downstairs is a good place for lunch or tea. Admission to the house is £5 ($10) for adults and £2.50 ($5) children 5 to 15. The house is open mid-March to October Saturday through Thursday from 11 a.m. until 4:30 p.m. (Nov 1–11 until 3 p.m.); it's closed December to mid-March.

Almost 5km (3 miles) of **medieval city walls** enclose York, and walking along them is one of the best ways to enjoy the historic ambience of this ancient city. Fortified gateways (or *bars*) still serve as entrances to the old part of town. A path (open daily 8 a.m. to dusk) runs along the top of the walls, with plenty of great views along the way. You find stairways up to the top of the walls at the four gates. Micklegate, the southern entry used by royalty, is a good place to start your wall walk.

Until 150 years ago, **The Shambles** (www.yorkshambles.com) was a street where butchers displayed their finest cuts in open windows on wide shelves called *shammels.* Today, this narrow, winding lane, with buildings so close that they shut out the light, is England's most famous medieval street. Gift shops have replaced the butcher shops, so you can get in a bit of retail therapy as you stroll. No. 35 The Shambles is a shrine to St. Margaret Clitheroe, a butcher's wife executed during the Reformation for hiding Catholic priests in her attic; she was canonized in 1970.

If you want to revisit the Viking Age, hop into one of the time cars at **Jorvik Viking Centre** (Coppergate; ☎ 01904/643-211; www.jorvik-viking-centre.co.uk) to be transported back to A.D. 948, when Eric Bloodaxe was king and York was Jorvik, a thriving Viking port and trading town. The scenes you see — of village life, market stalls, crowded houses, and the wharf — are meticulously re-creations based on archaeological finds in this area; even the heads and faces of the animatronic characters were modeled on Viking skulls. Artifacts unearthed on this site are also on display. Give yourself about an hour. Admission is £8 ($16) adults, £7 ($14) seniors and students, and £5.50 ($11) for children 5 to 15. Jorvik is open daily from 10 a.m. to 5 p.m.; in winter until 4 p.m. Allow about 30 minutes.

In the Medieval Era, guilds ran English towns. The 14th-century stone and half-timbered **Merchant Adventurers Hall** (Fossgate; ☎ 0194/654-818; www.theyorkcompany.co.uk) belonged to York's most powerful guild (the Merchant Adventurers controlled trade into and out of the city). This building, one of the largest and best-preserved guildhalls in the country, has a great hall for business, a hospital for charitable work, and a chapel for worship. Allow 30 minutes for a tour with an audio guide. Admission is £2.50 ($5) adults, £2 ($4) seniors and students, £1 ($2) children 5 to 15. The guildhall is open April through September Monday through Thursday 9 a.m. to 5 p.m., Friday through Saturday 9 a.m. to 3:30 p.m., Sunday noon to 4 p.m.; October through March Monday through Saturday 9 a.m. to 3:30 p.m.

The great exhibits at the **National Railway Museum** (Leeman Road; ☎ 08448/153-139; www.nrm.org.uk) appeal to both adults and children. The earliest train cars on display in this museum devoted to England's railroad system date from the 1840s and look like stage-coaches on tracks. You can peek into the windows of private royal coaches, from Queen Victoria's of 1869, with its bulky furniture (the engineer had to stop when the queen wanted to move from one car to the next), to Queen Elizabeth II's streamlined, functional carriage, used until 1977. You see a replica of the first steam locomotive (1830) and a display of the new Eurostar high-speed train. You need at least an hour for a thorough visit of this fascinating museum. On some trains, kids can climb up into the engineer's area. Admission is free. The museum is open daily 10 a.m. to 6 p.m.; it's closed December 24 to 26.

England's most popular folk museum, the **York Castle Museum** (☎ 01904/653-611; www.yorkshiremuseum.org.uk) is located in the area called Eye of York, near Clifford's Tower. Using a treasure-trove of now-vanished everyday objects, the exhibitions re-create slices of life from past historical eras. The museum took over York's 200-year-old prison buildings, with graffiti still on the walls of the dingy cells. You can walk down a reconstruction of Kirkgate, a cobbled Victorian shopping street; see a Jacobean dining room; visit a moorland cottage and a gypsy caravan; call in at a Victorian police station and an Edwardian pub; and check out the Jane Austen Costume Collection's fashion and fabrics. Kids love the giant dollhouses. Allow at least an hour. Admission is £5 ($10) for adults, £3.50 ($7) for children 5 to 15, and £12 ($24) for families (two adults, one child). It's open daily from 9:30 a.m. to 5 p.m., and is closed January 2 and December 24 to 26.

Ghostly legions

In 1953, apprentice heating engineer Harry Martindale was working in the basement of the Treasurer's House when he heard what sounded like marching feet. As he watched in amazement, a battalion of ghostly Roman soldiers marched right through the cellar. As it turns out, the Treasurer's House was built over the main Roman road. You can check out the haunted cellar of Treasurer's House yourself on one of the daily cellar tours, which cost £2 ($4).

The **Yorkshire Museum** (Museum Gardens; ☎ 01904/551-800; www. yorkshiremuseum.org.uk) is somewhat old-fashioned and heavy on the text panels, but if you start in the Roman section and walk through to the end, you get a sound presentation of Yorkshire's history from two millennia ago through the 16th century. You can view elegant Roman jewelry, mosaics, and Anglo-Saxon silver. Viking treasures include swords and battleaxes. The Middleham Jewel, a 15th-century pendant decorated with a large sapphire, was found in 1985 in North Yorkshire. The museum lies in 10 acres of landscaped gardens amid the ruins of St. Mary's Abbey, once the wealthiest abbey in the north. On the grounds, you can see a 15th-century timber-framed building known as The Hospitium. Give this museum about an hour. Admission is £5 ($10) for adults, £3.50 ($7) for children 5 to 15, and £12 ($24) for families (two adults, one child). You can purchase a joint ticket that allows admission to the Yorkshire Museum and the York Castle Museum. These tickets are £9.50 ($19) adults, £6 ($12) for children 5 to 15, and £24 ($48) for families (two adults, one child). The museum is open daily from 10 a.m. to 5 p.m., and is closed January 1 and December 25 to 26.

The **York Art Gallery** (Exhibition Square; ☎ 01904/687-687; www. yorkshiremuseum.org.uk), with freshly refurbished galleries and a new cafe, is in an Italian Renaissance–style building completed in 1879. The collections on view span seven centuries of Western European painting and include pictures by Parmigianino, Bellotto, Lely, and Reynolds, and a small collection of 20th-century studio pottery. You can see the entire collection in less than an hour; if your time is limited, don't make this a priority. Admission is free. The museum is open daily from 10 a.m. to 5 p.m., and is closed January 1 and December 25 to 26.

York's big wheel

York's newest attraction is a giant Ferris wheel located at the National Railway Museum. Rising 54m (114 feet), the **Yorkshire Wheel** (www.nrm.org.uk) offers great views of the city center, York Minister, and the River Ouse from enclosed, air-conditioned pods similar to those of the British Airways London Eye (see Chapter 11). The wheel operates daily from 10 a.m. to 6 p.m. (until 8 p.m. in summer). Cost is £6 ($12) for adults, £4 ($8) for children.

Dining locally

Founded in 1919, **Betty's** (6–8 St. Helen's Sq.; ☎ 01904/659-142; www. bettys.co.uk) is a wonderfully old-fashioned Art Nouveau tearoom, patisserie, and restaurant. Sandwiches, salads, and a dozen or so hot dishes (both fish and meat) are available. Specialties include smoked salmon muffins, Yorkshire rarebit, locally made sausages, and haddock and prawns in white-wine cream sauce. The pastries, all made according to secret recipes, are superb. At the shop in front, you can buy specialties, such as Yorkshire fat rascals: warm scones with citrus peels, almonds, and cherries. Main courses go for £6.50 to £10 ($13–$20); cream tea costs £7 to £15 ($14 to $30). American Express, MasterCard, and Visa are accepted. The restaurant is open daily from 9 a.m. to 9 p.m.

If you're looking for atmosphere and good Modern British cooking, try **The Blue Bicycle** (34 Fossgate; ☎ 01904/673-990; www.thebluebicycle. com), an appealing restaurant overlooking the canal-like Ouse River. It has a brasserie-style menu with a few standard menu items, daily specials, and a grill for meat and fish dishes. The dinner menu usually features several varieties of fish cooked various ways, plus chicken, beef, and a vegetarian offering. Reservations recommended for dinner. Main courses run from £11 to £20 ($22–$40). American Express, MasterCard, and Visa are accepted. The restaurant is open daily from noon to 2:30 p.m. and 6 to 9 p.m. The Blue Bicycle also rents out two self-contained luxury rooms in the center of York for £150 ($300) per room per night.

If you're looking for simple pub grub, stop in at **Harkers** (St. Helen's Square; ☎ 01904/672-795), in the former Yorkshire Insurance Company building dating from 1824. The menu features traditional dishes, such as chicken-and-onion pie, fish and chips, ploughman's lunch (bread, cheese, and salad), and Cumberland sausages. The place can become something of a mob scene after work. Main courses cost £5.50 to £9.95 ($11 to $20). MasterCard and Visa are accepted. Food is served daily from noon to 7 p.m.; the pub is open Monday through Saturday from 11 a.m. to 11 p.m. and Sunday from noon to 10:30 p.m.

Spending the night

The Bar Convent (17 Blossom St.; ☎ 01904/264-902; www.bar-convent.org.uk), a hotel in a former convent building, is an inexpensive, unusual, and convenient place to stay. The accommodations are in a Georgian building on the corner of Nunnery Lane and Blossom Street, a five-minute walk from the train station. The seven rooms, refurbished in 2005, are comfortable but nothing fancy; only one has a private bathroom. The convent, which houses a neoclassical chapel and a museum, was founded in 1686 and was active as a school until 1985. The on-site cafe serves inexpensive meals. A double room with shared bathroom costs £57 ($114); the double room with private bathroom costs £70 ($140). Rates include continental breakfast. The hotel accepts MasterCard and Visa.

Created from a classical Regency brick town house, **The Grange** (1 Clifton; ☎ 01904/644-744; www.grangehotel.co.uk) is a small, elegant hotel close to the city walls and a few minutes' walk from York Minster. The 30 individually designed rooms use antique furniture and convey a comfortable English charm. Bathrooms are nicely done. The hotel offers room service and two good restaurants: The Ivy, serving classic French and Modern British cuisine, is considered one of the best restaurants in York; the Brasserie offers informal dining in the old brick vaulted cellars. A double room with English breakfast costs £125 to £220 ($250 to $440). American Express, MasterCard, and Visa are accepted.

Ghouls and ghosties galore: York's ghost walks

If you're spending the night in York, check out the city's array of Ghost Walks. Apparently, plenty of supernatural activity takes place in York, which some claim is England's most haunted city. Evening ghost walks, with entertaining commentary and sometimes a bit of spookery thrown in, are a regular year-round industry. You have several tours to choose from and you can buy your tickets on the spot. Tours cost £4 to £5 ($8–$10) for adults, £2 to £3 ($4–$6) for seniors, students, and children 5 to 15.

✔ **The Ghost Hunt of York** (☎ 01904/608-700; www.ghosthunt.co.uk): "Andy Dextrous," ghost hunter, leads this fun, one-hour walk and performance. Walks leave nightly at 7:30 from The Shambles, York's medieval street.

✔ **The Ghost Trail** (☎ 01904/633-276; www.ghosttrail.co.uk): You get more traditional ghost-storytelling on this walk, which leaves nightly at 7:30 from the front entrance of York Minster.

✔ **Original Ghost Walk of York** (☎ 01759/373-090; www.theoriginal ghostwalkofyork.co.uk): This tour started in 1973 and features great storytelling that explores the area's folklore, legend, and dreams. Walks leave nightly at 8 from The King's Arms Pub, Ouse Bridge.

Part V
Living It Up after Dark: London Nightlife

The 5th Wave   By Rich Tennant

CRICHTENNANT

I love visiting London. There's so much history there — my first boyfriend, my second divorce, my third facelift...

In this part . . .

London, for some people, is synonymous with the performing arts. Planning a night out here isn't the problem — choosing among all the possibilities is where the difficulty lies. So, in Chapter 15, I give you the scoop on London's world-class performing arts scene, tell you how to find out what's going on and how to get tickets, and provide information on the main venues for theater, music — including opera and symphony concerts — and dance. The performing arts are only part of London's pulsing nightlife, so, in Chapter 16, I introduce you to some of the many places where you can rub elbows with Londoners and have a pint or two — pubs, bars, clubs, discos, and jazz spots.

Chapter 15

Applauding the Performing Arts

. . . .

In This Chapter

▶ Getting the inside scoop on London's theater and performing arts scene

▶ Going to the symphony, listening to chamber music, and hitting rock concerts

▶ Seeing opera and dance performances

▶ Finding out what's on and getting tickets

. . . .

*L*ondon is a mecca of the performing arts, offering world-class the-ater, several symphony orchestras, rock concerts, operas, modern dance, and classical ballets. In a city renowned for its theater scene, you can enjoy every kind of play or musical. Or take your pick from the city's own **Royal Opera, Royal Ballet, English National Opera,** or **London Symphony Orchestra.** This chapter gives you the information that you need to plan a trip that includes the performing arts.

Getting the Inside Scoop

From a global perspective, London may hold the title of world perform-ing arts capital, based on the number of offerings and the quality of the performances. Of course, London didn't attain this stature overnight. The city has been building its theatrical reputation since the Elizabethan Era, when Shakespeare, Marlowe, and others were staging their plays in a South Bank theater district. A strong musical tradition has been in place since the 18th century.

The performing arts scene, in general, gives London a buzz for residents and visitors alike. Major British stars with international screen reputa-tions regularly perform in the West End, although you're just as likely to see a show starring someone that you've never heard of but who's well known in England. You can also expect to find a few American plays and musicals, because the crossover between London and New York is increasing.

And here's some more good news: Tickets are still cheaper here than in New York. In London theaters, you rarely pay more than £50 ($100) for the best seats in the house. The price is dramatically less for symphony concerts, too: £5 to £20 ($10–$40) for excellent seats at the Barbican, for example. The same goes for that priciest of art forms, opera — you can get special day-of-performance seats for as little as £10 ($20).

Plays and performances in London have varying curtain times. Evening performances may begin at 7:30 p.m., 8 p.m., or 8:30 p.m., and matinees at 1:30 p.m., 2 p.m., or 2:30 p.m. Check your ticket to be certain, because if you're late, you won't be admitted until the second act or a suitable pause in the action occurs. If you come laden with packages, you can check them in the coatroom. Talking and noisily unwrapping pieces of candy during the performance will be frowned upon — especially if I'm in the audience.

Wondering what to wear to the theater? London theater audiences are, generally speaking, pretty well dressed. Although no hard and fast rules apply, if you arrive in a sweat suit and running shoes, you'll be conspicuous. A "smart casual" approach is best.

Finding Out What's Playing and Getting Tickets

For the most comprehensive listings of London performances, buy a copy of the weekly magazine *Time Out,* available at London newsstands on Wednesdays. You can find details for all London shows, concerts, and other performances in the daily London newspapers: the *Daily Telegraph,* the *Evening Standard,* the *Guardian,* the *Independent,* and the *Times.* Another good source is the free booklet *London Planner,* available at the British & London Visitor Centre (1 Lower Regent St., SW1), or from a VisitBritain travel office (see the Quick Concierge, at the end of this book, for contact info).

To find out the performance schedule for an entire season, check out the Web sites that I list for specific opera, symphony, and ballet groups throughout this chapter. Many venues let you book online.

The Web is one of the best places to search in advance for information on plays and performances currently running in London. You may find the following sites useful:

- ✔ **Albemarle of London:** www.albemarle-london.com
- ✔ **Keith Prowse:** www.keithprowse.com
- ✔ **London Theatre Guide:** www.londontheatre.co.uk
- ✔ **Official London Theatre Guide:** www.officiallondontheatre.co.uk

Getting tickets

If you are in London and decide that you want to see a show, you'll probably be able to get a seat. Even if an announcement has been made that a show is sold out, you can usually buy a ticket from the theater's box office, most of which open at 10 a.m. Ticket cancellations occur, and last-minute house seats go on sale the day of the performance or an hour before.

If you don't have time to go to the box office and you have a major credit card handy, call the theater directly. Box office phone numbers are listed in the papers and in *Time Out.* Many London theaters accept telephone credit card bookings at regular prices (plus a minimal fee of about £1.50/$3). They'll hold your tickets at the box office, where you pick them up any time up to a half-hour before the curtain. By buying directly from the box office, you don't have to pay the commission fee (up to 30 percent) that ticket agencies charge.

Buying a ticket in the "stalls" doesn't mean that you'll be seated in the ladies' powder room. It means that you may have one of the best seats in the house. *Stalls* is the British term for first-floor orchestra. Most of the West End theaters are fairly old, which means that they may have *boxes* for sale as well; these box seats are on the sides of the second or third tiers.

Using ticket agencies

Ticket agencies are used for commercial West End plays and musicals, not for opera, ballet, or other performing arts. All over the West End, and particularly around Leicester Square, ticket agencies boldly advertise that they have tickets to the sold-out hit shows. Most of these places are legitimate, but their commission fees vary.

If you choose to use the services of a ticket agency instead of booking directly with the box office (see the preceding section), I recommend that you call, stop in, or book online at one of the following trustworthy agencies:

- ✔ **Albemarle of London** (74 Mortimer St., W1; ☎ 020/7637-9041; www.albemarle-london.com; Tube: Oxford Circus or Goodge Street) is a long-established agency, open Monday through Friday 10 a.m. to 6 p.m. and Saturday 10 a.m. to 5 p.m. Albemarle maintains dedicated theater desks at several of London's ritzier hotels, including the **Savoy,** the **Park Lane** the **Dorchester,** and **Claridge's** (see Chapter 9). Its commission fee of 25 percent on top of the ticket price is what you can expect to pay for just about any theater booking made through a hotel concierge.

- ✔ **Keith Prowse** maintains a counter at the Britain & London Visitor Centre (1 Lower Regent St., SW1; ☎ 020/7808-3871; www.keithprowse.com; Tube: Piccadilly Circus). The counter is open Monday through Friday 10:15 a.m. to 6:15 p.m. and Saturday and Sunday 10 a.m. to 4 p.m. You pay a variable commission on top of the ticket price.

Before you buy any ticket from any agency, the agent must tell you the face value of the tickets (you can ask to see them). Before you sign the charge receipt, be sure to check the seat numbers, the face value of the tickets, and the agent's booking fee. If you're making a telephone booking, the agent must disclose the face value of the tickets, their locations, and whether you have a restricted view.

Beware of unlicensed ticket agencies that charge far more than the face value of the ticket plus a very hefty commission fee. A commission fee should *never* be more than 30 percent of the regular ticket price. Reputable ticket agencies belong to the Society of Ticket Agents and Retailers (STAR) and always advertise this fact.

The **Society of London Theatres** (☎ 020/7836-0971; www.solt.co.uk) operates the **tkts** half-price ticket booth in the clock tower building by the gardens in Leicester Square (Tube: Leicester Square). The booth has no telephone info line, so you have to show up in person to see what's on sale that day. One of the notice boards at tkts lists available theater tickets for matinee performances (which may be on Wed, Thurs, Sat, or Sun); the other notice board lists tickets available for evening performances. Check the signs above each of the ticket windows and make sure you join the correct line, because tickets for matinee and evening shows are sold from different windows. The booth is open Monday through Saturday 10 a.m. to 7 p.m. and Sunday noon to 3 p.m. Tickets are sold the day of the performance only; you can pay with cash or by MasterCard or Visa. You pay exactly half the price plus a nominal fee (usually about £3/$6). The most popular shows usually won't be available, but you may luck out. Tickets for the English National Opera and other events are sometimes available as well. You may want to stop by, in any case, to pick up a free copy of *The Official London Theatre Guide,* which lists every show with addresses and phone numbers and includes a map of the West End theater district.

Ticket agencies advertising half-price or reduced-price tickets are located around Leicester Square. Keep in mind that the Society of London Theatres operates the only official half-price ticket booth (tkts), and wave away those pesky scalpers who hang out in front of megahits. They may, indeed, be selling (for an astronomical price) a valid ticket. But some of these *touts,* as they're called, also forge tickets, which means that you'll be out of cash and out of a show. By law, any tout must disclose the face value of the ticket, so you know exactly what the markup is. The best advice: Don't deal with them.

Raising the Curtain on the Performing Arts

London is famous for the scope and excellence of its theater scene, but this world capital offers visitors a wealth of possibilities for enjoying all the performing arts.

Theater

Plays and musicals are staged all over the city in approximately 100 theaters, but the commercial hits are centered in the **West End theater district** — also called Theatreland — concentrated in the area around Piccadilly Circus, Leicester Square, and Covent Garden. The theaters at the **Barbican** and the **South Bank Centre** (see the following section) also provide major theater venues. Just like New York, London is the home of many *fringe venues* (the equivalent of off- or off-off-Broadway theaters).

London's theater offerings always include new plays and musicals, long-run favorites, and revivals of the classics, as well as Shakespeare. Some of the shows in the West End — such as Agatha Christie's *Mousetrap* and Andrew Lloyd Webber's *Phantom of the Opera* — have been running for years and show no sign of winding down. The newest long-running musicals are *Mary Poppins, Wicked, The Sound of Music,* and *Billy Elliot.* In general, evening performances are Monday through Saturday, and, depending on the show, matinees are on Wednesday or Thursday, and Saturday. Some shows have added Sunday performances, too. Matinees are a couple of pounds cheaper than evening performances.

In London, theaters don't hand out play programs free of charge to every patron. If you want a program, you must buy it. They usually cost £3 to £5 ($6–$10).

Major stages beyond the West End

I can't list all the theaters in Theatreland, but I can highlight three standout venues. They're geographically outside London's West End, but they're still considered part of the West End theater community.

- ✔ **The Old Vic** (The Cut, Waterloo, SE1; ☎ 020/7928-7616; www.oldvictheatre.com; Tube: Waterloo), on the South Bank near Waterloo Station, has long been known as "the actors' theatre." Many of England's greatest performers have played on its stage, including Laurence Olivier, Maggie Smith, and Judi Dench. The American actor Kevin Spacey is the artistic director and appears in some of the shows. Its adjunct theater, the **Young Vic** (☎ 020/7928-6363; www.youngvic.org), hosts productions of the Royal Shakespeare Company. The box office for both venues is open Monday through Saturday 10 a.m. to 7 p.m.

- ✔ **Shakespeare's Globe Theatre** (New Globe Walk, Bankside, SE1; ☎ 020/7401-9919; www.shakespeares-globe.org; Tube: Cannon Street or London Bridge) is the newest addition to the South Bank theater scene. The Globe presents a May-through-early-October season of the bard's plays (and, now, contemporary works as well) in a reconstructed oak-and-thatch, open-air, Elizabethan theater. (Performances may be cancelled because of rain.) You can stand (700 £5/$10 seats are available for every performance) or sit on benches; any discomfort is worth the opportunity to see Shakespeare performed not far from the original theater and right beside the Thames. Check out the Web site for current performances.

✔ **The South Bank Arts Centre** (South Bank, SE1; Tube: Waterloo) is home to the **Royal National Theatre** (☎ 020/7452-3000; www.nationaltheatre.org.uk), which performs in three theaters — the **Olivier** (1,160 seats), **Lyttelton** (890 seats), and **Cottesloe** (a smaller theater-in-the-round). The Royal National performs Shakespeare, but it also offers revivals of big Broadway musicals and new plays. Tickets cost slightly less than at the commercial theaters on the other side of the river, generally £10 to £40 ($20–$80) for evening performances and £9 to £35 ($18–$70) for matinees. You can get unsold seats at even lower prices two hours before curtain. The facility also houses cafes, bars, and a good bookstore. The box office is open Monday through Saturday from 9:30 a.m. to 8 p.m. You can find all performances and an online booking form on its Web site.

The fringe

In many ways, fringe theater is London's real theatrical heartbeat. The *fringe,* London's equivalent to New York's off- or off-off-Broadway, is now commonly called *Off West End.* (When my own play, *Beardsley,* was produced in London, it was on the fringe.) Groups performing on the fringe don't have the big bucks to mount lavish West End productions.

With the overabundance of acting talent in London, the fringe is where you may see tomorrow's stars acting today and next season's hit in its original, bare-bones form. The plays performed on the fringe are sometimes controversial or experimental, but for true theater lovers, they can provide a stimulating alternative to the tradition and glamour of the West End.

The performance spaces for fringe productions are usually smaller than for West End shows (sometimes tiny, sometimes above a pub), and the ticket prices are usually much lower (rarely more than £12/$24). Fringe theaters and spaces adapted to fringe productions are scattered far and wide, so consult a *London A–Z* or *Time Out* to find out what's on and call the theaters directly for directions on how to find them.

Royal Shakespeare shake-up

The prestigious **Royal Shakespeare Company** (RSC; ☎ **01789/403-444**; www.rsc.org.uk), headquartered in Stratford-upon-Avon (see Chapter 14), dropped a theatrical bombshell when it announced that it was leaving its long-time London home, the Barbican Centre, and would mount its London productions in West End theaters. The RSC now mounts productions in the **Gielgud Theatre** (Shaftesbury Avenue, W1; ☎ **020/7494-5085**; www.gielgud-theatre.com; Tube: Piccadilly Circus) and the **Theatre Royal Haymarket** (Haymarket, SW1; ☎ **0870/901-3356**; www.trh.co.uk; Tube: Piccadilly Circus).

Outdoor theater

What could be more fun than watching a good play performed under the stars? The **Regent's Park Open Air Theatre** (Inner Circle, Regent's Park, NW1; ☎ 020/7486-2431; www.openairtheatre.org; Tube: Baker Street), located on the north side of Queen Mary's Rose Garden, has a May-to-August season. This large venue offers theater seats but no roof, so rain may cancel the show. Ticket prices range from £10 to £33 ($20–$66); you can check out the program on the theater's Web site. **Shakespeare's Globe** (see the "Major stages beyond the West End" section, earlier in this chapter) is another venue that's open to the heavens.

Opera

Two major opera companies call London home. The **Royal Opera** enjoys international prestige, performs operas in the original languages, and boasts the most famous international singers. Its home is the **Royal Opera House** (Covent Garden, WC2E; ☎ 020/7304-4000; Tube: Covent Garden), which recently reopened after a state-of-the-art refurbishment that added two smaller venues — the **Linbury Studio Theatre** and the **Glore Studio Theatre.** Ticket prices for the grand opera run £10 to £150 ($20–$300); 200 tickets in all price ranges are always available on the day of performance, starting at 10 a.m. For a summary of the opera (and ballet) season, check the Web site www.royalopera.org. If you have your heart set on seeing an opera at the Royal Opera, book as far ahead as you possibly can — I'm talking weeks, not days. The season runs September through July.

The **English National Opera** (usually referred to as the ENO) offers more inventive productions than the Royal Opera. It performs at the freshly refurbished **London Coliseum** (St. Martin's Lane, WC2N; ☎ 0870/145-0200; Tube: Leicester Square). All the operas are sung in English. Seats sell for £10 to £79 ($20–$158). The opera season runs September through July. You can see the ENO program and book online by going to its Web site at www.eno.org.

The following two venues also offer you the opportunity to see opera during your time in London:

- ✔ **The D'Oyly Carte Opera Company** (☎ 020/7793-7100; www.doylycarte.org.uk): For nearly 150 years, this company has been performing the comic operas of Gilbert & Sullivan. Venues change, and the schedule is irregular; it's best to check out the company's Web site for current information.

- ✔ **The Holland Park Theatre** (Holland Park, W8; ☎ 0845/230-9769; www.operahollandpark.com; Tube: Holland Park): London's most charming stage uses the ruins of a Jacobean mansion in Holland Park as a backdrop for a mid-June-to-August season of opera and ballet. Tickets run £10 to £46 ($20–$92). You can view the performance schedule and book tickets online.

Four orchestras, one hall

The biggest and most exciting cultural news in London in 2007 was the reopening of the newly refurbished **Royal Festival Hall,** the major concert venue in the **South Bank Centre** (Tube: Waterloo). Royal Festival Hall, which first opened in 1951 as part of the Festival of Britain, is now home to four resident orchestras: the **London Philharmonic,** the **Philharmonia Orchestra,** the **London Sinfonietta** and the **Orchestra of the Age of Enlightenment.** The South Bank Centre is also the home of **Queen Elizabeth Hall,** a smaller venue that offers chamber music concerts and dance programs, and the **Purcell Room,** an intimate setting used for recitals. You can get tickets and information on all three venues at the box office (Foyer, Queen Elizabeth Hall), open daily 10 a.m. to 8 p.m., or online at www.sbc.org.uk; prices vary for each event. For credit card bookings, call ☎ 0871/663-2500.

Symphony

London offers some of the world's finest classical and chamber music. The home base for the **London Symphony Orchestra** (www.lso.co.uk) is the **Barbican Hall** at the Barbican Centre (Silk Street, EC2Y; ☎ 020/ 7638-8891; Tube: Barbican), the concert hall portion of a giant performing arts complex in the City. They also perform at St. Luke's, 16 Old St. (Tube: Old Street). Seats in these acoustically fabulous halls sell for £6 to £30 ($12–$60). At the Barbican you may also catch a performance by the **Royal Philharmonic Orchestra** (www.rpo.co.uk), which plays concerts here and at the Royal Albert Hall, another all-purpose venue for classical music.

The **Royal Albert Hall** (Kensington Gore, SW7; ☎ 020/7589-8212; Tube: High Street Kensington) is an enormous, circular, domed concert hall that has been a landmark in South Kensington since 1871. The box office is open daily 9 a.m. to 9 p.m.; ticket prices vary by event.

Wigmore Hall (36 Wigmore St., W1; ☎ 020/7935-2141; Tube: Bond Street) is a beautifully renovated, century-old concert hall used for chamber music and solo concerts and recitals. You can find performance information on the Web at www.wigmore-hall.org.uk.

Concerts by candlelight

Evening candlelit concerts of baroque music are performed weekly (usually on Thurs–Sat nights) at 7:30 p.m. in the lovely church of **St. Martin-in-the-Fields** (Trafalgar Square, W1; ☎ 020/7839-8362; www. stmartins-in-the-fields.org; Tube: Charing Cross; see Chapter 11). Lunchtime concerts are usually held on Monday, Tuesday, and Friday at 1 p.m. Tickets are generally £15 ($30).

Music under the stars

Kenwood House (Hampstead Lane, NW3; ☎ **0870/890-0146;** Tube: East Finchley), a picturesque lakeside estate on Hampstead Heath, is the setting for **Kenwood Lakeside Concerts,** a series of outdoor concerts held at 7:30 p.m. on Saturdays in July and August. A free shuttle bus runs between the East Finchley Tube station and the concert bowl. From Central London, you need at least 20 minutes to get to the Tube stop and another 15 minutes for the ride on the shuttle bus. Tickets cost £15 to £20 ($30–$40). You can find more information online under "Kenwood House" at www.english-heritage.org.uk. *Note:* This venue closed in 2007 but was expected to reopen in 2008.

Dance

The **Royal Ballet** performs at the **Royal Opera House,** and the **English National Ballet** and other visiting companies perform at the **London Coliseum** (see the "Opera" section, earlier in this chapter, for details).

Sadler's Wells (Rosebery Avenue, Islington EC1R; ☎ **020/7863-6000;** Tube: Angel) is well known for its contemporary dance, theater, and music productions and as a venue for solo performers. Sadler's Wells also manages the **Peacock Theatre** (Portugal Street, WC2; ☎ **020/7863-8222;** Tube: Covent Garden), a home for dance in the West End, and the **Lillian Baylis Theatre** (Arlington Way, EC1; ☎ **020/7713-6000;** Tube: Farringdon), a smaller venue for dance and performance. Programs for all three theaters are listed on the Web at www.sadlerswells.com.

The Place Theatre (17 Duke's Rd., WC1; ☎ **020/7387-0161;** www.theplace.org.uk; Tube: Euston) is the main venue for contemporary dance in the United Kingdom. **Riverside Studios** (Crisp Road, W6; ☎ **020/8237-1111;** www.riversidestudios.co.uk; Tube: Hammersmith) is an arts center that showcases theater, cinema, and dance.

Summer Proms

From mid-July through mid-September, fans of classical and pops concerts attend the wildly popular concert series called the *Proms.* Featuring musicians from all over Europe, Proms concerts are held at the **Royal Albert Hall** (see the "Symphony" section, earlier in this chapter), where they began in 1895. For Proms concerts, all seats are removed from the orchestra and gallery levels. Reserved seats are available, but devotees stand for a close look at the orchestras. Starting in July, you can book seats through the Royal Albert Hall box office at ☎ **020/7589-8212.** To get one of the 1,000 standing-room places (£6–£13/$12–$26), you have to queue up on the day of the performance (Door 12, 9 a.m.–9 p.m.). You can check out the Proms schedule on the Web at www.bbc.co.uk/proms.

Rock concerts

When the rock and pop stars play London, they need a *huge* arena to hold their shrieking fans. The two biggest venues are **Wembley Stadium** (Empire Way, Wembley, Middlesex; Tube: Wembley Park) and the **Earl's Court Exhibition Centre** (Warwick Road, SW5; Tube: Earl's Court). Tickets for large-scale events in these venues are sold through ticket agencies.

A much smaller (by that I mean less than 70,000 seats) rock and pop venue is the **Carling Academy Brixton** (211 Stockwell Rd., SW9; ☎ 020/7771-3000; Tube: Brixton; www.brixton-academy.co.uk).

Another big-event hall is **Shepherd's Bush Empire** (Shepherd's Bush Green, W12; ☎ 020/7711-3000; www.shepherds-bush-empire.co.uk; Tube: Shepherd's Bush). And sometimes the old **Royal Albert Hall** (see the "Symphony" section, earlier in this chapter) rocks, too.

Dining before or after the performance

Will you eat dinner before or after going to the theater? Many of the restaurants in the West End that I review in Chapter 10 serve pre-theater meals. These places are geared for the theater crowd, so they know your time is limited. Restaurants usually serve their pre-theater menus from 5:30 p.m. to 7 p.m. The restaurant limits your choices to a set menu, but you can be done with your meal and out of the restaurant by 7:30 p.m. or earlier. You find post-theater menus less often; they go into effect around 9:30 p.m. You can usually find a good value in pre- and post-theater fixed-price menus.

The following restaurants (all of which you can read more about in Chapter 10) are close to West End theaters and have pre-theater or post-theater menus:

✔ **The Ivy:** 1–5 West St., Soho, WC2; ☎ 020/7836-4751; Tube: Leicester Square

✔ **Joe Allen:** 13 Exeter St., Covent Garden, WC2; ☎ 020/7836-0651; Tube: Covent Garden

✔ **Rules:** 35 Maiden Lane, Covent Garden, WC2; ☎ 020/7836-5314; Tube: Covent Garden

✔ **Simpson's-in-the-Strand:** 100 The Strand (next to the Savoy Hotel), WC2; ☎ 020/7836-9112; Tube: Charing Cross

Just be certain to book a table beforehand. If you're dining outside the West End, allot extra time to order, eat, pay the bill, get your coats, and then hop on the Tube or hail a taxi to make the curtain.

If you're not fussy about what you eat and just want to keep your stomach from growling during the performance, fast food joints are plentiful in Leicester Square and Piccadilly Circus. And if you're going farther afield — to the **Barbican** or **South Bank Centre** — you can ward off impending hunger pangs with a light meal or a sandwich at one of the cafes or restaurants on the premises.

Chapter 16

London's Best Pubs, Clubs, and Bars

*M*aybe your idea of a perfect evening is going to an elegant hotel bar for a cocktail or sitting back in a historic pub and quaffing a pint of ale. In this chapter, I help you find a fun and fitting nightspot. And if you need music to make you happy, this chapter can point you in the direction of your kind of beat. For locations, see the "London Pubs, Clubs, and Bars" map on p. 308.

Enjoying a Pint: London Pubs

A great way to experience real-life London is to do a *pub crawl* — that is, walk from pub to pub and sample the different brews. If you're accustomed to ordering one particular type of beer with a rather conventional name, you may be bowled over by the colorful names and vast assortment of British beers on tap in a pub. You can find Brakspears, Courage Best, Friary Meux, Ind Coope Burton, Old Speckled Hen, and Wadworths 6X, to name just a few. Although you can get a hard drink at both bars and pubs, when you're in a pub you're better off confining yourself to beer because pubs don't generally carry all the ingredients necessary for a fancy cocktail. Of course, if you find just the right pub, you can order a pint, get comfortable, and even order a good meal (see Chapter 10 for restaurants that serve pub grub).

Opening hours are regulated by Parliament. You can count on most pubs being open Monday through Saturday, from 11 a.m. to 11 p.m. and Sunday noon to 10:30 p.m. Last call is ten minutes before closing, signaled by a bell.

London Pubs, Clubs, and Bars

0   1 Mi

0   1 Km

✝ Church

ⓘ Information

⊖ Tube stop

*Note: not all Tube
stations are featured
on this map*

Admiral Duncan's **19**
Ain't Nothing But
  Blues Bar **12**
Anchor Inn **40**
Atlantic Bar & Grill **20**
Bar Italia **16**
Bar Rumba **21**
Black Friar **36**
Bracewells Bar
  (Park Lane Hotel) **10**
Café Boheme **17**
Churchill Arms **4**
Cittie of Yorke **32**
Coal Hole **30**
Comedy Café **37**
The Comedy Store **23**

The Complex **33**
Compton's of Soho **18**
Equinox **22**
G.A.Y. **24**
George Inn **41**
Glass Bar **13**
Hanover Grand **11**
Heaven **29**
Jazz Café **2**
King's Head
  and Eight Bells **6**
Koko **1**
Ladbroke Arms **3**
Lamb and Flag **25**
The Library
  (Lanesborough Hotel) **8**

Lillie Langtry Bar
  (Cadogan Hotel) **7**
Olde Mitre **34**
Pizza Express Jazz Club **14**
Pizza on the Park **9**
Red Lion Public House **28**
Ronnie Scott's **15**
Salisbury **27**
Seven Stars **31**
606 Club **5**
Venom Club/
  The Zoo Bar **26**
Williamson's Tavern **38**
Ye Olde Cheshire
  Cheese **35**
Ye Olde Watling **39**

A movement is afoot to abolish the strict pub hours throughout the United Kingdom. The laws restricting pub hours were passed during World War I so that munitions workers and others involved in the war effort couldn't spend too much time drinking at their "local." The change requires an Act of Parliament to deregulate pub hours, but the drinkers who want pubs to remain open till the wee hours have a great deal of public support.

Remember: Never tip your bartender. Instead, you can offer to buy him or her a drink.

When you're in the City, try these pubs (all of which you can see on the "London Pubs, Clubs, and Bars" map on p. 308):

✔ **Black Friar** (174 Queen Victoria St., EC4; ☎ 020/7236-5474; Tube: Blackfriars) is an Edwardian wonder made of marble and bronze Art Nouveau. The interior features bas-reliefs of mad monks, a low-vaulted mosaic ceiling, and seating carved out of gold marble recesses.

✔ **Olde Mitre** (Ely Court, Hatton Garden, EC1; ☎ 020/7405-4751; Tube: Chancery Lane), named after an inn built on this site in 1547, is a small pub with an eccentric assortment of customers.

When you're in West London, check out these pubs (which appear on the "London Pubs, Clubs, and Bars" map on p. 308):

✔ **Cittie of Yorke** (22 High Holborn, WC1; ☎ 020/7242-7670; Tube: Holborn or Chancery Lane) has the longest bar in Britain and looks like a great medieval hall — an appropriate look because a pub has existed at this location since 1430.

✔ **Churchill Arms** (119 Kensington Church St., W8; ☎ 020/7727-4242; Tube: Notting Hill Gate or High Street Kensington) is loaded with Churchill memorabilia. The pub hosts an entire week of celebration leading up to Sir Winston's birthday on November 30. Visitors are often welcomed like regulars here, and you'll find the overall ambience to be down-to-earth and homey.

✔ **Ladbroke Arms** (54 Ladbroke Rd., W11; ☎ 020/7727-6648; Tube: Holland Park) strays a bit from a traditional pub environment with its jazz in the background and rotating art prints, but it makes for a pleasant stop and a good meal. The pub's changing menu may include such items as chicken breast stuffed with avocado and garlic steak in pink peppercorn sauce.

✔ **Seven Stars** (53 Carey St., WC2; ☎ 020/7242-8521; Tube: Holborn) is a tiny and modest pub with a collection of Toby mugs and law-related art. You can find the pub at the back of the law courts, so a lot of barristers drink here — you can pick up some British legal jargon while having a pint.

For more information on pubs and British beer, see Chapter 2. If you want to try a truly historic pub, check out my suggestions in Chapter 19.

Focusing on the Music: The Best Jazz and Blues Clubs

Small, smoky jazz clubs are common in London. In Soho, **Ronnie Scott's** (47 Frith St., W1; ☎ **020/7439-0747;** www.ronniescotts.co.uk; Tube: Tottenham Court Road) has been London's preeminent jazz club for years, with dependably high-caliber performances and some big-name stars. Bring a full wallet because you have to order food (meals or snacks) on top of the £15 to £75 ($30–$150) admission.

In Earl's Court, the **606 Club** (90 Lots Rd., SW10; ☎ **020/7352-5953;** www.606club.co.uk; Tube: Earl's Court or Fulham Broadway) is a basement club where young British jazz musicians play. You have to order food if you want to drink; to pay the musicians, the establishment adds to your bill an additional charge of £8 to £12 ($16–$24). You can find good food and diverse music (Afro-Latin jazz to rap) at the **Jazz Café** (5 Parkway, NW1; ☎ **020/7916-6060;** Tube: Camden Town). Admission runs £15 to £20 ($30–$40).

In Soho, try the **Pizza Express Jazz Club** (10 Dean St., W1; ☎ **020/7439-8722;** www.pizzaexpresslive.co.uk; Tube: Tottenham Court Road). Big names from the American jazz scene regularly perform in this intimate venue, and you can enjoy pizza, too. The club is open daily 7:45 p.m. to midnight, and the admission is £15 to £20 ($30–$40). In Knightsbridge, you can hear mainstream jazz performed in the basement Jazz Room of **Pizza on the Park** (11 Knightsbridge, SW1; ☎ **020/7235-5273;** Tube: Hyde Park Corner). The club is open daily from 7:30 p.m., with sets at 9:15 p.m. and 11:15 p.m.; admission is £16 to £20 ($32–$40). Neither club's cover charge includes food.

London's only authentic blues venue is the **Ain't Nothing But Blues Bar** (20 Kingly St., W1; ☎ **020/7287-0514;** www.aintnothinbut.co.uk; Tube: Oxford Circus). The club features local acts and touring American bands. Expect long lines on weekends. Hours are Monday through Thursday 6 p.m. to 1 a.m., Friday and Saturday 6 p.m. to 3 a.m., and Sunday 7:30 p.m. to midnight. Free every night except Friday and Saturday after 8:30 p.m.; cover charge varies from £5 to £10 ($10–$20).

Laughing the Night Away: Comedy Clubs

The Comedy Store (1A Oxendon St., off Piccadilly Circus, SW1; ☎ **0870/060-2340** to reserve by phone; www.thecomedystore.co.uk; Tube: Piccadilly Circus) is London's best showcase for established and rising comic talent. Visitors must be 18 or older. Doors open at 6:30 p.m., and shows start at 8 p.m.; cover charge is £12 to £20 ($24–$40). You can't reserve seats, so arrive early to get a good spot.

You can also sample standup, London-style, at the **Comedy Cafe** (66 Rivington St., EC2; ☎ **020/7739-5706;** www.comedycafe.co.uk; Tube: Old Street). Doors open at 7 p.m., and shows start at 8:30 p.m.; the cover is £3 to £15 ($6 to $30).

Shaking Your Groove Thing: The Best Dance Clubs

London is a large, multicultural city, and its music scene reflects its diversity. In the London clubs, you can listen to drum 'n' bass, indie, Asian underground (or *tabla 'n' bass,* as it's called), chemical beats (don't ask), break beats, techno, trance, psychedelic, and many others.

Cover charges vary according to the day of the week and what band is playing. For more options, check out the music and club listings in *Time Out,* a weekly entertainment magazine.

The Complex, in Islington (1–5 Parkfield St., N1; ☎ **020/7288-1986;** Tube: Angel), frequently books live bands. The club has four floors with different dance vibes on each. Hours are Friday and Saturday 10 p.m. to 7 a.m.; admission is £10 to £12 ($20–$24).

The **Equinox** (Leicester Square, WC2; ☎ **020/7437-1446;** Tube: Leicester Square) boasts London's largest dance floor and one of the largest lighting rigs in Europe. A diverse crowd dances to equally diverse music, including dance hall, pop, rock, and Latin. The hours are Monday through Saturday 9 p.m. to 3 a.m., and the cover is £7 to £12 ($14–$24).

Venom Club/The Zoo Bar (13–17 Bear St., WC2; ☎ **020/7839-4188;** Tube: Leicester Square) features a trendy Euro-androgynous crowd and music so loud that you have to use sign language. The club boasts the slickest, flashiest, most psychedelic decor in London, and even 35-year-olds come here. The hours are daily 9 p.m. to 3 a.m., and the cover (charged only after 10 p.m.) is £3 to £5 ($6–$10).

Bar Rumba (36 Shaftesbury Ave., W1; ☎ **020/7287-2715;** www.barrumba. co.uk; Tube: Piccadilly Circus) is all over the map, musically. Every night, this club features a different type of music, including jazz fusion, phat funk, hip hop, drum 'n' bass, soul, R&B, and swing. The minimum age for admittance is 21 on Saturday and Sunday and 18 Monday through Friday. Hours are Monday through Thursday 10 p.m. to 3 a.m., Friday 10 p.m. to 4 a.m., Saturday 9 p.m. to 6 a.m., and Sunday 8 p.m. to 1 a.m. The cover is £3 to £12 ($6–$24).

The **Hanover Grand** (6 Hanover St., W1; ☎ **020/7499-7977;** Tube: Oxford Circus) is funky and down and dirty on Thursday, but otherwise, it's cutting edge and always crowded. Age and gender are not always easy to distinguish here. Hours are Monday through Saturday 10 p.m. to 4 a.m., and the cover is £10 to £12 ($20–$24).

Housed in a former theater, **Koko** (1A Camden High St., NW1; no phone; www.koko.uk.com; Tube: Camden Town) draws a young all-night crowd addicted to trendy, downtown costumes. The music varies from night to night, so check online in advance. The club is open Tuesday and Wednesday 9 p.m. to 2 a.m., Friday 10 p.m. to 6 a.m., and Saturday 10 p.m. to 8 a.m. The cover is £5 ($10) on Tuesday and Wednesday, and £7 to £20 ($14–$40) on Friday and Saturday.

Unwinding in Elegance: Posh Hotel Bars

Maybe you just want a quiet, romantic spot where you and your significant other can enjoy a cocktail and actually talk to one another. Or perhaps you're looking for a sophisticated place to enjoy a pre- or post-theater drink. The following establishments are just the ticket. They're located in grand hotels and offer a bit of privacy from the crowds. A "smart casual" dress code is in effect at these establishments, so leave your jeans and sneakers in the hotel room.

Bracewells Bar (in the Park Lane Hotel, Piccadilly, W1; ☎ 020/7499-6321; Tube: Green Park or Hyde Park) is chic and nostalgic, with a plush décor of Chinese lacquer, comfortable sofas, and soft lighting.

Looking for high ceilings, leather chesterfields, oil paintings, grand windows, and old-world charm? Visit **The Library** (in the Lanesborough Hotel, 1 Lanesborough Place, SW1; ☎ 020/7259-5599; Tube: Hyde Park Corner), one of London's poshest drinking retreats, known for its collection of ancient cognacs.

At the **Lillie Langtry Bar** (in the Cadogan Hotel, Sloane Street, SW1; ☎ 020/7235-7141; Tube: Sloane Square or Knightsbridge), you can go back in time to the charm and elegance of the Edwardian Era, when Lillie Langtry, an actress and a society beauty (and a mistress of Edward VII), lived at the Cadogan (see Chapter 9 for a description of the hotel). Writer Oscar Wilde — often a guest in Lillie's home and in this hotel — is honored on the drinks menu by his favorite libation, the Hock and Seltzer.

Seeking Spots for Night Owls

Except for the die-hards in the all-night discos, Londoners retire to bed fairly early. Restaurants and bars routinely close before midnight. But a few places in restless, nightclub-heavy Soho stay open late to accommodate night owls (you can see these places on the "London Pubs, Clubs, and Bars" map on p. 308):

✔ **Atlantic Bar & Grill** (20 Glasshouse St., W1; ☎ 020/7734-4888; Tube: Piccadilly Circus) is open for drinks Monday through Saturday until 3 a.m. You may have to wait in line for a place to sit.

- **Bar Italia** (22 Frith St., W1; ☎ 020/7437-4520; Tube: Tottenham Court Road) is open 24 hours for coffee and serves a limited snack menu.

- **Café Boheme** (13–17 Old Compton St., W1; ☎ 020/7734-0623; Tube: Tottenham Court Road or Leicester Square) offers a chance to get a drink Monday through Wednesday until 3 a.m., Sunday until 11:30 p.m., and Thursday through Saturday 24 hours.

Stepping Out: Gay Clubs and Discos

Check the gay listings in *Time Out* for nightclubs that have dedicated gay nights. Gay bars and pubs frequently have fliers for reduced-price admission to big dance venues like G.A.Y.

To be where it's happenin', stroll along Old Compton Street in Soho (Tube: Leicester Square). You may want to duck into **Admiral Duncan's** (54 Old Compton St., W1; ☎ 020/7437-5300) or the two-floor **Compton's of Soho** (53–55 Old Compton St., W1; ☎ 020/7479-7961; www.comptons-of-soho.co.uk). Both of these gay bars/pubs are Soho institutions, open Monday through Saturday noon to 11 p.m. and Sunday noon to 10:30 p.m.

The city's largest women-only bar is the bilevel **Glass Bar** (West Lodge, Euston Square Gardens, 190 Euston Rd., NW10; ☎ 020/7387-6184; Tube: Euston). The bar has a "smart casual" dress code and is open Tuesday through Friday 5 p.m. until "late," Saturday 6 p.m. until "late," and Sunday 2 to 7 p.m.; you can't get in after 11:30 p.m. Monday through Saturday.

In terms of size, central location, and continued popularity, the best gay (and everyone else) disco in London is **Heaven** (Under the Arches, Craven Street, WC2; ☎ 020/7930-2020; www.heaven-london.com; Tube: Charing Cross or Embankment). The place is open Monday and Wednesday 10:30 p.m. to 3 a.m., Friday 10:30 p.m. to 6 a.m., and Saturday 10:30 p.m. to 5 a.m. Admission varies from £3 to £10 ($6–$20).

G.A.Y. (London Astoria, 157 Charing Cross Rd., Soho, WC2; ☎ 0906/100-016; Tube: Tottenham Court Road) is the biggest gay dance venue in Europe. Hours are Saturday 10:30 p.m. to 5 a.m., and admission is £10 ($20).

Part VI
The Part of Tens

The 5th Wave   By Rich Tennant

In this part . . .

This part contains plenty of suggestions for having more fun and delving deeper into the fascinating city of London. You can have a wonderful time in London without reading a word of this part, or you can use this part to enhance your trip. If you've been to London once or twice already and you're ready to expand your explorations, turn to these chapters for a few super ideas.

I unveil the stories behind ten famous London statues in Chapter 17. In Chapter 18, I describe ten historic London churches. In Chapter 19, you get the goods on ten extra-special London pubs. And in Chapter 20, I introduce you to ten notable royals.

Chapter 17

Striking a Pose: Ten (Or So) Famous London Statues

In This Chapter

▶ Enjoying the statues of royalty: The good, the bad, and the ugly

▶ Checking out London's other statues: From Abraham Lincoln to Queen Boudicca

*U*nlike pigeons, people don't really pay too much attention to statues of public figures anymore. The whole idea of casting a bronze of an important public figure just doesn't fit with the modern worldview. Who'd qualify for such an honor in this day and age? In London, the only person today who may be considered deserving of such a monument is the late Princess Diana (at least in the general public's opinion), but it's the late Queen Mother who will get the official royal tribute, in the form of a statue placed off the Mall (Diana got a fountain named after her in Hyde Park). The city is filled with all sorts of other bronze statues commemorating all sorts of individuals from the past. This chapter offers ten (or so) statues that you may find interesting or that you may run into at some point during your London stay and think "Who *is* that?" (For the location of each statue, see the "More London Sights" map in Chapter 11.)

Admiral Lord Nelson

In Trafalgar Square (Tube: Charing Cross), perched atop the 145-foot Nelson's Column, one of London's most famous monuments, is a statue of (you guessed it) **Admiral Lord Nelson.** Horatio Viscount Nelson defeated the French and Spanish at the 1805 Battle of Trafalgar and is Britain's best-known naval hero. On the column, he's 17 feet high (and had to be hoisted up in three sections), but in real life, he was all of 5'4" tall. (Also in Trafalgar Square, you can see an equestrian statue of **George IV,** who considered himself a gentleman but was nobody's idea of a hero.)

Charles 1

In 1633, French sculptor Hubert Le Sueur completed the equestrian statue of **Charles I** that stands (or rather sits) at the north end of Whitehall, just south of Trafalgar Square (Tube: Charing Cross). For no discernable reason, royals seem to have elevated egos and think of themselves as larger than life. So Charlie, who came in at just 5 feet tall, had the sculptor tack another foot onto his frame. In real life, alas, the monarch lost whatever symbolic stature the extra foot gave him when Cromwell chopped off his head in 1649.

However, history has many strange twists and turns: This statue was sold to a scrap dealer who was supposed to destroy it but instead shrewdly buried the piece in his garden. In 1660, when the monarchy was restored and Charles II ascended the throne, the scrap dealer was able to sell the new king the undamaged statue. The figure didn't go up in its present spot on Whitehall — with a pedestal by great architect Sir Christopher Wren — until 1765.

Duke of York and Edward VII

Just north of St. James's Park, at the midpoint of Carlton House Terrace (Tube: Charing Cross), you can find the **Duke of York Monument.** Why did the Duke of York (not Prince Andrew) warrant this massive 7-ton statue? That's a very good question that I'm completely unable to answer. He was the second son of George III (who was on the throne when America gained its independence from Britain), and when he died, he was massively in debt. Sir Richard Westmacott's 1834 sculpture, which rests on a column of pink granite, was funded by withholding a day's pay from every soldier in the Empire. I ask you, was that fair? Some wags have speculated that the duke's statue was placed high up so his creditors couldn't reach him.

The monument looms over Waterloo Place, an enclave of aristocratic elegance and one of London's greatest examples of urban planning. At the entrance of Waterloo Place, you find a statue of **Edward VII,** chiseled by Sir Bertram Mackennal in 1921 to honor the king who gave his name to the Edwardian Era. The son of Queen Victoria, "Eddie" had to wait until he was 60 before he could ascend the throne, and he died nine years later.

But not all is royal in Waterloo Place: You also find a **statue dedicated to the victims of the Crimean War.**

Henry VIII

Wouldn't you say that Henry VIII is England's best-known king? You may have "seen" him in plays, movies (such as *Anne of the Thousand Days* and *A Man for All Seasons*), and that great *Masterpiece Theatre* TV series, *The Six Wives of Henry VIII.* Henry VIII was a huge man, with huge appetites, and he wouldn't take no for an answer. (He didn't have to — he was king.) The much-married monarch has never been considered anyone's idea of a role model, so maybe that explains why London has only one statue of him. You can see it atop the **Henry VIII Gateway** on West Smithfield (Tube: Barbican). In 1702, the stonemasons who built St. Paul's Cathedral built the gateway, which commemorates Henry's giving of St. Bartholomew Hospital to the city — a gift made possible by his dissolution of the monasteries.

James II and George Washington

Two notable statues flank the main entrance of the National Gallery, across from Trafalgar Square (Tube: Charing Cross). On the left, you can see British sculptor Grinling Gibbons's fine statue of **James II,** from 1636, a year after James ascended the throne. Because he immediately levied new taxes and sought to restore Catholicism to England, this monarch never caught on in the public popularity polls. In fact, he was ousted from the throne and spent the rest of his life in exile in France.

The **George Washington** statue on the right is a Jean Antoine Houdon replica of a statue in the capitol building in Richmond, Virginia. A gift from that state, the statue arrived in London with boxes of earth for the base, so the first American president would always stand on American soil.

Oliver Cromwell

The small garden in front of the Houses of Parliament (Tube: Westminster) contains a statue of **Oliver Cromwell,** Lord Protector of England from 1653 to 1658. This fanatical Puritan led the Parliamentary armies during the Civil War that dethroned Charles I. Under Cromwell's "protectorate," at least 30,000 Irish men, women, and children were massacred, and vast tracts of Ireland were handed over to the English. Small wonder that Irish members of Parliament were outraged when Cromwell's statue, by Hamo Thorneycroft, was unveiled in 1899. In fact, Parliament ultimately refused to pay for it, and Lord Rosebery, the prime minister, shelled out the money himself. Cromwell, a sword in one hand and a Bible in the other, appears to be averting his eyes from the bust of **Charles I** (the king whom he had beheaded — see "Charles I," earlier in this chapter), which you can see across the street above the doorway of St. Margaret's Westminster church.

Peter Pan

Children love the famous statue of **Peter Pan,** north of the Serpentine Bridge in Kensington Gardens (Tube: High Street Kensington). Commissioned in 1912 by Peter Pan's creator, J. M. Barrie, the bronze sculpture by George Frampton marks the spot where Peter Pan touched down in the gardens. Of course, this kid could fly — he didn't have to take the Tube like the rest of us.

320 Part VI: The Part of Tens

Peter Pan was an adored fantasy hero long before he became a psychological syndrome for men who refuse to grow up. He was to children of earlier generations what Harry Potter is to the kids of today. Maybe someday there'll be a Harry Potter statue in King's Cross Station.

Prince Albert

Prince Albert of Saxe-Coburg-Gotha (a name that the royals changed to Windsor at the onset of World War I) was the handsome German consort of Queen Victoria. When he died at age 42 in 1861, the grief-stricken queen donned the black widow's weeds she wore for the rest of her long life. London has two statues of Prince Albert. You can find one at the rejuvenated **Albert Memorial** in Kensington Gardens (see Chapter 11). The other stands in the center of Holborn Circus (Tube: Holborn). The latter has been dubbed "the politest statue in London" because the prince is raising his hat.

Queen Boudicca

Who, you may wonder, is the superwoman in the horse-drawn chariot at the north end of Westminster Bridge (Tube: Westminster)? She's **Queen Boudicca** (or Boadicea), that's who, with her fearless warrior-daughters. "Bo" was a fierce Celtic queen who fought back the invading Romans and died in A.D. 60. Thomas Hornicraft created the sculpture in the 1850s; the figure was placed at its current site in 1902. For more on Queen Boudicca, turn to Chapter 20.

Winston Churchill and Abraham Lincoln

Parliament Square (Tube: Westminster) boasts more outdoor sculptures than any other place in London. Unless you're a student of British history, most of the bronze gentlemen (**Sir Robert Peel, Benjamin Disraeli, the 14th Earl of Derby,** and **General Jan Smuts**) ranged around the square won't mean anything to you.

But you may recognize two of them. **Sir Winston Churchill,** the prime minister during World War II (you can find info on the Cabinet War Rooms, which Churchill used during the war, in Chapter 11), is at his most bulldoggish in Ivor Roberts-Jones's 1975 sculpture, standing in the square's northeast corner.

A statue of **Abraham Lincoln,** by Augustus Saint-Gaudens, stands across the street on the west side of the square. The statue of America's 16th president was a gift from the city of Chicago, which has the 1887 original in Lincoln Park.

Chapter 18

Making Amens: Ten Noteworthy London Churches

*W*estminster Abbey and St. Paul's Cathedral (both of which you can read about in Chapter 11) are giant repositories of English history and get the lion's share of visitor attention in London. But the city boasts scores of smaller churches also worth visiting. The area known as the City of London is especially rich in neoclassical churches designed by Sir Christopher Wren (1632–1723) after the disastrous Great Fire of 1666. One of England's greatest architects, and certainly its most prolific, Wren designed St. Paul's.

This chapter explores ten London churches that you may want to check out on your ramblings around town. (For their locations, see the "More London Sights" map in Chapter 11.)

Church of St. Bartholomew the Great

On the east side of Smithfield Square, EC1 (Tube: Barbican), you can see a rare 16th-century gatehouse, and perched atop the gatehouse sits an even rarer late-16th-century timber-frame house predating the Great Fire. The gatehouse opens onto the grounds of the **Church of St. Bartholomew the Great,** a little-visited gem that just happens to be the oldest parish church in London. The church was part of an Augustinian priory founded in 1123. Over the centuries, the building has somewhat miraculously escaped major damage — despite being used at various times as stables and a printing office (where Benjamin Franklin worked in 1725). The

15th-century cloisters are to your right as you enter. Inside the church is a "weeping" 17th-century statue of Edward Cooke (the marble condenses moisture from the air); the tomb of Rahere, the priory's founder; and a lovely *oriel* (projecting bay) window.

If you leave the churchyard by using the gate in the far-right corner, you come out on **Cloth Fair,** a street with gabled houses from 1604. Like St. Bartholomew's, they're among the very few surviving buildings predating the disastrous Great Fire that leveled much of London in 1666.

Church of St. Stephen Walbrook

Walbrook, EC4 (Tube: Cannon Street), a lane in the heart of the City, was the site of a brook that was paved over in medieval times. Today, the lane houses the **Church of St. Stephen Walbrook,** one of Sir Christopher Wren's finest works. By the 18th century, the fame of this church had spread throughout Europe, and many still consider it the most beautiful church in London. Its splendid dome served as a model for the one at St. Paul's Cathedral. The travertine altar beneath the dome was sculpted in 1956 by British sculptor Henry Moore, who had reservations about tackling the job because he was an agnostic. "Henry, I'm not asking you to take the service," said the rector who offered Moore the commission. "I understand that you're a bit of a chiseler; just do your job."

St. Botolph's

I think it's appropriate to include in this chapter a church dedicated to England's patron saint of travelers: **St. Botolph's** on Aldersgate Street, EC1 (Tube: Barbican), close to the **Museum of London** (see Chapter 11). The church interior has a fine barrel-vaulted roof. Actually, three city churches are dedicated to St. Botolph, and all are located beside now-vanished gates into the city. At one time, instead of being greeted by ATMs and currency-exchange windows, travelers could pause and give thanks to Botolph for their safe journey to London.

St. Dunstan's-in-the-West

The octagonal **St. Dunstan's-in-the-West,** on Fleet Street, EC4 (Tube: Temple), is a fine early example of Gothic Revival architecture. That style was in fashion when an earlier church that survived the Great Fire of 1666 was replaced between 1829 and 1833. The large clock on the tower is something of a historical curiosity: The clock dates from 1671 and was installed by the congregation as an offering of thanks because the church hadn't burned down. Every 15 minutes, two giant clubs strike a bell that has been tolling for more than 330 years. People take clocks, watches, and timepieces for granted nowadays, but this clock was the first in London to have a double face and to have minutes marked on the dial.

St. George the Martyr Church

In Southwark, next to the remains of Marshalsea Prison on Borough High Street, SE1 (Tube: Borough), you can find **St. George the Martyr Church.** The church is probably more famous for its literary associations than for any beauty of the structure itself. This church is where Dickens's fictional heroine Little Dorrit is baptized and, at one point, is forced to spend the night when she's locked out of the Marshalsea debtors' prison; later she's married in this church. A stained-glass window in the east wall shows her at prayer.

St. Margaret's Westminster

St. Margaret's Westminster, the parish church of the House of Commons since 1614, is on St. Margaret Street, SW1 (Tube: Westminster), and is often mistaken for Westminster Abbey next door. St. Margaret's is notable for its glorious above-the-altar East Window, the stained glass of which was presented by King Ferdinand and Queen Isabella of Spain to commemorate the marriage of their daughter, Catherine of Aragon, to Arthur, the son of Henry VII. By the time the glass arrived, Arthur had died and Henry VIII, his younger brother, had wed Catherine, the first of his eight wives. (He divorced her to marry Anne Boleyn.) The weddings of poet John Milton (1656) and statesman (and future prime minister) Winston Churchill (1908) were held in this church.

St. Martin-in-the-Fields

St. Martin-in-the-Fields, on Trafalgar Square, WC2 (Tube: Charing Cross), was a stylistic prototype for hundreds of churches constructed in 18th-century New England. James Gibbs, who was influenced by the churches of Sir Christopher Wren, designed the church in 1726. Furniture designer Thomas Chippendale, painters Sir Joshua Reynolds and William Hogarth, and Nell Gwynn, mistress of Charles II, are buried within. For details about the concerts held here, see the description of St. Martin in Chapter 11.

St. Mary-le-Bow

Established in the 11th century, **St. Mary-le-Bow,** on Bow Lane, EC4 (Tube: Mansion House), is one of London's most venerable churches. The structure that originally stood here was a casualty of the Great Fire of 1666; the steepled church that you see today is a work by Sir Christopher Wren, who modeled it after Rome's Church of the Basilica of Maxentius. According to tradition, a true *Cockney* (a native of the East End of London) is someone born within hearing distance of the bells of St. Mary-le-Bow. In the churchyard's garden is a statue of Captain John Smith, a one-time parishioner who left London to become one of the first settlers of Jamestown, Virginia. (He's the one who was saved by Pocahontas.)

Southwark Cathedral

Southwark Cathedral, on Montague Close, SE1 (Tube: London Bridge), is one of the oldest buildings in Southwark and also one of the most beautiful (see Chapter 11). A church has occupied this site for at least a thousand years; before that, a Roman villa stood here.

London's second-oldest church, after **Westminster Abbey,** Southwark Cathedral, in the 12th century, was the first Gothic church to be erected in London. Today, you can see the 15th-century cathedral (with Victorian restorations) that once served London's rowdy South Bank theater district. Chaucer and Shakespeare both worshiped here, and Shakespeare's brother Edmund was buried here in 1607.

Besides a memorial to the immortal bard, the church contains a 13th-century wooden effigy of a knight, one of the oldest surviving wooden effigies in England. John Harvard, founder of Harvard University, was baptized in this church.

Temple of Mithras

Not far from **St. Stephen Walbrook** (see "Church of St. Stephen Walbrook," earlier in this chapter), at the entrance to Temple Court on Queen Victoria Street (Tube: Mansion House), you can find the remains of what's probably London's oldest church site. This church isn't a Christian church, however, but a 3rd-century Roman temple. Unearthed during 1954 excavations and raised to its present level, the **Temple of Mithras** is shaped like a tiny Christian basilica with a central nave and two aisles.

The Mithraic cult, which had its origins in Persia and was brought to London by Roman soldiers in the 2nd century, used this temple. At one time, when the Roman Empire still ruled the Western world, Mithraism was as popular as Christianity. Archaeologists speculate that the pagan temple was destroyed in the 4th century, when Christianity became the official religion of the Empire. Some of the sculptures that were found in the temple are displayed in the **Museum of London** (see Chapter 11).

Chapter 19

Ale's Well That Ends Well: Ten Historic London Pubs

*P*ublic houses, better known as pubs, have been a way of life in London and throughout the United Kingdom for centuries. Chapters 2, 10, and 16 offer information about London pubs. But I could write an entire book just on the pubs of London — the city has hundreds of them. Not all these pubs are old, of course, and not all have the kind of character that accumulates over centuries of drinking, talking, smoking, and eating. But dozens upon dozens of these pubs date back anywhere from a century to more than 400 years.

This chapter offers descriptions of ten more pubs. Each of these places has some special story, history, or association attached to it. (For their locations, see the "London Pubs, Clubs, and Bars" map in Chapter 16.) All these pubs are open regular pub hours (Mon–Sat 11 a.m.–11:30 p.m.); some are open Sunday noon to 10:30 p.m. And as of 2007, smoking is no longer permitted in any of them.

Anchor Inn

Eighteenth-century figures, such as Samuel Johnson, who produced the first *Dictionary of the English Language,* playwright Oliver Goldsmith, whose most famous work is *She Stoops to Conquer,* and painter Sir Joshua Reynolds, the first president of the Royal Academy, frequented the **Anchor Inn** (34 Park Street, SE1; ☎ **020/7407-1577;** Tube: Southwark). It has a nice riverside terrace.

Coal Hole

Opened in the early 19th century, the **Coal Hole** (91 The Strand, WC2; ☎ **020/7379-9883;** Tube: Covent Garden) got its name from the coal haulers who unloaded their cargo on the Thames nearby. One of Central London's larger pubs, the Coal Hole has many theatrical connections because of its West End location. Famous mid-19th-century Shakespearean actor Edmund Kean used to hire rowdies, get them drunk here, and then send them off to heckle his rivals in other theaters.

George Inn

You can find one of the city's most historically important pubs in the **George Inn** (in George Inn Yard off Borough High Street, SE1; ☎ 020/7407-2056; Tube: Borough). It's the last remaining example in London of an old-style coaching inn, with balconies (called *galleries*) around the inner court. The George was doing business during the reign of Henry VIII, and some claim it actually dates back to Chaucer's era.

King's Head and Eight Bells

Chelsea's intimate, clublike **King's Head and Eight Bells** (50 Cheyne Walk, SW3; ☎ 020/7352-1820; Tube: Sloane Square) opened more than 400 years ago, around 1580. Back then, of course, the area was rural; Henry VIII's country house stood nearby. Later, celebrated artists and writers, such as Dante Gabriel Rossetti, Thomas Carlyle (whose house is now a museum; see Chapter 11), Oscar Wilde, Laurence Olivier, and Vivien Leigh made their homes in Chelsea, one of the prettiest (and now one of the most expensive) parts of London. The neighborhood's still filled with literary and other luminaries, so keep your eyes open if you stop in here. You never know who may pop in.

Lamb and Flag

The **Lamb and Flag** (33 Rose St., WC2; ☎ 020/7497-9504; Tube: Leicester Square) was once known by the grisly name "Bucket of Blood" because prizefighters battered one another into a bloody pulp during matches held for betting customers. The pub, a rare survivor of the Great Fire of 1666, has a couple of literary associations to offset its unsavory past. In the 19th century, this place was one of Charles Dickens's favorite taverns. A couple of centuries earlier, poet John Dryden was attacked and beaten just outside, probably because of a lampoon that he directed at the earl of Rochester. Every year on December 16, the pub commemorates the anniversary of the attack with a Dryden Night.

Red Lion Public House

Civil servants and members of Parliament (MPs) frequent the **Red Lion Public House** (48 Parliament St., SW1; ☎ 020/7930-5826; Tube:

Westminster). So many MPs stop in here that the pub rings a special bell before a vote is taken, allowing the lawmakers to get back in time. Charles Dickens stopped in once for a pint of beer — he was 11 years old at the time. (Life was different back then.)

Salisbury

I'm partial to the **Salisbury** (90 St. Martin's Lane, WC2; ☎ 020/7836-5863; Tube: Leicester Square) because I used to hang out there. The pub sits right in the heart of the West End theater district, dates from 1852, and has a beautifully preserved Art Nouveau interior with marble fittings, cut-glass mirrors, and brass statuettes. Like the Lamb and Flag noted earlier, the Salisbury was once famous for bare-knuckle prizefights — but that was long before my time.

Williamson's Tavern

Williamson's Tavern (in Groveland Court, off Bow Lane, EC4; ☎ 020/7248-6280; Tube: St. Paul's) was the residence of the lord mayor of the City of London before the nearby Mansion House was built. The tavern stands behind a 17th-century gate presented to the lord mayor by William and Mary. The building later served as an inn. Inside, you can have a drink and one of its famous steak sandwiches.

Ye Olde Cheshire Cheese

Ye Olde Cheshire Cheese (Wine Office Court, 145 Fleet St., EC4; ☎ 020/7353-6170; Tube: Blackfriars) was established in 1667, but a tavern stood on this site as early as 1590 (see Chapter 11). The earlier tavern burned down in the Great Fire of 1666 and was quickly rebuilt — in fact, Ye Old Cheshire Cheese was the first pub to reopen after the fire. Downstairs, you can see charred wooden beams bearing witness to the massive fire that destroyed a large portion of London. This pub was one of Charles Dickens's favorite hangouts, and he usually sat at a table to the right of the fireplace on the first floor.

Ye Olde Watling

Ye Olde Watling (29 Watling St., EC4; ☎ 020/7653-6252; Tube: Mansion House) is a 17th-century pub that the great architect Sir Christopher Wren used as an office when St. Paul's Cathedral was being constructed. The pub was built from timber taken from dismantled sailing ships.

Chapter 20

Ten Important Royals — Past and Present

I am not a royalist, but the kings and queens of England fascinate me. These are people whose lives encapsulated ultimate power and humiliating defeat, people who killed to stay on the throne and were killed by others who wanted it, people who inspired their subjects and treated them like dirt, people who sometimes changed the course of history and sometimes disgraced the nation they ruled.

I had a hard time choosing just ten, but in the thumbnail sketches that follow, you can get at least a glimpse of how the rulers of England — and the rule of England — have changed over the past 2,000 years.

Queen Boudicca (A.D. 30?– A.D. 60): Braveheart of the Britons

I've always thought Boudicca's story would make a fantastic film, but who would play this fierce Celtic queen who painted her face blue and led 100,000 British troops against the invading Romans in A.D. 60? Angelina Jolie?

Boudicca's story harks back to the earliest period of Britain's recorded history. Historians think that she was born about A.D. 30. In A.D. 48, she married Prasutagus, king of the Iceni, and bore him two daughters. The Iceni were a Celtic tribe that had been made a Roman client-state in A.D. 43. When Prasutagus died, he left his kingdom — as required by Roman law — to the Roman emperor. But hoping to provide for his two daughters, he left a portion of his personal estate to them. For the Romans, that inheritance gave them a perfect excuse to confiscate all of Prasutagus's belongings and punish the Iceni for "disobeying" Roman law. Just days after her husband's death, Boudicca was stripped and publicly whipped, her teenaged daughters raped by Roman soldiers.

The outrages committed by the invading foreigners changed Boudicca's life forever. As more Roman troops arrived to begin the job of conquering all the native Britons, Boudicca managed to raise an army among formerly warring local tribes. The Celts were much feared by the Romans because Celtic women fought alongside the men, painting their faces blue to frighten the enemy and uttering terrifying shrieks as they attacked with swords, axes, and clubs. Boudicca and her army marched to Roman forts and settlements, laid waste to them, and killed their inhabitants. Finally, at a site that was probably somewhere in the West Midlands, Boudicca faced the army of Suetonus Paulinus, the Roman governor of Britannia. She had more troops, but Suetonius and his legionnaires had the discipline that helped Rome conquer the Western world. The Celts under Boudicca were slaughtered. No one knows what happened to Boudicca herself. Some accounts say that she took poison. The alternative, had she lived, would have been worse. She would have been paraded in chains at a public triumph in Rome and then publicly tortured in the Coliseum.

Next time you're crossing Westminster Bridge in London, look up and you can see a bronze statue of Boudicca on the north side. A mid-19th-century work by Thomas Hornicraft, it shows a wild-haired superwoman in a horse-drawn chariot with her two daughters.

Alfred the Great (849–899): A Warrior and a Scholar

If you make a trip to Winchester, the capital of the old Anglo-Saxon kingdom of Wessex, you can see a statue of Alfred the Great on Bridge Street. Alfred is the only English monarch to carry the title "the Great," and that alone makes him an intriguing character. His story goes back to the 9th century A.D. when the Danes, more commonly known as the Vikings, were relentlessly attacking and terrorizing England.

Youngest son of King Æthelwulf, Alfred became king of Wessex in 871. Wessex was an Anglo-Saxon kingdom patched together in southern and southwestern England after the departure of the Romans in A.D. 410. Following a series of attacks led by the Dane Guthorm, Alfred finally defeated the Danes decisively at the Battle of Eddington. As a condition of the peace treaty, Guthorm withdrew his forces from Wessex and Alfred recognized Danish control over East Anglia and parts of Mercia. This partition of England was called the *Danelaw,* and though the English kings soon brought the Danelaw back under their rule, they did not attempt to interfere with the laws and customs of the area, many of which survived until after the Norman Conquest in 1066.

Alfred created a series of fortifications to surround his kingdom and provide security from invasion. You can still find traces of *burh,* the Anglo-Saxon word for these forts, in the common English place-name suffix *–bury.* The reign of Alfred was known for more than military success, however. He promoted better education and helped make learning important in an age when education had gone into a decline because of Danish looting of monasteries and churches, traditional centers of learning. Alfred was also a codifier of law and a patron of the arts. A warrior and a scholar, he translated Latin books into the Anglo-Saxon tongue. With the kind of leadership that he provided, it's no wonder he was proclaimed "the Great."

William the Conqueror (1028–1087): Winner Takes All

The illegitimate son of the Duke of Normandy, William received the duchy of Normandy upon his father's death in 1035. He spent the next several years consolidating his strength on the Continent through marriage, diplomacy, war, and savage intimidation. By 1066, Normandy was in a position of virtual independence from William's feudal lord, Henry I of France, and the disputed succession in England offered William an opportunity for invasion.

When Edward the Confessor died childless, the English crown was offered to Harold Godwinson (an Anglo-Saxon), even though Edward had purportedly promised the throne to William, his second cousin. Insisting that Harold had sworn allegiance to him in 1064, William prepared for battle. But as the new King Harold anxiously awaited William's arrival on England's south shores, Harold Hardrada, the king of Norway, invaded England from the north. Harold's forces marched north to defeat the Norse at Stamford Bridge on September 25, 1066. Two days after the battle, William landed unopposed at Pevensey, forcing Harold to move south to a new battle. What has come to be known as the Battle of Hastings took place on October 14, 1066. Harold and his brothers died fighting, thus removing any further organized Anglo-Saxon resistance to the Normans. The Anglo-Saxon earls and bishops soon submitted and crowned him William I on Christmas Day, 1066.

William's acquisitive nature never left him. His forces ruthlessly crushed uprisings until, by 1072, the whole of England was conquered and united. William confiscated lands and reallocated them to the Normans. In 1085, William commissioned the *Domesday Book* to survey land ownership, assess property, and establish a tax base. Although he began his invasion with papal support, William refused to let the Church dictate policy within English and Norman borders. Ruthless and cruel, the Conqueror exacted a high toll from his subjects, but he also laid the foundation for the economic and political success of England. Buildings from his reign include Windsor Castle and the Tower of London (both of which you can read about in Chapter 11), but you can find perhaps the most atmospheric reminder of William the Conqueror in Battle, a town in Sussex, where you can visit the battlefield that was William's first conquest in England.

Henry II (1133–1189): Family Plots

Henry II, the first Plantagenet king, was one of the most effective of England's monarchs, refining Norman government and creating a self-standing bureaucracy that could keep the country running even if it had a weak or incompetent monarch. But Henry's personal life was one unending soap opera, with more plots and counterplots than I can possibly detail here.

A grandson of Henry I, Henry was raised in the French province of Anjou. His vast continental possessions more than doubled when he married Eleanor of Aquitane, the ex-wife of King Louis VII of France. Eleanor was 11 years older than Henry and was rumored to have slept with his father. Crowned King of England in October 1154, Henry was technically a feudal vassal of the king of France but, in reality, owned more territory and was more powerful than his French lord.

Throughout his reign, Henry instituted reforms meant to weaken traditional feudal ties and strengthen his position, but in the process of strengthening the royal courts, he became involved in the murder of his best friend, Thomas Beckett. The church courts instituted by William the Conqueror had become a safe haven for criminals, and Henry wanted to transfer sentencing in such cases to the royal courts. Thomas Beckett, named archbishop of Canterbury in 1162, vehemently opposed the weakening of church courts. He also angered Henry by opposing the coronation of Henry's eldest son. When an exasperated Henry publicly conveyed his desire to be rid of the contentious archbishop, four thuggish knights took the king at his word and murdered Beckett in his own cathedral on December 29, 1170. (You can see the exact spot if you visit Canterbury Cathedral; see Chapter 14.)

Henry's plans for dividing his myriad lands and titles evoked treachery from his sons, who, with the encouragement of their mother, repeatedly rebelled against their father. Eleanor, equally ruthless and scheming, was kept a virtual prisoner for 16 years. Henry died in 1189, two days after being attacked and defeated by his son Richard, with the assistance of Philip II Augustus of France, forcing Henry to accept a humiliating peace.

Henry VIII (1491–1547): Take My Wife — Please!

The significance of Henry's reign is generally overshadowed by his six marriages, a record topped only by Elizabeth Taylor. Something is scarily pathological about Henry's many marriages, even if they *were* in pursuit of an elusive male heir.

His first wife was Catherine of Aragon (widow of his brother, Arthur), whom he married in 1509 and divorced in 1533; the union produced one daughter, Mary. Henry married the pregnant Anne Boleyn in 1533; she gave him another daughter, Elizabeth, but was executed in 1536 on trumped-up charges of infidelity, a treasonous charge in the king's consort but never for the king. The same month that Anne was beheaded, the monarch married Jane Seymour, who died giving birth to Henry's lone male heir, Edward, in October 1536. After viewing Hans Holbein's beautiful portrait of the German princess Anne of Cleves, Henry arranged a marriage with her early in 1540. When Anne arrived, however, Henry found her so homely that he never consummated the marriage. In 1540, with Anne scratched off the list, he married Catherine Howard, who was executed for infidelity two years later and reputedly haunts Hampton Court Palace to this day. Catherine Parr became Henry's sixth and last wife in 1543, and she provided for the needs of both Henry and his children until his death in 1547.

So what did Henry do besides bed and wed? Most notably, he altered England and the whole of Western Christendom by separating the Church of England from Roman Catholicism. The separation actually happened because of Henry's obsession with producing a male heir. When Catherine of Aragon failed to produce a male, Henry sought an annulment from the pope in order to marry Anne Boleyn. When Cardinal Wolsey failed to secure a legal annulment, Henry summoned the Reformation Parliament, which passed 137 statutes in seven years, influencing political and ecclesiastical affairs in a way previously unknown. By 1536, all ecclesiastical and government officials were required to publicly approve of the break with Rome and take an oath of loyalty. Henry's dissolution of the monasteries filled royal coffers, as revenues from the sale of monastic lands went either to the crown or to the nobility. The break with Rome, coupled with an increase in governmental bureaucracy, led to the royal supremacy that lasted until the execution of Charles I and the establishment of the Commonwealth a century after Henry's death.

Elizabeth 1 (1533–1603): Heart and Stomach of a King

In contrast to her much-married father, Henry VIII, Elizabeth I never wed and was known as the Virgin Queen. When she ascended the throne in 1558, dissension between Catholics and Protestants tore at the very foundation of society, and the royal treasury had been bled dry by Mary, Elizabeth's Catholic half-sister, and Mary's advisors.

Instead of being a fanatic like Mary, Elizabeth was strong-willed, tolerant, and intelligent. In religious matters, she devised a compromise that basically reinstated her father's Protestant reforms. Another potentially volatile problem was her cousin, Mary Queen of Scots, who gained the loyalty of Catholic factions and instituted several plots to assassinate or overthrow Elizabeth. After irrefutable evidence of Mary's involvement in such plots came to light, Elizabeth sadly succumbed to the pressure from her advisors and had the Scottish princess executed in 1587.

The persecution of continental Protestants forced Elizabeth into war, a situation which she desperately tried to avoid. She sent an army to aid French Huguenots (Calvinists who had settled in France) after a 1572 massacre in which over 3,000 Huguenots lost their lives, and she assisted Belgium in its bid to gain independence from Spain. After Elizabeth rejected a marriage proposal from Philip II of Spain, the indignant Spanish monarch, incensed by English piracy and forays in the New World, sent his much-feared Armada to raid England. "I know I have but the body of a weak and feeble woman," Elizabeth told her troops, "but I have the heart and stomach of a king." England won the naval battle and emerged as the world's strongest naval power.

In many ways, Elizabeth's reign has come to be regarded as a Golden Age. Literature bloomed through the works of Spenser, Marlowe, and Shakespeare. Francis Drake and Walter Raleigh expanded English influence in the New World. Elizabeth's religious compromise laid many fears to rest and sought to avoid murderous strife. Fashion and education came to the fore because of Elizabeth's penchant for knowledge, courtly behavior, and extravagant dress. Good Queen Bess, as she came to be called, maintained a regal air until the day she died, at 70 years of age and after a very successful 44-year reign. Few English monarchs enjoyed such political power while still maintaining the devotion of the whole of English society.

George III (1738–1820): "My Lords and Peacocks . . . "

George III was in no way an exemplary ruler, but I've long been fascinated by him because he was king at the time of the American Revolution and because he went mad. The only thing he really excelled at was procreation. He married Charlotte of Mecklenburg-Strelitz in 1761, and the prolific couple produced 15 children.

George was descended from the Hanoverian (German) line of succession that first came to the English throne in 1714. Determined to recover royal prerogatives lost to the Whig Party by George I and George II, George III methodically weakened the Whigs through bribery, coercion, and patronage, hand-picking yes-men of mediocre talent and servile minds to serve as cabinet members.

George's commitment to taxing the American colonies to pay for military protection led to hostilities in 1775. The colonists proclaimed independence in 1776, but George obstinately continued the war until the final American victory at Yorktown in 1781. The Treaty of Paris, signed in 1783, ensured British acknowledgment of the United States of America.

Bouts with madness (attributed to a disease called porphyria) and the way he handled the American Revolution eroded his support.

Other major events and people marked George III's reign. The British Army under the Duke of Wellington (whose London residence, Apsley House, you can visit; see Chapter 11) and the British Navy under Lord Horatio Nelson (honored by Nelson's Column in London's Trafalgar Square; see Chapter 11) defeated French forces under Napoleon. England also went to war again with the United States between 1812 and 1814, this time over the British practice of pressing American seamen into service in the British Navy.

It's safe to say that by the time he began an address with "My Lords and Peacocks," it was time for George to step down. Personal rule was given to his son George, the prince regent, in 1811. George III died blind, deaf, and mad at Windsor Castle (see Chapter 11) on January 29, 1820. You can see Kew Palace, his favorite residence, on a visit to the Royal Botanic Gardens (also known as Kew Gardens; see Chapter 11).

George IV (1762–1830): A Dandy King for the Regency

George IV, eldest son of George III and Charlotte, was the antithesis of his father (are you starting to see a pattern here?): conservative in his infrequent political involvement and licentious in affairs of the heart. As prince regent, he had many mistresses until he secretly married the Catholic widow Maria Fitzherbert in 1785. When George III found out about it, he had the marriage declared illegal because his son would have been ineligible to reign with a Catholic wife. In 1795, George IV married again, this time to his cousin Caroline of Brunswick, who was something of a slob and whom he detested. Caroline took their only child and moved to Italy, returning to England to claim the rights of queen when George succeeded his father in 1820. George created one of the greatest scandals of his reign when he had Caroline barred from his coronation.

Bright, witty, and able on the one hand, indolent, spoiled, and lazy on the other, George was in some ways the psychological forerunner of many modern royals. Although he was scandalous with his mistresses and extravagant in his spending, he was also a patron of the arts and donated his father's immense book collection as the foundation of the British Museum Library. His penchant for building projects inspired the Regency style of architecture, at its most fanciful in the Royal Pavilion in Brighton (see Chapter 14). But his extravagances came at a time of social distress and general misery, following the Napoleonic Wars and the tremendous changes brought forth by the Industrial Revolution. He was basically a party boy who couldn't transcend his sense of royal entitlement to provide true leadership.

Queen Victoria (1819–1901): Mother of Monarchs

Victoria, who gave her name to an era, was the daughter of Edward, Duke of Kent and Strathearn, and Victoria of Saxe-Coburg-Saalfeld. Her father died when she was an infant, and her mother enacted a strict regimen that turned its back on the scandal-ridden courts of Victoria's uncles, George IV and William IV. Popular respect for the Crown was at a low point at her coronation in 1837, but the modest and straightforward young queen, just 18 years old, eventually won the hearts of her subjects. She refused any further influence from her domineering mother, and though she had no direct input in policy decisions, she wanted to be informed of political matters. (After the Reform Act of 1832, legislative authority resided in the House of Lords, with executive authority resting within a cabinet formed by members of the House of Commons; the monarch was essentially powerless.)

Victoria married Prince Albert of Saxe-Coburg in 1840, a marriage that was apparently happy and certainly fecund: She bore nine children. The public, however, was not fond of Victoria's German prince, and Albert was excluded from holding any official political position, was never granted a title, and was named prince consort only after 17 years of marriage. Victoria did nothing without her husband's approval. His interests in art, science, and industry spurred him to organize the Crystal Palace Exhibition in 1851, a highly profitable industrial convention whose proceeds were used to purchase lands in Kensington for the establishment of several museums (one of which is the Victoria & Albert Museum; see Chapter 11). Following his death from typhoid in 1861, Victoria went into seclusion for more than 25 years, not emerging until the Golden Jubilee of 1887. An entire generation had never seen the face of their queen. In that period, she had the Albert Memorial erected in Kensington Gardens (see Chapter 11).

During her reign, the British Empire doubled in size, encompassing Australia, Canada, India, and various locales in Africa and the South Pacific. Victoria was named Empress of India in 1878. England's success in avoiding European conflicts for almost a century (1815–1914, the Crimean War of 1853–1856 being the major exception) was due, in large part, to the marriages Victoria arranged for her children. Either directly or by marriage, she was related to the royal houses of Belgium, Denmark, Germany, Greece, Norway, Romania, Russia, and Sweden. Nicholas II of Russia married Victoria's granddaughter Alexandra, and the dreaded emperor of Germany, Kaiser Wilhelm II, was her grandson "Willy."

The era we now call Victorian England was one in which the queen's rigid ethics and uninspired personal tastes generally reflected those of the middle class. When she died of old age, an entire era died with her.

Queen Elizabeth II (1926–): Monarchy Amidst Media

Elizabeth II, who became queen in 1952, is the best known of the seven remaining monarchs in Europe. The eldest daughter of George VI and Elizabeth Bowes-Lyon, she married a distant cousin, Philip Mountbatten, in 1947 and had four children: Charles, Prince of Wales; Anne; Andrew; and Edward. (For an account of some recent royal scandals involving Elizabeth's kids and grandkids, see Chapter 2.)

In the modern world, where wealth and celebrity have taken the place of actual accomplishment, monarchs are basically privileged show dogs whose pedigrees allow them to amass enormous fortunes, live in a rarified world, and be regarded as newsworthy for no reason other than that they're royal. Seen in the unflattering light of her children, Elizabeth shines like an old-fashioned beacon of virtue and traditional values. She has never embarrassed her nation, and she is a hard and disciplined worker, the most widely traveled head of state in the world. She celebrated her Golden Jubilee in 2002 and appears determined to remain on the throne for quite some time — perhaps as long as Victoria.

And yet, overall, the popularity of the English monarchy is in sharp decline. In large part, this is because the disliked and derided Windsor children have tarnished the royal name. (Princess Diana was the only recent royal to reach the hearts of the public.) But it also has to do with a growing sense that the monarchy is simply irrelevant. The monarchy provides an enormous boost to tourism and sells a lot of books and newspapers, but in a world of democratic models and historical amnesia, how can an elitist monarchy achieve any meaningful relationship to the public it is expected to serve?

It's hard to imagine England without a king or a queen and the traditions associated with royalty. And perhaps the monarchy is worth preserving for that reason alone.

One of my favorite stories about Elizabeth II appeared in a book by Paul Burrell (the queen's butler), *A Royal Duty*. One night, the queen asked if he would like to accompany her as she viewed the latest likeness of herself sent from Madame Tussaud's for her approval. The queen and her butler walked through the hallways and corridors of Buckingham Palace until they came to an enormous, dark drawing room. When the lights were switched on, they saw a lifelike effigy of the queen standing in the center of the room. Elizabeth slowly circled her wax twin, carefully scrutinizing her image, then pronounced herself satisfied, turned off the lights, and left her twin in the dark.

Appendix

Quick Concierge

Fast Facts

American Express

You can find Amex foreign exchanges in Terminal 3 and Terminal 4 at Heathrow (☎ 020/8759-6845) and in London at 78 Brompton Rd., Knightsbridge SW3 (☎ 020/7761-7905).

ATMs

You can access ATMs, also called *cash-points,* at banks throughout Central London. The most popular networks are Cirrus (☎ 800/424-7787; www.mastercard.com/atmlocator/index.jsp) and Plus (☎ 800/843-7587; www.visa.com/atms).

Baby Sitters

Universal Aunts (☎ 020/7386-5900; www.universalaunts.co.uk) is a trustworthy babysitting agency that's been around for nearly two decades.

Business Hours

Banks are usually open Monday through Friday 9:30 a.m. to 3:30 p.m. Business offices are open Monday through Friday 9 a.m. to 5 p.m. London stores generally stay open 9 a.m. to 6:30 p.m., staying open to 7 p.m. one night a week.

Pubs are allowed to stay open Monday through Saturday 11 a.m. to 11 p.m. and Sunday noon to 10:30 p.m. With a special permit, some bars stay open past midnight.

Camera Repair

Sendean, 9–12 St. Anne's Court, W1 (☎ 0871/750-2463; www.sendeancameras.co.uk), gives free estimates and does quick work. It's open weekdays 10 a.m. to 6 p.m. and accepts MasterCard and Visa.

Credit Cards

American Express, Diners Club, MasterCard, and Visa are widely accepted in London and throughout the United Kingdom. If your card gets lost or stolen in London, call the following numbers: American Express ☎ 01273/696-933 (☎ 800/221-7282 in the U.S.); Diners Club ☎ 0800/460-800 (☎ 800/525-7376 in the U.S.); MasterCard ☎ 01702/362-988 (☎ 800/307-7309 in the U.S.); Visa ☎ 01604/230-230 (☎ 800/645-6556 in the U.S.).

Currency

Britain's unit of currency is the pound sterling (£). Every pound is divided into 100 pence (p). Coins come in denominations of 1p, 2p, 5p, 10p, 20p, 50p, £1, and £2. You can get notes in £5, £10, £20, and £50 denominations.

Currency Exchange

In London, you can easily exchange cash or traveler's checks by using a currency-exchange service called a *bureau de change.* You can find them at the major London airports, any branch of a major bank (including

Barclays, HSBC, Midland Bank, and NatWest), all major rail and Underground stations in Central London, post offices, and American Express or Thomas Cook foreign-exchange offices.

Customs

For complete Customs information, see Chapter 12.

Dentists and Doctors

Dental Emergency Care Service, Guy's Hospital, St. Thomas St., SE8 (☎ 020/7188-7188; Tube: London Bridge), is open Monday through Friday 8:45 a.m. to 3:30 p.m. for walk-in patients. Most hotels have physicians on call. Medical Express, 117A Harley St., W1 (☎ 020/7499-1991; www.medicalexpressclinic.com; Tube: Oxford Circus), is a private clinic with walk-in medical service (you don't need an appointment) Monday through Friday 9 a.m. to 6 p.m. and Saturday 10 a.m. to 2 p.m.

Electricity

British electrical current is 240 volts, AC cycle. You can't plug North American or Australian appliances into the holes of British wall outlets without suitable con-verters or adapters (available from electri-cal-supply shops). You can destroy the inner workings of your appliance (and pos-sibly start a fire) if you plug foreign appli-ance directly into a European electrical outlet without a transformer.

Embassies, Consulates, and High Commissions

London is the capital of the United Kingdom and therefore the home of all the embassies, consulates, and high commissions: United States, 55/56 Upper Brooke St., W1 (☎ 020/7499-9000; www.usembassy.org.uk; Tube: Bond Street); Canada, MacDonald House, 38 Grosvenor St., W1 (☎ 020/

7258-6600; www.canada.org.uk; Tube: Bond Street); Ireland, 17 Grosvenor Place, SW1 (☎ 020/7235-2171; www.ireland.embassyhomepage.com; Tube: Hyde Park Corner); Australia, Australia House, Strand, WC2 (☎ 020/7379-4334; www.australia.org.uk; Tube: Charing Cross or Aldwych); New Zealand, New Zealand House, 80 Haymarket at Pall Mall, SW1 (☎ 020/7930-8422; www.newzealandhc.org.uk; Tube: Charing Cross or Piccadilly Circus).

Emergencies

For police, fire, or an ambulance, call ☎ 999.

Holidays

Some local holidays won't be familiar to non-Brits, particularly the spring and summer Bank Holidays (the last Mon in May and Aug), when everyone takes off for a long weekend. Most banks and many shops, museums, historic houses, and other places of interest are closed on Bank Holidays, and public transport services are reduced. The same holds true for other major British holidays: New Year's Day, Good Friday, Easter Monday (the day after Easter), May Day (first Mon in May), Christmas, and Boxing Day (Dec 26). The London crowds swell during school holi-days: mid-July to early September, three weeks at Christmas and at Easter, a week in mid-October, and a week in mid-February.

Hospitals

The following hospitals offer 24-hour emer-gency care: Royal Free Hospital, Pond Street, NW3 (☎ 020/7352-8121; www.royalfree.nhs.uk; Tube: Hampstead Heath), and University College Hospital, Cecil Fleming House, Grafton Way, WC1 (☎ 020/7387-9300; www.uclh.nhs.uk; Tube: Warren Street or Euston Square).

Many other London hospitals also have accident and emergency departments.

Hot Lines

The Rape Crisis Line at ☎ 020/7837-1600 accepts calls after 6 p.m. Samaritans, 46 Marshall St., W1 (☎ 020/7734-2800; Tube: Oxford Circus or Piccadilly Circus), maintains a crisis hot line that helps with all kinds of troubles, including threatened suicides. Doors are open daily 9 a.m. to 9 p.m., but phones are open 24 hours. Alcoholics Anonymous, 3–5 Cynthia St., N1 (☎ 020/7833-0022), answers its hotline daily 10 a.m. to 10 p.m.

Information

The main Tourist Information Centre, Britain & London Visitor Centre, 1 Lower Regent St., Piccadilly Circus, SW1 (Tube: Piccadilly Circus), provides tourist information to walk-in visitors Monday 9:30 a.m. to 6:30 p.m., Tuesday to Friday 9 a.m. to 6:30 p.m., and Saturday and Sunday 10 a.m. to 4 p.m. You can find another Tourist Information Centre in the Arrivals Hall of the Waterloo International Terminal (open daily 8:30 a.m.–10 p.m.). For general London information, call ☎ 0870/156-6366.

Internet Access and Cybercafes

easyInternet (☎ 020/7241-9000; www.easyeverything.co.uk) has cybercafes all over London. Try one of the following: 358 Oxford St., W1 (Tube: Bond Street); 9–16 Tottenham Court Rd., W1 (Tube: Tottenham Court Road); 160–166 Kensington High St., W8 (Tube: Kensington High Street); and 456–459 Strand, WC2 (Tube: Charing Cross).

Legal Aid

In every case where legal aid is required by a foreign national within Britain, the British Tourist Authority advises visitors to contact their embassy.

Liquor Laws

No one under 18 can be served alcohol legally. Children under 16 aren't allowed in pubs, except in dining rooms, and then only when accompanied by a parent or guardian. Restaurants are allowed to serve liquor during the same hours as pubs (see "Business Hours," earlier in this appendix, for these hours); however, only people who have a meal on the premises can be served a drink. In hotels, liquor may be served between 11 a.m. and 11 p.m. to both guests and non-guests; after 11 p.m., only guests can get a drink.

Mail

A postcard or airmail letter to North America, Australia, and New Zealand costs 54p ($1.10) for 10 grams. You can send mail within the United Kingdom first or second class. See "Post Offices," later in this appendix.

Maps

You can get the best all-around street directory, *London A–Z,* at most newsstands and bookstores. You can obtain a bus and Underground map at any Underground station.

Newspapers and Magazines

The *Times, Telegraph, Daily Mail,* and *Evening Standard* are all dailies carrying the latest news. You can get copies of the *International Herald Tribune,* published in Paris, and an international edition of *USA Today* daily. You can also buy copies of *Newsweek* and *Time* at most newsstands. Magazines such as *City Limits, Time Out,* and *Where* contain useful information about the latest happenings in London. You can pick up a copy of *Gay Times,* a high-quality, news-oriented magazine covering the gay and lesbian communities, at most newsstands and news agents. See "Where to Get More Information," later in this appendix, for more info.

Pharmacies

They're called *chemists* in the United Kingdom. The chain Boots (www.boots.com) has outlets all over London. Bliss the Chemist, 5 Marble Arch, W1 (☎ 020/7723-6116; Tube: Marble Arch), is open daily 9 a.m. to midnight. Zafash Pharmacy, 233–235 Old Brompton Rd., SW5 (☎ 020/7373-2798; Tube: Earl's Court), is London's only 24-hour pharmacy.

Police

In an emergency, dial ☎ 999.

Post Offices

The Main Post Office, 24 William IV St., WC2 (☎ 020/7930-9580; Tube: Charing Cross), is open Monday through Saturday 8:30 a.m. to 5:30 p.m. Other post offices and *sub-post offices* (windows in the backs of news agents) are open Monday through Friday 9 a.m. to 5:30 p.m. and Saturday 9 a.m. to 12:30 p.m. For general post office information, go to www.royalmail.com. Look for red POST OFFICE signs outside.

Restrooms

The English often call toilets *loos*. Loos are marked by PUBLIC TOILETS signs on streets, in parks, and in a few Tube stations. You can also find well-maintained lavatories that anybody can use in all larger public buildings, such as museums and art galleries, large department stores, and rail stations. You can usually use public lavatories for free, but you may need a 20p coin to get in or to use a proper washroom. In some places (like Leicester Square), you can find coin-operated "Super Loos" that are sterilized after each use. If all else fails, duck into the nearest pub.

Safety

Security in the London Underground was dramatically increased following the 2005 terrorist attacks. In general, London is a safe city. As in any large metropolis, use common sense and normal caution when you're in a crowded public area or walking alone at night. The area around Euston Station has more purse snatchings than anywhere else in London.

Smoking

As of July 2007, smoking was prohibited in all public areas throughout the United Kingdom, including restaurants and pubs. Nonsmoking rooms are available in more and more hotels, and many B&Bs are now entirely smoke-free.

Taxes

The 17.5 percent value-added tax (VAT) is added to all hotel and restaurant bills and is included in the price of many items that you purchase. You can get this tax refunded if you shop at stores that participate in the Retail Export Scheme (signs are posted in the windows of participating stores). See Chapter 12 for more information on receiving a VAT refund.

Taxis

You can hail a cab from the street; if the FOR HIRE light is lit, the cab is available. You can phone for a cab at ☎ 020/7272-0272.

Telephone

The country code for the United Kingdom is **44**. London's telephone area code is **020** within the United Kingdom or **20** outside the United Kingdom. If you're calling a

London number from outside the city, use 020 followed by the eight-digit number. If you're calling within London, leave off the 020 and dial only the eight-digit number.

For directory assistance in London and the rest of Britain, dial ☎ **192.**

To call England from the United States, Canada, and Australia dial 011-44, then the city code (20 for London), and the eight-digit phone number. For calls from New Zealand, dial 00-44, then the city code and the eight-digit phone number.

If you're dialing a London number within London, drop the 020 city code.

You can find three types of public pay phones: those that take only coins (increasingly rare); those that accept only phone cards; and those that take phone cards, credit cards, and coins. You can get phone cards in various values — from £3 ($6) up to £20 ($40) — and you can reuse them until you use up the total value of the card. You can buy the cards from newsstands and post offices. At coin-operated phones, insert your coins before dialing. The minimum charge is 40p (80¢). The credit card pay phone operates on credit cards — Access (MasterCard), American Express, Diners Club, and Visa.

To make an international call from London, dial the international access code (00), the country code, the area code, and the local number. Or call through one of the following long-distance access codes: AT&T USA Direct (☎ 0800/890-011), Canada Direct (☎ 0800/890-016), Australia (☎ 0800/890-061), or New Zealand (☎ 0800/890-064). Common country codes are: United States and Canada, 1; Australia, 61; New Zealand, 64.

Time Zone

England follows Greenwich mean time (five hours ahead of United States eastern standard time). Most of the year, including summer, Britain is five hours ahead of the time observed on the East Coast of the United States. Because the United States and Britain observe daylight saving time at slightly different times of year, for a brief period (about a week) in autumn, London is only four hours ahead of New York, and for a brief period in spring, London is six hours ahead of New York.

Tipping

In restaurants, service charges of 15 percent to 20 percent are often added to the bill. Sometimes, this tip is clearly marked; other times, it isn't. When in doubt, ask. If service isn't included, adding 10 percent to 15 percent to the bill is customary. Sommeliers get about £1 ($2) per bottle of wine served. Tipping in pubs isn't done, but in cocktail bars, the server usually gets about £1 ($2) per round of drinks. Tipping taxi drivers 10 percent to 15 percent of the fare is standard. Barbers and hairdressers expect 10 percent to 15 percent. Tour guides expect £2 ($4), although this tip isn't mandatory. Theater ushers are not tipped.

Transit Info

For 24-hour information on London's Underground, buses, and ferries, call ☎ 020/7222-1234 or go online to www.tfl.gov.uk.

Water

London's water is safe to drink. Tap water is free in restaurants, so be sure to ask for it if you don't want to pay for bottled water.

Weather Updates

For the daily London weather report before you go, check the Visit London Web site at www.visitlondon.com.

Toll-Free Numbers and Web Sites

Airlines

Air Canada
☎ 888/247-2262 (U.S. and Canada)
☎ 0871/220-1111 (U.K.)
www.aircanada.ca

Air New Zealand
☎ 800/262-1234 (U.S.)
☎ 800/663-5494 in Canada
☎ 0800/737-767 (New Zealand)
☎ 0800/028-4149 (U.K.)
www.airnewzealand.com

American Airlines
☎ 800/433-7300 (U.S.)
☎ 020/7365-0777 (U.K.)
www.aa.com

British Airways
☎ 800/247-9297 (U.S.)
☎ 0845/77-333-77 (U.K.)
www.british-airways.com

British Midland
☎ 800/788-0555 (U.S./U.K.)
☎ 1332/64-8181 (outside U.S./U.K.)
www.britishmidland.com

Continental Airlines
☎ 800/625-0280 (U.S.)
☎ 0800/231-0856 (U.K.)
www.continental.com

Delta Air Lines
☎ 800/221-1212 (U.S. and Canada)
☎ 0845/600-0950 (U.K.)
www.delta.com

Icelandair
☎ 800/223-5500 (U.S. and Canada)
☎ 354/50-50-100 (Iceland)
☎ 0870/787-4020 (U.K.)
www.icelandair.is

Northwest Airlines
☎ 800/225-2525 (U.S. and Canada)
☎ 0870/507-4074 (U.K.)
www.nwa.com

Qantas
☎ 800/227-4500 (U.S.)
☎ 612/9691-3636 (Australia)
☎ 0845/774-7767 (U.K.)
www.qantas.com

United Airlines
☎ 800/241-6522 (U.S. and Canada)
☎ 0845/844-4777 (U.K.)
www.united.com

Virgin Atlantic Airways
☎ 800/862-8621 (U.S. and Canada)
☎ 0870/380-2007 (U.K.)
www.virgin-atlantic.com

Major hotel chains

Hilton Hotels
☎ 800/445-8667 (U.S.)
☎ 0800/88844 (U.K.)
www.hilton.co.uk

Hyatt Hotels & Resorts
☎ 800/228-9000 (U.S.)
☎ 0845/888-1234 (U.K.)
www.hyatt.com

Le Meridien Hotels & Resorts
☎ 888/625-5144 (U.S.)
☎ 0800/028-2840 (U.K.)
www.starwoodhotels.com

Macdonald Hotels & Resorts
☎ 888/892-0038 (U.S.)
☎ 0870/830-4812 (U.K.)
www.macdonaldhotels.com

Moat House Hotels
☎ 800/641-0300 (U.S.)
☎ 0870/225-0199 (U.K.)
www.qmh-hotels.com

Red Carnation Hotels
☎ 877/955-1515 (U.S.)
☎ 0845/634-2665 (U.K.)
www.redcarnation.com

Relais & Chateaux
☎ 800/735-2478 (U.S.)
☎ 0800/2000-0002 (U.K.)
www.relaischateaux.com

Sheraton Hotels & Resorts
☎ 800/325-3535 (U.S.)
☎ 0800/3253-5303 (U.K.)
www.sheraton.com

Thistle Hotels Worldwide
☎ 800/847-4358 (U.S.)
☎ 0800/181-716 (U.K.)
www.thistlehotels.com

Major car rental agencies

Alamo
☎ 800/327-9633 (U.S.)
☎ 0800/272-200 (U.K.)
www.goalamo.com

Avis
☎ 800/331-1212 (U.S.)
☎ 0990/900-500 (U.K.)
www.avis.com

Budget
☎ 800/527-0700 (U.S.)
☎ 0541/156-5656 (U.K.)
www.budgetrentacar.com

Hertz
☎ 800/654-3131 (U.S.)
☎ 0870/844-8844 (U.K.)
www.hertz.com

National
☎ 800/227-7368 (U.S.)
☎ 0990/565-656 (U.K.)
www.nationalcar.com

Where to Get More Information

For general information about London, contact an office of VisitBritain (formerly the British Tourist Authority) at one of the following addresses:

✔ **In the United States and Canada:** The main VisitBritain office for North America is at 551 Fifth Ave., Suite 701, New York, NY 10176-0799 (☎ 800/462-2748 in U.S., ☎ 888/847-4885 in Canada).

✔ **In Australia:** Level 2, 15 Blue St., North Sydney, NSW 2060 (☎ 1300/858589).

✔ **In Ireland:** ☎ 8456/443010; phone and Web enquiries only.

✔ **In New Zealand:** ☎ 0800/700-741; phone and Web enquiries only.

The Web gives you a great place to find information on London. For general information on London, try these sites:

✔ www.visitbritain.com: You may find the Web page for the official British tourism agency, VisitBritain, a good resource for visitors to London and the United Kingdom, in general.

✔ www.visitlondon.com: The city's official London Web page has all kinds of special information for visitors to London.

✔ www.londontown.com: This site features special offers on hotels, B&Bs, and theater tickets.

- ✔ http://news.bbc.co.uk: You can find national and international BBC news reports and features on this site.

- ✔ www.guardian.co.uk: *The Guardian,* London's left-of-center daily newspaper, provides up-to-the-minute online news coverage.

- ✔ www.timesonline.co.uk: *The Times,* the oldest and most traditional of London papers, is a good source for general news and cultural information.

- ✔ www.gaylondon.co.uk: This site provides a useful list of gay and gay-friendly hotels, services, clubs, and restaurants.

- ✔ www.baa.com: You can get information on London's Heathrow and Gatwick airports on this site.

- ✔ www.tfl.gov.uk: This is the Web site for Transport for London, which is in charge of all forms of public transportation in the city: the Tube, buses, and ferry service.

- ✔ www.royal.gov.uk: If you want more history, information, and trivia about the Windsors and the British monarchy, in general, check out the official royal Web site.

Not all travelers have the same needs or interests. For more specialized travel reading, here are three recommended titles for travelers with special interests:

- ✔ *Suzy Gershman's Born to Shop London* **(Wiley Publishing, Inc.)** is a must for travelers eager to cruise London with a credit card. This book covers everything from top department stores to tiny boutiques and helps you find the best, most unusual, and most quintessentially English goods.

- ✔ *Frommer's London with Kids* **(Wiley Publishing, Inc.)** is filled with recommendations for families seeking kid-friendly accommodations, restaurants, and unique attractions. And, it's all written by a local London parent.

- ✔ *Frommer's Memorable Walks in London* **(Wiley Publishing, Inc.)** is an excellent resource for those travelers who want to explore the city in depth and on foot. Each walking tour provides clear, easy-to-follow directions and describes important sights along the way.

Index

• B •

B&Bs, 103–104
baby sitters, 62–63, 337
ballet, 15
Bank of England (bank), 92
Bank of England Museum, 217
Bank Holidays, 338
Bar Italia (nightclub), 314
Bar Rumba (dance club), 312
Barbican Centre, 92
bars, 313. *See also* pubs
Bath, day trip to
  accommodations, 269
  dining, 269
  map, 267
  overview, 266
  sightseeing, 268–269
  tours, 268
  transportation to, 266
BBC Henry Wood Promenade
    Concerts, 35
Beefeaters, 205
beer types, 25
Belgravia, 95
Benjamin Franklin House, 217
Big Ben, 192–193, 260. *See also* Houses of
    Parliament
Big Bus Company tours, 231
Black Friar (pub), 310
Blair, Tony, 22, 213
Bliss the Chemist drugstore, 243
blues clubs, 311
boat tours, 232–233
The Body Shop, 252
Bond Street shopping, 253
books, recommended, 26–27, 344
bookstores
  Children's Book Centre, 248
  Gay's the Word, 68
  Hatchards, 249
  Murder One, 14, 254
  Siver Moon, 254
  W & G Foyle, 14, 254
  Waterstone's, 14, 254
Boots the Chemist drugstore, 243, 340
Boudicca, Queen, 320, 328–329
Boyz (magazine), 68
Bracewells Bar (hotel bar), 313

Brick Lane Market, 244
Brighton, day trip to
  accommodations, 273
  dining, 272
  map of, 271
  overview, 270
  sightseeing, 270–272
  tourist information, 270
  transportation to, 270
Britain & London Visitor Centre,
    97–98, 109
British Airways, 53, 59, 342
British Hotel Reservation Centre,
    107, 109
British Library Exhibition Centre, 215
British Midland airline, 342
British Museum, 11, 93, 188–190, 258
British Travel International package
    tours, 58
Brown, Gordon, 213
Brown, Tina, *The Diana Chronicles,* 26
Brown's Hotel high tea, 176
bucket shops, 54
Buckingham Palace. *See also*
    Royal Family
  event calendar, 36
  overview, 10
  Queen's Gallery, 191
  Royal Mews, 190–191
Budget car rental agency, 343
budgeting
  cutting costs, 45–47
  dining, 43–44
  lodging, 43
  nightlife, 44–45
  overview, 41–42
  shopping, 44–45
  sightseeing, 44
  transportation, 42–43
Burberry (clothing store), 249
bureau de change, 48, 337–338
Burlington Arcade, 249, 252
bus travel
  24-hour clock, 89
  from Gatwick airport, 87
  from Heathrow airport, 85
  around London, 100–101
  tours, 231–232

restaurants listed by cuisine, 179–180
restaurants listed by neighborhood,
177–179
restaurants listed by price, 181
Salisbury and Stonehenge, 284
service charge, 44
snacking, 171–174
Stratford-upon-Avon, 280–281
styles, 24–25
tea rooms and patisseries, 175–176
tipping, 42, 44, 145, 341
VAT (value-added tax), 145
wine bars, 144
York, 292
Disability Discrimination Act (2004),
65–66
disabled travelers
access issues, 65–66
escorted tours, 65
health precautions, 67
tips and resources, 64–65
wheelchair accessible attractions,
208–209
Docklands Light Railway (DLR), 88
doctors, 338
downtown. *See* West End
D'Oyly Carte Opera Company, 303
Dr. Martens Department Store, 255
drugstores, 243, 340
Duke of York Monument, 318

• E •

Earl's Court
Exhibition Centre, 306
overview, 96
Early English Gothic architectural
style, 23
easyInternetCafe, 76, 339
Edward VII statue, 318
Elderhostel, 63
electricity, 338
Elizabeth I, Queen, 332–333
Elizabeth II, Queen, 20–21, 336
Elizabethan England, 18, 23
ELTExpress consolidator, 54
E-Mail communication, 76–78
Embankment Gardens, 177
embassies, 338
emergencies, 338

English National Ballet, 15, 305
English National Opera, 15, 303
Equinox (dance club), 312
escorted tours
choosing, 56–57
companies, 57–58
disabled travelers, 65
travel insurance, 57
ethnic cuisine, 13
Eurostar train service, 55–56, 88
exchanging money, 47–49
Expedia online travel agency, 54

• F •

fairs/festivals
Chelsea Antiques Fair, 36
Chelsea Crafts Fair, 36
King's Road Antiques Fair, 33
London Lesbian and Gay Film
Festival, 67
Notting Hill Carnival, 36
Summer Rites, 67
Thames Festival, 36
fall season, traveling during, 32
families. *See* children, traveling with
Family Travel Forum Web site, 61
Farlows (sports equipment store), 249
Fashion Museum (Bath), 268–269
Fenwick of Bond Street department
store, 241
ferry travel, 56
films, recommended, 27–28
The Filofax Centre (store), 252
First Option Hotel Reservations, 109
five day itinerary, 259
Floris (toiletry shop), 14, 249
flower shows, 34–35
FlyCheap consolidator, 54
Flying Wheels Travel escorted tours, 65
Football Association FA Cup Final, 34
The Forsythe Saga (series), 27
Fortnum & Mason department store,
14, 176–177, 241
Fox, Kate, *Watching the English,* 27
Franklin, Benjamin, 217
French cuisine, 13
Frommer's London with Kids (Carrier), 344
Frommer's Memorable Walks in London
(Jones), 102, 344

• *P* •

Restaurant Index